Uncle John's Bathroom Reader®

VROOM!

A WORLD OF MOTORIZED MARVELS

By the
Bathroom Readers'
Institute

Bathroom Readers' Press
Ashland, Oregon

UNCLE JOHN'S BATHROOM READER®
VROOM!

For information, write:
The Bathroom Readers' Institute, P.O. Box 1117,
Ashland, OR 97520
www.bathroomreader.com • 888-488-4642

Cover design by Michael Brunsfeld, San Rafael, CA
(*Brunsfeldo@comcast.net*)

ISBN-13: 978-1-60710-184-0 / ISBN-10: 1-60710-184-X

Library of Congress Cataloging-in-Publication Data

Uncle John's bathroom reader vroom!.

p. cm.

ISBN 978-1-60710-184-0 (pbk.)

1. Motor vehicles—Miscellanea. 2. Motor vehicles—Humor. 3. American wit and humor. I. Portable Press (Ashland, Or.) II. Title: Vroom!

TL146.5.U53 2011

388.3'4—dc23

2011020178

Printed in the United States of America
First Printing
1 2 3 4 5 6 7 8 15 14 13 12 11

THANK YOU!

The Bathroom Readers' Institute sincerely thanks the people whose advice and assistance made this book possible.

Gordon Javna
Malcolm Hillgartner
Jahnna Beecham
Sharilyn Carroll
Amy Miller
Jeff Altemus
Kim Griswell
John Dollison
Jay Newman
Brian Boone
Thom Little
Michael Brunsfeld
Angela Kern
Myles Callum
Michael Conover
Michael Kerr
John Gaffey
Brandon Hartley
Maggie McLaughlin
Rob Proctor
Amber Goodspeed
Lt. Matt "Chuppet" Powers, USN
Lt. Col. Kirk Reagan, USAF
Maj. Rob "Trip" Raymond, USAF
Claire Breen
Claudia Bauer
Susanna Sturgis
JoAnn Padgett
Melinda Allman
Monica Maestas
Annie Lam
Ginger Winters
Jennifer Frederick
Maggie Javna
Tom Mustard
Sydney Stanley
David Calder
Erin Corbin
Media Masters
Publishers Group West
Bloomsbury Books
Raincoast Books
Felix the Dog
Thomas Crapper

Hiya, Sam! Hiya, Gideon!

CONTENTS

Because the BRI understands your reading needs, we've divided the contents by length as well as subject.

Short—a quick read

Medium—2 to 3 pages

Long—for those extended visits, when something a little more involved is required

* **Extended**—for those leg-numbing experiences

INTRODUCTION

LADIES AND GENTLEMEN!

Start your engines and strap into your thrones for an all-new *VROOM!* edition of *Uncle John's Bathroom Reader*. This time around the track, we're moving into the fast lane with articles about nearly every kind of motorized vehicle you can think of: planes, trains, boats, motorcycles, scooters, hot-tub limos, and, of course, that universal obsession: the automobile.

Admit it. Like us, you're fascinated with fast. We bet that you remember the first time you drove a car, as if it were yesterday. Uncle John does. He learned to drive—and to ignore speed limit signs—in his mom's '66 metallic blue Mustang. It was a fantastic car...right up to the time he drove a little *too* fast, lost control, and flipped it. But don't worry—nobody got hurt...except the Mustang. It was totaled.

(Sorry, Mom.)

Uncle John's not the only one at the BRI with fond memories of first cars. Amy had a green '67 Cougar with fat tires, mag wheels, and air shocks, that caught fire...twice. Brian got the family junker, a 1985 Oldsmobile, after it was passed down three times. He remembers one thing: the mold. Jay was only five feet tall when he learned to drive, which explains why he couldn't see over the front quarter-panels of his dark green 1972 Ford Mustang Grande. And Kim never did get all of the duck poop out of that red-and-white Metropolitan her sister inherited from their grandfather. (Don't ask.)

We'd love to hear about your first car, Big Wheel, helicopter, motorcycle, or dirigible, so drive over to *www.bathroomreader.com* and share the story. In the meantime, we've got the right fuel for hours of bathroom reading. And all you have to flip are the pages.

During quick pit stops, you'll discover . . .

• The man who plans to dive head-first from a balloon 23 miles above the earth (and which high-energy drink dares to sponsor him)

• How many Kias, Volvos, and BMWs have been lost at sea
• And whether it would really be a good idea for us to start flying our cars to work.

When you need more time at the gas station, learn about…

• Whose ride has more safety features, the President's or the Pope's
• Which highways to avoid (because they're haunted)
• And who has to "find the meatball" on an aircraft carrier.

And for those really long hauls, check out…

• How far a helicopter will fly on human muscle power
• The 1930s French showgirl who went *Va-va-vroom!*
• And the "flying pancake."

While you're warming up your engines, we'd like to take a moment to thank our dedicated team of writers, researchers, editors, and designers. Our special thanks go to longtime contributors Jahnna and Malcolm. These two went the extra mile to bring you story after story guaranteed to keep your brain firing on all 4, 6, 8, or 16 cylinders.

From take off to landing, from starting line to checkered flag, *VROOM!* will give you the inside track on every mud-chugging, sound-barrier-breaking, mother-scaring vehicle the wonderful world of motors has ever known. Caution: Fasten your seatbelts before reading.

And as always…

Go with the Flow!

—Uncle John and the BRI Staff

MONSTERS INC.

Monster trucks are the automotive equivalent of body builders. Here's a short history.

MUD BOGGING

Monster trucks would not exist were it not for the peculiar sport of mud-bogging. This off-road motorsport is basically a race through a big mudhole. The vehicle that makes it to dry land on the other side the quickest (or, as is often the case, goes the farthest before getting stuck) is the winner. Mud-bogging started in the 1950s in North America, then took off in popularity with the onset of organized racing circuits in the late 1970s.

Competitors hoping to up their chances of traversing the mucky courses at these rallies began modifying their vehicles with heightened suspensions and large tires. After a while the modifications became an end in themselves as 'boggers competed to see who could build the tallest, toughest truck.

BIGFOOT

The first monster truck was built in 1979 by auto-shop owner Bob Chandler of St. Louis, Missouri. It took him four years to turn the family 1974 Ford 250 pickup into an outsized behemoth with heavy-duty military axles and 48-inch tires. Chandler, an avid off-roader, named his truck Bigfoot and began taking it to off-road rallies and tractor pulls, where it caught the attention of promotor Bob George, who announced to the crowd, "*That* is a monster truck!" The name stuck.

As Bigfoot's popularity grew, other monster trucks with names like King Kong and Bear Foot started to appear at similar events around the Midwest. Shortly after his machine appeared in the 1981 film *Take This Job and Shove It*, Chandler came up with an idea that would change motor sports forever. He set two junked cars in the middle of a field and drove over them with Bigfoot until they were smashed flat. A friend videotaped the stunt, and Chandler began showing the clip on a VCR in his shop. When customers pleaded with him to do it again, only this time in public, he gave in.

Racecar driver Lee Petty once did a full lap with a pit crew member still on the hood.

SUPER SMASH

After some initial smash-fests that were resounding successes, Chandler debuted an even bigger truck at Michigan's Pontiac Superdome in 1982. The capacity crowd howled with delight as Bigfoot 2 crushed another batch of cars with its 66-inch wheels. The event drew national press, and a sponsorship from the Ford Motor Company followed. Imitators quickly built their own super monster trucks, eager to top Chandler's creation. Events popped up at state fairs and rallies across the heartland, featuring new brutes with names like King Krunch, Mad Dog, and Virginia Giant. By 1985 monster trucks were featured in races on obstacle-lined courses in addition to the audience-pleasing car-crush sideshows.

In the years that followed, monster-truck racing teams created Equalizer, Tarus, and other increasingly innovative trucks, equipping them with cutting-edge coil springs and shock absorbers that dramatically improved their suspension and handling. Chandler made history again in 1989 with Bigfoot VII. This beast's cantilevers, full tubular chassis, and nitrogen shock absorbers were considered landmark innovations and set the standard for future trucks.

BIG WHEELS KEEP ON TURNIN'

If Bigfoot is the Hulk Hogan of monster trucks, Grave Digger is the Macho Man Randy Savage. The two trucks have enjoyed a friendly rivalry over the years, trading the title of "World's Most Famous Monster Truck" back and forth. Grave Digger, a 1951 Ford Panel truck monster-modified by Dave Anderson, debuted in 1986 and beat Bigfoot for the first time in front of a national ESPN audience in 1987. Anderson's go-for-broke driving style resulted in spectacular crashes that often knocked his truck out of contention for trophies but wowed audiences. The emergence of freestyle events in the early '90s allowed drivers a proper venue to show off theatrical jumps and often-intentional crashes. Meanwhile Bigfoot, now in its 16th iteration, continues to win races and events. Bigfoot 16 set the speed record for a monster truck at an indoor race in 2010 with a top speed of 85 mph. (The average speed for monster trucks in stadium races is around 70 mph.) Not half bad for a truck that tips the scales at over 10,000 pounds!

Monster trucks can cost as much as $250,000—the engine alone casts about $35,000.

FEAR OF FLYING

These great sci-fi minds wrote the book about interstellar space travel—yet they're afraid to set foot on an airplane.

"I do not use airplanes. They strike me as unsporting. You can have an automobile accident—and survive. You can be on a sinking ship—and survive. You can be in an earthquake, fire, volcanic eruption, tornado, what you will—and survive. But if your plane crashes, you do not survive. And I say the heck with it."

—Isaac Asimov

"Call it enlightened cowardice, if you like. I am afraid of airplanes. I've been able to avoid flying for some time but, I suppose, if I had to I would. Perhaps it's a case of a little knowledge being a dangerous thing. At one time, I had a pilot's license and 160 hours of solo time on single-engine light aircraft. Unfortunately, all that seemed to do was make me mistrust large aeroplanes."

—Stanley Kubrick

"My first flight was at age 62. I needed three double martinis. After we landed, I realized I was not afraid of flying. I was afraid of running up and down the aisle screaming: 'Stop the jet, I want to get off.' I took a second flight, and I didn't scream or yell or panic.... I've now been to every major city and three times across the Atlantic."

—Ray Bradbury

"The flight you have to be afraid of is the flight where there's nobody on who's afraid of flying. Those are the flights that crash. Trust me on this. You have three or four people who are terrified right out of their minds. We hold it up...it's some kind of a psychic thing because, OK, this shouldn't work anyway. Anybody with half a brain knows that [flying] shouldn't work."

—Stephen King

Since 1900 the price of crude oil has risen by 200,000%.

THE BLACK BEETLE

What do you get when you cross a jet with a commuter train?

SUPER ENGINE

In 1966 the New York Central Railroad had a problem: how to get drivers out of their cars and back into trains. NYCR's president, Alfred E. Perlman, decided faster "jet" trains could be the answer. First, the existing rails needed to be tested to see if they could handle high-speed trains.

Lab engineers at Collinwood Yard in Cleveland took a month to assemble a prototype super engine. They ripped out the seats and motor engine of a 1956 Budd RDC3 self-powered diesel commuter coach and attached a streamlined cowling (which looked a lot like a black welding mask with 2 square eyeholes) across the front. Two J47 GE-19 jet engines were stripped from a retired B-36 "Peacemaker" bomber and installed on the roof of the train, which was named the M-497.

MAKING TRACKS

On July 23, 1966, Perlman and engineer Donald C. Wetzel climbed into the cab of the "Black Beetle" (the M-497's nickname) and fired up the jets. A straight length of track between Butler, Indiana, and Stryker, Ohio, had been chosen for the test run. On four runs over the next two days, the M-497 hit a top speed of 183.68 mph, an American light-rail record that remains unbeaten to this day.

Although the M-497 tests yielded useful data about the stresses of high-speed travel on conventional equipment, the experiment went no further. In 1968, New York Central merged with the Pennsylvania Railroad, which decided that high-speed rail travel was not cost-effective. Its jet engines removed, the Budd RDC3 was returned to service, where it remained until 1984. However, the new company, Penn Central Transportation, did find a use for the jet engines. They were rigged to the front of a locomotive for use as a high-performance snow blower.

In Europe, demolition derbies are called "banger races."

DUSTED

Crop dusters are a breed apart, putting on dazzling air shows every day for an audience of...no one.

AERIAL ASSAULT

On August 3, 1921, former Army Air Corps pilot Lt. John A. Macready climbed into the cockpit of his Curtiss JN-6J "Jenny" biplane and prepared to attack the enemy. Only this time it wasn't the Germans he was fighting. The Catalpa sphinx moth had infested a grove of trees near Dayton, Ohio. Armed with a hopper full of powdered lead arsenate bolted to the fuselage of his Jenny, Macready pumped the moths full of lead—literally. Most of the bugs were wiped out in the first pass. Macready didn't know it, but he'd not only demonstrated a new practical use for the airplane, he'd created a new industry: crop dusting.

Macready was one of a small force of World War I pilots who, along with their surplus biplanes, had come home looking for work. Farmers immediately saw how "aerial application" (the preferred industry term) could save them money and time, and the practice spread quickly across rural America.

In 1925 Huff Daland Manufacturing of Macon, Georgia, added a chemical tank and spreader system to a modified Petrel 5 biplane and created the Huff Daland Duster, the first airplane built specifically as a crop duster. The company later moved its operations from Macon to Monroe, Louisiana. By 1928 Huff Daland Dusters had 25 aircraft, the largest private fleet in the world at the time. (Woolman renamed the company Delta Air Service, and it eventually became Delta Airlines.)

LOW AND SLOW

Flying the crop dusters required a special breed of pilot: a little reckless, but very careful. They had to drop in "low and slow" over the fields, wheels almost brushing the crops (this was necessary to reduce "chemical drift," pesticide or fertilizer that drifted where it wasn't meant to go), all the while keeping a sharp eye out for fence posts, telephone and electrical wires, and their own flagmen. Being a flagman was as dangerous as being a

Despite higher speed limits, fatality rates on German autobahns are lower than on US interstates.

pilot: The flagman's job was to stand at the end of a field and signal to a diving crop duster with a white flag which rows had been dusted and which hadn't. Flagmen ran a constant risk of being sprayed.

THE PLANES

In spite of the Huff Daland planes, most crop dusters in the 1930s were still WWI relics that had been jury-rigged to deliver pesticides and fertilizers. But those early planes had lightweight frames that couldn't hold up to the pressures of dusting. Accidents were common; deaths, frequent. The end of World War II delivered an unexpected but welcome dividend in the form of surplus military training planes like the Boeing/Stearman "Kaydet" and Piper "Cub." Thousands became crop dusters, many of them flown by veterans who had trained in them. Nonetheless, they were repurposed planes.

Starting with the Ag-1 in 1950, new planes tailor-made for crop dusting became the norm. With a high cockpit positioned above its single wing, the Ag-1 gave its pilot maximum visibility, something the old biplanes didn't have. The Ag-1 was followed by the Grumman Ag-Cat, which became an industry workhorse for over 40 years, and the Piper PA-25 Pawnee and PA-36 Brave.

Planes used today, like the Ayres Turbo-Thrush and Air Tractor AT-400 Turbo Crop-duster require shorter runways for takeoffs and landings, a useful thing when the "runway" is often a dirt track along the edge of field. As for flagmen, they're not needed anymore: Today's dusters use GPS technology to track which fields they've sprayed.

AIRPLANE DRIVERS

John "Dusty" Dowd of Syracuse, Kansas, spent four decades crop dusting. "To be a good crop duster," he says, "a pilot has to be intimate enough with the airplane that flying it becomes second nature." Commercial pilots, he says, rely on instruments too much, not their own senses. Dowd tells his students to "quit looking at the instruments and watch where you're going." For Dusty, it's a matter of life and death. Although the new planes are far superior to the planes of old, the hazards of flying "low and slow" remain as deadly as ever.

The phrases "brownie points," "make the grade," and "side-tracked" all began as railroad terms.

CLOWN CARS

A clown named Otto came up with the now-classic gag of piling lots of guys into a tiny car. So how does he do it?

OTTO-MATIC DRIVE

You're at the circus, enjoying a night under the big top. Suddenly a little car roars to the center of the ring, spewing pink and blue smoke. After much honking, the clown driver gets out, followed by a fellow clown. Then another clown. And another...and another. Eventually as many as 20 clowns emerge from an impossibly tiny car, and the crowd goes wild. Kids of all ages have been applauding the clown car trick for more than 60 years, ever since it was first introduced in 1950 by master clown Otto Griebling at the Cole Brothers Circus. Other clowns quickly incorporated the bit into their own acts, and it's been a mainstay of big-top mayhem since then. According to Greg DeSanto, executive director of the International Clown Hall of Fame and Research Center in Baraboo, Wisconsin, the trick remains the most requested of all clown gags.

SO WHAT'S THE CATCH?

"There's no trick to the clown car gag," DeSanto insists. "No trap doors, and the cars are real." He should know: He studied at the renowned Barnum and Bailey Clown College in Sarasota, Florida, and went on to perform with "The Greatest Show on Earth." According to DeSanto, the typical clown car is a fully functional automobile (VW Beetles are especially popular) with a stripped-out interior. Everything is removed: seats, door panels, and any barrier to the trunk. Windows are painted over, with only a small space on the windshield left clear for the driver, perched on a milk crate, to see through. Carefully placed handles and ledges allow the other 14 to 20 clowns to cram themselves, and their props and costumes, into about three cubic feet of space each. Once inside, these clown contortionists need only endure a few minutes of discomfort before they're released...to the delight of the crowd.

Car salesmen refer to a cheap but very ugly car as a "clown car."

BIKER FLICKS

Moviegoers in the late '60s and early '70s were hot for motorcycle gangs and girls gone bad. Often the best part of a biker movie was the tag line on the poster.

Leather on the outside...
All woman on the inside.
(*The Hellcats*, 1968)

Kitten on wheels with
her bike...her boots...
and her bikini!
(*Born Losers*, 1967)

He's a cycle PSYCHO!
(*Angels from Hell*, 1968)

They laid waste to
the flesh and blood of
America's daughters.
(*Rebel Rousers*, 1970)

Riding their men
as viciously as they ride
their motorcycles!
(*She Devils on Wheels*, 1968)

Their credo is violence...
their god is hate!
(*The Wild Angels*, 1966)

The roar of their pipes
is their battle cry...
the open road
their killing ground.
(*The Savage Seven*, 1968)

He squealed on his
gang...and the world was
out to WASTE HIM!
(*Run, Angel, Run!*, 1969)

They're hog-straddling
female animals on
the prowl!
(*The Mini-Skirt Mob*, 1968)

Meet the debutante
in a leather skirt.
(*Hell's Belles*, 1969)

A howling hellcat humping
a hot steel hog on a roaring
rampage of revenge.
(*Bury Me An Angel*, 1972)

If you're hairy, you belong
on a motorbike.
(*Werewolves on Wheels*, 1971)

The cycle jungle of hot
steel and raw flesh!
(*Devil Rider*, 1970)

He'll take his chopper and
ram it down your throat.
(*Chrome and Hot Leather*,
1971)

Louis Chevrolet, who co-founded the company, lost everything in the 1929...

LE FLOP

Renault's Le Car was sporty, economical, and cute. And, according to NPR Car Talk's *Tom and Ray Magliozzi, it was also so badly engineered that it "would put you in mortal danger if you ran into anything larger than a croissant."*

LE COMPANY

By 1976 giant French automaker Renault had been trying to break into the North American market for nearly two decades. The company had been producing cars since 1897—almost from the birth of the automobile—and knew a thing or two about selling them to fuel-conscious Europeans. But the U.S. was a different market, saturated with gas-guzzling models. Then the energy crisis of 1973 pushed Americans to trade in their Camaros and T-Birds for more-economical Honda Civics and VW Rabbits. Working in partnership with American Motors (AMC), Renault decided the time was right to introduce its 41-mpg 55-hp supermini, the Renault 5. The car featured a sporty look that included a steeply sloped rear hatchback and dashboard, and Renault believed it finally had a sure winner.

LE DEBUT

The Renault 5 debuted in grand fashion at the Silverado Country Club in Napa Valley in October 1975. Famed chef Paul Bocuse was on hand dishing out hors d'oeuvres and foie gras to the press, and racecar driver Marie-Claude Beaumont demonstrated a sports version of the 1976 model 5 on a track. Dealers were charmed. But the first models were rolled out in showrooms on the East Coast, not the booming California market where the car had just been so favorably previewed. And Renault decided not to put in an appearance at the influential L.A. Auto Expo, which specialized in trendy imports. Those two moves would prove to be marketing miscalculations of epic proportions.

LE SILENCE

The Renault 5 hit the market with a thud. Of 13,458 cars sent to the U.S. in 1976, nearly half remained on the lot by the time the

...stock market crash and had to work as a line mechanic in a Chevrolet factory.

'77s were introduced in September. The company blamed its advertising agency for the weak sales and promptly fired it, only to be informed by its new agency, Marsteller, that Renault's problem was its image: It didn't have one. The Renault name was unknown to most American buyers, so the number 5 meant nothing to them. Marsteller convinced Renault's director of publicity, Pierre Gazarian, to rename the vehicle, adding that "the name should not only convey the car's French heritage, but be easily digestible for a less sophisticated American consumer." After several names were tested—including Frog—Renault settled on Le Car.

LE SUCCESS

A new marketing campaign inspired by Le Car's Gallic roots began in earnest. Ads for Le Car touted "Les Features," "Le Performance," and "L'Economy." Buyers could expect "Le Fantastic Ride" at a reasonable "Le Price." It worked—Americans sick of waiting in gas lines began snatching up Le Cars. In February 1977, 862 were sold. In March, Americans purchased another 1,377. In April, the number shot up another 2,503. By the end of the year, Renault had sold 12,645 Le Cars, doubling its sales from the previous year. Five years later, annual sales had reached 37,000.

LE DEMISE

Then cracks appeared in the import's fortunes—literally. Before long, Le Cars gained a reputation for rusting and flimsiness. Said one owner, "I'm convinced that the body metal for this car was supplied by Reynold's Aluminum Foil." Head gaskets were prone to failure, and owners found themselves waiting for months for expensive replacements to be shipped from France. Soon Le Car became known as Le Throwaway Car, as dissatisfied owners complained that they couldn't drive what they couldn't fix. Renault, losing money to the tune of one billion francs per month, decided to pull the plug. With little fanfare, the automaker ceased production in 1983. By 2000, when *Car Talk*'s Tom and Ray named Le Car the sixth-worst car of the millennium, there were only a handful left on the road. But there may be Le Car Nouveau in the near future. In 2014 Renault will offer an all-new Le Car to compete with the popular Mini Cooper and Volkswagen Beetle. No plans have been announced for a U.S. release—yet.

New York City's subway cars travel about 350 million miles per year.

TOP GUN: FACT OR FICTION?

Uncle John asked some real military pilots the burning question: Is all that stuff in Top Gun *real?*

PLAYING VOLLEYBALL

Hollywood: The men oil up, get half-naked, and play volleyball in dramatic lighting.

Reality: According to former naval flight officer Lt. Matt Powers, NFOs do *not* get oiled up and play volleyball together. And they wear regular clothes when they go out.

FLYING UPSIDE DOWN CLOSE TO AN ENEMY

Hollywood: In the most famous scene of the movie, Maverick (Tom Cruise) and Goose (Anthony Edwards) fly their F-14 "inverted" less than two meters from an enemy MiG. (Note: In 2006 the Navy replaced the F-14 "Tomcat" with the F/A-18 "Super Hornet.")

Reality: This upside-down move is aeronautically possible but according to Major Rob Raymond, an F-16 pilot with 1,800 flight hours' experience, 300 in combat, the answer is, "No. The MiG-28 would have been a willing participant with very steady hands, and even then they probably would have swapped paint."

"HIT THE BRAKES, HE'LL FLY RIGHT BY"

Hollywood: Maverick has an adversary at his "dead-6" (directly behind him). He slows down, pulls up, and a few seconds later when he's directly behind his adversary...whoo-hoo, Jester's dead!

Reality: Lt. Colonel Kirk Reagan, a test-pilot at Edwards Air Force Base, California, says that the movie got the aeronautics right. "By applying idle power and popping the speed brakes, you could cause the other aircraft to over-pursue." But it's a bad idea, unless your adversary is a terrible pilot. "You would only want to 'hit the brakes' after your primary game plan fails against an adversary who demonstrates he can maintain position at your 6 [tail],"

Oldest active fighter pilot: Uri Gil of the Israeli Air Force, born in 1943.

Raymond explains. "If he continues to threaten you, you are most likely pretty slow at that point, as he will have been threatening you with air-to-air missiles, causing you to perform a high-G break turn with your throttle back to minimize your heat signature. If he knows what he is doing, he will keep his distance to allow range for either missiles or a controlled gun attack. Putting the brakes on may be your only hope to draw him in closer or cause an overshoot once you are too slow to turn effectively, but it would not occur in the crisp, abrupt manner portrayed in the movie."

SPINNING OUT OF CONTROL

Hollywood: On a training mission Maverick and Goose fly through the jet-wash (the turbulent air behind a plane's engines) of a friendly plane, sending their plane into an uncontrollable spin out to sea. They eject, and Goose dies when he slams into the canopy.

Reality: Major Raymond has been in a spin or two, and he says the depiction of the spin is pretty close but having the spin send the plane out to sea is "just plain silly." Once an aircraft is in a spin, it quickly runs out of forward momentum and will hit the ground close by.

SUSTAINING 20-MM GUN DAMAGE

Hollywood: An enemy shoots a handful of 20-mm rounds into the engine of Iceman's plane. He bravely carries on, taking even more rounds before landing safely on the carrier.

Reality: The kind of damage Iceman (Val Kilmer) takes in the movie's final dogfight would effectively end that aircraft's viability, and it would have crashed 30 seconds later.

REQUESTING A FLY-BY

Hollywood: Maverick has a history of high-speed passes by the control tower with an uncanny knowledge of exactly when his commander will be drinking coffee.

Reality: Pilots request fly-bys all the time and are often allowed to do them. But Lt. Matt Powers says the movie got it way wrong. When the "pattern is full," he explains, "there are a bunch of other fast, expensive jets in the way and if you do a fly-by you may crash and die. So let's say you go ahead and perform the for-

Vasilii Hazkevich of Russia set a world record in 2005 when he drove 13,172 miles on a tractor.

bidden fly-by. You get in SERIOUS trouble. You don't get sent to Top Gun. Your skipper gets an earful, and you get stuck on duty for a month."

FLYING CLOSE TOGETHER

Hollywood: In the movie, the F-14s, F-5s, and A-4s (simulating MiGs) all fly at over 300 knots (345 mph) only a few hundred feet from each other, especially when going in for the kill.

Reality: Not a special effect. The planes really did fly that close. But they wouldn't in actual combat. An F-14 pilot wouldn't go to guns inside 1,200 feet, so images of planes fighting that closely are pure Hollywood. If a pilot shot down a plane at that range, the exploding target would send debris into the motor of any plane behind it, and they'd both crash. When Iceman said, "I'm too close for missiles, I'm switching to guns," he was already too close for guns.

COACHING COUGAR

Hollywood: Maverick's wingman has a nervous breakdown after a close call and can't land his plane. Maverick calms him down and talks him through it.

Reality: Another pilot would not be doing the coaching; it would be the Landing Signal Officer. The military is very good at keeping unnecessary chatter off the radio.

TRAVELING AT THE SPEED OF SOUND

Hollywood: When Maverick rushes to help Iceman in the last battle, he says he is "supersonic." The next shot shows the F-14's wings in the wide, extended position.

Reality: To travel that fast, the F-14 would need its wings in a swept-back position. The wing position is automatically controlled by onboard computers, so Maverick wasn't quite at the speed of sound yet.

* * *

REJECTED NAMES FOR THE BLUE ANGELS

Jaxcats, Jaxateers, Com-Bats, Death-Cheaters, Blue Bachelors, Cloud Busters, Strat-O-Cats, Cavaliers, Blue Lancers

FATAL FIRSTS

Unfortunately, someone has to go first.

FIRST DEATH BY TRAIN

Among the many celebrities attending the September 15, 1830, launch of the Liverpool and Manchester Railway in England were the Duke of Wellington and William Huskisson, Member of Parliament. The two were to ride a succession of trains to Liverpool, with the first stop at Parkside railway station to water the steam engine. Ignoring the engineer's warning to remain on the train, Huskisson joined the other passengers who'd disembarked to gawk at the parade of engines lined up on parallel tracks. He stepped onto an empty track just as an engine called *The Rocket* barreled into the station. Huskisson fell beneath the wheels of *The Rocket* and lost his leg. As his own train transported him to the nearest hospital, the MP declared, "My death is near." He died moments later, unaware that he'd made history.

FIRST DEATH BY CAR

On September 14, 1899, Henry Bliss stepped down from a streetcar at W. 74th and Central Park West in New York City. As he turned to help a female passenger down the stairs, he was struck by a passing cab, making the 68-year-old realtor the first pedestrian killed by an automobile in the United States.

FIRST DEATH BY PLANE

Five years after their historic first flight at Kitty Hawk, the Wright brothers took their new plane, the *Wright Flyer*, on a cross-country tour to prove it could safely carry passengers. Their third stop was at Ft. Myer, Virginia on September 17, 1908. As a crowd of 2,000 cheered, Orville Wright and his passenger, Lt. Thomas E. Selfridge of the U.S. Signal Corps, lifted off into the sky. Then the propeller snapped in two and the *Wright Flyer* nose-dived 150 feet to the ground. Selfridge was killed outright; Wright suffered multiple hip and leg fractures that plagued him with chronic pain for the rest of his life.

PISTOL-PACKIN' TRUCKER

Lillie Drennan's hardscabble life prepared her well for the challenges she faced as America's first female truck driver.

TRUCK-DRIVIN' MA'AM

A trucker's life is a hard one: miles of road and hours of tedium broken only by the occasional truck stop or roadside diner. When you add the days or weeks away from family, frustrating breakdowns, and even-more-frustrating regulations, it rarely equals the romantic image glamorized in country songs. You have to be tough to make it as a long-haul trucker. You have to be even tougher to overcome barriers like sexism.

HARD-KNOCK LIFE

Born in 1897 in Galveston, Texas, Lillie Drennan dropped out of the fifth grade to earn money for her family. A childhood infection left her with impaired hearing. By 17 she was a single mom with a child. She married Willard Drennan, a businessman in Hempstead, Texas, just as big oil came to town in 1928. That March the couple purchased a beat-up Ford Model T truck with an open cab and started the Drennan Truck Line.

Although Willard drove the truck, it soon became clear that Lillie was the driving force behind the enterprise. She went door to door soliciting business from every merchant in town. Through persistence and hard work, Drennan Truck Line developed a reputation as the go-to company for on-time deliveries— no small feat given the rutted, potholed dirt roads of the day. They paid off the first truck and bought another one. The second truck—a closed-cab Chevrolet—was Lillie's.

DON'T MESS WITH THIS TEXAS GIRL

Lillie's growing reputation as a hard-charging, no-nonsense businesswoman became too much for Willard, and the couple split up in 1929, and Lillie got the business in the divorce settlement. Realizing the big money was in the oil fields, Lillie decided to

...the car slows by one-millionth of a mile per hour.

get her commercial truck-driver's license. When the Texas Railroad Commission, which ran the state's motor-freight business, tried to deny her a license due to her hearing impairment, Lillie took them to court and claimed sex bias. "If any man can beat my record, I'll just get out of here!" she exclaimed. Lillie's driving record was spotless, so the commission granted her the license.

NOBODY DID IT BETTER

For the next 24 years, Lillie hauled oil-field equipment, general freight, and explosives all over East Texas. In all that time, neither Lillie nor the drivers she employed had a single accident. She insisted on training each driver herself and only half-jokingly threatened to "pistol-whip" them or "brain them with an iron bar" if they broke her rules. In her 10-gallon hat, khaki pants and shirt, and work boots, a loaded revolver strapped to her hip, she was one of the most colorful characters in a state full of them. When criticized for her "cussin'," she shrugged it off, saying, "Me 'n' God have an understanding."

During World War II, Lillie gained national attention for teaching other women how to drive trucks. Dubbed a "dry-land Tugboat Annie" by the L.A. *Times*, she received safety awards from the Texas Motor Transportation Association and her old nemesis, the Railroad Commission. In 1946 the town of Hempstead honored Lillie with a banquet on Six-Shooter Junction Day, calling her a "20th-century pioneer who has all the color of an Annie Oakley, and who lives the life of a hard-hitting frontierwoman."

ENDURING LEGACY

Lillie died in 1974 at the age of 77. Today an estimated 200,000 women in the United States are long-haul truckers, roughly 5 percent of all drivers. Drawn to the industry for the good pay as well as the independence of working for themselves, women truckers nonetheless face the chronic risk of sexual assault in poorly lit, unpoliced truck stops. Professional associations like Women In Trucking are helping to reform an industry once reserved for men into a safer, more welcoming environment. They may not know it, but these women owe a nod to a feisty pioneer trucker named Lillie Drennan.

The taxi was named after the taximeter, originally used on horse-drawn carriages.

THE TAXI MONOPOLY

A tale of corporate greed from the dawn of the automobile age.

BACKGROUND

In 1897 a fleet of 13 electric taxi cabs took to the streets of New York City. Built by the Electric Carriage and Wagon Company of Philadelphia, the cabs had a range of 30 miles and a cruising speed of 9 mph, and were equipped with quick-change battery boxes. Twelve cabs and drivers were in service at any given time, supported by a team of six at a battery-charging station. The lead batteries weighed a ton (literally) and were removed for recharging after almost every trip. At the time, the cabs represented the cutting edge of modern technology. Clean, quiet, and comfortable, they made the horse-drawn hacks of the day look positively last century. Profits soared, and soon Electric Carriage and Wagon Company had expanded its fleet to 100 cabs.

But owner Isaac Rice wanted much, much more. He partnered with Wall Street financiers William C. Whitney, P. A. B. Widener, Anthony N. Brady, and others, and the renamed Electric Vehicle Company became a holding company with a single purpose: to create a taxicab monopoly, first in New York City and then in every metropolitan area in the United States.

BATTERY EMPOWERED

Using its investors' big wallets, EVC snapped up the Electric Storage Battery Company, which controlled the rights to most existing battery patents from General Electric and Consolidated Electric Storage. Now EVC could refuse batteries to any competing cab or car company. The "lead cab syndicate" (so-called because of the lead batteries used in the cars) put the pressure next on electric car designers and manufacturers, making them offers they couldn't refuse if they wanted to stay in business. Within the year, the EVC fleet had 1,000 taxis. In 1899 EVC bought the rights to George Selden's "liquid hydrocarbon motor carriage" patent, in effect giving the company the right to receive royalties from the manufacture of any internal combustion engine in America.

From 1916 to 1920, Girl Scouts could earn an Automobiling Badge.

The future looked rosy for EVC. The company had its monopoly: Their distributors and manufacturers had no place else to do business, and competitors were hamstrung by the vise-like control EVC had on industry patents. As profits soared, EVC used the money to gobble up any innovator or company that seemed a potential threat to what had now become complete control of the infant automobile industry.

A TITAN FALLS

Then came the Bank Panic of 1907 and the closing of 93 banks across the country. EVC had leveraged future profits to borrow $20 million (about $461 million today) to keep expanding its reach. Now investors and lenders, facing bankruptcy themselves, wanted their money back. Without the cash to pay up, EVC collapsed. Its investors lost millions, its taxi monopolies were broken up, and the electric car industry faltered and never recovered. Saddled with lawsuits from competitors like Henry Ford, the company filed for bankruptcy. The coup de grace came in 1911, when its rights to the Selden patent were overthrown in court. The Electric Vehicle Company was history, a victim of its own corporate gluttony.

* * *

TAXI!

• The word *taxicab* comes from the French *taximeter cabriolet*. *Taximeter* is a derivation of the German *Taxameter*, which itself comes from the Medieval Latin *taxa*, meaning "to tax or charge." *Meter* comes from the Greek word *metron*, meaning "to measure." A *cabriolet* is a type of horse-drawn carriage. Put it all together and you get "to tax or charge the measure of (distance traveled) by a horse-drawn carriage." Over time, the *-meter* and *-riolet* fell away, leaving us with the modern English word *taxicab*, and the universal *taxi*.

• Ancient Romans had taximeters that measured distance by balls dropped out of a cart's axle into a receptacle. The number of balls used by the end of the ride determined the fare.

World's largest battleships: the Japanese WWII vessels *Yamato* and *Musashi*, at 863 feet long.

THE ORIENT EXPRESS

In the Golden Age of travel, nothing said glamor, intrigue, and romance like the fabled train that ran from Paris to Istanbul.

VIPS ONLY

Georges Nagelmackers (1845–1905) was a wealthy Belgian with friends in high places. His father, a railroad financier, taught him the business and especially how to exploit royal connections with King Leopold and his court. Nagelmackers dreamed of offering a train service that catered to those high-society VIPs. His dream came true on October 4, 1883, when he launched *L'Express d'Orient*, a private train that was touted as the most luxurious in the world. The inaugural trip's guest list of 40 was a veritable Who's Who of Europe's elite. Diplomats and bankers, a Romanian general, a Belgian cabinet minister, an esteemed author from Alsace, and a smattering of journalists gathered at the Gare de l'Est in Paris, anxious to begin their journey. Each one of the gentlemen carried a revolver.

CRÈME DE LA CRÈME

Nagelmackers's vision of a state-of-the-art luxury train was inspired by the time he'd spent traveling on Pullman railroad cars in the United States. In the 19th century, these were the best in the world, with unparalleled service and amenities. By contrast, Nagelmackers found European trains to be overheated, overcrowded, and lacking adequate toilets or decent food service. If you wanted to eat, you had to grab a sandwich on the run at station stops, and sleeping cars found strangers lying head to toe and shoulder to shoulder. Tedious stops at every border made long-distance travel all but unbearable.

After his U.S. trip, Nagelmackers envisioned a European train that would run smoothly from country to country with passengers riding in what he called *boudoir* cars. In 1870 he formed the Compagnie Internationale des Wagons-Lits and for several years simply attached his boudoir cars to existing trains. But in 1883 he was able to put together an entire train.

LAP OF LUXURY

Each compartment, or *coupe*, was an individual sitting room replete with Turkish carpets, silk wall coverings, and two red plush armchairs. In the evening, stewards made up the double bed that folded out of the wall with silk sheets and eiderdown duvets. Each *coupe* had its own toilet with marble counters, porcelain sinks, gilt fixtures, and scented toiletries. Showers were at the rear of the train. Social cars included a smoking lounge, ladies' boudoir, and library. The ceiling of the dining car was sheathed in embossed Cordoba leather, its walls lined with tapestries and velvet curtains. Every evening, the master chef, who hailed from Burgundy, prepared a five-course *haute cuisine* meal.

BON VOYAGE!

The train route itself was exotic. For most Victorians, traveling farther east than Vienna or Budapest was unimaginable, like going to the edge of civilization. But the premiere voyage of the Orient Express went all the way to Istanbul, fabled capital of the mysterious, decadent Ottoman Empire. That initial run turned out to be quite an adventure.

Reportedly, as the train rolled into Augsburg, Germany, the dining car's axle overheated, so the diner had to be replaced by a much plainer one in Munich. In Bucharest, King Charles of Romania invited all of the passengers to his "summer palace" for brunch, which ended up being a four-hour side trip that involved slogging through mud up a steep hill to reach the king's country chalet.

At the Danube River, the passengers were told to disembark. They were ferried across to Bulgaria (a railroad bridge wouldn't be built for five more years), where they boarded a new train. At Votova Station, the story goes, they found that brigands had murdered the stationmaster, kidnapped his daughter, and tried to set fire to the station. Gentlemen passengers were instructed to keep a tight grip on their revolvers that night, lest the murderers return. At the Black Sea port of Varna, the inaugural party disembarked once again, and traveled the final leg of their 1,896-mile journey to Istanbul by steamship.

C'EST MAGNIFIQUE

According to some accounts, the return trip featured the happy addition of a few new passengers, all female and all dressed to the nines. The correspondent from *The Times* of London wrote that "the train's corridors became like the pavement of the Rue de la Paix" as beautiful young ladies emerged from their rooms to promenade among the gentlemen. A gypsy band boarded at Tsigany, Hungary, and presented a lively concert in the dining car, which had been cleared of furniture. When the band played "La Marseillaise," the chef popped out of the gallery to lead the singing. By the time *L'Express d'Orient* made its triumphant return to Paris, word had spread about this glamorous and exciting new way to tour the Continent.

RIDING HIGH

L'Express d'Orient was definitely for the very wealthy. The price tag was outrageous: fare for a couple and servant was enough to feed and clothe a working-class family for a year. But the extravagance only increased its cachet.

By 1889 the route from Paris to Istanbul was complete, with no changes required in trains, ferries, or steamship rides. Nonetheless, travel on the Orient Express (the English version was made the official name of the train in 1885) was always full of surprises. King Boris III of Bulgaria viewed it as his own personal plaything. When the train entered his domain, he often came onboard in a tailored white engineer's suit and insisted on driving. After he set the fireman's clothes on fire by stoking the engine too high, engineers were given instructions never to let him drive again.

Nagelmackers died in 1905, but his Orient Express continued to run until 1977, only stopping service during the world wars. During the 1930s, its route made it a hotbed of international intrigue, which, of course, only made it more desirable. And it became the glamorous setting for best-selling novels by Bram Stoker, Agatha Christie, Ian Fleming, and Graham Greene, as well as Alfred Hitchcock's 1938 thriller *The Lady Vanishes*.

Today a private company continues the fabled run under the name Venice-Simplon Orient Express, using original carriages from the 1920s and '30s. The train still runs from Paris to Istanbul, and it remains one of the most expensive, luxurious train rides in the world.

ACCESSORIZE ME

With countless auto products to choose from, Uncle John picked these five essentials for a tricked-out ride.

CARSTACHE

What every car needs: a mustache for its grille. This must-have accessory from Carstache of San Francisco is made of fuzzy faux fur and comes in many colors and styles to match every personality, like classic Firestache Orange: "Your heat is intense. You are molten. You are liquid hot magma. You are the match that lit the torch that set the 'stache on fire."

BULLET HOLE STICKERS

From Prank Place, the company who brought you the Remote Control Fart Machine, Cockroach Gum, the Fake Parking Ticket, and the $5 Box of Crap, comes a set of extreme Rapid Fire Bullet Hole stickers to apply to auto windows or doors.

CARLASHES

Imagine giant plastic eyelashes framing your VW Beetle's headlights. Turbo Style Products of Park City, Utah, offers these flirty lashes that also look cute on BMWs and Mini Coopers. Sparkly eyeliner available separately.

FRENCH FRY HOLDER

For the drive-through gourmet, a constant issue is: Where do I put my fries? The Improvements company offers a French Fry Holder with a non-slip rubber base that fits right in your cup holder. There's even a clip-on ketchup cup for easy dipping and driving.

CAR TEETH

These inserts fit over a car's grille to make it look like a cartoon car. Not all car smiles are alike: You can choose a friendly opened-mouth smile, the "Alley Gator" pointy-teeth version, or the "Mako" shark-toothed smile. AutoXpressions of Lancaster, California, also offers buckteeth, missing teeth, and, of course, vampire fangs.

The first American ambulance service was established in Cincinnati in 1865.

PROPELLER CARS

Why put a propeller on a car? For starters, it eliminates the need for a transmission or clutch. No traction problems in snow or mud. And, oh yeah, speed.

PLANES WITHOUT WINGS

Airplanes and cars entered the 20th century together, so it's not surprising that technological progress in one often found its way to the other. One early air-car was the Sizaire-Berwick Wind Wagon, an armored truck powered by a rear-mounted propeller developed for use in rough terrain by the British Army in 1915. But it was only after the Great War that propeller cars began to appear on the road with some regularity, particularly in France.

Leading the way was Marcel Leyat (1885–1986), who started out making airplanes but in 1913 switched to building a line of propeller-powered cars called Helica. His "planes without wings," as Leyat called them, looked much like a fuselage with the wings stripped off. An 8-hp Scorpion radial engine and a wooden propeller were mounted in front of the driver. The passenger sat behind the driver, as in a two-seater airplane. Some models had a protective shroud around the propeller, but most were completely open. Leyat's prototype 1914 Helicycle was a three-wheeler that proved unstable, so all future Helicas were four-wheeled. The front wheels were fixed, and the rear wheels were controlled by the steering wheel. The car's body was made entirely of plywood, making it very light (only 550 pounds) and thus very fast. In 1927 a Helica set a speed record of 106 mph at the Montlhéry racetrack. However, Leyat sold only 30 of his air-cars before stopping production at his Paris factory in 1926. The car-buying public saw the Helica as an interesting novelty but not as a viable family car.

VIVA ARGENTINA

Nonetheless, auto innovators continued to develop air-cars throughout the 1930s and '40s. Most were one-offs that appeared with a splash, only to vanish shortly after, like the 1932 Helicron that can be seen today at the Lane Motor Museum in Nashville,

The Antonov An-124 Ruslan has a 290-foot wingspan, the greatest of any plane currently flying.

Tennessee, and the 1938 German Maybach luxury sedan, fitted with a seven-cylinder radial airplane engine above the trunk.

The Russians built hundreds of propeller-driven sleds for winter use during both World Wars and well into the 1960s, leading directly to the development of the modern snowmobile. But over time, propeller power gave way to track or half-track systems.

In 1953 Eugenio Grosovich and Gianfranco Bricci of Argentina piqued the interest of the U.S. auto industry with the Aerocar. Sleek and aerodynamic (it was often compared to the Czech Tatra in style), the Aerocar was powered by a rear-mounted 90-hp Chevy engine. Tests showed it hitting highway speeds of over 100 mph. However, its sluggish acceleration from 0 to 40 mph, along with safety fears associated with its five-foot propeller, convinced Detroit to pass on the Aerocar.

CHIMERA

For the past 50 years, the propeller car has remained an object of fascination for mechanical tinkerers and enthusiasts but has been pretty much ignored by the auto industry. However, in 2005 Atair Aerospace debuted the Chimera, billed as a "fast attack, light strike" vehicle designed specifically for Special Forces operations. Powered by what Atair calls a "ducted fan propulsion system" (read: propeller) the Chimera can be airdropped to a landing site, converted in minutes to a light jeep by folding up the 100-foot elliptical parasail, propeller-driven wherever it needs to go on the ground at 60 mph, then flown back to base at 30 knots (40 mph). With its capability of driving or flying over any obstacle, be it a river, gorge, jungle, or swamp, the Chimera is the ultimate off-off-road vehicle.

* * *

THEFT BY TOW TRUCK

Thieves in Florida have discovered a unique way to steal cars: hire tow trucks and let them do it. Posing as fed-up car owners, they hire towing services to haul the designated cars to a junkyard, where they get some cash for their "trash." How can they get away with this? Salvage yards in Florida don't require the car's owner to present a title.

GM's head of research, Charles Kettering, invented freon refrigerant (1928) and leaded gas (1924).

TALES OF THE TUBE

An estimated three million people ride the London Underground every day. But it turns out there may be a few more...things...down there as well.

BRING OUT YOUR DEAD

Eerie stories about the London Underground have their roots in a time long before the subway tunnels were built, long before there were even trains. Back in 1665, the bubonic plague swept through London, and 100,000 people—a fifth of the city's inhabitants—succumbed to the disease. To prevent the epidemic from spreading, corpses were buried by the thousands in what were known as "plague pits." In the centuries that followed, the location of these mass graves was forgotten. But when tunneling began on the new subway in the 1860s, workers began uncovering the grisly remains of plague victims. As late as the 1960s, tunneling machines routinely crunched through human skeletons mixed in with rock and dirt. And where the dead lie buried, ghost stories surely follow...

SOUTH KENSINGTON WHISTLE STOP

In December 1928, passengers at South Kensington station boarding the final westbound train of the evening were startled when a loud whistle announced another train pulling in. A man in a peaked cap and reefer jacket (naval coat) was hanging on to the side of the unexpected locomotive. The mysterious train and its ghostly passenger disappeared as quickly as they had appeared, never to be seen or heard from again.

THE UNDEAD OF CRYSTAL PALACE

When it was built in 1865, Crystal Palace station in south London was a marvel of Victorian architecture. At its peak, 7,000 to 8,000 passengers passed beneath its majestic iron-and-glass roof with corner spires. By 1890, however, the station's elegant terra cotta brickwork had fallen into disrepair. By the late 1920s, it served only a few hundred daily passengers. During World War II, Crystal Palace was used as an air raid shelter. German bombing during the

The mayor of Boston's official car has had the same license plate number, 576, since 1914.

Blitz shattered what was left of the glass roof, and by the time the war ended, rats far outnumbered commuters. The station was closed for good in 1954 and demolished in 1961. The area is now covered by apartments and houses. All that remains of the station is a high retaining wall, a lone building, and a stretch of tunnel beneath the road...and perhaps some ghostly zombies.

Legend has it that buried somewhere beneath the rubble of Crystal Palace station is a bricked-up train wreck from the early days of the line. The dead were purportedly entombed where they perished, along with the shattered remains of the locomotive. They are not resting in peace, however. Locals claim ghostly hands occasionally reach up from below to grab unwary pedestrians passing by aboveground.

DON'T MIND THE GHOUL

Strange noises, footsteps with no source, doors flinging themselves open, and the sight of a ghostly girl are par for the course at the Elephant and Castle station of the Bakerloo line. Northbound passengers often report seeing the reflection of someone sitting in the seat beside them on the train, even though no one is there. These events are so common, in fact, that longtime employees take the sounds and sightings in stride. When one new employee reported to his driver that a young girl had brushed past him on the train and vanished, presumably down the tunnel, the driver replied, "Oh, her. We hear about her all the time. She's even been in the papers."

* * *

CAUTION: HUMAN CROSSING

As a man stepped off the curb to cross a street, a car came screaming around the corner and headed straight for him. The alarmed man tried to hurry across the street, but the car changed lanes and maintained its collision course. So the guy turned around to run back to the curb, but the car changed lanes again. Panicked, the old man froze in the middle of the road. The car pulled up beside him and the window rolled down. The driver was a squirrel. "See?" it said. "It's not as easy as it looks."

Minnesota has one recreational boat per every six people, more than any other state.

PARLEZ-VOUS DRAGSTER?

If you want to impress the pit tootsies, better learn how to talk like a big weenie. Then head down to Broadway, hop in your Hauling Henry, and cut a fat one.

Anchors: brakes

Baby moons: wheel covers

Bad news: good running car

Balloon the balonies: put air in the tires

Barn door bash: race

Bicycle big arm: stroker crank

Big weenie: top driver

Bird catcher: fuel injector

Blown hemi: engine equipped with a supercharger

Broadway: drag strip

Buzz box: mag timer

Chizler: Chrysler

Christmas tree: lighting device used to start a race

Cut a fat one: hit top speed

Dead player: broken car

Digger diver: crew member

Donovan: engine

Drilled him on the tree: beat another driver off the line with a faster reaction time

Flatty: flathead V8, usually a Ford

Galloping hinge: connecting rod

Go juice: fuel

Goat: GTO

Hauling Henry: fast Ford

Hiccup: backfire

Hole shot win: victory due to having the fastest reaction time at the start of the race

Lunched: wrecked

Mouse: small-block Chevy

Pipe: chassis

Pit tootsies: girls

Plastic fantastic: funny car

Railbirds: fans

Railcar: dragster

Rat: big-block Chevy

Set on kill: tune up for optimal racing

Shoe: driver

Treed: having a slower reaction time than your opponent

Wally: National Hot Rod Association Championship trophy

Weenie roaster: jet car

Unglue: blow an engine

Zoomies: short exhaust pipes with no mufflers

CAT TRACKS

A small British company put tracks on a tractor and changed agriculture—and war—forever.

MAKING TRACKS

In 1903 the British War Office offered £1,000 to the maker of a tractor that could haul 25 tons for 40 miles without stopping for fuel or water. The tiny agricultural manufacturer Hornsby & Sons (est. 1815) won with a tractor that went 58 miles. Chief engineer and manager David Roberts realized that if the British Army wanted to make full use of his 80-hp, 12-ton tractor, the machine could not get stuck in mud.

By 1906 Roberts had come up with a novel chain track that he fitted onto the tractor. When British soldiers saw this rolling track in action, they dubbed the machine a "caterpillar." Two years later, the War Office purchased four chain-track tractors to tow artillery pieces. Encouraged, Roberts worked to expand the caterpillar tractor's working applications, fitting it with wooden wheels for desert travel and boosting its top speed to 25 mph.

LOSING TRACK-TION

Hornsby & Sons wanted to share their caterpillar tractor with not only the army but also the general public. They commissioned a film to advertise it (the first commercial ever filmed). Audiences at the Empire Theatre of Varieties in London attended the premiere on April 27, 1908, and were impressed by the new vehicle. Unfortunately, soldiers in the Royal Artillery were not. One gunnery officer sniffed, "A team of eight horses in my opinion is far superior under every condition." Roberts was devastated. When another officer suggested that they might be interested in the caterpillar if it could carry some kind of large gun protected by bulletproof armor, Roberts chose not to pursue it—a decision he was to regret. He only made one sale to the public and came to the conclusion that the caterpillar tractor was a loser. He decided to sell the caterpillar-track patent to cover Hornsby & Sons' losses. Enter C. H. Holt.

Braess's paradox, a mathematical formula, shows that adding more lanes to roads...

TRACK STAR

While Hornsby & Sons was developing engines and tractors in England, C. H. Holt Manufacturing was building wagon wheels and frames in the United States. Founded in California in 1864, Holt quickly evolved into a large-scale farm equipment manufacturer, building 20-ton machines capable of hauling 50 tons. Holt tried to keep his heavy machines from sinking into deep mud by equipping them with tires seven feet in diameter and six feet wide. When that didn't work, he built redwood tracks for the tractors to ride on, which was cumbersome, time-consuming, and expensive. In 1909 he went to England to see what other farm-equipment manufacturers were doing to combat the mud problem. Holt saw the potential in the caterpillar tractor and snapped up the patent from Hornsby & Sons for a mere £4,000 pounds ($86,000 today). Holt also had the foresight to trademark the name "Caterpillar."

Hornsby & Sons lost out due to bad timing—the British War Office decided within the year that they needed lots of caterpillar tractors to tow their heavy howitzers across the uneven fields of France and Belgium during World War I. They purchased 420 from Holt Mfg. for the hefty sum of $5,500 each ($118,000 today). By 1914 Holt had shipped 1,200 Caterpillar tractors to the English, French, and Russians, who sent them off to war. Most importantly, the Holt Caterpillar became the inspiration for the British tank. Today, Caterpillar, Inc. is the largest manufacturer of construction and mining equipment, diesel and natural gas engines, and industrial gas turbines in the world, putting it at #66 on the 2010 Fortune 500 list.

STILL A-TRACK-TIVE

Although Hornsby & Sons missed the business opportunity of a lifetime when Roberts sold the Caterpillar patent, the company prospered with the Hornsby-Akroyd "hot bulb" engine. An early diesel engine designed by Herbert Akroyd Stuart, it was used to power tractors, locomotives, boats, submarines, and lighthouses for a generation. Hornsby-Akroyds powered the lights that originally lit the Statue of Liberty, Rock of Gibraltar, and Taj Mahal.

FLIGHT TRICK

Ever wondered how planes stay up in the air? Here's how it works, along with a little experiment that proves it. All you'll need is…a square of toilet paper.

MAY THE FOUR FORCES BE WITH YOU

Everything that flies—an airplane, a bird, a butterfly—is subject to the same four forces of aerodynamics: to stay aloft, it needs enough *lift* and *thrust* to overcome its *drag* and *weight*. *Thrust* is what powers the aircraft or creature—an engine, flapping, and so on. *Weight* is how gravity affects it, and *drag* is how much it's slowed down by friction with the air. But *lift* is the key—it's the force that keeps the plane or bird from falling out of the sky. How does lift work? For centuries it was a mystery, but in the 18th century, Swiss scientist Daniel Bernoulli figured it out.

LIFT ME UP

Bernoulli's theory went like this: "As the velocity of a fluid or gas increases, its pressure decreases." To picture this, think of a wing slicing through the air like a knife, with some air going over it and some under it. Air particles moving over the wing take the same amount of time to pass over it as the particles below it take to pass under it. So a wing that is *curved* on top will force the air going over it to travel faster than the air below—the higher air speed makes the air pressure *above* the wing less than the air pressure *below* it. The resulting higher pressure below pushes toward the lower pressure above in an attempt to equalize, and the force from below literally "lifts" the wing. With enough lift, anything can be made to fly, no matter how much it weighs.

THE PAPER TRICK

Remember that square of toilet paper? Drape it over your fingers and hold it to your chin just beneath your lower lip. Now blow horizontally over the top of it. See how the paper rises up? That's Bernoulli's Principle in action. By speeding up the air on top of the TP, you decreased the pressure over it. The higher pressure from below pushed the paper upward toward the area of lower pressure. Result: flight. And the rest is aviation history.

Longest race on an oval track: the 600-mile Coca-Cola 600. It takes 400 laps to complete.

FEARLESS FRED

In the early 1960s, helicopter traffic reporters awed audiences by bringing the adventure of flying right into their living rooms. It was hip, it was "now"—and Fred Feldman started it all.

FLIGHT PATTERNS

The first guy to file a traffic report from the sky had no journalism skills whatsoever. What landed Fred Feldman the job as the world's first helicopter reporter was that he could fly and talk at the same time. Others followed, most notably Gary Powers, the U-2 spy plane pilot shot down over the USSR in 1960 who became a pilot/reporter in L.A. in the 1970s. But Fred Feldman was the first "sky jock" to emerge as a beloved radio personality.

The Queens, New York, native had such a strong passion for flying that a college roommate cracked, "You hang one more model from the ceiling and the entire dorm room will take off." After seven years in the Air Force, Feldman went to work for a helicopter service in New York City. In 1962 the 29-year-old pilot was chartered by radio station WOR-AM to fly a reporter over the city during morning rush hour. When the station forgot to hire the reporter, they asked Feldman to make the report himself.

TRAFFIC JAMMIN'

Feldman and Helicopter 710 became a fixture to millions of rush-hour commuters. Balancing a clipboard on his knee, he swooped over the city, delivering reports and quips at 10-minute intervals. Soon "Fearless Fred," as WOR DJ John A. Gambling dubbed him, was getting hundreds of letters from adoring female fans. It was Feldman who called the Long Island Expressway "the world's longest parking lot." Phantom bottlenecks became "rubbernecking delays" because traffic would suddenly slow to gawk at a traffic accident, or, in one instance, at a couple necking on a blanket in Riverside Park, causing a 4-mile backup. When the lights went out in NYC on November 9, 1965, Feldman was the first to tell the world that the blackout covered the entire Northeast. A heart attack grounded him at the age of 45, but "Fearless Fred" continued to work in communications until his death in 1996.

An airbag deploys at about 250 mph.

AUTO NUMMER EINS

The first practical automobile was created in Germany in 1886. One of these guys was the proud papa...but which one?

WHO CAME FIRST?

On March 8, 1886, Gottlieb Daimler of Cannstatt, Germany, powered a stagecoach with a new gasoline combustion engine he had invented. The first automobile? Not quite. A patent for a similar contraption had already been registered in Berlin two months earlier. *Patentschrift* #37435 was granted to Karl Benz of nearby Mannheim, on January 29, 1886, for his *Fahrzeug mit Gasmotoren-betrieb*, or "vehicle with gas engine operation."

THE CHICKEN...

Born in Schorndorf, to a family of successful bakers, Daimler (1834–1900) decided early in his career as an engineer that combustion—not steam—engines were the wave of the future. Headstrong, he bounced from company to company until he found a home in 1872 at Deutz Gasmotorenfabrik, the firm that had invented and mass-produced the four-stroke engine. After parting ways with them in 1882, Daimler worked with his friend William Maybach for four years to build what is considered the first Daimler motorcar.

Daimler's invention looked like an engine strapped to a modified horse carriage, because that's exactly what it was. The four-wheeler had a black metal body with leather seats built by carriagemaker Wimpf & Sohn. The one-cylinder 28-ci gas engine generated up to 1 hp, and maxed out at 11 mph.

...OR THE EGG?

Benz (1844–1929) grew up poor in Karlsruhe. His father died when he was two, and his mother barely got by on a small widow's pension, but she made sure Benz graduated from the local trade school. At age 27, he partnered with a friend to open a foundry, but his friend proved unreliable, and within a year they almost lost the business. Benz's fiancée, Bertha, saved the partners from ruin by convincing her parents to let her use her dowry before the wedding. (Bertha was not afraid to stand by her man, and her hands-on approach was to pay off for Benz years later.)

In 1882 Benz reorganized as Benz und Cie. The new company sold enough engines to allow him time to experiment, and by 1885 he was ironing out the kinks on a three-wheeled, gas-powered vehicle (which meant accidentally driving it into the wall of the garage on occasion). By 1886 Benz had a vehicle he felt was good enough to bring to the patent office in Berlin: the Benz Patent-Motorwagen.

Benz's three-wheeler burned the benzene vapor of a petroleum byproduct called ligroin. The driver steered with a handcrank that turned a rack-and-pinion device attached to a fork of the wheel. Unlike Daimler, Benz integrated the engine into the chassis to make for better steering. Top speed was 10 mph, curb weight 584 pounds, and the price a mere 600 Imperial Deutsche Marks (about $4,440 today).

WORLD'S FIRST AUTO ROAD TRIP

There they were—the first automobiles, poised to change history. But sales were hard to come by. It took Benz a year to find his first customer, a business associate who bought one of the vehicles in 1887 for private use. Even winning the Gold Medal at the Munich International Exhibition of 1888 didn't boost sales for Benz. Daimler didn't close a sale until 1892, when the Sultan of Morocco decided he had to have one of the horseless carriages.

Bertha Benz decided to save the family business—again. One August morning, she grabbed the kids, hopped in a Benz und Cie car, and drove the 102-mile round-trip between Mannheim and Pfozheim, stopping along the way to visit her mother and see her baby nephew. It was the world's first road trip by auto.

The impact of Bertha's exploit was staggering. This was 1888. Few men were willing to trust their own safety to Benz's new device, and here was a woman driving one alone—with her children, no less. By 1900 Benz und Cie was the production leader in automobiles. (Today motorists can relive history by driving the Bertha Benz Memorial Route, part of which goes over an original Roman road called the Via Montana.)

In most US cities, just hailing and getting into a cab will cost you at least $2.50.

THE RACE IS ON

Daimler didn't suffer because of Benz's success. His company—Daimler Motoren Gesellschaft, or DMG—was selling not only cars but also the first fire trucks and commercial buses.

Benz introduced two new four-wheelers called the Viktoria and the Velo, which revved up sales, but he couldn't keep up with the innovations coming out of Daimler works. Also, disagreements between Benz and his board of directors about whether or not to expand the product line got so heated that Benz and his son Eugen quit in 1903, only to return after certain board members resigned. The first thing they did was to expand their line, to great success. World War I destroyed the German economy but helped the company.

But DMG maintained its edge over Benz by constantly upgrading their luxury roadsters, gaining a cult following of rich thrill-seekers like Austrian business magnate Emil Jellinek. Jellinek was fond of racing the latest Daimler sports car, and he soon became the primary Daimler dealer in much of Europe and America. He even insisted that the 1901 model—which introduced the low-mounted engine and trademark radiator grill that attracts drivers today—be named after his 10-year-old daughter, Mercedes.

FOOTNOTE: THE IRONY OF FATE

Daimler died in 1900, and 26 years later, Benz und Cie officially requested "cooperation" with the steady and sturdy DMG. The new union was called Daimler-Benz. Benz died shortly after the merger, in 1929. As rivals and competitors, Daimler and Benz had helped make the automobile become the machine of the modern age. The cars they invented, and the companies they founded, combined to become one of the most respected names in automobiles the world over. Yet even though their workshops were only 60 miles apart and their companies eventually joined, Benz and Daimler never met.

* * *

"I used to work in a fire hydrant factory. You couldn't park anywhere near the place."

—**Steven Wright**

HIGH-SEAS HIGH TECH

Using GPS units and camouflaged frigates, modern pirates have been capturing ships and headlines around the globe. Their targets have begun to fight back.

SITTING DUCKS

When Somali pirates began seizing freighters in the Gulf of Aden in the 1990s, they sailed in small, wooden fishing skiffs. Flimsy and slow, the makeshift craft were easy to spot and avoid, so the pirates' victims were limited to the slowest freighters—other ships could easily slip away. But at the turn of the 21st century, the pirates stepped up their game.

They turned the trawlers and small freighters they captured into "motherships" that blended in with other sea traffic in the crowded shipping lanes of the Persian Gulf. The pirates would release skiffs full of men from a mothership. Coordinating their attack with satellite phones and GPS devices, they would converge and swarm over a target before its crew knew what was happening. With the pirates outfitted with an array of modern weapons, ranging from machine guns to rocket launchers to grenades, there was no incentive for crewmembers to resist an attack.

Advances in technology have made cargo ships more vulnerable to such attacks, because while ships have grown in size, their crews have gotten smaller. Onboard systems control everything from water supplies to fuel to air-conditioning, all of which used to require monitoring by several sailors from multiple stations throughout a ship. Now one crewmember can run them all from a computerized control panel on the bridge. The result is that a 1,000-foot supertanker may have a crew of just 10 or 11 sailors, who can be easily overwhelmed by well-armed pirates.

PUSHBACK

The upsurge in pirate attacks on cargo vessels in the mid-2000s led to an outcry from shipping companies all over the world. In 2008 a multinational coalition created the Maritime Security Patrol Area to help secure the Gulf of Aden. Warships from India and Russia began regular joint patrols throughout the region and

...The military bomber Northrop Grumman B-2 Spirit, at $2.2 billion per plane.

reduced the number of incidents there from 86 in 2009 to 33 in 2010. Elsewhere, the Combined Task Force has deployed military-grade vessels to protect the Panama Canal. Coalition patrol ships rarely engage the pirates directly. Instead, they deploy search-and-seizure teams in high-speed raider boats. Taking a page from the pirates' own playbook, they deploy these smaller vessels, loaded with marines packing machine guns and rifles, from motherships such as the Royal Navy's HMS *Cumberland*, a frigate that has been patrolling the waters off Somalia since 2008. But maintaining standing fleets of ships and marines in international waters is very expensive, causing maritime nations to become more efficient and creative in their anti-piracy campaigns.

NEW ERA, NEW TACTICS

Cargo-ship defenses are being bolstered in non-lethal ways:

• Water cannons mounted front and aft have proven especially effective at repulsing attacks.

• The Long Range Acoustic Device by American Technology Corporation lets a crew blast the eardrums of approaching pirates with sonic waves "50 times greater than the human threshold for pain."

• The U.S. Air Force research lab is developing a similar weapon, dubbed the "Dazzle Gun," that temporarily blinds oncoming pirates with intense bursts of laser lights.

• A lower-tech but equally effective defense is spreading an industrial-strength goo along the sides of the ship, making it too slippery for pirates to board.

• Newly developed early-warning alarms utilize high-tech cameras and radar to protect ships from would-be buccaneers. Companies like the U.K.'s BAE Systems have designed software capable of warning crews of suspicious boats and activity up to 15 miles away, allowing them time to contact naval warships in the area or take evasive action.

• In 2011 the U.S. Navy started using a computer system that takes into account weather, ocean currents, shipping routes, unmanned drone aircraft, and intelligence data to determine where raiders may head next. The Piracy Attack Risk Surface is

Harry Houdini drove a car only once in his life.

updated every 12 hours, and the information is made available to every commercial vessel in the area.

SEA ROBOTS

• In 2007 the U.S. Navy a began testing an Unmanned Surface Vessel—in other words, a high-speed robotic patrol boat. Named the *Predator*, this 30-foot craft is designed to increase the patrol range of a destroyer or frigate. Remotely controlled and armed with a 7.62-mm machine gun, the Predator can go up to 55 knots to intercept pirates closing on a freighter. Versions of the *Predator* are already being used by the Israeli and Singaporean navies.

• The Interceptor, built by Marine Robotic Vessels International, is autonomous, meaning it can be programmed to patrol a quadrant on its own without direct radio control. If it spots a suspicious craft with its sensors, it will send a warning to its parent ship or to nearby commercial shipping vessels that might be vulnerable to attack.

• British defense tech firm QinetiQ has built a Jet-Ski–size drone called the Stryker that can be used to investigate suspicious rafts and boats without putting human crew at risk.

CIRCLING THE SHIPS

In addition to cargo ships, yachts are routinely targeted, especially off the coasts of Brazil, Africa, and southern China. Since 1996 over 300 yachts have been attacked by pirates around the world. Many yachts now travel in clusters with bodyguards, watch patrols, and elaborate security systems. Currently there is a patent pending for a 9,000-volt marine fence that can be installed around the perimeter of a single yacht, or a group of them.

Even as maritime nations become more effective in countering pirate attacks, the brutal truth is that this global scourge hasn't stopped and now has a horrific new aspect. Sea pirates of the past, whether in the Malacca Straits or around the Horn of Africa, were marine robbers. They looted a ship and sold the contents, and that was it. Now the preferred mode is to kidnap ships and crews and hold them for ransom. Hijackings rose from 46 in 2008 to 62 in 2010. Only time will tell whether the new weapons will stem the tide and force modern-day pirates off the seas forever.

Kingda Ka, a hydraulic launch roller coaster at Six Flags in NJ, reaches 128 mph in 3.5 sec.

TIRE TRIVIA

Here's the scoop on the rubber that hits the road.

• "Tire" is thought to be derived from the word "tie," the outer steel ring of a wooden cart wheel that holds, or ties, the segments together.

• It takes a half-barrel of crude oil to produce the rubber found in one truck tire.

• A "road alligator" is a strip of a tire that's come off and is left on the highway.

• Race car tires are often inflated with nitrogen. The moisture present in air can make them contract or expand erratically during a race. A 1/2-pound difference in tire pressure can affect how a car handles, so many racers think nitrogen, which is steadier under pressure, gives them an edge.

• A "T" on a tire's sidewall stands for "temporary," meaning that it's a "space-saver" spare wheel.

• A tire on a top fuel dragster has a life span of 30 seconds.

• If all tires in America were properly inflated, an estimated two billion gallons of gasoline could be saved per year.

• If you're buying only two tires, put them on the rear axle. Putting new tires on the drive-wheel position makes a vehicle more susceptible to fishtailing.

• An estimated 290 million tires are thrown away each year in the United States, mostly into landfills.

• 80% of the discarded tires in Iowa are used to make *tire derived fuel* (TDF). The rest are ground into rubber crumbs to make doormats, roofing, playground materials, and asphalt.

• In 1983 seven million tires in a Winchester, Virginia, tire dump burned for nine months, polluting the area with lead and arsenic. A tire fire in Heyope, Wales, burned for 15 years before it was finally put out in 2004.

The first 24-hour car race took place in 1907 at Brooklands, England.

SEEING IS BELIEVING

The controversy over whether UFOs are real continues. Some votes on the "yea" side...

TESTIMONY

From Cdr. Malcolm Scott Carpenter, USN, Mercury 7 astronaut:

> *"At no time, when the astronauts were in space were they alone: there was a constant surveillance by UFOs."*

Carpenter photographed a UFO while in orbit May 24, 1962. NASA has never released the photograph.

From Mercury 7 and Gemini Astronaut Col. Gordon Cooper, USAF, addressing the United Nations in 1985:

> *"I can now reveal that every day, in the USA, our radar instruments capture objects of form and composition unknown to us. And there are thousands of witness reports and a quantity of documents to prove this, but nobody wants to make them public."*

Capt. Robert Salas, USAF Air Traffic Controller & Missile Launch Officer, describing events that occurred March 16, 1967:

> *"The security guard called and said, 'Sir, there's a glowing red object hovering right outside the front gate. I've got all the men out here with their weapons drawn.' We lost between 16 and 18 ICBMs at the same time UFOs were in the area."*

From a 1951 interview with test pilot, astronaut, and NASA Director of Flight Crew Operations Maj. Donald "Deke" Slayton:

> *"I was testing a P-51 fighter in Minneapolis when I spotted this object....As I got closer it looked like a weather balloon, gray and about three feet in diameter. But as soon as I got behind the darn thing it didn't look like a balloon anymore. It looked like a saucer, a disk. About the same time, I realized that it was suddenly going way from me—and there I was, running at about 300 miles per hour. I tracked it for a little way, and then all of a sudden the (expletive) thing just took off. It pulled about a 45-degree climbing turn and accelerated and just flat disappeared."*

A gas station is a *petrol bunk* in India, a *petrol kiosk* in Singapore, and a *servo* in Australia.

From *Apollo 14* Astronaut Capt. Edgar Mitchell, USN:

> *"The evidence points to the fact that Roswell was a real incident and that indeed an alien craft did crash, and that material was recovered from that site. We all know that UFOs are real. All we need to ask is where do they come from, and what do they want?"*

From Air Chief Marshal Lord Dowding, Commanding Officer, RAF, in World War II:

> *"More than 10,000 sightings have been reported, the majority of which cannot be accounted for by any 'scientific' explanation... They have been tracked on radar screens and the observed speeds have been as great as 9,000 mph. I am convinced that these objects do exist and they are not manufactured by any nation on earth. I can therefore see no alternative to accepting the theory that they come from an extraterrestrial source."*

From testimony before Congress in 1968 by Dr. James McDonald, senior physicist, Institute for Atmospheric Physics, University of Arizona:

> *"My own present opinion, based on two years of careful study, is that UFOs are probably extraterrestrial devices engaged in something that might very tentatively be termed 'surveillance.'"*

From Col. Philip Corso, head of Foreign Technology, U.S. Army Research and Development Department, 1961:

> *"Let there be no doubt. Alien technology harvested from the infamous saucer crash in Roswell, New Mexico, in July 1947 led directly to the development of the integrated circuit chip, laser and fibre optic technologies, particle beams, electromagnetic propulsion systems, depleted uranium projectiles, stealth capabilities, and many others. How do I know? I was in charge! I think the kids on this planet are wise to the truth, and I think we ought to give it to them. I think they deserve it."*

From former President Jimmy Carter, 1976:

> *"I don't laugh at people anymore when they say they've seen UFOs. I've seen one myself."*

Ken Warby's *Spirit of Australia* is the only speedboat racer to break 300 mph...and stay intact.

PUMP & CIRCUMSTANCE

The story of America's first drive-through filling station.

GOT GAS?

At the turn of the 20th century, when folks referred to automobiles as "horseless carriages" and "gasoline buggies," gasoline was delivered to homes and businesses by horse-drawn tankers. Customers provided their own containers and had to guess how much fuel they would need for the month. Savvy merchants soon realized if they installed a gas pump outside their shops, they could get in on the gasoline bonanza. But these store pumps were often inconveniently located and caused friction with nearby shop owners who didn't like the noise, exhaust, or traffic jams created by the new machines. Enter two Standard Oil men from Columbus, Ohio: B. A. Mathews and H. S. Hollingsworth.

LITTLE GAS SHACK

Mathews and Hollingsworth came up with an elegant solution: a barnlike shed where automobile owners could drive in one end, refuel, and drive out the other. They built a 14-by-20-foot structure on the corner of Oak and Young streets in Columbus, just three blocks east of the State Capital. On June 1, 1912, the world's first drive-through filling station opened for business.

Customers entered from the front of the auto filling station, and then hand-cranked pumps were used to fill their tanks with Standard Red Crown gasoline. Automotive accessories like Polarine lubricating oil lined shelves on the interior walls. One of the first "specials" was a free grease job with the purchase of 25 cents' worth of grease. The filling station was an overnight success. Packards, Wintons, and Model Ts lined the street waiting to drive through, and nearly 1,800 gallons of gas were pumped the first week.

By 1918 the partners found that they could handle more cars if they placed the pumps along the front of the building. No longer a drive-through, the station became a full-service outdoor operation illuminated with electric lights and staffed by uniformed attendants who pumped gas, changed oil, and washed windshields. The modern gas station was born.

In 2007 a motorized sofa drove at 92 mph, setting a world record for "fastest furniture."

ALL IN THE FAMILY

Like thoroughbreds, great racecar drivers seem to be bred from great racing bloodlines. Here are some notable racing dynasties from around the world.

HOUSE OF UNSER

By far the most prolifically successful family in racing, the Unsers have particularly excelled at the Indy 500. **Bobby Unser** (b. 1934) is a three-time Indy 500 winner (1968, 1975, 1981), but younger brother **Al** (b. 1935) has one up on him with four wins (1970, 1971, 1978, 1987). Both are IROC national champions: Bobby in '75, and Al in '78. Bobby has two USAC Indy Car championships (1968, 1974) to Al's two CART championships (1983, 1985).

Then comes **Al Jr.** (b. 1962), with two Indy 500 wins (1992, 1994), three IROC championships (1982, 1986, 1988), two CART championships (1990, 1994), and something his dad and uncle don't have: a win at the 24 Hours of Daytona (1984).

Bobby's son **Robby** (b. 1968) has won the Pikes Peak Hill Climb nine times.

Bobby's daughter **Jeri** (b. 1969) broke the record for fastest time by an electric car at the Pikes Peak Hill Climb in 2003.

HOUSE OF PETTY

Lee Petty (1914–2000) was the first three-time NASCAR Champion (1954, 1958, 1959). He also won the first Daytona 500 in 1959.

Son **Richard** (b. 1937) holds seven NASCAR NEXTEL championships and a matching seven wins at the Daytona 500. He has won 200 NASCAR cup races, more than any other driver.

Richard's son **Kyle** (b. 1960) has won eight NASCAR NEXTEL races and remains a top NASCAR competitor.

Kyle's son **Adam** (1980–2000) had three top-five finishes and four top-tens when he died during a NASCAR practice run in 2000.

HOUSE OF ANDRETTI

Named "Driver of the Century" by the Associated Press, **Mario**

Andretti (b. 1940) is considered by many to be the greatest all-around driver America has ever produced, due to the fact that he's the only driver to win the Daytona 500 (1967), Indy 500 (1969), and the Formula One World Championship (1978).

Son **Michael** (b. 1962) was Rookie of the Year at Indy in 1984, and won the CART Indy Car World Series Championship in 1991.

The Andretti family was also the first in racing to have five relatives (father Mario, sons Michael and **Jeff**, cousin **John**, and grandson **Marco**) all racing in the same CART/Champ Car/Indycar series.

HOUSE OF HILL

England's **Graham Hill** (1929–75) was the only driver to win the Triple Crown of Motorsport: the Formula One World Championship (1962, 1968), Indy 500 (1966), and the 24 Hours at LeMans (1972).

His son **Damon** (b. 1960) won the Formula One World Championship in 1996, making the Hills the only father and son to both win the most prestigious title in motor racing.

HOUSE OF FITTIPALDI

Brazil's **Emerson Fittipaldi** (b. 1946) won two Formula One World Championships (1972, 1974), two Indy 500s (1989, 1993), and a CART championship (1989).

His nephew **Christian** (b. 1971) was Formula 3000 champion in 1991, Rookie of the Year at the 1995 Indy 500, and co-driver of the winning car at the 2004 24 Hours at Daytona.

HOUSE OF JONES

Stan Jones (1923–73) was one of the greatest amateur drivers in Australian history, winning the New Zealand Grand Prix (1954) the Australian Drivers Championship (1958), and the Australian Grand Prix (1959).

His son **Alan** (b. 1946) won the Formula One World Championship in 1980, as well as the Can-Am Challenge Cup (1978) and Australian GT Championship (1982).

Alan's son **Christian** (b. 1979) won the Asian Formula Three Championship in 2004.

ICEBERG COWBOYS

Considering a career change? Here's a job that may not pop up in the want ads.

CALVING SEASON

Every year between February and July, icebergs calve off the glaciers feeding into Baffin Bay, Canada, and drift south along the ocean corridor off the eastern coast of Newfoundland known as "Iceberg Alley." Some of these icebergs rise 240 feet above sea level and extend over an area the size of two football fields. Unfortunately, the world's largest oil rig, the Hibernia Platform, sits 200 miles off of St. Johns, Newfoundland, right in the middle of Iceberg Alley. The Hibernia Platform drills for oil for six major oil companies, including Exxon and Mobil. Even though the platform rests on a fortress of concrete, the drilling company doesn't want any iceberg bigger than a piano to get near their $5 billion dollar investment. That's why they hire iceberg wranglers.

HEAD 'EM UP, MOVE 'EM OUT

Once a wrangler receives a report of a rogue calf, or "bergie," drifting within range of the platform, he grabs his 3,600-foot-long, 8-inch-thick polypropylene rope, climbs aboard a 2,600-hp steel-reinforced boat, and motors out to lasso the quarter-million-ton ice cube. Lassoing a monster chunk of ice is complicated—icebergs are often giant towers of glass with hull-piercing shards extending below the water. The lasso can slip off, or worse, flip the iceberg, resulting in a miniature tsunami that can capsize the boat. Wranglers, along with a crew of 10 to 14 men, try to keep at least a half-mile distance from any iceberg under tow. Whereas cowboys on horseback may gallop along at a good clip, iceberg wranglers have to go slow—while pulling a massive iceberg, the tow ship may manage one knot, and it can take 10 hours to build up to that speed, so towing an iceberg away from the Hibernia Platform can take as long as three days. When wranglers aren't lassoing icebergs, they ferry supplies and equipment to the more than 280 technicians working and living on the platform.

The Uddeholm Swedish Rally is the only car race run entirely on snow.

HISTORY OF THE INTERSTATE

It's the largest highway system in the world and possibly the greatest public works project in history. You've probably ridden or driven on it. Here's its colorful story.

IKE HITS THE ROAD

On July 7, 1919, an Army convoy of 300 men and 70 vehicles left the White House, heading west for San Francisco. The Trans-Continental Truck Train was the first military expedition commissioned to study the nation's roads. The trip took 62 days, put 21 soldiers in the hospital, disabled 9 vehicles, and demolished 88 bridges. There were 230 accidents in all: Vehicles were flipped upside-down, driven into ditches, and sunk in quicksand. Along as an observer was a young lieutenant colonel named Dwight D. Eisenhower.

What Eisenhower and the other soldiers discovered was that the nation's roads were a disorganized, unsafe mess. There were lots of road maps but no uniform, consistent naming of highways, byways, and routes. Instead of numbers, a map might show "blue" routes, which towns would mark by painting blue strips on utility poles. Some highly traveled routes had names, like the Dixie Highway, Santa Fe Trail, Lincoln Highway, and National Road. Others were simply lines on a map. Many well-traveled roads were in terrible condition—one highway near Denver had so much traffic that 12-inch-deep grooves were cut into the rock roadbed.

HIGHWAY ACT

By 1956 Dwight Eisenhower had become president. On June 29 he signed the Federal-Aid Highway Act, which provided $30 billion for 41,000 miles of modern, safe roads crisscrossing the country. The new plan followed the 1922 map designed by General John Pershing to show which routes would be most helpful to the military in the event of war. The new interstate system would consist of four-lane expressways designed for sustained high-speed

Number of rest areas along the Interstate Highway System, as of 2011: 1,214.

travel. Instead of intersections, the new system would use underpasses and bridges, allowing traffic in all directions to continue safely without slowing down. The federal government was to pay 90% of the cost, with the states assuming the remaining 10%. Upon completion, each state would take ownership of the interstate within its borders and be responsible for maintenance and law enforcement—which is why state police patrol the interstates instead of local cops.

YOUR TAX DOLLARS AT WORK

• The first project to begin construction under the act was the I-70 Mark Twain Expressway in St. Charles County, Missouri, on August 13, 1956. The last to be completed was I-105 in Los Angeles, in 1993.

• Between 1997 and 2001, an average of 23,745 miles of interstate were under construction every year.

• In 1991 the final cost was figured to be $130 billion. The federal government paid $114 billion of the tab.

• The red, white, and blue interstate shield was adopted in 1957. It is 36 inches high and 36 inches wide. Shields for three-digit roads are 45 inches wide.

• Some interstates don't actually cross state lines. I-99 is completely inside Pennsylvania, and I-465 circles Indianapolis more than 60 miles from the state border. I-878, the shortest interstate, doesn't even cross city limits: all 3,696 feet of it are just outside JFK International Airport in New York City.

• In 1947 a UFO may or may not have crashed near Roswell, New Mexico. When the interstate system was designed a decade later, the section in New Mexico was placed 100 miles away from the area—making Roswell farther from an interstate than any other place in the lower 48 states.

• The official name of the U.S. interstate highway system is now the "Dwight D. Eisenhower System of Interstate and Defense Highways." Eisenhower's name was added in a 1990 Congressional bill introduced by Senator John Kerry and signed by President George H. Bush.

Temperatures inside a NASCAR cockpit can reach 120°F.

NEAR MISSES

In the decades preceding the Wright brothers' flight of 1903, aviation pioneers raced to be the first in flight. Their efforts were a combination of trial and (mostly) error.

AIRPLANE: Mozhaysky Monoplane (1884)
INVENTOR: Alexander Mozhaysky (1825–90)
NEAR MISS: In 1881 retired Russian naval officer Alexander Mozhaysky received a grant of 2,500 rubles ($50,000) to build a flying machine. The Mozhaysky Monoplane was 75½ feet long and driven by three propellers, powered by one 10-hp and two 20-hp steam engines suspended from a 74¾-foot wing. On launch day in 1884, Mozhaysky pushed his craft down a ski-jump-style ramp near St. Petersburg and hopped onboard for a ride of less than 100 feet—then crash-landed. Although the Mozhaysky Monoplane made only the second assisted takeoff of a powered aircraft in history (Félix du Temple had done it a decade earlier in France), the crash destroyed the wing and the now-penniless Mozhaysky gave up his dream. Decades later Soviet dictator Joseph Stalin gave it back to him—sort of. Stalin had the writers of the official Great Soviet Encyclopedia upgrade Mozhaysky's attempt to "the first true flight of a heavier-than-air machine in history." Mozhaysky never learned of his so-called achievement, having died in 1890.

AIRPLANE: Maxim Biplane (1893)
INVENTOR: Hiram Maxim (1840–1916)
NEAR MISS: This American-born inventor of the Maxim machine gun inherited a passion for flight from his father. In 1893, the Maxim Biplane was ready to test at Maxim's estate in Bexley, England. Two steam-driven 180-hp motors drove a pair of 17½-foot propellers. Maxim mounted his machine on a 7,000-pound test rig so that it could zip along a 1,800-foot track with guides like a roller coaster to prevent it from taking off. During its third test run, on July 31, 1894, with Maxim and three others aboard, the biplane generated so much lift that it

No. 1 on *Trains* magazine's list of "The 100 Greatest Train Movies": *The Train* (1964).

broke free and careened out of control two to three feet above the ground for nearly 200 yards before crashing to a halt. No one was injured, but Maxim was so shaken by the episode that he abandoned the project.

AIRPLANE: Pilcher Triplane (1899)
INVENTOR: Percy Pilcher (1866–99)
NEAR MISS: Percy Sinclair Pilcher was 29 in 1895, when he flew his first glider, the Bat, off a hill in Cardross, Scotland. In 1897 he flew his fourth glider, the Hawk, a world-record 250 yards over the grounds of Stanford Hall near Leicestershire, England. On September 30, 1899, Pilcher seemed destined to make history again. The propeller-driven Pilcher Triplane would have been the first engine-powered aircraft to fly, except for one glitch: Pilcher couldn't start the engine. Not one to let his audience down, Pilcher broke out the Hawk to give what should have been a routine demonstration of the famous glider. Instead, the crowd watched in horror as the glider's tail snapped in half and Pilcher plummeted to the ground. He died two days later. In 2003 the Pilcher Triplane was rebuilt for the BBC television program *Horizon* and flown for nearly 90 seconds, proving that Pilcher would have beaten the Wright Brothers into the skies by four years—had he been able to start his engine.

AIRPLANE: Kress Waterborne Aeroplane (1901)
INVENTOR: Wilhelm Kress (1836–1913)
NEAR MISS: After spending 20 years and his life savings perfecting a step-winged aircraft that he dubbed the Waterborne Aeroplane, Kress's efforts came to an abrupt end on October 3, 1901, on the Tullnerbach reservoir in Austria. Experts believe that the seaplane, equipped with three offset wings, two floats, and an oversized horizontal tail and rudders, should have flown. But Kress had run out of money shortly before the test flight, forcing him to abandon his plan to use a lightweight custom-built engine to power the twin propellers. Instead he opted for a cheaper and heavier 30-hp Daimler engine. Upon takeoff the plane hopped once, flipped over, and sank. Kress swam to safety, but his dream of soaring into the skies went down with his plane. He never built another.

First aircraft to land on a moving ship: A Sopwith Pup biplane. In 1917...

DRIVERLESS CARS

For years "Google cars" canvassed the country on photo-taking missions for mapping software. Today, they're up to something completely different.

A PECULIAR PRIUS

In November 2009, a Californian named Ben Tseitlin snapped a picture of an odd-looking Toyota Prius (pronounced "PREE-us") while driving on the freeway between San Francisco and Palo Alto. What caught his attention was a high-tech modified spoiler on the roof equipped with cameras and spinning sensors. Tseitlin posted the photo on his Facebook page, along with his suspicions about the car. Had he just stumbled on the secret test drive of a new wind-powered Prius?

HIDING IN PLAIN SIGHT

A year later, Google revealed that yes, it was a secret test drive...but not for wind-power technology. The car Tseitlin had seen was testing *self-driving* car technology. To date, six prototype driverless cars—with a human riding in the driver's seat as a backup—have logged 140,000 accident-free miles around California. The cars have driven up and down the notoriously bendy Pacific Coast Highway, over the Golden Gate Bridge, and all the way around Lake Tahoe. One even navigated the picturesque switchbacks on San Francisco's super-steep Lombard Street. There's also a driverless Audi TT being developed for off-roading.

Forty-three-year-old Sebastian Thrun, a professor at Stanford University, is the leader of the Google Driverless Car development team. He calls it the "Drive-Thru Manhattan Project." Google recruited Thrun after his Stanford Racing team won a robotic car competition in 2005 sponsored by the Defense Advance Research Projects Agency, the futuristic research-and-development arm of the U.S. military. Thrun also led the team that created Google StreetView. The other 15 members of the Driverless Car team are among the leading automotive robotics researchers in the world.

ROBOT CARS

Why create robotic vehicles? Google believes that limiting the human element will increase safety and decrease costs. Computerized cars can't get distracted, tired, or drunk. Smarter cars will mean fewer accidents, so cars can be built with lighter, cheaper materials. "It's amazing to me that we let humans drive cars," explains Google CEO Eric Schmidt. "Your car should drive itself. It's a bug that cars were invented before computers."

Google's futuristic cars use laser range finders, video cameras, and inertial sensors interconnected with mapping software. They scour databases for local driving laws, speed limits, construction delays, and traffic updates and feed the information into the brain of a car that can sense anything near it through fine-tuned radar. Google's programmers study the habits of drivers, and program their cars to adapt to be more cautious or more aggressive, as needed. True geeks, they built in a swooshing *Star Trek* warp-drive sound when the car is switched to the fully automated cruise mode.

BUT ARE THEY LEGAL?

Prior to testing, Google checked with local police, who gave them the go-ahead because the human backup drivers could override the cars manually at any time. The only accident so far occurred when another car (operated by a human) rear-ended a driverless Prius. The cars have also logged about 1,000 miles without a person in the car at all, on closed courses. Google-watchers point to possible disadvantages, though: A system crash could lead to dangerous consequences, like sudden acceleration. And programmers have yet to equip the cars with defensive skills against drunk drivers, darting children, or bicycle messengers. But Google contends that even in this early stage of development, their driverless technology is still safer than human-driven vehicles.

THE FUTURE IS HERE

The earliest predictions put driverless cars in showrooms no sooner than 2020, but Google's research technology might show up in cars before that. Semiautomated cruise control could adapt to shifting traffic patterns. Linking into the "Google Cloud" of up-to-date information could help a driver avoid road hazards such as disabled vehicles or fog. And computer sensors could warn a driver when they're speeding, tailgating, or dozing off.

Gentlemen, start your motherboards!

Google is lobbying to make Nevada the first state where driverless vehicles could be legally operated.

EL MAESTRO

Ask racing fans who the top 10 drivers of all time are, and you'll get 10 different answers. But one name—Juan Manuel Fangio—consistently heads any list of racing greats.

BACKGROUND

Born on June 24, 1911, to Italian immigrants in Balcarce, Argentina, Juan Manuel Fangio worked as a garage mechanic as a teenager. Soft-spoken and shy, he first showed his competitive fire on the soccer field, where he earned the nickname El Chueco (Bandy Legs). He was 18 when he entered his first pro car race, driving a 1929 Model A Ford taxicab that he'd rebuilt himself.

At that time, road racing in Argentina was a brutal test of man and machine over courses that crisscrossed the Andes Mountains and desert plains. Drivers had no pit crews, and any repairs had to be handled by the driver himself or, if he had one, his co-driver. In this trial-by-fire environment, Fangio was highly successful, winning the Argentine National Championship in 1940 and 1941. Plans were made to send him to the lucrative racing circuit in Europe, but the breakout of World War II put everything on hold.

WHO'S THE OLD GUY?

It wasn't until 1949 that Fangio went to Europe to race. By then he was 37, an age at which most professional drivers start thinking of retiring. But Fangio was just getting started. In 1950, the first year of Formula One racing, he placed second in the World Championship. The following year, after jumping from Alfa to Maserati, he took the first of an unprecedented five World Championship titles. His string was interrupted in 1952 when he broke his neck in an accident at Monza and was out for most of two seasons. But 1954 saw him back on top, winning his second championship in a Mercedes. That year he drove in eight Grand Prix races, winning six of them. When he won the World Championship again in 1955 and 1956, his teammate Stirling Moss declared him *El Maestro*—"The Master."

FINEST MOMENT

The 1957 German Grand Prix at Nurburgring looked to be El

Maestro's last hurrah. The 46-year-old Fangio worried publicly that he'd lost his competitive edge, that perhaps it was time to retire and go back to Argentina. Nonetheless, he turned in the fastest qualifying time over his top competitor, Mike Hawthorn.

Race fans awaited what they hoped would be an epic duel, and they weren't disappointed. Fangio was driving for Maserati that year, Hawthorn for Ferrari. Fangio started at a record pace, but Hawthorn stayed within reach. When Fangio was forced into the pits to refuel, things went wrong. The pit crew had trouble getting a wheel off during a tire change, and by the time Fangio got back on the track he was 45 seconds behind not only Hawthorn but the second Ferrari driver, Peter Collins. It was a seemingly insurmountable lead for even El Maestro to overcome, but Fangio drove like a man possessed. Soon he'd shattered the lap record he set in qualifying and, second by second, the gap began to narrow. The Ferrari pit crew started to panic, urging Hawthorn and Collins to go faster and harder. Meanwhile, Fangio chipped away at the Ferrari team's lead so methodically that a reporter commented later how the Argentine "might almost have been pulling them backwards on the end of a rope." Fangio made his move on the 20th lap, quickly slipping by Collins. The Englishman countered and regained second, but Fangio caught him on a straightaway and hurried after the leader, Hawthorn. The two racers played cat-and-mouse until finally Fangio bulled his way through the final turn to win the race, and his fifth World Championship. His margin of victory? Three seconds.

ODD MAN OUT IN HAVANA

Fangio had won the first Cuban Grand Prix held in Havana in 1957, but when he came back to defend his trophy in 1958, he stumbled into the most bizarre episode of his life. On February 23, 1958, the night before the race, he was kidnapped by armed gunmen in the lobby of the Hotel Lincoln. They were members of Fidel Castro's 26th of July Revolutionary Movement that 11 months later would overthrow the dictatorship of Fulgencio Batista. The rebels hustled Fangio off to a safe house, where they quickly reassured the driver that they had no intention of hurting him. Their goal was to embarrass the Batista regime by stealing the star of Cuba's greatest public event and drawing some worldwide publicity for their cause in the process. Fangio spent a pleasant couple of days with his captors, who brought in a radio so he could hear the race he was going to miss (he declined, saying later, "I did not want to listen because I felt nostalgic"). Afterward, the rebels dropped him off at the Argentine embassy, unharmed.

"IT IS FINISHED"

As it turned out, 1958 brought Fangio's career to a close. In the French Grand Prix at Rheims, he could do no better than fourth place. The eventual winner was Mike Hawthorn, the English driver Fangio had nipped to win the German Grand Prix the year before. Hawthorn could have lapped Fangio just before the finish line. Instead he braked and let Fangio cross just ahead of him. It was a touching show of respect by one driver for another. As for Fangio, he got out of his car, turned to his mechanic and said, "It is finished." He never raced again.

Fangio's record of five World Championships stood for 45 years, until Michael Schumacher won his fifth in 2002. Schumacher went on to win two more championships, prompting some critics to downplay Fangio's great accomplishment. But a side-by-side comparison of the two racers is revealing. Schumacher took 19 seasons to win his 7 titles; Fangio won 5 in only 9 seasons, 2 of which were shortened by his neck injury. Over his long career, Schumacher had a 33 percent winning percentage, which is superb. But Fangio's winning percentage was a stunning 48 percent, meaning he won almost one out of every two races he entered. No other Formula One driver has come close to matching him. El Maestro retired to his hometown in Argentina and died in 1995.

POSTSCRIPT

The year before his death, Fangio went to renew his driver's license and was turned down. The traffic bureau said he was too old—no one over 80 was allowed to have a license, and Fangio was 83. Furious, the old man challenged the bureau: Let him race a government representative from Buenos Aires to the seaside resort of Mar del Plata 250 miles away and see who was the better driver. The traffic bureau declined the challenge and made an exception to the law in Fangio's favor.

What are *rayguns*, *drag pipes*, and *pea shooters*? Mufflers, to motorcycle buffs.

LAND YACHTS

Wind power may be the green energy du jour in America, but it's been a "go-to" power source in China for centuries.

BLOWING IN THE WIND

In his *Book of the Golden Hall Master*, Chinese emperor Liang Yuan-ti (A.D. 552–554) described a carriage powered by wind. The emperor reported that the famous philosopher Kaots'ang Wu-Shu built a wagon with sails that could carry 30 men and travel hundreds of miles in a day. A larger version, said to hold a thousand men, was built for Emperor Yang of the Sui dynasty in A.D. 610. In those days farmers across China attached sails to their wheelbarrows and plows to ease their labor. Northern Chinese rigged sails to iceboats with small wheels to sail up and down frozen rivers in the wintertime.

SAILING, SAILING

European traders brought word of the Chinese "land yachts" to Europe. The Portuguese cartographer Gerardus Mercator drew one on his map of China in 1577, and John Speed's 1626 book, *Kingdom of China*, had illustrations of wind-powered sailing carriages, along with descriptions of their varied uses. Perhaps the most notable reference was made by English poet John Milton in *Paradise Lost* (1665): "...the barren Plaines of Sericana where Chineses drive With Sails and Wind thir canie wagons light."

Once Europeans "got wind" of the Chinese sail cars, they had to have them, too. In 1600 Prince Maurice of Orange had Flemish scientist Simon Stevin build him a bus-sized sail wagon so he could take 26 of his friends on beach rides along the North Sea. This wind-powered vehicle could go 30 mph, much faster than the first steam locomotives nearly 300 years later.

WIND WAGONS

In the 19th century, the land yacht craze spread to the United States, where merchants used "wind wagons" to transport goods across dry lake beds and along railroad tracks. Some forty-niners heading west during the gold rush were inspired by a pioneer named

In 2009 use of seat belts saved an estimated American 12,713 lives.

"Wind Wagon Thomas" to attach sails to their covered wagons and attempt to sail the prairies. A few managed to barrel across the plains from Kansas City to Denver, traveling at speeds up to 15 mph, but most broke down as soon as they hit rough terrain.

RACING WITH THE WIND

In 1898 land sailing caught on in Europe when the Dumont brothers of Belgium began to build and sell land yachts modeled after the classic Nile sailboats of Egypt. Ten years later, pilots were racing competitively down the beaches of France and Belgium. By the 1960s, a new breed of land yacht had emerged: three-wheeled polyester-fiberglass carts with nonadjustable sails, steered with pedals or hand levers. And 1967 brought a new level of competition, when a French Foreign Legion officer organized an epic race across the Sahara. Starting in Algeria, teams from seven countries "sailed" 1,700 miles through southern Morocco to the Atlantic coast of Mauritania. The first to cross the finish line: the American team.

And the U.S. has prestigious races of its own. Every year, land sailors gather at Ivanpah Dry Lake in Nevada's Mojave Desert for the sport's "America's Cup." Racers go head to head to set new speed records, the latest of which was set on March 26, 2009, when British engineer Richard Jenkins piloted his land yacht, *Ecotricity's Greenbird*, to a world-record 126.2 mph.

DIRTBOATS TODAY

Today's land yachts are made from high-tech lightweight materials like aluminum, Kevlar, and carbon fiber, with battened, flexible sails as long as 26 feet. The pilot rides in a recumbent position and sometimes, depending on the class or size of yacht, suspended from the chassis. Land yachts can sail downwind, crosswind, and upwind, like a sailboat, but they go faster quicker. The dry lake beds of California, Nevada, and eastern Oregon provide some of the best spots in the U.S., where sailors pilot a wide variety of sail cars, including sand yachts, parakarts, kitebuggies, speed sails, miniyachts, and "blo-karts." For those who find wind power alone a little disconcerting, there are "whikes"—tricycles with sails.

According to the FAA, US airlines are four times safer than those of any other country.

HISTORY OF AIRSHIPS, PART I

Look! Up in the sky! It's a blimp, it's an airship, it's…it's a dirigible!

BACKGROUND

An airship is a type of craft that stays aloft due to its lighter-than-air buoyancy. It also must be self-propelled and steerable. Otherwise it's just a balloon. French engineers pioneered the first successful efforts to fly airships, and they also gave them the name *dirigible*, from the French word *dirigeable*: "that which can be directed or steered."

There are three types of dirigible: the *nonrigid*, commonly called a blimp, has no frame. Its shape and volume are maintained entirely by the gas pressure inside the skin (called the envelope) of the blimp itself. A *rigid* airship has a complete internal metal skeleton that gives shape to the ship, as well as support for its multiple internal gas cells. The envelope is stretched over the framework. *Semi-rigid* ships have a keel either suspended beneath the bottom of a single fabric gas cell or attached to the underside. Gondolas and engines are usually attached or suspended from the keel. The keel structure helps to ensure even distribution of force to the envelope, while gas pressure gives shape to the envelope.

CONTINENTAL DRIFT

French inventor Henri Giffard (1825–82) made the first recognized flight of a proper airship in 1852 (see page 438). However, Giffard's airship was only a barely disguised balloon with an ineffectual steam-driven propeller attached to its gondola.

In 1872 German engineer Paul Haenlein lifted off from Brünn, Germany, in a dirigible with a difference—its propeller was driven by an internal combustion engine, a first for aeronautics. The *Haenlein* was 164 feet long and 29½ feet at its widest diameter. To ensure air-tightness, the fabric was coated inside and out with rubber. Like Giffard's airship, Haenlein's used coal gas for lift, but the gas also fueled the engine. As gas was pulled from the envelope, it was replaced with pumped-in air to maintain the envelope's volume. Over time this reduced the buoyancy of the dirigible, limiting its time aloft. The gondola, which ran the length of the envelope, was a mesh cage suspended by ropes. A five-hp, four-horizontal-cylinder engine drove a four-bladed, 15-foot-diameter propeller at 40 rpm. For its only flight, however, the *Haenlein* was held by a tether to the ground.

VIVE LA FRANCE

The first big improvement in design came from a pair of French Army engineers. *La France,* built by Charles Renard and Arthur C. Krebs, was the first airship that could actually be steered well enough to return to its point of departure. Roughly the same length and diameter as the *Haenlein*, La France was powered by a lightweight electric motor driving a massive 23-foot-diameter propeller. Its maiden flight in 1884 lasted only 23 minutes and covered a distance of barely five miles, but Krebs and Renard were in control of their craft the entire way, proving that a dirigible was capable of living up to its name.

A BRAZILIAN STEPS UP

It fell to a wealthy Brazilian playboy named Alberto Santos-Dumont to build a powered dirigible capable of fully maneuvering into and across the wind. Santos-Dumont (1873–1932) moved to Paris at age 18 to devote himself to the study of chemistry, physics, astronomy, and mechanics. Aeronautics became his passion, and he began to build dirigibles.

On November 13, 1899, piloting his hydrogen-filled airship the *Santos-Dumont No. 3,* he circled the Eiffel Tower several times. Over a three month period in 1901, he both frightened and delighted Parisians as he doggedly pursued the Deutch Prize, a 100,000-franc award offered by the Aero-Club of France to the first person to fly from St. Cloud to the Eiffel Tower and back—a distance of 14 miles—in less than 30 minutes. Few observers thought such a feat possible. Then again, this was the age of Jules Verne and H. G. Wells, and for a devotee like Santos, everything seemed achievable at the turn of the 20th century.

THIRD TIME'S THE CHARM

He pinned his hopes on his latest creations, the *Santos-Dumont*

...they were once found in the wreckage of a fatal crash.

Nos. 5 and 6. Each was 108 feet long by 19 feet at its widest diameter, with an envelope full of 15,755 cubic feet of hydrogen gas. They were powered by a four-cylinder, 12-hp gasoline engine located in mid-keel. A radiator sat atop the engine, with the driveshaft running back through the keel to the rear-mounted, two-bladed propeller, 13 feet in diameter. The base of the 60-foot keel held the engine and, well forward, a basket just wide enough for Santos-Dumont to stand and man the ropes controlling the large rudder. He cleverly replaced the heavy rope suspension rigging with piano wire, greatly reducing air resistance.

It took Santos-Dumont three attempts to succeed. The highly flammable hydrogen gas and thoroughly unreliable engine with its hot, spark-spewing exhausts made for a foolhardy combination. On his second try, *Santos No. 5* sprung a leak and crashed, exploded, and burned into the chimneys of Paris. Santos-Dumont was unfazed by the setback, and two months later *Santos-Dumont No*. 6 captured the prize. Ever the showman, he donated half of his award money to the beggars of Paris and the other half to his mechanics.

FIRST LADY OF DIRIGIBLES

Santos liked to fly a smaller dirigible, *Santos-Dumont No*. 9 "*La Balladeuse*" to his favorite Parisian restaurant and park it on the street while he dined. With a volume of only 6,300 cubic feet, the 50-by-18-foot airship was much easier to fly. In 1903 at the behest of dinner partner Aïda de Acosta, a 19-year-old Cuban-American society girl, he gave her a crash course in flying, lifted her into the basket of *La Balladeuse*, and set her loose. He bicycled along below, shouting advice. She put down in a polo field at Château de Bagatelle, watched a bit of the match with Santos-Dumont, then piloted the dirigible back to Neuilly-St. James. Her 90-minute excursion made her the first woman to fly a motorized aircraft—six months before the Wright brothers' flight.

Santos-Dumont built 14 dirigibles in all, but by 1905 his interest had switched to airplanes. Meanwhile another German inventor was preparing to take the lead in airship innovation—Count Ferdinand von Zeppelin.

For the next installment, go to page 177.

The canals in Venice, California, are "highways" maintained with state highway funds.

PATENTLY WEIRD

No mode of transport should be without one of these unique inventions.

INVENTION: Integrated Passenger Seat and Toilet apparatus (1988; patent no. 4,785,483)

Inventor: Paul H. Wise; Tucson, AZ

Details: This inventor figured when you gotta go, you gotta go, so he designed a way to conceal a toilet under a passenger swivel chair seat cushion. The setup includes a built-in privacy curtain, a foot pedal flush system, a holding tank mounted beneath the car, and an electric water pump.

Invention: Collapsible Riding Companion (1991; patent no. 5,035,072)

Inventor: Rayma E. Rich; Las Vegas, NV

Details: Afraid to drive alone at night? Want to drive in the car pool lane? Just want a little company? The Collapsible Riding Companion is a dummy head and torso complete with full head of hair, T-shirt, and zippered jacket that rides "shotgun" wherever you need to go. The head and torso collapse into a lightweight rectangular case for easy storage.

Invention: Motorcycle Safety Apparel (1989; patent no. 4,825,469)

Inventor: Dan Kincheloe; San Clemente, CA

Details: So you like to ride your hog, but you hate to wear those sweaty protective leathers. Dan Kincheloe's safety apparel is practically invisible until you need it. It looks like a regular jacket, but should an accident occur, the hood fills with compressed or liquefied gas to protect your head, and the jacket inflates and extends to cushion your torso and thighs. You may look like the Michelin Man lying by the side of the road, but hey—you'll be alive.

Invention: System for Protecting Against Assaults and/or Intrusions (1989; patent no. 4,281,017)

Inventors: Yari Tanami, Yoav Madar; Gedera, Israel

Love Bug: The first "Herbie" Volkswagen was a 1963 Model 115 Deluxe Sunroof Sedan.

Details: If you're worried that your passenger might assault you, then this is the invention for you. Electrodes over the front and back passenger seats are connected to a high-voltage ignition coil. If the driver is threatened (or, say, the kids ignore that final warning), a foot switch sends a charge of electricity through the offending passenger strong enough to temporarily stun them. Leaving your car parked in a bad neighborhood? Set the system on "FRY" and give some unsuspecting burglar the shock of his life.

Invention: Flushable Vehicle Spittoon (1991; patent no. 4,989,275)

Inventor: Dan L. Fain; Chancellor, AL

Details: Some drivers love to chew tobacco or munch sunflower seeds as they head down the road—but there's always the problem of where to spit. The Flushable Vehicle Spittoon attaches by Velcro to your door or dashboard, to be ready wherever and whenever you need it. Gravity drains the waste through a funnel into a tube that empties into the great outdoors. A separate line attaches to the windshield wiper fluid container, providing an extra flush should gravity fail to do the job. Unfortunate pedestrians walking nearby will just have to step lively to avoid being sprayed by any discharge.

*　　*　　*

COINCIDENCE

On October 15, 1952, Robert Paterson was boarding an train from Phoenix to Los Angeles when the conductor told him that a Robert Paterson was already onboard. They soon discovered that the two Robert Patersons resembled each other in height, weight, and appearance. On the journey to L.A., the train made an emergency stop in Barstow, California, to pick up a passenger: *another* Robert Paterson. This man was also similar in appearance to the first two. Once the train reached L.A., the three Robert Patersons disembarked and the conductor prepared to board passengers for the return trip to Phoenix. Who was on the passenger list? A fourth Robert Paterson.

"SPIRIT OF ECSTASY"

The year 2011 marks the 100th anniversary of the sleek statuette ornamenting the grille of every Rolls-Royce.

THE WHISPER

English nobleman John Walter Edward Douglas-Scott-Montagu, an early promoter of automobiles, founded and edited *The Illustrated Car* magazine in 1902. That was also the year he fell for his 22-year-old secretary, Eleanor Velasco Thornton, a renowned beauty. But since Montagu was already married, their love affair was kept under wraps. It was known only by a tight circle of friends—and Montagu's wife, who actually condoned the romance. Montagu, anxious to find some way to proclaim his passion for his lovely Thorn, as he called her, commissioned friend and noted sculptor Charles S. Sykes to create a special hood ornament for his Rolls-Royce Silver Ghost, and asked his secret love to pose for it. The small statue depicted Thornton draped in diaphanous material with a finger pressed to her lips, as if encouraging the viewer to keep a secret. It was christened "The Whisper."

SILVER LADY

Montagu had started a new trend. In the same way that bobble-heads adorn some dashboards today, statuettes of gargoyles, toy policemen, and popular dolls began to festoon the hoods of Rolls-Royce motorcars. Claude Johnson, director of Rolls-Royce, Ltd., claimed to be appalled. To maintain quality and elegance of design, Johnson turned to Sykes to craft an official, Rolls-Royce hood ornament. Instructions were to create "the spirit of the Rolls-Royce, namely speed with silence, absence of vibration, the mysterious harnessing of great energy and a beautiful living organism of superb grace." The model who could embody all of this? Surprise! Eleanor Thornton.

The new statuette turned out to be a variation of Sykes's "The Whisper." This time, Thornton, in a fitted gown, was shown leaning into the wind, her arms stretched out behind her. Fabric, like delicate silver wings, draped her body and arms and billowed off her fingertips. Sykes presented "The Spirit of Ecstasy" to the company in February 1911 with these words: "A graceful little goddess, the Spirit of Ecstasy, who has selected road travel as her supreme delight and alighted on the prow of a Rolls-Royce motor car to revel in the freshness of the air and the musical sound of her fluttering draperies."

The public loved the new statue, which they called the "Silver Lady." (Those in the know referred to her as "Ellie in Her Nightie.") Charles Royce, owner and chief engineer of Rolls-Royce, Ltd., had been ill during the commission of the flying lady and didn't like the idea of anything standing on the nose of his car. He argued that she would block the driver's view and refused to drive a car bearing the ornament. But public opinion triumphed, and "The Spirit of Ecstasy" has adorned the hood of almost every Rolls-Royce since. The only two Rolls-Royce cars produced without "The Spirit of Ecstasy" hood ornament were made in 1954 and presented to Queen Elizabeth and her sister, Princess Margaret. The queen's ornament was St. George slaying the dragon, and Margaret's was Pegasus.

THROUGH THE DECADES

Sadly, Eleanor Thornton died a few years after the debut of her statuette. On December 30, 1915, while traveling with Montagu to India on the S.S. *Persia*, she was drowned when a German U-boat torpedoed their ship off the coast of Crete. Montagu survived by clinging to an overturned lifeboat for 36 hours.

Over the years, Rolls-Royce has crafted 11 variations of "The Spirit of Ecstasy." To keep from obscuring the driver's sight, she has been shrunk in stature and now leans a little more forward. From 1936 to 1939, she knelt on the hood of the Phantom III. She currently stands three inches tall and, for safety, is mounted on a spring-loaded mechanism designed to retract into the radiator shell if struck from any direction. There is a button inside the Rolls-Royce that can retract or extend the statuette when pressed. Buyers can choose a stainless steel, sterling silver, or 24-Karat-gold model. The National Motor Museum in Hampshire displays a number of the various "Spirits of Ecstasy," along with Montagu's one and only silver statuette of his beloved Thorn as "The Whisper."

All Rolls-Royce cars are still pinstriped by hand by a single artist, Mark Court.

THE VIN FIZ FLYER

A daredevil pilot, a brand-new soft drink, and a coast-to-coast flight all play a part in this tale from the early days of aviation.

A MOGUL'S CHALLENGE

William Randolph Hearst liked to generate a good story for his chain of tabloid newspapers, and he was willing to pay for it. In October 1910, just seven years after the Wright brothers made their first flight, Hearst threw down the gauntlet to pilots around the United States: If one of them could fly a plane in short hops from coast to coast in less than 30 days, Hearst would pay the aviator the astounding sum of $50,000 ($1,150,000 today). When told of Hearst's dare, Orville Wright said, flatly: "The machine hasn't been built that can do that." But it didn't stop Wright or other intrepid aviation pioneers from trying. In the end, eight pilots entered the contest, five of them actually flew, and only one reached the finish line: Calbraith Perry Rodgers.

CAL GETS HIS TICKET

Cal Rodgers liked competition. The Pittsburgh native had spent his post-college years racing anything he could get his hands on: motorboats, yachts, autos, motorcycles. His competitive streak might have come from being related to a long line of U.S. naval heroes like Oliver and Matthew Perry, or it might have been a result of his deafness and the resultant speech impediment that made him more of a doer than a talker. Whatever the reason, Rodgers loved to race, loved to win, and was always up for any sporting challenge.

When Rodgers was 32, a cousin in Dayton, Ohio, introduced him to Orville Wright, who taught him how to fly a plane. Rodgers was a quick study: He soloed after a mere 90 minutes of training. Two months later, on August 7, 1911, he became the 49th aviator in the country to "get his ticket" (pilot's license). Five days later, Rodgers entered the Great Chicago Air Meet, an endurance competition. After keeping his plane aloft for 27 hours, Rodgers took third place and earned a cash prize of $11,285. His feat caught the attention of promoter Stewart de Kraft, who contacted him and suggested that he enter the Hearst contest.

First US traffic accident: New Yorker Henry Wells hit a bicyclist with his Duryea motorcar in 1896.

GRAPE EXPECTATIONS

De Kraft lined up a group of backers, including Orville Wright, who built Rodgers a Model EX biplane for the trip. In 1910 there were no airports or control towers, so a cross-continent airplane trip would require lots of ground support. De Kraft and Rodgers persuaded meatpacker J. Ogden Armour to sponsor the flight in exchange for naming the plane after Armour's new grape-flavored soft drink, Vin Fiz. The plane became the *Vin Fiz Flyer,* and the private three-car train that served as a mobile fuel tank/hangar/repair station was dubbed the *Vin Fiz Special.* The train carried a support team of three mechanics, Rodger's wife Mabel, and his mother, as well as reporters and representatives of Armour and Vin Fiz. When a reporter asked Rodgers why he was attempting the journey, he replied, enigmatically, "It's important...because everything else I've done before was not important."

FIZZ OUT

On September 17, 1911, the *Vin Fiz Flyer* took off from Sheepshead Bay near New York City. The plane, made of light-weight spruce and canvas, sported a 35-horsepower engine. It had no heater and no navigation aids, except for a shoelace dangling from the roof of the cockpit to determine vertical and horizontal alignment. Rodgers carried a bottle of Vin Fiz, the first airborne mail pouch, and a pair of crutches...just in case. The second morning he crashed into a chicken coop on take off and nearly totaled the plane. Luckily, the *Vin Fiz Special* was loaded with spare parts and engines. The mechanics rebuilt the plane in two days, and Rodgers was back in the air. Following the railroad tracks west, he steered away from mountains and bad weather. Nonetheless, the trip was fraught with problems: Eagles attacked him twice, and a souvenir-seeking crowd stole vital parts from his plane while it was on the ground.

Rodgers had planned 40 stops on the 2,500-mile journey; he ended up making 75, including 16 crashes. When the *Vin Fiz* arrived in Pasadena, California, the only thing left of the original plane was the rudder and some struts. Did Rodgers win the $50,000? Nope. His many stops and numerous repairs had cost him dearly—he was 19 days past the Hearst deadline. But that didn't bother Cal Rodgers, who said, "What matters is, I did it, didn't I?"

James Ramsey demonstrated the first motor boat to George Washington in 1784.

STOP THE WORLD

The story of the stop signal and the remarkable man who invented one of the first ones.

STOP THE BLEEDING

In the early 1920s, Garrett Augustus Morgan liked to cruise around Cleveland in his automobile. But the newfangled vehicles were making the city's streets—already crowded with bicyclists, pedestrians, and horses, and carriages—more dangerous than ever. Traffic cops helped at major intersections, but there weren't enough of them. After watching a car race through an intersection and collide with a horse-drawn carriage, injuring the horse so badly that it had to be put down, Morgan decided to do something about it. He would invent a simple, automated, traffic-control system.

DON'T STOP 'TIL YOU GET ENOUGH

Morgan was more than up to the job. Born in 1877 in Paris, Kentucky, to former slaves, Garrett had left home at 14 to seek his fortune up north. He found work as a handyman in the home of a rich landowner, where he hired a tutor to make up for his lack of education. In 1895 he moved to Cleveland and became a sewing machine repairman. He soon made a name for himself in the industry by inventing one of the first the automatic zigzag stitches. By 1909 he had his own tailoring business with 32 employees. The next year, after noticing how certain chemicals used in his workshop loosened tightly curled hair, he opened the G. A. Morgan Hair Refining Company, selling hair straighteners and similar products.

Branching out, in 1912 he patented an early version of the gas mask, and in 1916 used it to save more than 20 miners trapped in a tunnel under Lake Erie. In 1920 he founded the *Cleveland Call* newspaper, which remains today (as the *Call & Post*) a fixture in Cleveland's African-American community. Morgan had an unusual knack for creative thinking and was a rare commodity in 1920s America—self-made, self-educated, prosperous, and black.

World's first flight attendant: Heinrich Kubis, employed by the DELAG zeppelin company (1912).

DON'T STOP ME NOW

By February 1922, Morgan had a workable design for a lighted, semaphore-based traffic signal, which he patented the following year. Patent #1,475,024 was a three-armed device providing "a signal wherein the direction indicating arms are...moved vertically for stopping the flow of traffic and then to be revolved and dropped to indicate a right of way to vehicles moving in another direction." Among the Morgan Traffic Signal's innovations:

- **"All-Stop" position:** Both arms up, which reset traffic before allowing any direction to move along, making it easier for pedestrians to cross.
- **"Half-Mast" position:** Used in light traffic like a blinking yellow light today to tell all directions to proceed carefully through the intersection.
- **Alarm bell:** Operated by a traffic cop who also turned the entire machine by means of a hand-crank.
- **Electric lights to illuminate the arms at night:** These could be powered by internal batteries or overhead electrical lines, eliminating dangerous kerosene tanks. (Earlier traffic signal prototypes used kerosene to illuminate red and green lenses rotated in a lantern by a lever. In 1868 the kerosene tank in a unit in England exploded, badly injuring the constable working the lever.)

In 1924 city engineers installed the first Morgan signal at the intersection of Vine and Erie Streets in Cleveland, and by 1925 they lined Euclid Avenue, one of the city's main thoroughfares.

DON'T STOP BELIEVIN'

Other inventors, like Detroit's William Potts, had created working traffic signals before Morgan, but since Morgan was the first to patent the safety concepts still used today (Potts never patented his), the Federal Highway Administration gives him credit for being first. Also, he made his design the cheapest to manufacture, enticing General Electric to buy the rights to his patent for $40,000 (about $500,000 today). GE took advantage of having a clear patent under their control and soon cornered the stop signal market across the country.

STOP, STOP, STOP

• Morgan's original design did not have a yellow light, but the "All-Stop" and "Half-Mast" positions served the same purpose. He added a yellow light soon after 1923.

• Clear light signals were used at first, but abandoned when motorists had trouble seeing them during daylight hours.

• Morgan continued to invent things for the rest of his life. One of his last inventions was a self-extinguishing cigarette.

• Shortly before Morgan's death in 1963, he was given a citation from the U.S. government recognizing his invention of the stop signal.

• In the 1920s, vandals kept destroying traffic lights in an Irish neighborhood in Syracuse, New York. It turns out local residents didn't like that the red light was on top. They thought it represented Great Britain's oppression of the Irish. City officials put in lights with green on top.

• As of 2006, New York City had 11,871 traffic signals, 4,100 in Brooklyn alone.

DON'T STOP THINKIN' ABOUT TOMORROW

Modern traffic signals bear little resemblance to Morgan's invention. They have become dangling computers aware of almost everything around them, adjusting instantly to give an emergency responder the right of way, even adjusting light sequences to facilitate evacuations. Many city stoplights double as surveillance equipment, recording audio data and taking photographs and video of speeders and other lawbreakers in order for tickets to be issued.

* * *

Bonus quiz: You may have noticed something familiar about the title and subheads in this article. They're all song titles. Can you guess the artist who recorded each one? (Answers below.)

"Stop the World"—Extreme; "Stop the Bleeding"—Tourniquet; "Don't Stop 'Til You Get Enough"—Michael Jackson; "Don't Stop Me Now"—Queen; "Don't Stop Believin'"—Journey; "Stop, Stop, Stop"—The Hollies; "Don't Stop Thinkin' About Tomorrow"—Fleetwood Mac

JUST DUCKY

The DUKW "Duck" may not have been the first amphibious vehicle ever made, but it was certainly the most successful—and it inspired a host of imitators.

A DUCK BY ANY OTHER NAME

In 1942 the U.S. military machine was in full gear preparing to strike back at the German and Japanese occupiers of Europe and the Pacific. Both strategies involved beachhead invasions on a scale unprecedented in history. But these invasions presented a challenging tactical problem: How do you unload soldiers and cargo in places where there are no docks or piers? General Motors was given the contract to develop a new amphibious vehicle, with the simple directive: Build us a truck that can swim.

GMC turned to yacht designers Sparkman & Stephens for assistance, and the result was the DUKW. The initials, utilizing GMC's corporate naming terminology, stood for: D (vehicles designed in 1942), U (utility, which meant amphibious), K (having four-wheel drive), and W (having two powered rear axles).

UGLY DUCKLING

There was nothing fancy about the DUKW's utilitarian design. The designers started with a GMC six-wheeled military truck chassis and welded a watertight hull onto it, topped off with a propeller. Powered by a straight six-cylinder engine, it had a top speed of 50 mph on land and 5.5 knots (6.3 mph) on water. Instead of armor it was plated with light sheet metal to save weight, and fitted with a high-capacity bilge pump system that would keep it afloat even with bullet holes in the hull as wide as 2 inches.

But the DUKW was, frankly, an ugly duckling: ungainly, underpowered, and initially unwanted. When military brass got the first look at it during a demonstration off Cape Cod, their first reaction was to reject it. But a twist of fate saved the "Duck" from the scrap heap. A Coast Guard patrol ship ran aground on a sandbar nearby. Normal boats couldn't reach the seven stranded seamen due to the 70-mph winds and high seas, but the DUKW chugged through the heavy chop with no trouble. After the rescue, there was no more talk of canceling the DUKW program.

MIGHTY DUCKS

The first DUKWs to see action landed at New Caledonia in March 1943. They performed so well that by the invasion of Italy at Salerno in September, more than 150 DUKWs joined 90 LST landing craft to bring ashore 190,000 troops, 30,000 vehicles, and 12,000 tons of supplies. Duck brigades came ashore at Normandy, unloading 40% of all supplies during the first four months after D-Day. They helped lift the siege of Manila, where they were the only vessel that could safely navigate a bay strewn with sunken wreckage. In 1945 they turned into moving bridges across the Rhine to ferry men and materiél into Germany.

More than 21,000 Ducks served in WWII, with over 12,000 troops to operate and maintain them, in not only the U.S. military but the British, French, Canadian, Australian, and Russian as well. The Russians liked them so much that they built a knock-off DUKW of their own called the BAV-45.

DUCKS TODAY

After the war, many DUKWs were made surplus but only a few were scrapped. Most were snapped up for search-and-rescue units in coast guard, police, and fire units all over the world. The Australian government took several on expeditions to Antarctica in 1953 and 1955. Many of the original DUKWs still remain in service.

Today they are a familiar sight in harbor cities as amphibious tour buses. The first "Duck Tour" company, founded in Wisconsin in 1946, is still giving tours of the Wisconsin Dells, and similar tours can be found in Boston, Seattle, Philadelphia, Miami, London, and Singapore.

THE SEEP

After the success of the DUKW, the Army asked Sparkman & Stephens to design a smaller, jeep-sized version. The Seep (seagoing jeep) was produced in a hurry and in large quantities by Ford but proved to be a bust in the field. Too heavy to swim well, too slow on land to keep up with conventional Jeeps, the Army dumped as many as they could on the Russians. It turned out the Russians liked the Seep just fine—so much so that they began developing their own, which they exported throughout the 1950s to other Communist nations.

...to prevent blood from rushing from their heads while flying.

GEEZER JOKES

We know that the "elderly driver" is a tasteless stereotype...but still, we love a good joke.

An elderly Florida man was driving his Volvo down I-95 when his cell phone rang. "Frank, Frank! Be careful," his wife shouted. "I just heard on the radio that there's a car going the wrong way down I-95!"

"It's not just one car," Frank shouted back. "There are hundreds of them!"

A highway patrol officer pulled alongside a speeding car on the interstate. Glancing into the car, he was astounded to see that the old woman behind the wheel was knitting, completely oblivious to the patrol car's flashing lights and siren. The officer shouted over his loudspeaker, "Pull over!"

"No," the old lady yelled back, "it's a scarf!"

Four codgers were enjoying a cup of coffee at the local diner when one of them said, "Do you realize my hands hurt so much I can hardly hold this coffee cup?"

"Oh, that's nothing," said another. "My cataracts are so bad I can barely see my coffee cup."

"I got you two beat," said the third. "I got arthritis and can't turn my head to the left or right."

"Aw, quit your complaining!" ordered the fourth. "At least we can still drive."

Norma and Hazel were driving to the store in their Lincoln. At the first intersection, the light turned red and Norma powered right through it. Hazel was speechless. Norma ran the next red light as well. As they sailed through the third light, Hazel cried out, "Norma! We just ran three red lights! You're going to get us both killed."

"Me?" Norma gasped. "I thought *you* were driving!"

The first gas-powered tractor was built in 1892 by the Waterloo Company, now John Deere.

READY? GO!

America's very first automobile race was held in Chicago on Thanksgiving Day 1895.

MOTORCYCLE RACE

Sponsored by the Chicago *Times-Herald*, the first automobile race in the United States followed a 54-mile course from downtown Chicago to Evanston and back. In 1895 "horseless carriages" were so new that they didn't have an official name—so the *Times-Herald* offered a $500 prize to whoever came up with the best moniker for the new contraptions. The winning name was "Motocycle."

But the Motocycle Race was almost over before it began. When two out-of-town contestants drove into Chicago, they were stopped by cops who ordered, "Get those things off the street!" The drivers were forced to hire teams of horses to tow their machines out of town. This infuriated the *Times-Herald*'s publisher, H. H. Kohlsaat, who had a little talk with his cronies at City Hall. The situation was promptly straightened out, and the race was scheduled for November 28. The night before, the city was blanketed with a heavy snow, prompting most of the 83 entrants—many of whom were still struggling to finish building their "motocycles"—to pull out.

AT THE STARTING LINE

At 8:55 on Thanksgiving morning, despite freezing temperatures and ice-covered roads, six motocycles took their places on the starting line at Chicago's Jackson Park. Two of the competitors were battery-powered Electrobats, one from Morris and Salom of Philadelphia, and one from Sturgis of Chicago. Macy's Department Store and the De La Vergne Refrigerating Machine Co. of New York entered gasoline-powered Benz machines from Germany, as did H. Mueller & Co. of Decatur, Illinois. Frank Duryea and his brother Charles came from Springfield, Massachussets, to race the only car built in the USA—an old horse carriage they had hurriedly converted with a two-cylinder gasoline engine and three-speed transmission. They

Workers on Ford's 1913 production line could assemble a car in 93 minutes.

called it the Duryea Motor Wagon. All of the entries were open carriages with no protection from the elements, and each carried the driver plus a passenger chosen by the judges, to ensure that no cheating occurred.

IN A RUT

The Duryea Motor Wagon was first off the mark. The two Benz cars from New York caromed into each other as they sped through downtown Chicago, causing one to hit a horse and eliminating the driver from the race. Shortly after, the other New York Benz dropped out with engine trouble. The steering arm on the Duryea broke off, but Frank Duryea quickly found a blacksmith shop, replaced it, and motored off after the remaining three cars.

When not dodging frightened horses and boys hurling snowballs, the drivers spent a good portion of the race pulling their cars out of icy ruts and snowdrifts. The Stugis electric car's battery froze up; Pedro Salom's, cruised smoothly for 36 miles until the charge ran out. Mueller's Benz led the entire way to Evanston, where Duryea overtook him.

AND THE WINNER IS...

A little over 10 hours after the race had begun, Frank Duryea sputtered across the finish line, to win the $2,000 prize ($49,500 in today's money). His average racing speed was 7.3 mph. Mueller's Benz crossed the line almost two hours later, but Mueller was no longer driving it. He had collapsed from exhaustion in the passenger seat. The driver was C. Brady King, the passenger appointed by race organizers.

The next morning, the front page of the *Times-Herald* proclaimed that the "motocycle" was here to stay. A race official stated:

> Persons who are inclined...to decry the development of the horseless carriage...will be forced...to recognize it as an admitted mechanical achievement, highly adapted to some of the most urgent needs of our civilization.

Duryea and his brother invested the prize money into the Duryea Motor Wagon Company, which became the first domestic carmaker. It delivered 15 vehicles the following year.

WALL OF DEATH

"Oh, let me take my chances on the Wall of Death!"
—Richard Thompson, songwriter/guitarist

ON THE BOARDS

During the first two decades of the 20th century, motorcycle and car races often took place on board tracks, wooden concourses built out of tons of 2-by-4s stacked on edge and joined together to form a smooth, fast racing surface. Based on French velodromes used for bicycle races, they ranged from very tight ⅛-mile to two-mile-long ovals with straightaways and banked turns. The first board track to open in the United States was the Los Angeles Coliseum motordome, which opened on April 8, 1910. To get fast speeds, corners were banked at up to a 60-degree angle. Grandstands perched at the very edge of the tracks, with spectators looking down on the action. Accidents often took the lives of drivers and spectators alike. One crash in New Jersey in 1912 left four dead and 10 injured, prompting the press to refer to the shorter tracks as "murderdromes." At one time there were more than two dozen board tracks around the country, but by the 1940s only a few remained. It took the gritty glamor of the ride known as the Wall of Death to keep the board track alive.

DEFYING GRAVITY

The first carnival motordrome opened at Coney Island in 1911. By the following year, portable dromes had become a fixture of traveling carnival shows, with over 100 of them in parks and shows by the 1930s. The first drome with vertical walls (called a "drum") appeared in 1915, heralding the advent of the carnival sideshow known as the Wall of Death, or Thrillarena. Spectators stood around the open rim of the drum to see the shows. Inside, motorcycle riders rode up a transitional ramped section on the lower wall until they were circling the drum parallel to the floor. Typical dromes were 20 to 30 feet in diameter. The vertical sides of the drum ranged from 12 to 20 feet in height. Circling counter-clockwise at speeds of 60 mph or more, the bikers performed tricks such as steering with their feet, sitting side-saddle with arms up and legs out, facing backwards, and standing.

There were acts with tandem riders, as well as two or three vehicles performing simultaneously with drivers weaving in and out from one another.

LADIES AND LIONS

The Wall of Death is still a popular attraction at carnivals around the world. And women have often featured prominently in the shows. The most renowned American rider was Samantha Morgan, who thrilled audiences in the 1970s and '80s and was known as the "Motordome Queen." The Wall of Death act tended to run in families, like the Pelaquins of the United States and Messhams of England, who have been riding for 80 years. The husband-and-wife team of Joe and "La Vonnie" Pelaquin regularly performed a stunt that had them switching bikes in mid-ride, still considered the hardest trick on the wall.

As if going around in circles parallel to the ground at 60 mph wasn't daring enough, some shows introduced lions into the act. "Fearless Eggbert's Lion Drome" in the 1920s featured big cats that rode the Wall in sidecars, in cages on running boards, and even in the riders' laps. The last lion drome carnival act ended in 1964.

SCOUTS ONLY

The bike of choice to ride the Wall of Death has long been the American-made Indian Scout, first introduced in 1920 and culminating with the 1928 Series 101 Scouts. Heavy, with a long wheel base and a low center of gravity, the bright red bikes were the epitome of motorcycle engineering excellence, style, and reliability throughout the '20s and '30s. "You Can Never Wear Out an Indian Scout" was the company motto, and Wall of Death riders today still stake their lives on their vintage Indian Scouts.

Only three year-round motordromes still operate in the U.S., with about 15 in the U.K. and around the world. But the Wall of Death remains a staple of county fair and carnival sideshows, with traveling companies like the Diamond Maruti Car Circus of India and California's American Motor Drome Company.

The Triumph motorcycle that Marlon Brando rode in *The Wild Ones* was his personal bike.

SPACE FREIGHT

Some unusual stuff has found its way into the cargo bays of NASA spacecraft.

WRIGHT BROTHERS AIRPLANE

OK, just parts of it. Orville Wright never got more than 10 feet off the ground during his historic first flight in 1903, but 66 years later the crew of *Apollo 11* took a small wooden strut and a bit of fabric from the wing of the original *Kitty Hawk* plane all the way to the moon—slightly more than a billion feet off the ground.

17th-CENTURY CARGO TAG

Onboard the Shuttle *Discovery* on its 2007 mission to the International Space Station was a lead cargo tag, unearthed at the site of the Jamestown Colony in Virginia. The tag took several months to cross the Atlantic by boat in 1611; the return trip by space shuttle took only a few minutes.

JEDI LIGHTSABER

Also onboard *Discovery* in 2007 was the prop lightsaber used by actor Mark Hamill as Luke Skywalker in *Return of the Jedi* (1983), in honor of the 30th anniversary of the original *Star Wars* movie.

INDY 500 FLAG

When the Space Shuttle *Atlantis* lifted off from Cape Canaveral on November 26, 1985, it carried a checkered flag from the Indianapolis Motor Speedway with an inscription from track owner Mari Hulman George that read, "With you all the way!" Astronaut Jerry Ross returned the flag to George so she could use it to wave in the winner of the 1986 Indy 500. The flag is now on display at the Speedway's Hall of Fame.

GOLF CLUB HEAD AND GOLF BALLS

In 1971 Alan Shepard famously played golf on the moon. He fit the head of a Wilson six-iron onto a lunar sample scoop handle and, as he put it, tried to hit "a little sand trap shot." His suit was so stiff that he was forced to one-hand the shots. The first, as he reported to Mission Control, "hit more dirt than ball." The second connected and went "miles and miles and miles" into the Fra Mauro crater. Legend says Shepard snuck the club head and balls aboard in his sleeve, but NASA flight directors admitted that they were aware of his plans. The improvised club is now at the U.S. Golf Association Museum in New Jersey. As for the two golf balls, they're still on the moon.

SHEET MUSIC

Astronaut Stephanie Wilson once worked in a music store in Tanglewood, Massachusetts, summer home to the Boston Symphony Orchestra. So when she went into space onboard the Space Shuttle *Discovery*, she took a page of sheet music from one of the BSO's favorite concert pieces, Beethoven's "Ode to Joy."

KITE

In 1996 NASA honored the 10th anniversary of One Sky, One World, an organization that promotes world peace through kite flying, by sending up a kite with the Space Shuttle *Endeavor*. The kite, the first to fly around the world, remains on display at the National Air and Space Museum in Washington, D.C.

CURIOUS GEORGE T-SHIRT

Leland Melvin identified so much with the inquisitive monkey character he had loved as a child that, when he went into space on the 2008 Shuttle *Atlantis* mission, he brought along a T-shirt with a picture of his childhood hero.

ROSE

Rex Walheim brought a dried rose aboard *Atlantis* in February 2008 that was given to him by his brother, a horticulturalist and rose breeder. The preserved bloom was later featured in the 2009 Tournament of Roses Parade in Pasadena, California.

METEORITE

Astronaut Stan Love is responsible for the first meteorite to land on Earth twice. A group of scientists he had worked with at the University of Hawaii before joining NASA gave him the space rock to take on the Shuttle *Atlantis* in 2008.

...is named after comedian Stephen Colbert.

CELEBRITY YACHT QUIZ

Match the celebrities with the names of their yachts and then go to page 454 to see if you're right—and get details about the boats.

CELEBRITY

1. Paul Allen
2. Humphrey Bogart
3. Jimmy Buffet
4. Al Capone
5. Johnny Carson
6. Johnny Depp
7. David Geffen
8. Ernest Hemingway
9. Saddam Hussein
10. Howard Johnson
11. Dmitry Medvedev
12. Aristotle Onassis
13. Marge Schott
14. Elizabeth Taylor
15. Donald Trump
16. Tiger Woods

YACHT

a. *Ocean Breeze*
b. *Serengeti*
c. *Rising Sun*
d. *Cosmic Muffin*
e. *Sirius*
f. *Riptide*
g. *Octopus*
h. *Privacy*
i. *Flying Cloud*
j. *Vajoliroja*
k. *DSV*
l. *La Diva*
m. *Santana*
n. *Pilar*
o. *Christina O*
p. *Kalizma*

IT REALLY HAPPENED

Real excuses submitted on real car insurance claims.

"I saw a slow-moving, sad-faced gentleman as he bounced off the roof of my car."

From a questionnaire submitted after hitting a cow:

Q: What warning was given by you?

A: Horn.

Q: What warning was given by the other party?

A: Moo.

"I was on my way to the doctor with rear end trouble when my universal joint gave way causing me to have an accident."

"I was thrown from my car as it left the road. I was later found in a ditch by some stray cows."

"A truck backed through my windshield into my wife's face."

"The accident happened because I had one eye on the truck in front, one eye on the pedestrian, and the other on the car behind."

"The car in front hit the pedestrian, but he got up so I hit him again."

"A cow wandered into my car. I was later informed that the cow was half-witted."

Q: Could either driver have done anything to avoid the accident?

A: Traveled by bus.

"My car was stolen and I sent up a human cry, but it has not been recovered."

"There was no damage to the car, as the gatepost will testify."

"She suddenly saw me, lost her head, and we met."

"I left my Austin 5 outside and when I came out later to my amazement there was an Austin 12."

"The other man altered his mind so I had to run into him."

"A pedestrian hit me and went under the car."

SWAMP BUGGIES

Part tractor, part boat, these giant-wheeled contraptions can go through the worst mud and muck imaginable.

GETTING BUGGY

In the early 1930s, Ed Frank was a 19-year-old from Florida trying to strike it rich in California. He cobbled together a buggy for hunting from parts of old Model T Fords, surplus World War I airplanes, and some tires. Frank called the thing "Skeeter," after the mosquitoes he remembered from the Florida Everglades.

When Frank moved back to Florida, he brought Skeeter. An avid hunter, he set about modifying the buggy to traverse the swamps around his 220-acre farm near Naples. Frank swapped out the wheels and tires for a set from an old tractor and, after much trial and error, devised a vehicle capable of getting into and out of the worst parts of the swamps. Seeing this, his neighbors were soon welding their own swamp buggies out of whatever they had lying around.

TUMBLE BUGS

Just before hunting season in late October, Frank and his fellow buggy builders liked to get together to tune-up and waterproof their "tumble bugs," as the buggies were sometimes called. A hunter could end up as an alligator's dinner, so swamp-worthiness was important in a swamp buggy. A local named Sidney Griffin knew of a piece of property in east Naples that was used to grow sweet potatoes. When the potatoes were dug up, the field became a boggy mess—the ideal proving ground. Owner Raymond Bennett agreed to let them use the field, and it soon became an annual event for townsfolk to come out and watch the hunters race each other around the mudhole. The races started out with only a dozen or so buggies, but after 1943, when a local merchant donated a new shotgun as a grand prize for the overall winner, the field grew to 30 to 40.

BUGGY TECH

Buggies continue to be made out of junked cars, old aluminum boats, and rider-lawnmowers. They're usually built in two sections: upper and lower decks separated by a frame. Older frames were usually welded together from tubular steel, but today's racers use aluminum. The lower deck holds the engine (often a 4- or 6-cylinder Jeep engine), transmission, heavy-duty axles, independent front and rear suspension with lift kit, and tires (most builders prefer 35-inch or larger tractor tires). Three-speed two-by-four transmissions are chosen over automatic four-wheel-drive transmissions because they're more durable and easier to maintain. The upper deck is where the driver sits and operates the vehicle, and its design is limited only by the imagination of the builder. Some newer racing buggies are 1,000-hp V8 behemoths with tires six feet tall. Some buggies stand 12 feet high.

SWAMP BUGGY DAYS

In 1947 Frank had an idea to get even more people to come down to the 'tater patch "for some laughs." He suggested that the buggies parade through the town of Naples on their way to the race. So in 1949, civic leaders organized the first "Swamp Buggy Days" in Naples. All the shops in town closed as upwards of 50 buggies—everything from boats with balloon tires to jeeps on tractor frames—paraded from the Naples Hotel to Cambier Park for festivities before heading down to the mud. Hundreds of fans turned out to cheer Dirt Dobber, Tumblebug, Turkey Buzzard, Big John, Cold Duck, Outlaw II, and of course Skeeter, as well as dozens of other wacky-looking swamp crawlers. Local girl Joan Ozier was crowned the first "Swamp Buggy Queen," and local boy Johnny Jones won the shotgun.

In the mid-1950s, the annual swamp buggy races had caught the attention of ABC'S *Wide World of Sports*, and soon celebrities like Gary Cooper were seen riding around Naples on swamp buggies. Thousands of out-of-town fans began showing up as well. The 'tater patch was fashioned into a ⅞-mile track known as the "Mile O' Mud." Along most of the track the mud was a foot deep, but in three places it dipped to well over five feet. The deepest pit, located right in front of the grandstand, became known as the Sippy Hole, after racer "Mississippi" Milton Morris. For five years in a row, Morris bogged down in that hole. The crowd would howl with glee as Morris's bright red buggy sank deeper into the muck

At 55 mph, 50% of the average car's energy is used just combatting wind resistance.

with every attempt to dig himself out. Finally all that was left was his floppy hat on top of the mud. The name caught on—today all deep mudholes are called sippy holes.

In 1957 racer H. W. McCurry got so excited after winning the race that he grabbed the current Swamp Buggy Queen and dunked her in the Sippy Hole, gown and all. That started the Mud Bath, a tradition that continues to this day. The '50s also saw the shotgun grand prize replaced with money—first hundreds and now thousands of dollars.

BIGGER THAN EVER

In the 1960s, drivers began building buggies that could not only churn through the mud but go fast doing it. Far too noisy to be useful for hunting, the new breed of buggy was designed for one thing only—racing. By the 1970s, the sport had grown so popular that races were held twice a year, then three times. By 1982 Swamp Buggy Days had outgrown the 'tater patch. In 1985 the board of directors bought a local shooting range and converted it into the Florida Sports Park, where the buggy race has been held ever since.

Amy Lynn Chesser, whose father Leonard won the event 24 times, won the Big Feature in 2008 in her buggy, *Aches 'n Pains*—the first woman to take the event. (Ironically, founder Ed Frank never won an official race.) The muddy mayhem continues to draw tens of thousands of U.S. fans, as well as a global television audience on channels like National Geographic, Discovery, and Travel. Unlike the original swamp buggy, Skeeter, the 8-cylinder behemoths today are not made of scrap. It's not uncommon for racers to spend more than $100,000 on a finely tuned machine capable of turning mud into gold. And teams will often field more than one buggy in the race…just in case the first one gets lost down a sippy hole.

*　　*　　*

SMALL COMFORT

"Every time I fly and am forced to remove my shoes, I'm grateful Richard Reid is not known as the Underwear Bomber."

—Douglas Manuel, aerospace executive

RACING FLAGS

In the days before two-way radios, signal flags were the only way for officials and pit crews to communicate with drivers during a race. Today they remain a time-honored part of auto racing.

THE LANGUAGE OF RACING

The use of flags as a form of communication was adopted in the very earliest days of automobile racing. The basic signals were adopted from those used by ports to communicate with ships, and new flags were created to deal with situations specific to racing. Most races use the same basic flags:

• **Green:** "Go!" A green flag starts every race, practice, and restart. It signals that the track is clear, and conditions are safe for racing.

• **Yellow:** "Caution." Used to tell drivers to slow down; the track is no longer to safe to race on, due to accident or road condition. Once a yellow flag has been waved, drivers maintain their position in the race at slower speeds, usually behind the pace car. No passing is allowed (except for the IndyCar Series, where passing is allowed in the pit lane). A "furled" yellow flag—wrapped around the stick—means the caution is about to end.

• **Red:** "Stop." The race is stopped, usually temporarily, and all drivers must head to the pit lane. A red flag may be waved for bad weather, unsafe track conditions, and severe car wrecks. No car may pass another, and sometimes the race is over for good.

• **White:** "Last lap." A white flag means the leader has entered the final lap. Usually this is the same driver who wins the race, but not always. At the 2011 Indy 500, rookie J. R. Hildebrand took the white flag nursing a comfortable lead, into the final turn, where he lost control, hit the wall, and was passed by Dan Wheldon, the eventual winner.

• **Checkered:** "The race is over." A black-and-white checkered flag is recognized the world over; every racing league uses it to declare the winner. Historian Fred Egloff, in his book "The Origin of the Checker Flag," says the flag came into use during the Glidden Tours, a series of open-road rallies held across the United

What are "tiger teeth" and "alligator teeth?" Other names for tire-deflating spikes.

States in the early 1900s. The courses covered hundreds of miles of hazardous roads, and the cars were prone to breakdowns. To help with safety and scoring, officials installed a series of checkpoints along the route. In 1906 a Packard employee named Sidney Waldon designed a symbol to signify the checkpoints, a highly visible black-and-white checkered flag.

SELDOM-SEEN FLAGS

• **Blue with yellow stripe:** It means a driver is about to be passed by a faster car. In Formula 1, the driver being lapped must let the other driver pass at the earliest opportunity. IndyCar and NASCAR racing don't use the flag—drivers are allowed to block other cars.

• **Yellow with red vertical stripes:** This flag flies near sections of track that have lost adhesion due to an oil, fuel, water, or debris spill. It's essentially a road alert signal.

• **Red with yellow *X*:** An IndyCar exclusive, it tells drivers that the pits are closed. The flag usually appears when the entire track is under caution due to an accident or adverse conditions. At the Indy 500, the flag is sometimes red with a black *P*.

FLAGS DRIVERS NEVER WANT TO SEE

• **Black:** When displayed to a specific driver (with the car's number on the pole below), this means, "Get into the pits—we gotta talk." The cause could be a mechanical problem or a rule violation. If the driver ignores the black flag, it's time for…

• **Black with diagonal white cross:** This flag means, "Hey you! Yes, YOU! Get in here NOW!" In NASCAR this flag means the driver is temporarily suspended until the problem is rectified. In F-1 and IndyCar racing, that driver is done for the day.

• **White with red cross:** An IndyCar Series exclusive. It means a medical vehicle is on the track. Passing is unwise, and usually prohibited, but racers and officials can agree to suspend that rule.

• **Black with orange disc:** A driver shown this flag must come into the pit immediately—the car has some problem that makes it a hazard to other drivers. Often referred to as the "Meatball Flag," which may stem from the derogatory nickname American GIs gave to captured Japanese flags during WWII.

Why is it called a HEMI engine? Because the top of the combustion chamber is hemispherical.

JET MAN

When Yves Rossy straps his jet-propelled wing onto his back, he can do what no other human in history could—he can fly like a bird.

BORN TO FLY

Yves Rossy got the flying bug at age 13. The Swiss native went to an air show in 1972 and was hooked. He became a fighter pilot for the Swiss Air Force and later a commercial airline pilot, but his real ambition was to fly, open to the elements, without the surrounding body of an airplane.

He became an expert sky diver, parasailor, hang glider, wingsuit flyer, and skysurfer (performing aerobatic tricks with a board attached to his feet during freefall). In 1994 Rossy skysurfed over the Matterhorn with a small-scale replica of the Mirage III fighter he flew in the air force strapped to his feet. He skysurfed the famous *jet d'eau* ("jet of water") on Lake Geneva and off the top of a hot air balloon at 7,500 feet. In 2002 he built an inflatable wing that he could strap onto his back to increase the distance he could travel in freefall. Using the wing allowed him to glide the $7\frac{1}{2}$ miles (12 kilometers) across Lake Geneva between the borders of France and Switzerland. These stunts won him notoriety, which enabled him to raise money for his pet project.

WINGING IT

In 2003 Rossy decided to *power* his wing. He added two JetCat P200 model jet engines, each providing 52 pounds of thrust. But the prototype was a failure because the inflatable wing wasn't rigid enough to handle the power. By 2004 Rossy was experimenting with a fixed wing made of carbon fiber. With a span of roughly eight feet (2.4 meters), it was strong and rigid, but it took months of tinkering before he was able to complete a successful test flight. Realizing that the wing was underpowered, he added two more engines. On November 28, 2006, Rossy realized the dream of his life when he flew for an exhilarating 5 minutes, 40 seconds over Bex, Switzerland.

British Airways passengers consume about 6 tons of caviar per year.

Two years later, again at Bex, Rossy demonstrated his jet-propelled wing to the press. With the wing folded up on a pack, he jumped from a plane at 8,000 feet, deployed the wing, and began an amazing five-minute flight during which he looped the loop, dove and climbed, and performed figure eights using only his hands and body to steer (he controlled the jets with a throttle control in one hand). Then he popped the parachute, folded the wing, and landed on the airfield.

CHANNEL SURFING

Rossy's success made him look for bigger challenges. He decided to retrace the pioneering first flight across the English Channel by French aviator Louis Bleriot in 1909. Taking off in a single-engine plane from Calais, Rossy was flown to 8,000 feet, where he climbed out on the wing, started his engines, and let go. As soon as he stabilized his wing, he hit the throttle and rocketed toward Dover 22 miles (35 kilometers) across the ocean. It took him 13 minutes, after reaching a top speed of 186 mph (299 km/h). When the famous white cliffs of Dover loomed in sight, he cut his engine, opened his parachute, and landed near the South Foreland Lighthouse on the cliffs.

Rossy's next flight was a setback. Hoping to be the first person to fly by jet wing between two continents (in this case, across the Strait of Gibraltar from Tangier, Morocco, on the African side to southern Spain), Rossy started his flight at 6,500 feet but encountered a stiff head wind that forced him to ditch his jetwing in the Atlantic. Rescued by helicopter, he was unhurt but frustrated.

OVER THE CANYON

The failure of the intercontinental crossing caused Rossy to reexamine the design of his wing. He reconfigured his jet system for greater power and reduced the span on his wing by over a foot to 6 feet, 6 inches (2 meters). He hoped the shorter span would give him greater control. He decided to test his theory by flying over the Grand Canyon. On May 10, 2011, Rossy successfully completed the 8-minute flight, skimming 200 feet above the rim at 190 mph, before descending in his parachute, as one reporter put it, "like a high-tech, Lycra-clad Icarus."

BIG SHIPS

Oceangoing tankers from the 1970s and '80s were the largest vessels ever built.

STEEL LEVIATHAN

In December 2009, one of the world's biggest ships made its final voyage from the Persian Gulf to the west coast of India. It was a supertanker—also known as a ULCC, or "Ultra Large Crude Carrier"—called the *Knock Nevis*, after a hill in Scotland. The huge tanker was built in Japan in 1979, was sunk in the Persian Gulf during the Iran-Iraq War, was refloated, and served another 13 years before becoming permanently moored in storage off Qatar. On arriving in India, the *Knock Nevis* was intentionally beached and then scrapped, a process that took an entire year and 18,000 laborers.

- 1,504 feet long (The Empire State Building is 1,250 feet tall.)
- Dead-weight tonnage: 564,763 tons
- Capacity: 4.1 million barrels of crude oil
- Too wide to pass through the Panama or Suez canals
- Turning radius: 2 miles
- Stopping distance: 5½ miles
- Steam turbine engine generated 50,000 hp to a 30-foot, 5-blade, 50-ton propellor
- Cruising speed: 16.5 knots (18.99 mph)

SISTER SHIPS

Eighty supertankers, ranging in capacity from 320,000 to 550,000 tons were built between 1970 and 1985, but only four *Knock Nevis*–class ships were ever made. Two have since been converted to permanently moored oil-storage vessels; the other was scrapped. With the demise of the *Knock Nevis*, the largest and longest ship afloat is the Danish E-class container ship *Emma Mærsk* (see "The Biggest" on page 429), a distinction she shares with seven sisters. Longer than the largest cruise ship afloat, they require a crew of only 13. Fully loaded, they can carry 15,000 14-ton containers—equivalent to a line of railroad cars 55 miles long.

AIRSTREAM DREAMS

After baseball, Mom and apple pie, what could be more American than the iconic, bullet-shaped aluminum Airstream trailer?

SONG OF THE OPEN ROAD

For most Americans 100 years ago, the yearning for travel was just that—a yearning. Popular magazines like *National Geographic* tempted readers with photographs of far-off lands, but even as appetites were whetted by the stories and photos of exotic places, the dream of going there seemed out of reach. Then in 1913 Henry Ford perfected the assembly-line method of mass-producing his horseless carriage. By 1920, 10 million automobiles were rolling along America's roads, forcing President Warren G. Harding to put $75 million into upgrading the nation's highways. In 1927 there were 15 million Model T Fords alone. Virtually overnight, automobile travel had become a reality for millions of Americans. Many of those travelers turned to camper trailers as a way to bring home on the road with them, and manufacturers scrambled to fill the need. By 1930 one brand had emerged as the undisputed king of the road—the Airstream.

BACKYARD TINKERING

Armed with a new law degree from Stanford University, Wally Byam arrived in Los Angeles in 1923. Instead of law, however, Byam went into magazine publishing. When one of his publications, targeted at do-it-yourselfers, received a flood of letters from disgruntled readers who'd tried and failed to build a travel trailer using the plans published in the magazine, he decided to try building one himself. His readers were right: the plans were flawed. Byam decided that he could do better, and soon he was making a living selling his own trailer plans by mail for a dollar apiece. He then began building the trailers in his backyard and selling them for $1,200 (about $15,000 today).

Always with an eye on innovation, Byam built the best trailers money could buy. He became so successful that he was able to move the business out of his backyard and into a factory space in 1932. He dubbed his venture the Airstream Trailer Company.

...climbing 14,258 feet above sea level.

That year, Airstream competed with 48 other trailer manufacturers around the country.

AN ICON IS BORN

By 1936—the year Airstream came out with its first bullet-shaped, riveted aluminum model—more than 300 companies were fighting for a piece of the travel trailer pie. The Airstream Clipper featured *monocoque* construction, a technique Byam had picked up by studying aircraft plans drawn by Hawley Bowlus, who designed Charles Lindbergh's Spirit of St. Louis. This structural-skin type of construction allowed the trailer's exterior to support the load, dispensing with the need for interior struts, posts, and braces. The Clipper was an instant hit with customers. Even the Great Depression couldn't slow the company's growth, and by 1940 Airstream was the only trailer manufacturer still in business.

World War II did to Airstream what the competition could not. Needing every bit of scrap metal for the war effort, the U.S. War Production Board ordered that "house trailers shall not be made for the duration of the war." Airstream was temporarily out of business. It wasn't until 1948 that Byam was able to revive the business.

THE CADILLAC OF TRAILERS

Soon back up and running, the company expanded its manufacturing to Ohio. Airstream developed a reputation as the "Cadillac of trailers" because of their high quality and the attention to detail. Airstream models like Bubble, Flying Cloud, and Sovereign of the Road were built to suit practically every lifestyle. Byam told his employees, "Let's not make changes, let's make only improvements." Airstream managers scoured the world looking for items to make the trailers more livable. The ultimate goal was "self-containment," which meant complete freedom from outside power and water hookups. They procured state-of-the-art radiant heaters, chemical toilets, and gas refrigerators in their quest.

The company introduced a Way of Life department, and Byam began organizing caravans of Airstreams. Company engineers developed a harness that could load the trailers onto cargo ships for overseas travel. Scores of enthusiasts, known as "Airstreamers," traveled to faraway lands in a brilliant stream of gleaming alu-

Eww: Used diapers and turkey guts are all being considered as alternative fuel sources.

minum. Between the winter of 1951 and the spring of 1960, Byam personally led every caravan himself, including a six-month tour of Europe and an 18,000-mile trek across Africa. As a marketing ploy, it was sheer genius. Photos of the unmistakable Airstreams showed up in magazines back home. Airstreamers were shown picnicking in front of the pyramids in Egypt, towing their trailers along the Ganges River, and parking in front of the Eiffel Tower. Airstream became a juggernaut.

When the uninitiated questioned the seemingly exorbitant prices—a 1957 26-foot Overlander, for instance, sold for $4,450 (an inflation-adjusted $35,000 today)—Byam would retort, "Talk is cheap, Airstreams are expensive." Despite their cost, Airstream trailers far outsold everything else on the market.

STILL GOING STRONG

Byam died in July 1962, at the age of 66, but Airstream has lived on, along with its mystique. Following the first successful moon landing in 1969, Apollo 11 astronauts spent 21 days in a NASA-modified Airstream known as the Mobile Quarantine Facility. In 1979 Airstream introduced The Classic, its first-ever motor home. Ten years later, it introduced the Land Yacht motor home, which replaced the iconic aluminum construction with a patented laminated fiberglass. Today, a new custom luxury Airstream trailer sells for over $100,000. Vintage Airstreams remain as popular as ever. The 6,000-member Wally Byam Caravan Club, founded in 1955, holds 1,400 caravans and rallies each year.

According to the company, more than 60 percent of all Airstream trailers ever built are still on the road, including some of the ones built using the original one-dollar plan. Fifty years after Byam's death and eight decades after that first travel trailer, his words still echo in the hearts and minds of restless Americans: "To strive endlessly to stir the venturesome spirit that moves you to follow a rainbow to its end and thus make your travel dreams come true."

*   *   *

HARRUMPH!

Henry Ford II dismissed the Volkswagen Beetle as "a little box."

GOING BUGGY

More than 21 million VW Beetles were built between 1938 and 2003, making it the bestselling car model of all time.

• VW legend says that in 1932, while eating lunch in Munich, Adolf Hitler drew a sketch to illustrate his idea of a *Volkswagen* ("people's car") that could carry two adults and three children, go 62 mph, and get 42 mpg.

• Ferdinand Porsche was chief engineer on the VW design. The famous body shape was the work of designer Erwin Komenda.

• It was one of the first cars designed using a wind tunnel.

• The first Beetle test drive was on October 22, 1936.

• The famous name came from a remark attributed to Hitler: "It should look like a beetle. You have to look to nature to find out what streamlining is."

• The original name was the "KdF-wagen": *Kraft durch Freude* ("Strength through Joy").

• The Volkswagen Group also owns Audi, Bentley, Bugatti, Lamborghini, SEAT, Koda cars, and Scania trucks.

• Depression-poor Germans were urged to save for their new VW with this jingle: "Five Marks a week you must put aside, if in your own car you want to ride."

• Although the world knew it as the Beetle or Bug, VW didn't use either word until 1968. Until then, the car was referred to as the Type 1.

• Two words launched the Beetle in the U.S. in 1959: "Think Small" was later voted the best advertising campaign of all time.

• Other famous slogans: "It makes your house look bigger" (1966); "It's ugly, but it gets you there" (1969).

• The German word for beetle is *Käfer*.

• The last two German-made body shells, produced in Wolfsburg in 1974, are preserved in wax at a VW parts store in Milton-Keynes, England.

• VW is the world's third-largest automaker, behind Toyota and GM.

POWER TO THE PEOPLE

What super-efficient engine becomes more powerful with repeated use and has almost zero negative impact on the environment? Give up? It's you.

BACKGROUND

Human-powered vehicles have been around from the time some ancient monarch asked himself, "Why should I walk when I can command these servants to carry me?" A few thousand years later, the invention of the bicycle in the 1860s took "human power" to a new level: Cyclists cruising at 10 or 15 mph expend about as much energy as they would walking. Because pedal-pushing delivers up to 99 percent of a rider's energy to the wheels, a bike is still the most mechanically efficient form of transportation ever invented—10 times more than the most economical cars. But that hasn't stopped inventors from devising novel ways for humans to power themselves not just over land but also across the sea and through the air.

TRIKKE SCOOTER

The Trikke was thought up by Brazilians Gildo Beleski and Osorio Trentini in 1988. Their goal was to invent a stable scooter that could careen down hills like a skateboard. They figured a three-wheeled "carving machine" would be less wobbly than the traditional two-wheeled variety. What they didn't realize was that they'd come up with a completely new form of human-powered transportation. As on a regular scooter, a Trikke operator stands upright but, instead of placing one foot in front of the other, the feet are planted directly over each of the two rear wheels. Toggling the handlebars from side to side while shifting weight from one foot to the other, a Trikke rider can, with little effort, propel the scooter forward, even uphill. Today the Trikke is marketed primarily as a fitness aid, but its most useful application may be as a vehicle for older people with limited mobility. In 2002 *Time* magazine gave the Trikke its Invention of the Year award.

DAEDALUS AIRCRAFT

The big challenge in devising a human-powered aircraft is that, because of turbulence, energy efficiency drops significantly when the vehicle is in the air. A cyclist who routinely summons a 99-percent efficiency rate on a bicycle can expect only around 20 percent in a pedal-powered plane. This was the obstacle faced by a team of MIT students and faculty in the late 1980s when they created Daedalus, a superlight carbon-fiber craft that they intended to fly from the island of Crete to its northern neighbor Santorini. The craft's "engine" came in the form of Olympic cyclist Kanellos Kanellopoulos. Over the course of the 73-mile flight, Kanellopoulos had to pedal the aircraft's propellor at a constant 200 watts of power to stay aloft. That meant he burned a kilowatt of energy in the process—an enormous amount, even for an athlete. To counter that loss, Kanellopoulos drank a cocktail of water, salt, and glucose at a rate of one liter per hour—a lot of fluid, considering the MIT team estimated the flight to take more than seven hours. On April 23, 1988, Kanellopoulos and Daedalus shattered expectations by covering the distance in three hours, 54 minutes—a world record for human-powered aircraft that still stands.

DECAVITATOR HYDROFOIL

People have been paddling under their own power for centuries, in rowboats, kayaks, and canoes. Since rowing requires the weaker upper body muscles to provide much of the power to propel the craft, Bavarian engineer Julius Schuck thought it made more sense to invent a machine that better utilizes the stronger leg muscles. In 1953 he introduced the Wasserläufer, or Water Runner, a hydrofoil resembling a cross-trainer on water skis. When the standing rider pumped up and down with each leg, the craft moved over the water as intended—only sideways. Clumsy and unsteerable, the Wasserläufer sank into obscurity until the MIT team that created Daedalus took a second look at it 40 years later. In 1992 they came up with the Decavitator—a pedal-powered hydrofoil that, unlike the Wasserläufer, moved forward. The rider sat on a lightweight semirecumbent bike with low-drag pontoons beneath him and two pivoting takeoff wings submerged below those. A propeller placed behind the rider provided extra lift. When the rider worked the pedals, the wings rose out of the water and the Decavitator zipped along on the ski-shaped tips of the pontoons at a top speed of over 20 mph.

New York was the first state to require license plates on cars, in 1901...

FLYING FIRSTS

It takes years of training to become a successful test pilot. But it also took guts and determination to do what these historic flyers did.

TEST PILOT: Erich Warsitz (1906–83)
FIRST: To fly liquid-fuel rockets and turbojets
On June 20, 1939, *Flugkapitän* Warsitz of the German *Wehrmacht* became the first person to pilot a liquid-fuel rocket-powered aircraft—the super-secret Heinkel He 176. There was no time for showing off, as the plane had only enough fuel for one minute of flight. After a successful takeoff, Warsitz had to immediately concentrate on landing at over 310 mph. Said Warsitz of his achievement, "Once over the airfield boundary, I touched the runway a few times as prescribed and rolled the machine to a stop. The world's first manned rocket flight had succeeded!" Just two months later, on August 27, Warsitz became the first to pilot a turbojet airplane, the Heinkel He 178. Hans von Ohain, one of the inventors of jet propulsion, later said of Warsitz, "I admire him still and am firmly convinced that his brave preparedness to sacrifice himself...contributed significantly to the rapid development of the jet turbine and rockets for manned flight."

TEST PILOT: Hanna Reitsch (1912–79)
FIRST: Woman to fly a helicopter, jet plane, and rocket plane
Reitsch was the only woman to receive the Iron Cross First Class for her work as a test pilot with the German Luftwaffe. She became the first woman to fly a helicopter when she successfully demonstrated the Focke-Wulf Fw 61 in 1938. In 1942 she tested the infamous rocket-propelled Messerschmitt Me 163 Komet. After crashing during her fifth flight in the fast but ultimately unstable aircraft, Reitsch reportedly insisted on filing a post-flight report before falling into unconsciousness. She spent the next five months in a hospital. In the waning days of the war in 1945, Reitsch was captured by the Americans after a daring air escape from Hitler's bunker just hours before the Nazi leader took his own life. After her release, she went on to break several glider records, some of which still stand today.

TEST PILOT: Chuck Yeager (born 1923)

FIRST: To break the sound barrier

The name "Chuck Yeager" and the words "test pilot" are practically synonymous. Yeager became the most famous test pilot in history on October 14, 1947, when he flew faster than the speed of sound in a rocket-powered Bell X-1. Nicknamed "Glamorous Glennis" after his wife, the X-1 was dropped from the bomb bay of a B-29 bomber. Yeager flew the plane to an official top speed of 807.2 mph. In 1953 he broke another speed record by flying 1,650 mph (Mach 2.44—more than twice the speed of sound) in an experimental X-1A. In 1997 he used an F-15 fighter jet to repeat his historic first achievement on its 50th anniversary. He was 74.

TEST PILOT: Joseph A. Walker (1921–66)

FIRST: American to fly in space

"Oh, my God!" Walker yelled the first time he took off in a Bell X-15 experimental rocket plane in 1960. "You called?" the flight controller joked back. Walker had underestimated how much power the plane's engines would produce as he was smashed backward in his seat. He got used to it, flying that particular aircraft another 24 times. Two of those missions went higher than 62.2 miles in altitude, qualifying as space flights. That made him the first American in space, the first civilian in space, and the first person ever to go to space twice. Sadly, Walker died in a publicity photo shoot for GE when his F-104 Starfighter collided with another plane.

TEST PILOT: Nicholas "Hammer" Helms (born 1982)

FIRST: To fly unmanned drones

Unlike his predecessors, USAF Captain Helms doesn't strap into some futuristic aircraft and blaze across the sky at supersonic speeds. Instead, he sits at a desk at Edwards Air Force Base in California with a joystick and a monitor. In March 2011, the U.S. Air Force made the 29-year-old Helms its first drone test pilot. Helms admits that "flying at nine Gs is a lot more fun than sitting in a locked room." But few office workers get to remotely test planes like the new X-47B, a smaller, unmanned version of the stealth B-2 bomber that can fly 500 mph at 40,000 feet?

First air-conditioned car: the 1939 Packard.

DRAG RACING LEGENDS

Meet the kings of the quarter mile.

DON "BIG DADDY" GARLITS

Called the "father of drag racing" and "king of the dragsters," Don Garlits was first to top 170, 180, 200, 240, 250, 260, and 270 mph. He was also first to do 200 mph in the ⅛ mile. Garlits has won 144 major open events, 17 national championships, and 3 NHRA World Championships. After a horrific accident in 1970, where his dragster Swamp Rat XIII broke in half and he lost part of his foot, Garlits worked to perfect the rear-engine Top Fuel dragster design in use today. This put fuel processing and rotating parts behind the driver. Garlits was also one of the first drivers to promote the use of full-body fire-resistant suits, including gloves and socks.

Story Behind the Nickname: Garlits has had many nicknames in his lifetime: "The Floridian," "Don Garbage," "Tampa Dan" (not Don), and "Swamp Rat," all chiding him for being an outsider from Florida. (In drag racing's early days, when the sport was centered in California.) During a practice run at the 1962 Indy Nationals, where, as Garlits puts it, "I really smoked one, had a great run and the crowd went wild," track announcer Bernie Partridge bellowed, "Well, it looks like Big Daddy's gonna do aw-riiight!" The name stuck. The others disappeared over time except for Swamp Rat, which he named all 34 of his hand-built black dragsters. In 1987, Swamp Rat 30 was put on display at the Smithsonian. Garlits won his first race in 1955 at age 23. He retired four decades later and now runs the Don Garlits Museum of Drag Racing in Ocala, Florida.

TELEVISION TOMMY IVO

Tommy Ivo's status as a television star put a media spotlight on drag racing. Fans first came to the tracks to watch Ivo and his famed four-engine, four-wheel-drive Buick Showboat. When Ivo switched to Top Fuel dragsters, he beat "Big Daddy" Garlits in his first race at the Seattle World's Fair on July 1, 1962. He was 21 years old. His Top Fuel dragster, Barnstormer, was the first to record a seven-second run and first to officially reach 190 mph. On October 22, 1972, in Pennsylvania, Ivo posted a 5.97-second run, which made him the founding member of the Cragar 5-Second Top Fuel Club. Always the showman, Ivo was the first drag racer to tour the country. For years, he averaged 70,000 miles on the road and 80 to 100 races a year. In 1982 after 30 years of racing, he drove his refurbished Showboat at the Winston Finals at the Orange County International Raceway in one last, tire-smoking run. Then Ivo, in masterful showbiz fashion, climbed out, saluted the crowd, and burned his driving gloves on the starting line.

Story Behind the Nickname: As a young man, "TV" Tommy Ivo acted in nearly 100 movies and more than 200 television shows, including *The Donna Reed Show*, *The Mickey Mouse Club*, and *Margie*. Ivo would play Margie's boyfriend, Haywood Botts, during the week and scurry to the track to race on weekends. TV stardom helped propel him to the top in drag racing, but it was his skill that kept him there.

DON "THE SNAKE" PRUDHOMME

Rated #3 in the NHRA's Top 50 drivers from 1951 to 2001, Don "The Snake" Prudhomme started racing in high school as a member of Burbank's Road Kings car club in the late '50s. Prudhomme's career really began with his first Top Fuel victory at the Bakersfield March Meet in 1962. He was 21. He became the first racer to win four consecutive NHRA series titles, and won the prestigious U.S. Nationals seven times. A founding member of the Cragar 5-Second Funny Car Club (with a 5.98-second time), he's also the first Funny Car driver to break the 250-mph barrier. Prudhomme has come the closest of any driver to having an undefeated season. Driving his unstoppable Army Monza Funny Car, he won 6 of 8 national events in 1975, and seven of eight in 1976. "The Snake" retired in 1994, with 49 NHRA victories, at the time the sixth most in NHRA history. Today Prudhomme owns the Miller Genuine Draft Top Fuel Team. With his company, Snake Racing, he helped launch Larry Dixon into the Top Fuel winner's circle.

Howard Hughes' *Spruce Goose* was actually made of birch.

Story Behind the Nickname: Called "The Snake" because of his quick reflexes and intense focus, Prudhomme drove a yellow 1970 Plymouth Barracuda Funny Car with a cobra snake insignia. The Snake attracted big crowds who watched him go head-to-head with Tom "The Mongoose" McEwen in his red 1970 Plymouth Duster. (McEwen deliberately chose Mongoose as his handle because the animal is known for killing venomous snakes.) Their rivalry attracted crowds and helped secure sponsorship from Mattel, which released Hot Wheels toy versions of their cars in 1970. This opened the door for other nonautomotive sponsorships to enter racing.

* * *

HELLS ANGELS TRIVIA

- The Hells Angels Motorcycle Club (HAMC) was formed on March 17, 1948, in Fontana, California.
- Hells Angels say they are just an association of motorcycle enthusiasts; the FBI classifies them as one of the "Big Four" motorcycle criminal gangs dealing drugs, trafficking in stolen goods, and participating in widespread violence across the United States.
- The other three of the "Big Four" motorcycle gangs are the Bandidos, the Pagans, and the Outlaws.
- The "1%" patch worn by some Angels is a nod to the American Motorcycle Association's declaration that "99% of all motorcyclists are law-abiding citizens." Hells Angels are proud to call themselves "One Percenters."
- The Hells Angels insignia of the red-and-white-winged death's head is a registered trademark of the club.
- Other insignias include the number 81, which stands for the positions of the letters H and A in the alphabet.
- Journalist Hunter S. Thompson rocketed to fame in 1966 with the publication of *Hells Angels: The Strange and Terrible Saga of the Outlaw Motorcycle Gangs*. The founder of Gonzo journalism (in which a writer totally immerses himself in his subject) lived with the gang for a year, until some of them attacked him.
- As of 2011, there were Hells Angels chapters in 35 countries.

Germany, France, and England all pay a 70% gas tax. Americans pay only a 23% gas tax.

CRASH TEST DUMMIES

...or, as they're officially known, "anthropomorphic test devices."

ALL IN THE NAME OF SCIENCE

It's 1963. In a science building at Wayne State University near Detroit, a student rests his head sideways on his desk, his cheek on a textbook. A few inches above his head, a professor holds a solid metal rod he calls a "gravity impactor." The teacher drops it on the student's head. After the initial swelling goes down, he does it again. And again.

This was no bizarre classroom punishment. This was cutting-edge science, and the teacher dropping the metal rod was Lawrence Patrick. During the 1960s, Patrick was one of the leading biomechanics researchers on how the human body behaves in a car crash. (Patrick and his student volunteer had a sense of humor—the textbook the student rested his head upon was titled *Head Injuries.*) Like his colleagues, Patrick used human cadavers for his experiments whenever he could get them, but the supply was unreliable. So Patrick and his student assistants used the next best thing: their own bodies. Patrick himself rode a crash sled over 400 times, and—to test resistance levels and breaking points—slammed his own knee repeatedly into a metal pole with an attached sensor. Calling himself a human crash test dummy, Patrick and his lab produced helpful impact data for the auto industry. But testing on human bodies—even dead ones—has its limits.

LOOKING FOR A DUMMY

Patrick lived to the age of 85, but he probably wouldn't have if General Motors hadn't built the HY-GE, the world's first impact sled track designed specifically for automobiles. Soon after completion, they began looking for a simulated human being to strap into it. The Air Force had been using a human-shaped dummy called Sam for rocket-sled ejection tests since 1949, but GM wanted the latest technology. By the mid-1960s there were two competing dummies: the VIP-50 from Alderon Research Laboratories, and "Sierra Stan," Sam's successor. Neither model provided the consistency and reliability GM wanted.

So the engineers at General Motors took the best features of both designs and created the Hybrid-I in 1968. Four years later, they debuted an improved version, called the Hybrid-II. In an unusual move for a big automaker, they made their designs public, letting the auto industry take advantage of their research, an altruistic approach to auto safety.

DUMMY FAMILY

With the new dummies, impact research progressed quickly. In 1977 the Hybrid-III changed the game yet again. It had joints that could bend and flex; the ribcage and neck were "biofidelic," meaning they flexed and stressed exactly like a human ribcage and neck; and the head moved, and broke, the same way a real person's would. Best of all, the new dummy was equipped with sophisticated load sensors, accelerometers, and pressure gauges. Even the knees could produce impact data. Since its debut, there have been constant upgrades and innovations, but the basic design is still in use today. In September 1997, the U.S. government made the Hybrid-III dummy the industry standard for "occupant restraint compliance." Europeans adopted it a year later.

The Hybrid-III was a bachelor until 1987, when GM made a female Hybrid-III, and the Centers for Disease Control awarded a contract to Ohio State University to create a Hybrid-III family. OSU engineers created three prototypes: a six-year-old, a slightly smaller version, and a three-year-old. In recent years the family expanded again with a line of infant dummies ranging from 6 to 18 months old. Fittingly, these are called CRABI, or Child Restraint Air Bag Interaction dummies.

STAR DUMMIES

In 1985 the National Transportation Safety Board ran a TV ad campaign promoting the use of seat belts that featured a couple of talking crash test dummies named Vince and Larry. The commercials usually ended with a crash test vividly demonstrating what

...the Maternal Anthropomorphic Measurement Apparatus version 2B—or MAMA2B.

happens when one doesn't wear a seat belt: Larry would lose an arm and Vince would pull a piece of metal from his chest while informing the viewer that "thousands die in car accidents every year." The dummies even got musical. Vince grabbed a Fender guitar and sang "The Buckle-Up Blues," and Ray Charles joined the dummy duo for "Back Seat Baby," telling parents about the safest place to seat their children. The commercials ran until 1998. During the campaign, seat belt use in America increased from 14% to 79%. In 2010 the Smithsonian Institution installed an exhibit honoring the ads, with the original Vince and Larry costumes.

* * *

TEENY-TINY TRANSPORTATION

• The title of World's Smallest Piloted Airplane is held by the *Bumble Bee II*, built and piloted in 1988 by Robert H. Starr of Phoenix, Arizona. Only 8 feet, 10 inches long, it has a wingspan of a mere 5½ feet and weighs less that 400 pounds, but it can fly at speeds of up to 190 mph. It took Starr five years to design the plane, whose sole purpose was to set a world record. Sadly, the *Bumble Bee II* was destroyed in a crash not long after its historic flight.

• World's smallest car: the Peel P-50. At 52 inches long and 39 inches wide, this ultra-minicar is just big enough to hold a driver and a small shopping bag. With three wheels, one door, and one headlight, the P-50 weighs 130 pounds, less than some of its drivers. The 4.2-hp engine reaches a top speed of 10 mph. Originally built in 1962 by Peel Manufacturing on the Isle of Man, the P-50 was resurrected in 2011 as a collector's car. Ads tout that it is "the one car you can drive all the way to work," meaning it's small enough to drive right into your office.

• The smallest working toy railroad is 35,200 times smaller than a real train. The entire set—including the locomotive, five cars, and a track that goes through a mountain—is smaller than a thumbnail. Miniaturist David Smith of Tom's River, New Jersey, built it to go inside a model train shop in the village of his model train set. It's best viewed with a jeweler's eyepiece.

Thimphu, Bhutan, is the only capital city in the world with no traffic lights.

THE DYMAXION

The name sounds like classic sci-fi, but there was nothing fictional about this space-age vehicle. It may have been straight from the future...but it was totally for real.

DIRIGIBLE ON WHEELS

Philosopher, inventor, and futurist Buckminster Fuller (1895–1983), perhaps best remembered today for his geodesic dome, created other designs that were just as remarkable and functional—including a car that he called the Dymaxion. With a name derived by combining two words, *dynamic* and *maximum*, the car epitomized the Fuller philosophy of living: "Do more with less."

Fuller was fanatical about designing affordable, energy-efficient products that could be mass produced. His first Dymaxion design was actually a house that could be disassembled and reassembled like a fold-up tent. From there he moved on to the Dymaxion car. Built of balsa wood and aluminum, the Dymaxion was like nothing the world had seen before: a 20-foot-long three-wheeler with front-wheel drive, rear-wheel steering, and a 90-horsepower Ford engine. The car steered like a boat, had a periscope for rear vision, and was roomy enough to carry 11 people. Weighing only half a ton, it averaged 35 miles per gallon and had a top speed of 120 mph. Not only was it fast and light, it was agile: The Dymaxion (which one reporter said looked like a dirigible on three wheels) could make a U-turn in its own length and parallel park in a space only a few feet longer.

TOO GOOD TO BE TRUE?

A prototype Dymaxion made its debut at the 1933 Chicago World's Fair to much hoopla, and became a sensation. It looked like a Buck Rogers rocket on wheels, and the ease with which it passed other cars on the highway made it seem too good to be true. Perhaps it was.

Later that year, during an impromptu race with another car, the Dymaxion flipped over, killing the driver and wounding two passengers. Detroit carmakers quickly claimed that the car's design

The first farm tractors, introduced in 1868, were steam-powered.

was inherently unsafe—specifically, that its unique rear-wheel steering system was unstable. Fuller contended that the accident was caused by the other drivers coming too close, but the big automakers remained skeptical. In the face of relentless criticism from a media fed information from Detroit, Fuller hurriedly built two safer and improved prototypes, but the damage was done. His backers got cold feet and pulled their financial support.

A CONSPIRACY?

Although Fuller had already received many orders for Dymaxions—including from celebrity buyers such as famed aviator Amelia Earhart—without funding, he couldn't start production and was forced to close his factory. The final blow came when Chrysler, which had already agreed to mass produce the Dymaxion, reneged on its contract. In his 1996 book, *The Age of Heretics*, Art Kleiner claimed that the real reason Chrysler refused to produce the car was because bankers representing GM and Ford, fearing that the success of the Dymaxion would ravage the auto industry by giving consumers a real alternative, threatened to withdraw their loans to Chrysler. In other words, the auto industry needed to stop the Dymaxion before it stopped them.

BUCKY LIVES ON

The controversy continues to this day. Fuller himself never commented on the automaker conspiracy theory, and moved on to other projects such as the geodesic dome, for which he received a patent in 1954. Even though the Dymaxion quickly became a footnote in automobile history, it has had a major influence on car designers over the decades. Germany's "people mover" of the late 1940s, the Volkswagen Transporter van, was clearly inspired by the Dymaxion's body design. But it was the 1956 Fiat 600 Multipla that most closely resembled the Fuller original, with its rear-mounted engine, driver's seat over the axle, and capability of transporting six people at a time. Many of the three-wheeled, ultra-light hybrids of today, like the Aptera, give a strong nod to Fuller's innovative design and clean, green vision of the future. Of the three prototypes originally built by Fuller, only one survives. It's part of the car collection of casino magnate Bill Harrah in Reno, California.

GREAT TRAIN RIDES

There's no better way to watch the wonders of the world roll by than from the window of a train.

ALL ABOARD!

• **Flying Scotsman (1862–).** Has carried passengers on an express route between London and Edinburgh for the last 150 years.

• **Toy Train (1881–).** The only railway listed as a UNESCO World Heritage Site. The first and best example of a hill railway, this steam train rolls through the foothills of the Himalayas from Siliguri to Darjeeling, India.

• **Flåm Railway (1940–).** Travels a short but spectacular route: a 20-km descent from 3,000 feet down a cliff-hugging narrow gauge railroad into the longest, most spectacular fjord of Norway.

• **Blue Train (1939–).** Claims to be "a window to the soul of South Africa" as it carries passengers in five-star luxury over the 1,000 miles between Pretoria and Cape Town.

• **Trans-Siberian Railway (1916–).** Arguably the greatest train ride of all: 6,000 miles across the steppes of Russia, from Vladovostok in Siberia all the way to Moscow, in 19 days.

• **Hiram Bingham Express (2003–).** Visitors to Peru can get from Cuzco along the Urubamba River to the eye-popping magnificence of Machu Picchu in pampered luxury.

• **Ghan (1878–).** Formerly the Afghan Express, it travels 1,852 miles from Adelaide, Australia, through the rugged outback and Alice Springs all the way to Darwin on the north coast.

• **Glacier Express (1930–).** May be the slowest "express" on Earth, taking a poky 8 hours to roll 180 miles over 291 bridges and through 91 tunnels between the Swiss resort towns of Zermatt and St. Moritz.

• **Qingzang Railway (2006–).** Perhaps the only railroad where oxygen masks are standard passenger equipment. Leaving Golmud, China, it travels 1,142 km across the roof of the world (average trip elevation is 13,000 feet) to Lhasa, the capital of Tibet.

A car that shifts manually gets 2 more miles per gallon of gas than an automatic does.

FLYING 101

Uncle John asked some pilot pals to explain how they do the things they do in the wild blue yonder. Here are the basic maneuvers pilots must master when they learn how to fly.

AILERON ROLL

Without using the rudder or elevator, a pilot must perform a 360-degree roll using only the ailerons, which are panels on the trailing edges of the wings that move up and down. To avoid losing too much altitude, a pilot begins this move with the plane's nose 20 to 30 degrees above the horizon, then smoothly holds the stick to one side until the plane levels out again. An aileron roll isn't within the design specs of a commercial jet, but there is a legend that a test pilot in a 707 once completed one. A successful aileron roll causes an airplane to do a 360-degree turn directly along its longitudinal axis, an imaginary line going from the tail straight out through the cockpit. The maneuver requires hand-eye coordination along with an awareness of how the aircraft will behave, two good things for a pilot to know.

COORDINATED TURN

When flying a plane with a propeller, a pilot turns the craft by simultaneously working the rudder and the ailerons, making sure to add thrust to maintain speed and altitude. In a modern fighter jet, a pilot sets a bank angle, then pulls back on the stick to keep from losing altitude. The pull is what drags the nose around the horizon. The plane now faces in a different direction.

SIDESLIP

A pilot pushes the rudder steadily in one direction, banks slightly in the opposite direction to keep from turning, raises the nose, and adds a little extra power to make up for the drag. Now the plane's in a sideslip, going sideways and forward at the same time. Sideslipping is a great way to lose altitude quickly without changing course. A bomber, or a plane full of skydivers, can sideslip to get its payload on target. Often a pilot will sideslip to land in a crosswind.

LOOP

To perform a loop, a pilot pulls back the stick, causing the plane to climb and then invert (go upside down). At the top of the loop the pilot aims the plane back toward the ground, then finishes the circle by returning to the original heading. A proper loop requires the pilot to maintain "wings-level" throughout the entire maneuver. Students learn it to aid and enhance their skills. Students, pros, military pilots, and recreational pilots all do it for another reason too—it's fun!

STALL

Stalling an aircraft is different than stalling an engine, but both can happen in the air. An engine stall is usually the result of a mechanical malfunction. But stalling the aircraft is an aerodynamic malfunction that happens when a plane reaches what's called a "critical angle of attack": The nose is too high or low relative to the flight path, so the aircraft's wings are no longer generating sufficient lift. Outside of training, stalls are rarely done on purpose. Almost any aerodynamic stall can be recovered from if there's enough altitude. The trick is to get air flowing back over the wings, and having enough altitude is important. In a worst-case scenario, the pilot can use gravity to regain control and maneuverability (in other words, aim the plane at the ground and pull). Mechanical stalls are another issue—although rare in modern engines, the best bet is to have another engine.

SPIN

Yaw is an aviation term describing the left-right orientation of an airplane relative to the direction it is moving. A spin is essentially a stall with a yawing motion, and something to be avoided unless you're doing it to practice how to get out of one. Once the aircraft starts spinning, it stops flying. Spins develop when the wings stall (that is, they stop providing usable lift) and the plane begins to yaw, both of which can develop from things like mechanical failure or turbulence. A pilot can easily enter a spin from a sideslip—on purpose or not—by adding a slight rolling motion. The best way to learn to get out of a spin is to get into one, and then get out of it by aiming the nose down and adding throttle, increasing airflow over the wings, and then using the opposing rudder to straighten out.

...created by Australians Gary and Shirley Duval.

LOW-LEVEL FLYING

Flying close to the ground is one of the most exhilarating things pilots can do. In a fighter jet it gets even better. A USAF F-16, for example, has a standard training floor of 500 feet, and some pilots are cleared to fly lower during advanced training. They fly at 500 knots (over 570 mph). A good pilot can maintain this altitude in any terrain, including a mountainous battlefield, crossing ridges, and popping in and out of valleys. A civilian pilot will fly at low levels to help with visual navigation, for search-and-rescue operations, for sightseeing, or for aerial photography. A combat pilot will "hit the deck" to avoid radar, visual identification by the enemy, or surface-to-air missiles.

DOWNWIND-BASE-FINAL

An aircraft typically lands by descending in a defined pattern that forms three sides of a square. The first leg runs parallel to the runway and ideally in the same direction as the wind. (If an airport has multiple runways, the runway in use always favors the wind.) A 90-degree turn brings the pilot onto the base leg, which ends in another 90-degree turn into the wind and in line with the runway. Landing into the wind gives a pilot more lift at a slower airspeed, which makes for a safer, more controlled approach. A predictable landing pattern also helps air traffic controllers keep planes from running into each other.

For more advanced flight maneuvers, go to page 259.

* * *

GOING UP?

In 1870 Baron Leo Rothschild, a British banker, thoroughbred racehorse breeder, and member of the very prominent Rothschild family, installed one of the first hydraulic elevators in his West London home. The elevator cost more to run from floor to floor in his Gunnersbury Park Mansion than it did for the Baron to travel across London by Hansom cab.

How about you? About 21% of car owners never lock their car doors.

THE HISTORY OF THE VESPA

It's not the fastest or the quietest. It doesn't have the fanciest logo. But Vespa has become synonymous with "scooter" because it's always been one thing—cool.

THE WASP

The first Vespa was built by Piaggio & Co. in 1946. World War II had greatly diminished Italy's manufacturing capabilities, and the country's roads had been devastated by war. Enrico Piaggio gave engineer Corradino D'Ascanio his orders: Develop an affordable machine that can navigate the rubble-strewn back alleys of Italy. Drawing inspiration from the olive-green Cushman scooters U.S. Marines and paratroopers had used to elude the Nazis, D'Ascanio—who despised the look of the current motorcycles—came up with a "motorcycle of a rational complexity of organs and elements combined with a frame with mudguards and a casing covering the whole mechanical part." At least that's what the patent claimed. He nicknamed his creation the MP6 (for moto Piaggio number 6). When Piaggio saw the new scooter, he exclaimed, "*Sembra una vespa!*" ("It looks like a wasp!). The name stuck.

UNDER THE FAIRING

The first production Vespa—the 98—featured a 98cc two-stroke, single-cylinder engine mounted over the rear wheel, with drum brakes and a steel spring front suspension. At full throttle, it maxed out at just over 37 mph. Piaggio built 2,484 Vespas in 1946. The base model sold for 55,000 lira, a sum equal to $41 U.S. ($453 today). A luxury model went for 66,000 lira ($49.25 U.S.). The Vespa proved so popular that by 1947 a black market had formed to meet demand, with some machines commanding double the retail price. In 1949 Piaggio introduced a 125cc model that sped along at 43.5 mph. A shock absorber replaced the rubber pad above the rear wheel. A hydraulic shock was added in 1951 to the Vespa 125's front wheel, and it was on that more comfortable

The Japanese Gen H-4, the world's smallest helicopter, weighs only 155 pounds.

model that Audrey Hepburn and Gregory Peck famously romped around Rome in *Roman Holiday*.

THE HEPBURN FACTOR

Vespas sold well during the first few years of production—over 20,000 enthusiasts turned up for the first Italian Vespa Day in 1951—but sales exploded in 1953 after *Roman Holiday* hit the movie screens. Acclaimed for her cosmopolitan style and impish beauty, Audrey Hepburn almost singlehandedly generated an additional 100,000 Vespa sales that year. It was a breakout role not only for Hepburn but for the utilitarian scooter as well. The movie star permanently infused the little Italian scooter with her now-iconic image of class and style. Vespas have been considered cool and stylish ever since.

Membership in Vespa clubs shot up to 50,000 in the months following *Roman Holiday*'s release. By November 1953, half a million Vespas had been sold. In mid-1956, the millionth scooter rolled off Piaggio's production lines. When Enrico Piaggio died in 1965, there were roughly 3.4 million Vespas in Italy alone—one for every 50 citizens. Worldwide sales reached the 10 million mark in 1988, despite the fact that Vespa had quit the American market three years earlier rather than conform to emissions regulations.

ECO-COOL

By 2000 the now more eco-friendly scooter came back to the U.S., immediately cornering 20% of the market. Vespa's sleek, simple design—largely unchanged since its creation—seems as fresh as ever. Scooter sales continue to grow as a global recession and rising gas prices inspire people to take another look at two-wheeled transportation. It doesn't hurt that stars such as Sting, Antonio Banderas, Milla Jovovich, Matt Damon, and Owen Wilson make Vespa their ride of choice on location or vacation. Currently, Piaggio sells more than 100,000 Vespas per day, ranging from a 50cc model to the 80-mph 300cc GTS Super.

*   *   *

WORLD CAR-AUCTION RECORD

In 2011 the first '57 Ferrari Testa Rossa 250 sold for $16.4 million.

It would take 29 million years for a car traveling 100 mph to reach the nearest star.

FIRSTS

Here's a series of singular events that can only be described as "arresting," "speedy," and "electrifying."

FIRST CAR TO BREAK 100 KPH

Year: 1899

Details: Before the turn of the 20th century, no race car—gas, steam, or electric—had broken the 100-kilometers-per-hour (60-mph) speed barrier. Driver and car designer Camille Jenatzy was determined to be the first. Called the Red Devil because of his flaming red hair and flamboyant personality, Jenatzy built a race car that looked like something out of a Jules Verne novel. *La Jamais Contente* ("The Never Satisfied") resembled a torpedo on small Michelin tires. With two electric motors powering its rear wheels, the racer weighed in at a hefty 3,197 pounds. On April 29, 1899, at the track at Achères, outside Paris, Jenatzy reached the breathtaking speed of 105.88 kph (65.8 mph).

FIRST ELECTRIC TOY TRAIN

Year: 1896

Details: Thomas Davenport gets the credit for inventing the first miniature electric train in 1835, a three wet-plate battery-driven train car that traveled along its own circular track. When the Vermont blacksmith took his new toy to a convention of scientists to prove that real trains could run on electric power, he was laughed off the stage. A frustrated Davenport put his train in a closet and went back to blacksmithing. In 1894, a man named Murray Bacon patented a design for an electric toy train but never built it. It was the Carlisle & Finch company of Cincinnati that manufactured the first commercially successful toy electric train, in 1896. The seven-inch-long brass trolley had four wheels powered by a two-pole, 10-volt electric motor. The Electric Railway, as it was named, came with its own three-foot-diameter circular track and sold for $3.50 (about $90 today). The launch was hugely successful, and Carlisle & Finch went on to create many more highly detailed and colorful train sets right up until World War I, when the company focused its energy on its other business—searchlights.

FIRST POLICE CAR

Year: 1899

Details: One evening in 1899, Officer Louis Mueller Sr. of the Akron, Ohio, police got a call to pick up a drunk on the corner of Main and Exchange Streets. Officer Mueller hopped into his patrol car and sped off to arrest the intoxicated man. What made the event memorable is that Mueller was driving the very first police car in the United States. Built by the Collins Buggy Co. at a cost of $2,400 ($62,050 in today's money) and designed by city engineer Frank Loomis, the battery-powered squad car had a top speed of 18 mph (on level ground) and came equipped with electric lights, gongs, and a stretcher. Looking more like a trolley car with "Police Patrol" stenciled on its sides, this wagon was capable of transporting as many as 8 cops for 30 miles before it had to be recharged. Less than a year after Officer Mueller's historic pickup, race riots broke out in Akron and an angry mob pushed the patrol wagon into the Ohio Canal. It was fished out the next day and went on to "serve and protect" the citizens of Akron for several more years before making way for a newer, shinier gas-guzzling model.

*   *   *

POTTY TRAINER TO THE STARS

Using a toilet in the weightlessness of space is a challenge. It was Scott Weinstein's job to teach NASA astronauts at the Johnson Space Center how to use the specially designed shuttle toilet. The training toilet (really more of a space vac) was equipped with a potty cam to assist astronauts in correctly aligning their posteriors on the seat's 4-inch hole and ensure everything "goes" according to plan. The space shuttle commode looked more like a top-loading washing machine than a conventional toilet. The first astronauts used simple bags, but after Apollo astronauts returned from the moon, they insisted on a proper sit-down toilet—although in space it's more like hovering over a target.

The first Gemini capsule was nicknamed "Molly Brown" by astronaut Gus Grissom...

LUCKY SEVEN

NASCAR is a sport that's rich in traditions.
Here are seven of them.

1. KISSING THE BRICKS

The Indianapolis Speedway is called the Brickyard because it used to be made of bricks. The track was resurfaced with asphalt in 1937, but a yard-long stretch of the original bricks was left intact at the finish line. When Dale Jarrett won the Brickyard 400 in 1996, his exultant crew chief, Todd Parrott, told him, "We have to kiss the bricks!" Thus began the tradition of the winning team turning their hats around, kneeling down on the baked clay at Indianapolis, and placing a lip-lock on those hallowed bricks. The practice spread to other NASCAR races and eventually to the Indy 500 itself.

2. POLISH VICTORY LAP

On November 6, 1988, Alan Kulwicki won his first Winston Cup event at the Checker 500 in Phoenix. To celebrate, he took a victory lap going clockwise—the wrong way. Later, a Ford engineer asked him jokingly if that was his "Polish victory lap," and the name stuck. After Kulwicki was killed in a plane crash in 1993 on his way to a Cup event in Tennessee, winning drivers that season did a reverse victory lap in his memory. The Polish victory lap has since become the way NASCAR drivers honor people who have recently died. After winning the Cal Ripken Jr. 400 in 2001, Dale Earnhardt Jr. drove a Polish victory lap as a salute to the victims of 9/11.

3. HONORING THE MILITARY

At every Winston Cup event, U.S. men and women in uniform have a standing invitation to go behind the scenes and tour the garage and pit areas.

4. ALL-STAR RACE PIT CREW INTROS

At most Cup races, the drivers get all the glory. They're intro-

...in joking reference to the Mercury capsule, which sank and nearly drowned him.

duced to the crowd and paraded around the speedway in convertibles. The NASCAR Sprint All-Star Race is the one race where the "over-the-wall" guys—the pit crews—get to bask in the attention with their own intros. In 2005 Trent Cherry, a member of the #12 Penske Racing Dodge crew, dove into an infield crowd before a race and did a mosh pit dance. The crowd loved it. Crews have tried to top each other's antics ever since.

5. FORD CHAMPIONSHIP WEEKEND

Since 2001 the festivities in November during NASCAR's final race weekend at Homestead-Miami Speedway have become a must-see, must-do for diehard fans. The three-day blow-out includes crowning the winners of the Camping World Truck Series, Nationwide Series, and Sprint Cup Series, capped by a parade of race-team "haulers" (trailers used to transport race cars) bearing the Top 12 Sprint Cup and Top 10 Nationwide cars, as well as Homestead-Miami's Ford pace cars. There's plenty of red carpet strutting, champagne cork popping, and war whooping as drivers and fans wrap up another season of racing.

6. NIGHT RACE AT BRISTOL

Just try to get into the Irwin Tools Night Race at Bristol Motor Speedway in Tennessee! It's considered NASCAR's most sought-after ticket. Since 1978, the race has been held on a Saturday late in August (at night, to beat the heat), and fans come from far and wide to pack the 160,000 seats at the "Coliseum of NASCAR."

7. TAILGATING

Lots of sports fans throw tailgate parties, but NASCAR followers take it to the extreme, sometimes setting up their RVs and campers three to four days before an event. And NASCAR tailgating is souvenir heaven—there are logo grill covers, aprons, cooking mitts, lawn chairs, games, and even cookbooks, including one from top chef Mario Batali: *Mario Tailgates NASCAR Style*.

* * *

CAR-GO

The largest car-carrier ship, MV A *Ladybug*, can carry 7,600 cars.

The average American family spends about 50% of their yearly income for a new car.

THE BIGGEST...

Archimedes said, "Give me a lever and a place to stand and I will move the world." Or you could use one of these monster earth movers.

DIGGER: Bagger 293

This bucket-wheel excavator is the biggest industrial machine ever made. Standing 310 feet tall and stretching 722 feet long, it can dig 8½ million cubic feet of earth a day. That's like digging a hole the size of a football field to a depth of 25 feet. In one day. This mechanical colossus weighs just over 14,000 tons. Its bucket-wheel is 70 feet in diameter, and each of its 20 buckets can dig up 530 cubic feet of dirt. Built in eastern Germany, the Bagger 293 is used to strip-mine surface deposits of coal in Hambach. It has tracks that make it technically mobile, but they are powered by an external generator and can move the Bagger at only half a kilometer per hour.

MOVABLE MACHINE: Overburden Conveyor Bridge F60

It was designed to remove the layer of dirt and rock lying above a seam of coal in a strip mine. Because it's removed first and not contaminated by the mining process, the layer can be saved and then replaced over the spent coal seam to reclaim the site. At 1,647 feet in length, the F60 is longer than the Eiffel Tower is high; it's also 787 feet wide and stands 262 feet off the ground. One end has a cutting edge set at 60 meters above ground (hence the name F60), and the conveyor's nine moving belts carry dirt along the bridge to the opposite end, where it's dumped into waiting trucks. The whole structure rests on two *bogies* (wheeled chassis) that ride parallel stretches of narrow-gauge rail, allowing the entire bridge to be moved very slowly along a seam of coal.

SHOVEL: Bucyrus-Erie 1850B

"Big Brutus" is 160 feet high and weighs 11 million pounds, and during its heyday in the 1960s and '70s, the bucket hanging from its 150-foot boom could scoop up 150 tons at a time—enough to fill three railroad cars. However, it is only the second-largest

NASCAR's global TV audience per race: About 6 million. Formula One's: 150 million.

shovel ever built. The biggest is "The Captain," which also rates as the heaviest vehicle in history, at 28 million pounds. Built by the Marion Power Shovel Company in 1965, "The Captain" had a bucket capacity of 300 tons, twice that of "Big Brutus." But it was scrapped in 1992, leaving the title of Biggest Shovel in the World to Big Brutus, currently on display in West Mineral, Kansas.

BULLDOZER: Komatsu D575A-3SD Super Dozer

This huge bulldozer spends most of its time moving huge amounts of rock and dirt in pit mines. It is 16 feet tall, 41 feet long, and 24 feet wide, with an 1,150-hp engine. Its massive blade can push and shove 480,000 pounds of aggregate material. It also has a ripper arm, a spike that it can slam into rock or concrete, or rip across the ground. Too big to take on the road, the Superdozer is taken apart and transported in several trucks to its work site, then reassembled. Says the president of the company that leases the Superdozer to mining firms, "These things are made for knocking over mountains. It could push downtown Dallas into rubble in two weeks."

DUMP TRUCK: Three-way tie

Three trucks currently share the title—the Liebherr T 282B, the Bucyrus MT6300AC, and the Caterpillar 797F. Each is powered by a V-20 diesel-electric engine that can generate up to 4,000 hp, and each can haul up to 400 tons. All are around 25 feet high and 50 feet long, and have a curb weight of 1.3 million pounds.

TRACTOR: Big Bud 747

This tractor was custom built in 1977 by Ron Harmon of the Northern Manufacturing Company in Havre, Montana. It's 27 feet long, 20 feet wide, and 14 feet tall. The 16-cylinder Detroit Diesel engine generates 760 hp, and its 8-foot-diameter tires are special ordered from United Tire of Canada. When its 1,000-gallon fuel tank is full, this mammoth tractor weighs in at 100,000 pounds. Big Bud can cultivate an acre a minute at 8 mph and has been in continuous use since it went to work over three decades ago.

Saab is an acronym for "Swedish Aircraft, AB." (AB is for *aktiebolag*, or "stock company.")

TINY SPEEDSTERS

Today kids (and adults) get their vehicular kicks from video games, but remote-control cars used to be the toys of choice.

WOUND UP

The roots of remote-control toys lie in the windup clockwork cars popular during the early part of the 20th century. Some of them were fairly sophisticated, complete with intricate detailing and working horns. Meanwhile, less flashy "rubber cars" (powered by rubber bands) could reach over 40 mph in three seconds flat. The Model Car Racing Association was formed in Britain in 1936, and collectors young and old raced their windups on miniature tracks.

Gas-powered model cars began appearing in American hobby shops around the same time. Produced by Dooling Brothers and Ohlsson and Rice, they caught on with teens and miniature-racing aficionados, who converted them into "tether cars." Connected to a central post with cables, these vehicles blazed along circular tracks. Tether cars are still raced by hobbyists today at speeds of over 200 mph.

THE ADVENT OF REMOTE CONTROL

Although radio pioneer Nikola Tesla experimented with remote control vehicles in the 1890s, developing a toy boat that he operated from a distance, the idea of remotely controlling vehicles of any size didn't catch on commercially until decades later.

Fully functional remote-control model toys came on the market in 1966, when Italian manufacturer Elettronica Giocattoli released its 1:12 scale Ferrari 250-LM. The car was such a hit in toy and model shops in the United Kingdom that soon British company Mardave followed with its own gas- and nitro-powered models.

In the United States, K&B Veco McCoy released a kit line of remote-control cars, followed by planes, gliders, and boats. These initial kits required a lot of parental assistance to put together, which limited their appeal. But in 1976, Tamiya, a Japanese toymaker that had been selling model kits since the 1940s, began offering easy-to-use, battery-operated remote-control cars. The

Toy sales for the movie *Cars* (2006): a record-breaking $1 billion.

downside was that the Tamiya cars were limited to running on flat surfaces like parking lots and sidewalks. On uneven terrain they flipped over and were easily damaged. In 1979 Tamiya introduced the "Rough Rider," the first remote-control toy vehicle capable of going "off-road." Inspired by full-scale dune buggies, it sported rubber tires and a die-cast suspension system that had no problems with mud, dirt, sand, rocks—even water.

I LOVE TECHNOLOGY

Further advances in remote-control technology by manufacturers like Losi, Associated Electronics, and Traxxas made these vehicles go faster and farther than their predecessors, and they became increasingly popular during the 1980s. Remote-control cars even began to lead the way in electric motor technology: The hybrid Toyota Prius uses a brushless electric motor pioneered by those used in remote-control toys.

Cars favored by older fans grew more sophisticated while those geared towards kids became more gimmick-driven. In 1984 the toy company Galoob released "The Animal," a series of cars and trucks with retractable plastic claws on their wheels. The "Tamiya Rockbuster TLT-1" was a miniature monster truck designed to drive over the tops of its smaller brethren. Pint-size versions of nearly every automobile from sports cars to Army Jeeps to vans became available.

Starting in 1988, video designers began creating arcade games based on best-selling remote-control cars: "R.C. Pro-Am," released for the Nintendo Entertainment System in 1988, inspired future hit games like "Super Off-Road" and the ever-popular "Mario Kart" series.

REVVED UP

Since 1979 the International Federation of Model Auto Racing has sponsored team and individual world championship events in electric and fuel-powered classes across Europe and the United States. Masami Hirosaka of Japan has won 14 world titles, 6 more than any other racer, all in the electric divisions. Although electric toy cars remain the most popular, more and more hard-core devotees are racing nitro-fueled models with miniature two-stroke engines that roar and smoke like their full-size cousins.

STUNTS GONE WRONG

Despite being made as safe as possible, movie stunts involving cars are inherently dangerous. Here's proof.

THE CANNONBALL RUN (1981)

While driving in one of the stunts while making the film in 1980, driver Heidi von Beltz was struck by a van. She was thrown from her vehicle, and the resulting injuries left her a quadriplegic. An investigation revealed that von Beltz would not have been injured had she been wearing a seatbelt. Inexplicably, the safety belts had been removed from her car just prior to the accident.

TRANSFORMERS 3 (2011)

In 2010 wannabe actress Gabriela Cedillo took the day off from her day job at a Chicago bank to pick up some extra work on the popular action-movie series, which was filming in nearby Hammond, Indiana. Cedillo was sitting in her car (the producers had paid her $25 to use it in the shot) while a truck towed another car at high speed in the opposite direction. The cable snapped and whipped through Cedillo's windshield, slicing her skull open. She was airlifted to Loyola University Hospital and underwent brain surgery, which left her partially paralyzed and blind in one eye. Although Paramount promised to pay her medical bills, Cedillo's family has filed suit against the film company on her behalf.

TAXI 2 (2000)

As intended, stuntman Remy Julienne's Peugeot 406 became airborne as it sped out of a tunnel, but the special foils giving it extra lift caused the car to overshoot the pile of cardboard and fall instead in the middle of the crew, killing cameraman Alain Dutartre. A court ruled that the producer, EuropaCorp, had pressured the crew to cut corners. The company was fined 100,000 euros. But driver Julienne received the brunt of the punishment: along with a stiff fine and jail time (suspended), he was ordered to pay the victim's family 50,000 euros (about $12,000) in damages. Ironically, Julienne had pushed the producers to do trial runs of the stunt, which he later insisted would have prevented the accident. They refused.

MILLION DOLLAR MYSTERY (1987)

Over a career spanning two decades, Dar Robinson had a reputation of being a stuntman's stuntman. He held 21 stunt world records and had done it all without breaking a single bone. In 1986 he was making a high-speed run past the camera on his motorcycle, a simple procedure he'd completed successfully hundreds of times, when he lost control of the bike and flew off a cliff to his death.

THE DARK KNIGHT (2008)

While filming the Batmobile in action, a camera crew following the Caped Crusader's vehicle failed to make a left turn and crashed their 4x4 into a tree in Surrey, England. Cameraman Conway Wickliffe was thrown from the car and died instantly. Special effects coordinator Christopher Corbould, who went on to win an Academy Award for *Inception*, was accused of failing to follow health and safety rules. Prosecutor Pascal Bates told the court, "It was foreseeable and should have been foreseen by Christopher Corbould that, if the camera car crashed in any way, Mr. Wickliffe was likely to sustain an injury that might be severe." Corbould argued that it was Wickliffe's responsibility to fasten his own seatbelt. Corbould was cleared of any wrongdoing.

* * *

FIRST JET ENGINE?

Greek philosopher Archytas was a mathematician, geometer, undefeated general, and pal of Plato. He's said to have built the world's first heavier-than-air self-propelled flying craft, a bird-shaped model made of wood powered by "hidden and enclosed air." It's possible Archytas was describing a steam-powered glider. If so it would mean he invented the jet engine 2,400 years ago. Archytas' "Dove" purportedly flew over 600 feet, but the heat required to power a steam-engine wouldn't have worked well inside a wooden bird.

Ancient Roman roads had rest stops, with inns and stables for travelers, about every 15 miles.

RACE FOR YOUR LIFE

Notable for its anything-goes spirit, rally racing is the most enduring and popular form of road racing in the world. Here's a look at some of the greatest and craziest rallies, past and present.

TARGA FLORIO

First run in 1906, this Sicilian rally was one of the first great road races. A brutal combination of hill climb and endurance rally along Sicily's treacherous mountain roads, it quickly earned a reputation as the most difficult race in Europe. Drivers faced hairpin turns and abrupt changes in both climate and altitude, making the experience not only exhausting but also nauseating. To make things even more challenging, spectators and livestock gathered on the edges and even in the middle of the island's tiny roads to catch all the action.

The first race consisted of three laps around the island, totalling 277 miles. It took eventual winner Alessandro Cagno nine hours to complete the course, at an average speed of 30 mph. Austrian driver Helmut Marko set the all-time speed record in 1972, driving 128 mph in an Alfa-Romeo 33. (He described the Targa Florio afterwards as "completely insane.") Crashes and other safety issues in the early 1970s led the organizers to scale the race back, and the last formally recognized international race on the course was held in 1973. A fatal accident in 1977 put an end to the official rally, but it still lives on as an annual vintage car showcase in Palermo each May.

MILLE MIGLIA

This open-road endurance race tore along streets and roads across Italy from 1927 to 1957. The first iteration covered a figure-eight course of 930 miles long. Later events followed different routes of varying lengths. A true spectacle, the annual rally drew hundreds of thousands of fans and dozens of top drivers from across Europe, and was instrumental in making household names of the great Italian *scuderie* (racing stables) of Ferrari, Maserati, and Alfa-Romeo. The Mille Miglia provided a forum for legendary Italian aces like Tazio Nuvolari and Alberto Ascari to perfect their racing

Last man to win a Formula 1 race using a manual transmission: Michael Schumacher, in 1995.

skills. In those early days, little thought was given to the safety of drivers or spectators, and numerous accidents resulted. In 1938 Benito Mussolini was forced to call off the race after several spectators died when a driver lost control of his vehicle and ran into them. During World War II, a shorter rally in 1940 was won by two racers from Nazi Germany in a BMW 328. The Mille Miglia did not open again until 1947.

For a decade after the war, fearless racers took advantage of newer, more powerful cars to thrill spectators—who lined the roads by the thousands like fans of the Tour de France—with their sheer recklessness. In 1954 German racer Hans Herrmann, determined to keep up with the leaders, told his navigator to duck before shooting his car under a lowered railroad gate just ahead of a speeding train.

In 1957 a crash involving Ferrari driver Alfonso de Portago brought the annual melée to an abrupt end. In an act of crowd-pleasing bravado, the great Spanish driver stopped his 4.2-liter Ferrari along the route, jumped out to kiss his girlfriend, hopped back in, and hit the gas to catch up with the pack. He was going 150 mph when a tire blew. The Ferrari spun off the road, killing de Portago, his navigator, and 10 spectators (including five children). Public outcry over the lack of safety led to a ban on open-road racing in Italy.

The race lives on today in highly modified form. Beginning in 1977, a new group of organizers staged an annual series of revival rallies featuring classic cars that tour the traditional route of the race in a controlled, non-competive format.

24 HOURS OF LE MANS

Still held annually near the town of Le Mans, France, this rally tests the stamina and skill of driver and vehicle like no other in the world. Each team consists of three drivers, who alternate driving the same car around a set course non-stop until the end of 24 hours. The first rally took place in 1923 with an unusual set of rules. The original plan was to hold three rallies over the course of three years, with the driver with the highest combined finish to be declared the winner. That idea was scrapped in 1928, and the first-place trophy went to the team that covered the most miles within 24 hours.

The Gumball 3000 international road rally uses...

Le Mans turned out to be a great proving ground for auto manufacturers, who invested in new technology and in developing teams of drivers with the skill and discipline to last the race. Breakdowns, both mechanical and human, were frequent. French driver Marius Mestivier became the first casualty, in 1925, but it was the 1955 event that featured the most calamitous accident in motor sport history.

During the third hour of the rally, French driver Pierre Levegh clipped another vehicle, sending his Mercedes-Benz 300 SLR airborne into the crowd. The ensuing explosion killed Levegh and 80 spectators and injured more than 100 others. The fallout was immediate. Mercedes-Benz pulled its sponsorship and refused to race its cars for more than 25 years. Race organizers revised safety regulations, and eventually the 24 Hours of Le Mans regained its position as the world's most prestigious automobile road race.

DAKAR RALLY

Also known as "Paris to Dakar," this off-road race may be the world's most notorious rally. Since its birth in 1978, it has pitted teams from around the world in a thrilling battle that forces them to navigate some of the most treacherous terrain and climates on the planet. Up until 2009, competing teams drove their way from the City of Light all the way to Senegal in North Africa; the route now runs through South America. What happened after 2009? Often the racers' greatest challenges are not mechanical but political. Repeated threats by separatists in Mauritania led to the cancellation of the 2008 race. Although Osama bin Laden's son Omar suggested that the 2008 rally be replaced by a 3,000-mile horse race across North Africa, the race that year was held in South America.

Given the remoteness of the route, bizarre and sometimes tragic incidents have occurred. In 1982 British prime minister Margaret Thatcher's son Mark, his French co-driver and their mechanic disappeared for six days. An Algerian military plane found them, unharmed, wandering the desert 30 miles off-course. In 1988 a wildfire caused by a sparking engine led to a panic on a train in Mali, killing three passengers. Despite improved safety tactics, reduced speeds, and mandatory rest stops in recent years, the Dakar Rally continues as the world's most dangerous and controversial race.

...a different 3,000-mile route around the world every year.

ALL-WEATHER INNOVATIONS

Since the first horseless carriage, automakers have been trying to thwart Mother Nature with wacky gadgets.

RETRACTING WINDSHIELD

The July 1906 edition of Chilton's Automotive Industries magazine described a device that was "almost essential to comfortable touring in all sorts of weather." This miracle of automotive innovation protected passengers from the elements and provided a level of comfort theretofore unknown. It was a glass screen mounted above the dashboard: the "windshield." In those days, there were advantages to getting a windshield that folded down or slid out of the way to provide an unobstructed view of the road, especially in foggy weather. Perhaps no invention since has delivered on its promise to beat the weather like the windshield—but that certainly hasn't stopped automobile inventors from trying to create them.

THE IMPELERATOR

In 1928 car engines were notoriously difficult to start in cold weather. That year the Impelerator Corp. of Chicago announced a revolutionary new device that could start a car in two seconds regardless of the weather by putting "the vital vapor that spells POWER into the heart of your engine." Full-page ads in magazines like *Popular Mechanics* yielded few details about what the Impelerator actually did but were loaded with statements like "not a bit of exaggeration" and "no owner would sell it at any price if he could not secure another." Although installation did not require "any extra attachments of any kind," the ads claimed that the dash-mounted Impelerator would save gas, preserve your battery, prevent engine flooding, and even start a fickle car in a blizzard. The company bragged that it had already sold over 200,000 Impelerators and was looking for agents to sell more. Like the snake oil that came before and the late night infomer-

Adolf Hitler's Mercedes had a false floor to make him look taller.

cial gadgets that would come after, the Impelerator quickly evaporated like, well…vapor.

CUSTOM WILLYS

The April 1947 issue of *Popular Mechanics* featured Cecil Malone of Henderson, Tennessee, and his custom Jeep. Malone had covered his military surplus Willys with the cockpit of an Army training airplane to create the first 360-degree visibility all-weather automobile. Complete with streamlined sloping windshields that gave the driver a clear view in all directions ("Even overhead!"), the fuselage not only kept the driver warm and dry but also helped protect him in the event of an accident.

THE QUICKEE

The Safco Quickee Defroster hit the market in 1963. Although the device was little more than a hair dryer that plugged into a cigarette lighter, manufacturer A. C. Busch & Co. wanted consumers to believe that it was nothing less than magic. Ads claimed that the Quickee's blower, powered by an exclusive "nichrome heating element," would melt ice, snow, and frost in 30 seconds. Since dashboard auto defrosters were already commonplace, few motorists were willing to pay the asking price of $7.95.

TEFLON UMBRELLAS

Exiting a car in the rain has always been a messy proposition, but in 2003 luxury carmaker Rolls-Royce provided buyers of its new Phantom model with a simple, elegant solution: custom-made umbrellas that fit in tubes set in each rear door. Before getting out of the car, the chauffeur was to press a silver button that released a folded umbrella, which the exiting passenger opened by hand. On returning, the passenger simply folded the umbrella and slipped it back into the stow tube. Stray drops of water were drained away in specially built channels. The company assured buyers that their bumbershoots were top-of-the-line, with Teflon-coated fabric and brushed-aluminum handles. Asked if the umbrellas might be sold separately, company spokesperson Bob Austin said no. "But if you buy the umbrellas for $320,000," he added, "we'll throw in a Phantom for free."

The world's busiest train station: Tokyo's Shinjuku Station, serving 3.6 million people daily.

POWERBOAT QUEEN

Offshore powerboat racing is a brutal sport. Smashing against 10-foot swells at 80 mph can break your boat, snap your bones, and bruise your ego. But for a petite grandmother named Betty Cook, it was all in a day's work.

SPORT OF CEOs

Offshore powerboat racing has been a recognized sport for over a century, with its own international governing bodies, big-time sponsors, and legions of loyal fans. Until recently, with the emergence of new entry-level classes, it was, like polo, mostly a vanity sport for the wealthy. The primary reason is the high cost of entry. Purchasing and outfitting a boat, plus fuel and repairs, can cost upwards of $1 million per season. But it's no pleasure cruise. Combining the thrills of NASCAR racing with the hits of professional football, it's not for the faint of heart, and bloodied lips, broken bones, and concussions are par for the course.

Today most powerboat races take place close to shore, where tens of thousands of fans watch canopied dual-engine catamarans blast between and around buoys at speeds exceeding 200 mph. That wasn't always the case. In the 1970s, deep-V-hulled Scarabs, or cigarette boats, would race between checkpoints over hundreds of miles of open ocean. It was a sport where men fought the elements and each other to prove their mettle. Ironically, the person to beat wasn't a man at all. She was a 114-pound grandmother in her 50s named Betty.

MONGOOSE LESSONS

Betty Young met Paul Cook when she was a graduate student at MIT in the 1940s. After marrying and adopting two sons, the couple moved to California. Betty became a housewife and joined the PTA, which, she said, she flunked. "My cupcakes were very bad," she recalled. Paul made a fortune in plastics and decided to take up a new hobby—offshore powerboat racing. Betty became popular on the race circuit by serving drinks and sandwiches to the other racers from aboard the couple's yacht, which they used as a check boat for their team.

One day in 1974, Don Pruitt, her husband's race manager, talked her into taking a spin in one of his boats—a 32-foot Bertram nicknamed *Mongoose*. He handed her the keys and imparted the three most important lessons of powerboat racing:

- One: Never turn on the top of a wave.
- Two: Never let go of the throttles.
- Three: Always run in green water; that is, stay away from the wakes of other boats.

She loved it, and three days later, despite not knowing a thing about engines—"There could be five rabbits in there for all I know," she quipped—Betty entered the *Mongoose* in a race, a 60-mile dash from Long Beach to Newport Beach, and back—and won.

GOOD KAAMA

After that first win, Betty Cook was hooked. She went out and purchased a 38-foot deep-V-hulled Scarab she nicknamed *Kaama*, after a type of African antelope. Her husband's boat, *Kudu*, was named after another African antelope. In contrast to rival boats, which sported aggressive paint jobs and macho names like *Bounty Hunter*, *Intimidator*, and *Thunderball*, *Kaama* featured a stylized black painting of its namesake on the bow, complete with a slender neck, curved horns, and long eyelashes. It also featured a big red heart standing in for the antelope's lips—the only splash of color on the otherwise white boat.

Her competitors laughed when they saw her cute boat and its tiny female pilot, but once the racing began, the laughing stopped. Betty began racking up win after win, including the prestigious 193-mile Bushmills Grand Prix.

These were the days of "run what you brung" races, where teams often brought more than one boat to events in order to have an edge in unpredictable weather. Betty's second boat, the *Kaama II*, was a 38-foot Cougar catamaran with a pair of 482-cubic-inch, 700hp engines. *Kaama II* was capable of speeds of over

...in an F-14 Tomcat. He vomited during the first trip.

100 mph on glassy seas. "Once you get over 80 miles an hour on water, it's all fast," she said. "In fact, it's awesome."

WORLD CHAMPION

By 1977 Betty and her crew—throttleman John Connor and navigator Bill Vogel Jr.—were considered one of the teams to beat in offshore powerboat racing, but not everyone knew it yet. Before the race in Key West, Florida, that would determine the world champion that year, a competing throttleman named Jack Stuteville looked out at the stormy seas and muttered, "It'll get down to who has the most hair on his chest."

Once the race began, it became apparent that conditions were even worse than they looked from shore. Ninety-five miles into the race, Betty smashed into a wave that snapped her head backward and then forward into the wheel. Although she was spitting blood into the face mask of her crash helmet, she powered on toward the finish. Exhausted, she spotted the final check boat and eased into the harbor. Taking off her helmet, she asked, through bloodied lips, "Where is everybody?" Over the roar of the storm, race officials yelled that she was the first one in. They also informed her that she was the new open-class world champion, and the first female champion ever. The runner-up boat didn't come in for another 21 minutes. Only three of the nine starters in the top class even finished the race. As it turned out, the person with the least hair on her chest had won the day.

GEE, DID I DO THAT?

By the time she retired in 1982 at the age of 59, Betty Cook had won 17 races, including another world championship and three U.S. titles. She had also turned her boating skills to business, creating companies that built state-of-the-art engines, hulls, and boats for the sport.

When she was still racing, she was asked the secret of her success. Cook cracked, "I don't have a male ego to feed." Then she admitted that a part of her marveled at her accomplishments. "Whenever we win a race, I still jump up and down in the cockpit," she said. "I say, gee, did I do that?"

Sadly, Cook died of cancer in 1990, at age 67.

F-series trucks account for nearly one eighth of Ford's global sales.

HOT-TUB LIMO

Once a symbol of elegance, limousines today are modified with features ranging from the tacky to the absurd.

LONGEST LIMO

With its 26 wheels, this 100-foot land yacht has ample room for 75 of your closest friends. The "American Dream" is powered by two Cadillac V-8 engines and has a swimming pool, hot tub, tanning deck, putting green, and king-size bed, as well as a helipad on the trunk. This ultimate stretch limo splits in the middle to handle sharp corners. Owner "Hollywood Jay" Ohrberg of Burbank, California, rented it out for exhibitions and film productions but sold it in 2010. Now he intends to set a new record with a 105-foot Lincoln.

MIDNIGHT RIDER

Owned and operated by Irontree Management of California, this gigantic tractor-trailer limousine took seven years to construct. It's been called a "nightclub on wheels" and the "world's largest and most luxurious limo." Designer and engineer Mike Machado sought to combine 21st-century technology with décor representative of 19th-century "robber baron" luxury Pullman railcars. With enough room for 40 people, the Rider has three separate lounges, each with an 1,800-watt Sony surround-sound system, a full bar, and a bathroom with brass fixtures. At 50,560 pounds, it holds the Guinness record for "World's Heaviest Limousine."

ARMORED LIMO

Security-obsessed celebrities like Kim Kardashian and football star Terrell Owens like being chaffeured in the Armor Horse Vault XXL. This stretch armored truck (think Brinks truck crossed with an 18-wheeler) has bulletproof windows and composite ballastic panels for extra protection. Twenty-eight people can ride comfortably in the plush interior, which has two bars, seven televisions, emergency escape hatches, and gun ports. You can rent it for $8,000 per day or drive it home for only $149,900.

Daimler introduced the first electric car windows in 1948.

TALLEST LIMO

Seeking to break a record in another dimension, Gary and Shirley Duval of Colton, California, built the tallest limousine on Earth. More than 4,000 hours went into assembling the 10-foot, 11-inch high vehicle. Powered by two engines, this stretch Cadillac limo is jacked up above eight monster-truck tires ranged four per side, each controlled by its own suspension system.

TANK LIMO

U.K.-based Tanks-a-Lot rents out what is, literally, a tank-limousine. In addition to more everyday features like a refrigerator, television, and DVD player, this one also has a cannon turret on the roof. Built from sections of two armored personnel carriers, the Tank Limo has become a popular feature at weddings, proms, and corporate events around England.

COLOSSUS

Party buses with over-the-top, neon-lit interiors are the rage in Las Vegas, and Colossus stands above them all. Touted as the "Largest Limo in Sin City," it carries 45 passengers on three levels. Within its enormous steel belly are 11 flat-screen TVs, full karaoke and DJ mixing stations with an 8,000-watt Dolby surround-sound stereo system, full disco lighting with laser shows and a fog machine, Playstation 3 and Wii gaming area, and two stripper poles. Colossus took a year to construct and is said to have cost the equivalent of a private jet.

FASTEST LIMO

Tailor-made for the bridegroom who's running late, this 20-foot Ferrari 360 Modena limousine combines the sleekness and performance of the fabled Italian sports car with the size and turning radius of a bus. It was created by Englishmen Dan Cawley and Chris Wright, who stretched the original Ferrari by nine feet to "limo-ize" it. However, the modifications added only 350 pounds of extra weight, so this beast can still go from 0 to 60 mph in six seconds, with a top speed of 166 mph. Gentlemen, start your engines—and get that groom to the church on time!

Bea Muller, an 86-year-old retiree, has lived aboard the *Queen Elizabeth 2* cruise ship since 2000.

FASTEST JET

Imagine being able to fly from Los Angeles to Washington, DC, in a little over an hour. That flight would sure heat up the airwaves.

HOT STUFF

The Lockheed SR-71 Blackbird can fly at three times the speed of sound. This $34-million reconnaissance spy plane was in active service from 1966 to 1999 and remains the fastest jet airplane ever built. (The X-15 is a faster aircraft but is rocket-powered.) When the Blackbird is traveling at Mach 3 (2,280 mph) at an altitude of over 85,000 feet (16 miles), temperatures on the frame can rise to 1,000°F outside and 500°F inside. (Pilots were known to heat their rations simply by pressing them against the windshield.) Even with air-conditioning, the two-man crew was required to wear flight suits similar to those worn by astronauts.

SPECIAL TECHNOLOGY

Designer Clarence "Kelly" Johnson built 90% of the body with heat-resistant titanium alloy and composites. The landing gear is the largest single piece of titanium ever forged in the world. The blue-black paint coating the exterior made the airplane 75°F cooler than an unpainted frame. That black skin turned a cherry-red as the Blackbird approached Mach 3. Johnson kept the red-hot outer shell from disintegrating with an intricate system of pumps and pipelines that circulated fuel near the skin to absorb heat and carry it to cooler parts of the plane, where it was radiated away. He even created a masking technique that used the plane's heat emissions to confuse infrared tracking mechanisms of enemy surface-to-air missiles.

Normal tires would explode under such extreme temperatures, so the Blackbird sported six B.F. Goodrich 32-ply tires impregnated with aluminum powder and filled with nitrogen. If the crew didn't take the time to let the Blackbird cool down before it landed, it was literally too hot to handle for at least an hour.

The first electric railway opened in Germany in 1881. Top speed: 13 mph.

BYE BYE BLACKBIRD

Lockheed built 32 SR-71s that flew for a total of 29 years (1966–90; 1995–99). "Blackbird" was the unofficial nickname given the plane by the Air Force and Lockheed engineers, but flight crews had their own pet name, "Habu," a species of pit viper found on Okinawa. When satellites replaced the functions of the Blackbird, the world's fastest and hottest airplane was retired. Only nine of the billion-dollar SR-71 fleet exist today, most of them on display in air museums like the Smithsonian in Washington, D.C.

* * *

MOTORCYCLE MANIACS

"When my mood gets too hot and I find myself wandering beyond control I pull out my motor-bike and hurl it top-speed through these unfit roads for hour after hour."

—Lawrence of Arabia (T. E. Lawrence, who died in a motorcycle crash in 1935 at age 46)

"Faster, faster, faster, until the thrill of speed overcomes the fear of death."

—Hunter S. Thompson. journalist

"I'd rather be busted into the wind like a meteorite than just become dust. God made us to live, not just exist. I'm ready."

—Evel Kneivel, spoken moments before his motorcycle jump across the Snake River Canyon

"The real cycle you're working on is a cycle called yourself."

—Robert M. Pirsig, author,
Zen and the Art of Motorcycle Maintenance

"I believe many Harley guys spend more time revving their engines than actually driving anywhere; I sometimes wonder why they bother to have wheels on their motorcycles."

—Dave Barry

JUST HUMM ALONG

Here's the story of how an Austrian movie star talked a heavy-machinery company into selling its oversize military vehicles to civilians like you and me.

GENERAL INTEREST

Drive to a shopping mall today and you'll probably find at least one Humvee taking up a parking spot (or two, or three). Once upon a time, however, Humvees could be found only on the battlefield or military bases. The gas-guzzling jeep/tank hybrid was dreamed up by designers at the famed Italian team of Scuderia Lamborghini in the late 1970s. One prototype was built and lent to the U.S. Army, which was trying to find a replacement for its outdated transport vehicles. Dubbed "The Cheetah" by Lamborghini, the new vehicle wasn't very reliable, and the rigorous field tests destroyed the prototype. The Army decided that a company known for sports cars probably wasn't ideal to build a modified tank. So in 1979, Army officials wrote out a wish list of specifications for their ideal vehicle and invited bids for production.

The winner was Indiana-based heavy-vehicle manufacturer AM General. It received a $1.2 billion contract and an order for 55,000 "High Mobility Multipurpose Wheeled Vehicles"—or HMMWV, later simplified to "Humvee." These were to be delivered no later than 1985. After a lengthy series of field tests conducted in Washington State, followed by some factory modifications, the new vehicle made its combat debut in the U.S. invasion of Panama in December 1989.

MILITARY ISSUE

The Humvee was an instant hit with the troops, who liked the vehicle's solid craftsmanship, safety, and ease of use. It quickly became the military's go-to utility vehicle, and when 20,000 Humvees were filmed rolling into occupied Kuwait during Operation Desert Storm in 1991, its reputation as the new jeep of the modern military was secured. However, the initial M998 model was never designed or intended for front-line combat. A series of disastrous losses incurred during fighting in Somalia in 1993 convinced military brass to have AM General build an armored

...filed his first patent, for a multi-stage rocket, in 1914.

Humvee able to withstand small arms fire. The redesigned M1114 model featured a turbocharged engine and improved suspension, in addition to full armor plating and bullet-resistant glass.

THE HUMMINATOR

In the late 1980s, AM General considered marketing the Humvee to domestic consumers but worried that there wouldn't be much of a market for a super-sized SUV. Then Arnold Schwarzenegger got interested. While filming the 1990 comedy *Kindergarten Cop* near Astoria, Oregon, he spotted a convoy of Humvees headed back to base and was completely smitten. He asked a friend in the auto-body business to contact AM General on his behalf to see if he could buy one.

AM General turned Schwarzenegger down—but only because the actor wanted a full military-issue M1114. The camouflage paint, armor, and gun turret made it off-limits for civilian use. Undaunted, the actor flew to the company's South Bend headquarters and, after signing a lengthy liability agreement, came home with a sand-colored Humvee that had been modified to make it safe and legal for California highways. (It would later be featured in Schwarzenegger's 1993 movie *Last Action Hero*.)

Schwarzenegger had his Humvee—but he wanted more. He encouraged AM General to roll out a full-blown civilian model. Buoyed by the positive press the vehicles had received during Desert Storm, the company agreed. The new street version had un-military features like glossy paint, plush upholstery, wood trim, and a stereo system. In October 1992, Schwarzenegger flew to Indiana to buy the first two Hummers that rolled off the assembly line.

OUT OF GAS

In 1999 GM bought the brand. Sales jumped from 20,000 in 2002 to more than 71,000 in 2006. But sales plummeted the next year, when gas prices soared. GM tried to pawn off the brand on foreign manufacturers, but all the deals fell through, forcing the company to halt production altogether in 2010. Then governor of California, Schwarzenegger said through a spokesman, "It's a great vehicle that needs to be reintroduced with a more green engine like electric or bio-diesel." Until then, the giant SUVs will continue to gas-guzzle their way down the road.

On average, 51 cars a year accidentally drive into the canals of Amsterdam.

LIVE AND LET DRIVE

One of the highlights of any Bond film is the introduction of the latest tricked-out car.

ASTON MARTIN DB5

Issued by Q (Desmond Llewelyn), James Bond's first car made its debut in *Goldfinger* (1964), the third film in the series, starring Sean Connery. In addition to its standard 4.0-liter, 282-hp inline-six cylinder engine, the car had a few, shall we say, after-market parts. Gadgets included a passenger ejector seat, a homing beacon tracking device, front-mounted machine guns, bulletproof glass and rear shield, rotating license plates, rear-firing water jets, an oil slick, a smoke screen, wheel-splitters (a hubcap pop-out used to shred the tires of another vehicle), and—to really blow the audience's mind—a telephone. The DB5 reprised its role in the next Bond film, *Thunderball* (1965), and popped up three decades later in the 17th movie, *GoldenEye* (1995).

ASTON MARTIN DBS

For the sixth film, *On Her Majesty's Secret Service* (1969), the franchise introduced a new Bond (George Lazenby) and a new Aston Martin—the DBS. Aside from a hiding place in the glove compartment for a sniper rifle, the car lacked the gimmickry of its predecessor. The absence of bulletproof glass proves unfortunate for the brand-new Mrs. Bond, Tracy di Vicenzo (Diana Rigg).

ASTON MARTIN V8 VANTAGE VOLANTE

In the 15th film, *The Living Daylights* (1987), Bond (Timothy Dalton) drives another customized Aston Martin. Q "winterizes" a V8 Vantage Volante with ice-traction spikes and outrigger skis for snow driving, as well as some other handy options. Bulletproof glass is back, along with side-firing laser, forward-firing missiles, a rocket booster, and a self-destruct mode.

ASTON MARTIN V12 VANQUISH

In *Die Another Day* (2002), the 20th film, Bond (Pierce Brosnan) drives a 460-hp, 5.9-liter V12 Vanquish worth $200,000. At least,

In 1916, 55% of the world's cars were Model T Fords, a record that has never been beaten.

that was the sticker price before the Secret Service add-ons. The ejector seat and ice-traction spikes were standard options, along with some new high-tech devices including an "invisibility" cloaking device, auto-tracking dual shotguns, and heat-seeking missiles.

ASTON MARTIN DBS V12

The latest Aston Martin to feature in the series is an updated carbon-fiber DBS V12. Somehow surviving being ruthlessly driven by Bond (Daniel Craig) in *Casino Royale* (2006) and *Quantum of Solace* (2008), the DBS V12 comes back for the as-yet-unnamed 23rd film due in 2012. The DBS V12 is, in many ways, more practical: It features a high-tech first-aid kit that includes anti-toxins and (fortunately for Bond) a defibrillator.

LOTUS ESPRIT / ESPRIT TURBO

Lotus checked in as Bond's car of choice in a pair of films during the Roger Moore era (1973–85). What the four-cylinder Lotus Esprit lacked in horsepower, it made up for in customization. For the 10th Bond film, *The Spy Who Loved Me* (1977), Q turned the Lotus into a submarine complete with depth charges, surface-to-air missiles, explosive harpoons, and an inkscreen. For dry-land driving, the car came equipped with rear-firing windshield grease and an automatic self-destruct. In the 12th film, *For Your Eyes Only* (1981), the previously destroyed Esprit was replaced by an upgraded Esprit Turbo.

BMW Z3 / BMW 750iL / BMW Z8

BMW wrested away Aston Martin's longtime Bond-car status for a trio of films in the 1990s. Although the BMW Z3 roadster driven by Bond (Pierce Brosnan) in *GoldenEye* (1995) was cool, its features were more suited to a desktop PC—satellite linkup, an image scanner, and a printer. Bond's next BMW, a four-door 750iL he drove in *Tomorrow Never Dies* (1997), was more impressive: It came with an electric shocker to deter car thieves, a cellphone-activated remote control, GPS voice assist, bulletproof glass, a cable-cutter, forward-firing rockets, a tear-gas ejector, anti-tire spikes, and self-inflating tires. BMW's three-movie deal ended in 1999 with *The World Is Not Enough*, where Bond drives an upgraded Z8 featuring a keychain remote control, titanium armor plating, surface-to-air missiles, infrared tracking, and super-sensitive eavesdropping equipment.

The first commercial passenger airplane flew in 1914. The first with a bathroom: 1919.

007 GUIDE TO THE RIDE

These are either the modified cars provided by British Intelligence or Bond's personal vehicles. (* Denotes that no car played a significant role in the film.)

1. *Dr. No* (1962): Chevrolet Bel Air convertible
2. *From Russia with Love* (1963): Bentley Mark IV
3. *Goldfinger* (1964): Aston Martin DB5
4. *Thunderball* (1965): Bentley Mark II Continental, Lincoln Continental convertible, Aston Martin DB5
5. *You Only Live Twice* (1967): *
6. *On Her Majesty's Secret Service* (1969): Aston Martin DBS
7. *Diamonds Are Forever* (1971): Ford Galaxie 500
8. *Live and Let Die* (1973): Chevrolet Impala convertible
9. *The Man with the Golden Gun* (1974): *
10. *The Spy Who Loved Me* (1977): Lotus Esprit S1
11. *Moonraker* (1979): *
12. *For Your Eyes Only* (1981): Lotus Esprit Turbo
13. *Octopussy* (1983): Range Rover Classic convertible, Austin FX4 taxi
14. *A View to a Kill* (1985): Ford LTD
15. *The Living Daylights* (1987): Aston Martin V8 Vantage Volante, Audi 200 Avant, Audi 200 Quattro
16. *Licence to Kill* (1989): Rolls-Royce Silver Shadow, Lincoln Mark VII LSC
17. *GoldenEye* (1995): BMW Z3, Aston Martin DB5
18. *Tomorrow Never Dies* (1997): BMW 750iL, Aston Martin DB5
19. *The World Is Not Enough* (1999): BMW Z8
20. *Die Another Day* (2002): Aston Martin V12 Vanquish, Ford Fairlane
21. *Casino Royale* (2006): Aston Martin DBS V12, Ford Mondeo
22. *Quantum of Solace* (2008): Aston Martin DBS V12, Audi A6, Volvo S40T5
23. *"Bond 23"* (2012): ??

Five real DeLoreans were used in the filming of the *Back to the Future* trilogy.

AROUND THE WORLD IN 25 WAYS

How long it would take to go 25,000 miles (the Earth's circumference at the equator) in a…

RIDE (TOP SPEED	TIME
Voyager I space probe (50,000 mph)	30 minutes
Space shuttle (17,500 mph)	90 minutes
X-51 Scramjet (9,900 mph)	2 hours, 31 minutes
SR-71 Blackbird (2,133 mph)	11 hours, 23 min
Moto-GP Honda (349.288 mph)	2 days, 23 hours
Japanese bullet train (310 mph)	3 days, 8 hours
Bugatti Veyron sports car (270 mph)	3 days, 20 hours
Indy or NASCAR race car (227.472 mph)	4 days, 13 hours
Apache helicopter (192 mph)	5 days, 9 hours
Harley "Fat Boy" chopper (120 mph)	8 days
Hindenburg airship (82 mph)	12 days, 15 hours
Vespa GTV 300 scooter (80 mph)	12 days, 23 hours
Jetpack (60 mph)	17 days, 17 hours
Goodyear blimp (30 mph)	35 days
RMS *Titanic* (27.6 mph)	37 days, 14 hours
Sherman tank (24 mph)	43 days, 5 hours
German IXD U-boat (23.02 mph)	45 days
Segway (12.5 mph)	2 months, 13 days
Motorized wheelchair (11.6 mph)	3 months
New York City taxi* (10.07 mph)	3 months
Front-end loader (in reverse) (9.32 mph)	3 months, 21 days
Combine harvester (7 mph)	5 months
Zamboni ice machine (6.21 mph)	5 months, 2 weeks
Fishing trawler (4 mph)	10 months
Cellular robot (0.0003787 mph)	7,500 years

***ASSUMING YOU CAN HAIL ONE…**

A New York City taxi costs $2.50 to hire, then 40 cents for every one-fifth of a mile. So a trip the distance of the equator would cost $49,805.60. Plus the tip, of course.

RACE TO THE CLOUDS

When Zebulon Pike first saw the peak that would bear his name, he said, "No one will ever climb it." But not only have people climbed it, Pikes Peak is the site of one of the oldest, toughest auto races in the country.

BACKGROUND

At 14,110 feet, Pikes Peak juts majestically out of the southern Colorado plains. First climbed in 1820 by botanist Edwin James, the peak has a rugged beauty that inspired Katharine Lee Bates to write "America the Beautiful" while standing at its summit in 1893. The first road to the top was completed in 1901, prompting two Denver men named C. A. Yont and W. B. Felker to drive (and often push) their two-cylinder Locomobile Steamer car all the way up. It took them nine hours.

In 1915 a local businessman named Spencer Penrose saw the potential for tourist dollars at Pikes Peak if there were an easier access to the top. He spent $15,000 ($320,000 today) to improve the road, and then cast about for ways to make back his investment. To celebrate the first anniversary of the Pikes Peak Highway, on August 10, 1916, Penrose hosted the Hill Climb. Except for interruptions for the world wars, the Pikes Peak Hill Climb has been held every year since, making it the second-oldest race in the United States after the Indy 500.

THE FIRST HILL CLIMB

There were multiple classes to compete in, including motorcycles, with prizes ranging from $500 to $2,000. The overall winner would be awarded a 43-inch trophy gilded in Colorado silver and gold and worth $10,000 (but only on loan for a year). The course was grueling and dangerous: 12½ miles, two lanes, and mostly gravel, it began at 9,390 feet and climbed 4,078 feet through 156 unprotected turns bordering sheer cliffs. The drop-off at the Bottomless Pit turn was 6,000 feet. Weather conditions at those altitudes are fickle and constantly changing—a driver starting off in full sunshine might encounter sleet, high winds, hail, fog, and snow on the way to the finish.

Among the contestants were racing legend Barney Oldfield, fresh from becoming the first person to drive a 100-mph lap at the Indy 500 that May, and Eddie Rickenbacker, soon to become a flying ace in WWI and later owner of the Indy 500 Speedway. However, neither could challenge the eventual winner, the youngest driver in the field, 22-year-old Rea Lentz. He drove the course in 20 minutes, 55.6 seconds. (After collecting the prize money, he vanished and was never heard of in racing circles again.)

The "Race to the Clouds" was an instant success. As with the Indy 500, automakers were drawn to Pikes Peak as a means of testing and perfecting every aspect of their cars—durability, engine performance, handling under rugged conditions, braking—plus getting publicity for them. Open-wheel cars dominated the first 10 years, then a stock car division was added in 1929. From the beginning, the motorcycle division was one of the most hotly contested. In the inaugural race, 19 of the 29 motorcycle entries were Excelsiors, built by Ignaz Schwinn (who later turned his mechanical skills to making bicycles).

THE UNSERS

In 1915 three local boys—Louis, Joe, and Jerry Unser—were the first to drive a motorcycle and sidecar to the top of the peak. By 1926 they were regular competitors in the Hill Climb, with oldest brother Louis winning so many (nine wins starting in 1934, his last in 1953 when he was 57) that he was dubbed the "Old Man of the Mountain."

Nephews Al and Bobby Unser (both later to become racing legends for multiple wins at that other race, the Indy 500) picked up where their uncles left off. Al won back-to-back titles in 1964 and '65, while Bobby topped his uncle Louie with 13 career victories. Bobby's son Robby added eight more titles to the family's haul. Overall, the Unser clan has won 38 titles at Pikes Peak, a phenomenal string of victories.

In recent years, the father-son duo Leonard and Clint Vahsholtz have mounted a challenge to the Unser domination of Pikes Peak. They've amassed a total of 31 titles, with 17 for Leonard in the truck, sprint, and stock car divisions, and 3 motorcycle and 11 consecutive stock car wins for Clint.

First manmade object to reach the moon: the Soviet space probe *Luna Two* (1959).

RALLY TIME

Over the decades, the Hill Climb lost some of its luster and attendance dipped as other racing sports, like NASCAR and Formula 1, became more popular. The addition of the rally division in 1981 brought new competitors to the mountain, many of them from Europe and Asia, where rally racing has been hugely popular for decades. It also brought the first female champion to the peak, in the form of the "Flying Frenchwoman," Michele Mouton. She won her division in 1984, and then smashed the overall course record held by Bobby Unser in her 4-wheel-drive Audi Sport Quattro in 1985.

Bobby Unser quit racing at the peak in the 1970s and retired from racing entirely in 1981. Audi approached him and asked if he'd like another shot at the course record, this time behind the wheel of a specially prepared Quattro. Unser couldn't resist the challenge. In 1986 he regained the course record with a time of 11 minutes, 9.22 seconds—16 seconds faster than Mouton's record. It was the 52-year-old driver's last win. The following year, Walter Rohrl of Germany drove another Quattro to a new record of 10 minutes, 47.85 seconds.

CURRENT RECORDS

Most of the gravel sections have been paved, resulting in faster course records. The current overall record-holder is Nobuhiro "Monster" Tajima, who broke the 10-minute barrier in 2011 in his twin turbo-charged Suzuki SX4 with a time of 9 minutes, 51.278 seconds. Tajima, at age 62, is a racing marvel, having won 11 titles at the Hill Climb, including the last six in a row.

In the motorcycle division, Ducati has dominated in recent years. In 2011 Carlin Dunne set a new course record on his stock Multistrada 1200.

The electric car division has the potential to take over the race. Unlike combustion engines, electric motors don't require sophisticated carburetion to cope with the thin air of high altitudes. In 2003 Jeri Unser, Bobby's daughter, won and set a course record in her Compact Power ER3 electric car, a mark that stood for seven years until Ikuo Hanawa beat it by more than 1 minute, 15 seconds, in 2010 in a Sanyo battery-powered EV Sports Concept Vehicle HER-2.

PUZZLERS

Put on your thinking cap and give these a try. (Answers are on page 457.)

LEAVING ON A JET PLANE

Two jets take off from Andrews Air Force Base at midnight. Both fly at the same altitude and in the same direction. Air Force One is a Boeing 747 that averages 650 mph. Air Force Two is a Boeing 757 that cruises at 530 mph. *How many hours of flying until the planes are 600 miles apart?*

MECHANICS MANIA

The following is a monoalphabetic cipher, i.e., a randomized cipher that substitutes one letter with another. Each coded word is an auto part. Decipher the word to reveal the part. (Hint: The code's the same for every word, so if G=Z, that will be consistent for every other coded word. Decode the short words first.)

MCVVU	IGQIZIJQ	JIU OIUZVW
LANWY AUHG	SRUIQEVW	EWIXV DVUZ
WJZJW	WNEINZJW	DWNYV ANE
BHOOUVW	DNZZVWR	ZWNQLBILLIJQ

ALL ABOARD!

The *Coast Starlight* train, running between Seattle and Los Angeles, has an engine crew consisting of a fireman, brakeman, and engineer whose names are Davis, Johnson, and Smith—but not respectively. Three passengers share the same names as the crew.

1. Johnson lives in Los Angeles.

2. The brakeman lives halfway between Seattle and Los Angeles.

3. Smith earns $20,000 per year.

4. The brakeman's neighbor, one of the passengers, earns three times as much as the brakeman.

5. Davis beats the fireman in billiards.

6. The passenger with the brakeman's name lives in Seattle.

Question: What's the name of the engineer?

FINALLY, A FLYING CAR

The Terrafugia Transition is a car that's an airplane—or is it an airplane that's a car? Either way, the National Highway Safety Adminstration has cleared the innovative hybrid to take to the road (and sky).

LITTLE TRANSFORMER

Shortly after Carl Dietrich got his Ph.D from MIT in 2006, he and four classmates formed a company called Terrafugia (Latin for "escape the Earth"). Their goal? To build a flying car.

Three years later, their work came to fruition. Test pilot Phil Meeter took off from Plattsburgh, New York, in the first flight of the Transition Roadable Aircraft. It was a resounding success. Only 6 feet 9 inches tall and 80" wide (when its wings are folded), the two-seater craft can take off from any long, straight road and has a top airspeed of 115 mph. Upon landing, the pilot presses a button and the wings fold up automatically. Power from the 100-hp Rotax 912ULS engine is transferred to the front wheels, and the Transition can drive off the tarmac onto the highway. When in car mode, it's the size of a large sedan and reaches a top highway speed of 65 mph. The cargo area behind the side-by-side seats is just big enough to a hold a bag of golf clubs. Quips Dietrich, "It's like a little Transformer."

DOWN TO EARTH

The Terrafugia Transition was almost grounded before it took flight. In 2010 aviation authorities demanded changes to the design that would cost Terrafugia $18 million that it didn't have. They were saved by a $65 million contract from the Department of Defense, whose planners want to convert the Transition into a flying Humvee. The military design, expanded to carry four soldiers with gear, would run like a jeep on the ground but be able to lift off like a helicopter to bypass land-mined roads. Flight controls will be automated so non-pilots can fly the vehicle.

Meanwhile, over 100 eager buyers for the civilian Transition have put down $10,000 deposits on the first models to come off the assembly line in 2012. List price: $230,000.

The 1960s VW Beetle was so airtight that it could float.

PRESIDENTIAL RIDES

The first 24 U.S. presidents were carried to official functions in horse-drawn carriages. The next 20 rode in the premier automobile of their day.

President: William McKinley (1897–1901)
Ride: 1900 Stanley Steamer
McKinley was the first president to ever ride in an automobile. Though he refused to go to his inauguration in 1897 in an electric car, he did take a demonstration ride in a Stanley Steamer in July 1901. His second and final ride was to the hospital in an electric ambulance on September 6, 1901, the day he was shot by an assassin.

President: Theodore Roosevelt (1901–09)
Ride: 1901 White Steamcar
McKinley's successor also preferred horses to cars, but he permitted the Secret Service men to follow behind his horse-drawn carriage in a steam car manufactured by the White Motor Company.

President: William Howard Taft (1909–13)
Ride: 1909 Pierce-Arrow Brougham, 1909 Pierce-Arrow Landaulet, Baker electric, Model M steamcar
Called the "motoring president" because he fully embraced the automobile, Taft had two luxury Pierce-Arrows used for state occasions, a little Baker electric car preferred by Mrs. Taft, and a white Model M steamcar that became his favorite—because he could blast a cloud of steam to create a screen against the prying cameras of the press. Taft replaced the White House's presidential stables with a four-car garage and the feed bin with a gas tank.

President: Woodrow Wilson (1913–21)
Ride: 1919 "Series 51" Pierce-Arrow
Although Wilson rode to his inauguration in a traditional horse-drawn carriage, he was an enthusiastic supporter of the automobile and was the first president to join the American Automobile Association. In 1916 he acquired three Pierce-Arrows, including

one with a right-hand drive that he liked so much he bought it for $3,000 upon leaving office.

President: Warren G. Harding (1921–23)
Ride: 1921 Packard Twin-6
Harding is remembered for three things: the Teapot Dome scandal, his mysterious death during his second year in office, and his inaugural two-mile journey up Pennsylvania Avenue in an automobile, the first inaugural car ride by a president.

President: Calvin Coolidge (1923–29)
Ride: 1928 Cadillac Town Car
Coolidge's lavish Caddy was one of the first but not the last to be parked in the driveway at 1600 Pennsylvania Avenue. Coolidge, known for being a cautious man, instructed his driver not to exceed 16 mph in Washington, D.C.

President: Herbert Hoover (1929–33)
Ride: 1932 Cadillac 452-B V16 Imperial Limousine

President: Franklin D. Roosevelt (1933–45)
Ride: 1933 Cadillac, 1936 Packard Twin-6, many others
The presidential equivalent of Jay Leno, FDR collected cars the way some people collect coins. During his 12 years in office, Roosevelt's car collection included a 1936 Ford Phaeton equipped with hand controls so he could drive it himself (his legs had been crippled by polio). In 1938 Roosevelt received two Cadillac convertibles, each 21½ feet long, dubbed the "Queen Elizabeth" and the "Queen Mary," after the ocean liners. They featured back-up generators, two-way radios, and an arsenal of weapons. The following year, Roosevelt took delivery of a Lincoln convertible, which he called "the Sunshine Special" because he liked to ride in it with the top down. It was the first presidential limo to be built to Secret Service specifications and the first to be leased by the government instead of purchased. Its 160-inch wheelbase was capable of carrying 11 passengers. The Special sported extra-wide running boards for Secret Service agents.

The day after the bombing of Pearl Harbor in 1941, the Secret

World's fastest elevators: The ones in Taiwan's Taipei 101 building reach almost 40 mph.

Service was faced with a dilemma: how to safely ferry the president to Capitol Hill so he could make his speech to Congress. The Sunshine Special wasn't bulletproof. An agent thought of an armored car in the parking lot at the Treasury—Al Capone's black-and-green 1928 Cadillac 341A Town Sedan, which had been confiscated by the IRS. It had 3,000 pounds of armor plating and one-inch-thick bulletproof windows. Mechanics worked late into the evening of December 7 to make sure the car was fit to carry the commander in chief the next day. Capone's car was added to the First Fleet of limos, while the Lincoln was sent back to Detroit to be fitted with protective armor, bulletproof glass, a radio transceiver, a siren, red warning lights, and a compartment for submachine guns. After the protective upgrade, the car was six feet longer and weighed 9,300 pounds. The new, improved, and armored Sunshine Special carried Roosevelt to his historic war summits in Yalta, Casablanca, Tehran, and Malta.

President: Harry S. Truman (1945–53)
Ride: 1950 Lincoln Cosmopolitan convertible
Truman found no reason to dump FDR's car during his first term. But after his landslide reelection, he ordered his own custom Lincoln convertible, which included gold plating in the interior.

President: Dwight D. Eisenhower (1953–61)
Ride: 1953 Cadillac Eldorado
Ike rode to his 1953 inauguration in one of the first production Eldorados, painted Alpine White with East Indian red pepper leather seats and the first wraparound windshield. Eisenhower also had one of the Lincoln convertibles fitted with a glass roof and dubbed it the "Bubble Top." In 1956, FDR's '38 "QE" and "QM" convertibles were replaced with the QEII and QMII. They were slightly smaller than their predecessors but fully armored and featured state-of-the art communications. The tires were reinforced with narrow rims in case they were shot out. The "Queens" also served Kennedy and Johnson before the cars' retirement in 1968.

President: John F. Kennedy (1961–63)
Ride: 1961 Lincoln Continental convertible

The first London taxis, in 1897, were nicknamed "Hummingbirds"...

Read about it in "Famous Cars: The Kennedy Collection," on page 276.

President: Lyndon B. Johnson (1963–69)

Ride: 1965 Lincoln Continental Executive limousine, 1968 Lincoln Continental "Stretch" Executive limousine

Johnson shared one of the three Executives with Defense Secretary Robert McNamara; the "Stretch" was for his exclusive use.

President: Richard M. Nixon (1969–74)

Ride: 1969 Lincoln Continental, 1972 Chrysler Imperial LeBarons, 1972 Lincoln Continental

Nixon special-ordered his '69 limo from Lehman-Peterson of Chicago, who added a sunroof so the president could stand and wave to passing crowds. The two armor-plated Chryslers were the last of that brand to be used by the White House. The '72 Lincoln came heavily armored, with bulletproof glass and a powerful 460-ci V8 engine.

President: Gerald R. Ford (1974–77)

Ride: No new vehicles.

President: Jimmy Carter (1977–81)

Ride: No new vehicles.

President: Ronald Reagan (1981–89)

Ride: 1983 Cadillac Fleetwood

Reagan also used Nixon's 1972 Lincoln. He was getting ready to step into it when he was shot by John Hinckley, Jr. on March 30, 1981. In a bizarre irony, the assassin's bullet missed the president but struck the armored plating of the limo—and ricocheted to hit Reagan.

President: George H. W. Bush (1989–93)

Ride: 1989 Lincoln Town Car

The engine in Bush's limo was a 450-ci V8 from a Ford F-250 heavy-duty pickup.

...because of the sound their electric engines made.

President: Bill Clinton (1993–2001)
Ride: 1993 Cadillac "Presidential Series" Fleetwood Brougham
The last presidential car to be displayed in a presidential museum. The Secret Service now uses retired chief executive limos for security testing (which tends to demolish them).

President: George W. Bush (2001–09)
Ride: 2001 Cadillac Deville, 2005 Cadillac Deville Touring Sedan
The Cadillac DTS was the first armored SUV to be added to the White House stable of limos.

President: Barack Obama (2009–)
Ride: 2008 Cadillac DTS
President Obama's Cadillac has state-of-the-art protection, communication, and defense systems and is nicknamed "The Beast." Read about it on page 367.

* * *

YOU KNOW YOU'RE A BIKER WHEN...

...your best friends are named after animals.

...your wife has to ask you to move the bike so she can see the TV better.

...your three-piece suit consists of leather chaps, leather vest and leather jacket.

...you carry a picture of your bike in your wallet.

...your Christmas list has no words, just spare parts numbers.

...at least one of your children or pets has Harley or Davidson in their name.

...you own more black T-shirts than underwear.

...you are only sunburned on the back of your hands.

...you can identify bugs by their taste.

...it's OK to pile boxes and laundry on your car but your bike must have 6 feet of clearance on all sides at all times.

...your idea of a dream vacation is a trip to Sturgis, North Dakota, for the annual motorcycle rally.

John Lambert invented America's first automobile in 1891, but couldn't sell a single one.

ON THE AIR

What do air traffic controllers and pilots say to each other? Here are samples culled from actual flight recordings.

Tower: TWA 2341, for noise abatement, turn right, 45 degrees.

Pilot: Center, we're at 35,000 feet. How much noise can we make up here?

Tower: Sir, have you ever heard the noise a 747 makes when it hits a 727?

Tower: Delta 351, you have traffic at 10 o'clock, 6 miles.

Pilot: Give us another hint. We have digital watches.

(After waiting for a long time in a takeoff line)

Pilot: I'm f***ing bored!

Tower: Last aircraft transmitting, identify yourself immediately!

Pilot: I said I was f***ing bored, not f***ing stupid!

(After a DC-10 came in fast, with a very long roll-out)

Tower: American 751, make a hard right turn at the end of the runway, if you are able. If you are not able, take the Guadalupe exit off Highway 101, make a right at the lights, and return to the airport.

Tower: Eastern 702, cleared for takeoff, contact Departure on frequency 124.7.

Pilot: Tower, Eastern 702 switching to Departure. By the way, after we lifted off we saw some kind of dead animal on the far end of the runway.

Tower: Continental 635, cleared for takeoff behind Eastern 702, contact Departure on frequency 124.7. Did you copy that report from Eastern 702?

Pilot: Continental 635, cleared for takeoff, roger; and yes, we copied Eastern. We've already notified our caterers.

At 26 miles long, Colfax Avenue in Denver, CO, is the longest continuous street in America.

(At Munich International Airport, Germany)

Pilot (in German): Ground, what is our start clearance time?

Tower (in English): If you want an answer you must speak in English.

Pilot (in English): I am a German, flying a German airplane, in Germany. Why must I speak English?

Pilot from another plane (with a British accent): Because you lost the bloody war.

Tower: United 329 heavy, your traffic is a Fokker, one o'clock, three miles, eastbound.

Pilot: Approach, I've always wanted to say this…I've got the little Fokker in sight.

(While taxiing at London Gatwick Airport, US Air 2771, departing for Ft. Lauderdale, made a wrong turn and came nose to nose with a United 727.)

Tower (irate female): US Air 2771, where the hell are you going? I told you to turn right onto Charlie taxiway! You turned right on Delta! Stop right there. I know it's difficult for you to tell the difference between C and D, but get it right! God! Now you've screwed everything up! It'll take forever to sort this out! You stay right there and don't move till I tell you to! You can expect progressive taxi instructions in about half an hour and I want you to go exactly where I tell you, when I tell you, and how I tell you! You got that, US Air 2771?

Pilot, US Air 2771: Yes, ma'am,

Voice from another plane: Wasn't I married to you once?

* * *

"You know the part in the poem 'High Flight' where it talks about putting out your hand to touch the face of God? Well, when we're at speed and altitude in the SR, we have to slow down and descend in order to do that."

—Lt. Col. Gil Bertelson, USAF,
pilot of the SR-71 "Blackbird"

Smallest plane ever: The 1988 Bumble Bee biplane. It was 8'10" long, with a 5'6" wingspan.

EIGHT STRAIGHT LISTS

Eight lists of historical, hysterical, and hierarchical Vroom facts.

1 FACT ABOUT THE HELLS ANGELS PATCH

The "81" on the patch stands for the position of the letters H and A in the alphabet.

2 LONGEST ROADS

1. The Trans-Canada Highway starts on Vancouver Island, British Columbia, runs 4,860 miles across the Continental Divide, 10 provinces, and 5 time zones before reaching its end in St. John's, Newfoundland, making it the second-longest national highway in the world.

2. However, Australia's Highway 1 runs almost the entire way around that southern continent and, at over 14,500 km (9,000 miles) in length, is without question the longest national highway on Earth.

3 LEONARDO DA VINCI INVENTIONS THAT WOULD HAVE WORKED IF HE'D HAD AN ENGINE

1. Helicopter
2. Tank
3. Submarine

4 NICKNAMES FOR POLICE CARS

1. Black-and-white
2. Cherry top
3. Panda car
4. Gumball machine

5 MOVING PLOTS IN 10 WORDS

1. *The Grapes of Wrath* (1940): Dust bowl Okies head for California to not find jobs.

2. *Priscilla, Queen of the Desert* (1994): Drag queens cross the Australian outback in a pink bus and stiletto heels.

3. *A Streetcar Named Desire* (1951): How Stella didn't get her groove back. Neither did Blanche.

4. *D.C. Cab* (1983): When these guys hit the streets, this hits the fan.

5. *Taxi Driver* (1976): Insomniac Vietnam vet drives night shift, gets a Mohawk, and snaps.

6 CELEBS WITH REVVED-UP NAMES

1. Van Morrison

2. Cab Calloway

3. Chevy Chase

4. Freddie Mercury

5. Harrison Ford

6. Joan Jett

7 MASS-TRANSIT TUNES

1. *The Metro* (Berlin, 1983)

2. *Don't Sleep in the Subway* (Petula Clark, 1967)

3. *The Trolley Song* (Judy Garland, 1944)

4. *Taxi* (Harry Chapin, 1972)

5. *Crosstown Traffic* (Jimi Hendrix, 1968)

6. *Downtown Train* (Rod Stewart, 1989)

7. *Bus Stop* (The Hollies, 1966)

8 COLORS FOR 1970-MODEL FORDS

1. Original Cinnamon

2. Bring 'Em Back Olive

3. Anti-Establish Mint

4. Last Stand Custard

5. Hulla Blue

6. Counter-Revolutionary Red

7. Freudian Gilt

8. History Onyx

Grant Morton made the first parachute jump from an airplane,...

DRAG QUEEN

In a motor sport dominated by men, Shirley "Cha Cha" Muldowney not only held her own for over 40 years—she triumphed.

STREET RACING

A high school dropout at 16, Shirley Ann Roque took a job at a drive-in washing dishes and waiting tables in Schenectady, New York. This is where she met 19-year-old Jack Muldowney, who sometimes gave her a ride home after work. Better yet, he took her street racing. "I would sit as close to him as I could on that full front seat," Shirley recalled. "Jack would taunt the guys in the car next to us. He would turn and face them and hang both arms out the window. When the light turned green, he would swap feet, and I would shift and steer while he worked the pedals. It was crazy stuff." The two married in 1956. By the time Shirley was 17, they had a son, John.

JOINING THE BOYS' CLUB

Jack built Shirley her first official dragster—a 348hp 1958 Chevy—which they took to Fonda Raceway in New York. Jack tuned the engine and Shirley drove, and won. Some male fans did not like the idea of a woman driving a dragster, so they harassed her, sometimes throwing cans and beer bottles, but she kept on driving and winning, beating the boys at their game. She got the nickname Cha Cha when the numbers painter at the track wrote "Cha Cha" on the side of her car in white shoe polish. Shirley liked it and continued to paint "Cha Cha" on her soon-to-be-trademark pink Corvettes and dragsters. However, it wasn't until 1965, when she made history by becoming the first woman to be licensed to compete in the Top Gas professional division by the National Hot Rod Association, that this boys' club started to accept her. In 1971 Shirley decided to move up to the faster but more dangerous Funny Car division, and a new chapter in her life began.

BOUNTY HUNTRESS

Jack didn't want to work with the nitro-fueled Funny Cars and Shirley didn't want to stay married to Jack, so they divorced.

Shirley soon partnered with fellow Funny Car driver Conrad "Connie" Kalitta, and the two hit the match race circuit. Billing themselves as "The Bounty Hunter and the Bounty Huntress," they raced against each other in their matching Mustang Funny Cars.

In those days the driver's seat in a Funny Car straddled the engine. If a motor came apart, oil and fuel would spill onto the exhaust pipes and ignite, creating a 200 mph blowtorch in the driver's face. Muldowney endured numerous engine fires, but the worst occurred during the 1973 NHRA U.S. Nationals held at Indy Speedway, when a fire melted her goggles and singed her eyelids. After the accident, friends begged her to quit. Muldowney agreed that it was time for a change, but for her retirement was out of the question. She decided it was time to move up a division, to Top Fuel dragsters. *Their* engines were in the back.

TOP DOG

The NHRA was less than thrilled about Muldowney's decision. Top Fuel drivers were the elite of the boys' club: absolutely no girls allowed. Nonetheless, Muldowney's official licensing runs were verified by three of the best male drivers of the day: Connie Kalitta, "TV" Tommy Ivo, and Don "Big Daddy" Garlits, who later declared Muldowney to be "the greatest female race driver on the planet."

Driving her pink Top Fuel dragster, Muldowney became the first woman to win a Top Fuel title and the first driver of either sex to win three Top Fuel world titles (1977, 1980, 1982). She went on to rack up 18 national event victories in NHRA competition, and several more under International Hot Rod Association and American Hot Rod Association sanctions. Garlits had got it almost right: Shirley "Cha Cha" Muldowney was the best driver, male or female, on the planet, period.

HEART LIKE A WHEEL

On June 29, 1984, while racing in Montreal, Muldowney blew a tire at 250 mph and suffered a devastating accident. Her pelvis was shattered, both ankles and two fingers broken, and the cartilage in both knees torn. It seemed unlikely she'd ever walk again, let alone drive. But 18 months later, buoyed by the support of crew chief (and later, husband) Rahn Tobler, Muldowney was

Rhode Island Judge Darius Baker imposed the first jail sentence for speeding in a car (1904).

back in the driver's seat. It would take five years for her to return to the winner's circle, but at the 1989 NHRA Fall nationals, the first lady of drag racing drove to a dramatic victory over Darrell Gwynn, earning her 18th NHRA trophy.

THE HOLLYWOOD TREATMENT

The film biography *Heart Like a Wheel* (1983, starring Bonnie Bedelia) made Shirley Muldowney a household name to millions who didn't follow drag racing. Some of her old rivals, recalling her take-no-prisoners attitude on the track, suggested the title should have been *Heart Like a Bulldog.* Muldowney laughed the remarks off, saying, "I never would have survived if I had been a candy-ass."

Muldowney retired at 63 in 2003. She was inducted into the International Motorsports Hall of Fame in 2004, and is ranked fifth on the NHRA's list of "50 All-Time Greatest Drivers."

* * *

10-4, GOOD BUDDY

Long-haul truckers still use CB radios to communicate with each other. Here's some classic CB slang.

Driving award—A speeding ticket

Town clown—Local cop

Smoke detector—Radar detector

Weight watcher—Weigh station worker

Fifty dollar lane—The passing lane

Greasy side up—A flipped truck

Draggin' wagon—Tow truck

Gator guts—Pieces of shredded tire on the road

Pay the water bill—Use the restroom

Chew 'n' Choke—Restaurant

Flop box—Motel

Motion lotion—Fuel

Dream weaver—Drowsy driver weaving on the road

Boom wagon—Truck carrying hazardous materials

On your donkey—I'm right behind you

In 25 years, the space shuttle *Discovery* circled Earth 5,628 times.

FULL STEAM AHEAD

In 1899 the Stanley Steamer was seen as the car of the future. Easily the fastest machine on the road, it could hit 70 mph with ease, while getting up to 10 miles per gallon...of water.

BACKGROUND

Francis E. and Freelan O. Stanley were twin geniuses from Kingfield, Maine. They dressed alike in long black coats and stovepipe hats. In 1897 F. E. and F. O. built two cars with steam-powered engines that had only 13 moving parts and needed no clutch or transmission: the Stanley Steamers. They were as powerful as a small locomotive—they could accelerate from 0 to 60 mph in 11 seconds and maintain that speed going up or down hills. Whereas a horse-drawn trip to the top of New Hampshire's Mt. Washington took six hours, the Stanley Steamer made it in 2 hours, 10 minutes.

The twins zipped around the New England countryside in their mirror-image cars, irritating local policemen who couldn't tell one from the other. The Stanleys also piqued the interest of automobile owners anxious to give up the bone-breaking hand crank required to start combustion engines. By 1899, the Stanley brothers had made more than 200 steam cars, making them the largest automobile company in the U.S.

FLYING TEAPOT

The Stanley Steamer (or Flying Teapot, as it was affectionately called) had two main drawbacks: It took 30 minutes for its boiler to build up enough steam to operate, and it was very pricey. At a time when a Model T Ford cost from $500 to $850, the Stanley Steamer cost $3,950 (about $49,000 today).

As for the Stanley brothers, they had no interest in promoting their cars. Already wealthy retirees from the fortune they'd made patenting a gas-illuminating device, inventing the airbrush, and, most lucratively, selling a photographic dry-plate process to Eastman Kodak, they didn't need the money. Quirky and petulant, the brothers refused to advertise and insisted on full payment in cash in advance. If they didn't like a buyer, they simply refused to sell

When two cars collide, the average repair cost for each is about $3,000.

one of their cars to him. At an auto show, irritated by persistent criticism from bystanders that the Steamer's kerosene burner might catch fire (it never did), they exploded firecrackers under the car just to thumb their noses at their detractors. The Stanley twins also refused to upgrade their design and refused to make more than 1,000 cars per year. By 1914 the Ford Motor Company was producing twice as many Model Ts in a day as the Stanley Motor Carriage Company rolled out in 12 months. But the Steamer remained popular.

GOT SPEED?

Drivers enjoyed the smooth power of the Stanley steam engine that came without the noise and backfire of a gas-powered car. Once the Stanley was moving, it ran almost silently with only the occasional hiss of steam. Turn-of-the-century hot-rodders discovered that the Stanley could go just as fast in reverse, and other drivers were often startled to be passed on the road by a Stanley Steamer going backward. During a race in New York, a Stanley driver came around the curve and spotted bystanders on the track. He hit the reverse pedal and the chassis of the Stanley instantly went backward, but the body of the car—and the driver—continued forward and stopped just a few yards from the startled group. In 1906 the brothers built the Stanley Rocket, which hit a record speed of 127.7 mph on the sands of Ormond (Daytona) Beach, Florida, making it the fastest car in the world.

OUT OF STEAM

In 1912 the automotive world changed. General Motors debuted the Cadillac Model 30 with its revolutionary electric self-starter, invented by Charles Kettering. The clumsy, dangerous hand crank soon gave way to a key-operated starter nicknamed the "World Wonder." Now a driver could get in a car at any time and drive away immediately. No waiting a half hour for the boiler to heat up. The Stanley twins saw the writing on the wall and sold their company in 1917. Francis Stanley died a year later at age 69 in a car crash in Maine. Brother Freelan lived until 1940, splitting his time between Maine and the Stanley Hotel, which the brothers had built in Estes Park, Colorado. The last Stanley Steamer was made in 1924. The cars remain on display today at the Smithsonian and in private collections.

The Batmobile in the1989 *Batman & Robin* film was 30 feet long.

CRASH COURSE

Sure, accidents happen. But after taking this quiz, you may never want to get into another car again. *(Answers on page 458.)*

1. What percentage of fatal car accidents involve alcohol?

- **a)** 20 percent
- **b)** 32 percent
- **c)** 66 percent
- **d)** 90 percent

2. Who are better drivers?

- **a)** Men
- **b)** Women

3. Which of the following accidents is most likely to prove fatal?

- **a)** Head-on collision
- **b)** Side-impact collision
- **c)** Landing in water
- **d)** Vehicle rollover

4. Which profession accounts for the most car accidents per capita in the United States?

- **a)** Lawyer
- **b)** Dog groomer
- **c)** Doctor
- **d)** Bartender

5. Statistically, a person is how many times more likely to be killed in a traffic accident than in a commercial airline crash?

- **a)** 9
- **b)** 45
- **c)** 85
- **d)** 190

One Alaska Airlines plane is painted like a fish. Nickname: the "Salmon-Thirty-Salmon."

6. What's the world's most dangerous road? Hint: Its nickname is "The Road of Death."

- **a)** China National Highway 107 from Beijing to Shenzhen
- **b)** A682 between junction 13 of the M65 and Long Preston in the United Kingdom
- **c)** North Yungas Road near La Paz, Bolivia
- **d)** Highway 21 near St. Louis, Missouri

7. According to a recent study, which of the following cars (2007–'09 models) are the least safe to be riding in during an accident?

- **a)** Honda Accord
- **b)** Chevrolet Corvette
- **c)** Kia Rio
- **d)** Mitsubishi Lancer

8. In a recent poll, young drivers thought that driving while doing which of the following activities was the safest?

- **a)** Talking on a cell phone
- **b)** Texting
- **c)** Talking with a passenger
- **d)** Drinking

9. How many states in the U.S. have seatbelt laws?

- **a)** 26
- **b)** 35
- **c)** 48
- **d)** 50

10. Approximately how many car accidents occurred somewhere in the U.S. while you were reading this question?

- **a)** .5
- **b)** 2
- **c)** 3,700
- **d)** 6.5 million

The first known electric locomotive was built in 1837 by Scotsman Robert Davidson.

DER RAKETE-MANN

In 1928 Fritz von Opel sat on 265 pounds of rocket fuel—enough to blow up the neighborhood—and prepared to blast off into the future.

FEARLESS FRITZ

One sunny afternoon in May 1928 at Berlin's Avus racetrack, a crowd of 3,000 gathered to watch a bespectacled man in a shiny black car launch himself down a racetrack at a speed no human or machine had ever attempted before. He wore a flight jacket and goggles, but no helmet. If he crashed while going the speed he hoped to attain, a helmet wouldn't save his life.

The young man, Fritz von Opel, was no stranger to cars. For generations the Opel family, starting with his grandfather, had made machines: sewing machines in 1862, bicycles in 1886, and finally automobiles in 1899. But it was a serendipitous meeting with a scientist visionary named Max Valier that brought von Opel to this world-changing moment.

MAX-IMUM SPEED

In 1927 Valier, an astronomer from Austria's South Tyrol and author of *Advance into Space*, asked von Opel to finance his rocket engine research. Besides being head of marketing for the family business, von Opel was also an amateur pilot and very excited about the potential. Soon the Opel factory in Russelsheim was researching and testing Valier's designs for all forms of jet propulsion. Opel and Valier brought in Friedrich Wilhelm Sander from nearby Bremerhaven, whose solid-fuel rockets were the current state of the art. Sander was already famous for rockets he'd created for maritime rescuers to use to launch ropes to ships in distress.

In the spring of 1928, the company announced the debut of the RAK-1 (short for *Raketanwagen*), the world's first rocket-powered car. At its road test in April, the RAK-1 reached a speed of 62.5 mph in eight seconds, using eight rockets. What would happen, Valier and Sander wondered, if the car were powered by 24 rockets, firing in sequence?

A month later, von Opel assumed the job of test pilot in the RAK-2. The cigar-shaped racer had an additional component—wings. They were designed to act like airfoils and keep the car on the ground. Before blasting off, von Opel announced,

> Today we want to test the maximum speed the human body can take. We are here on the threshold of a new era: Soon man will travel in space. Imagine the day when the first manned rocket with our beautiful country's name on its fuselage will go round the earth faster than even the sun!

STAND CLEAR

Von Opel was sitting on enough explosives to blow up the race-track, fairgrounds, and everyone within range. However, the crowd, which included movie stars Lilian Harvey and Jackie Coogan and boxing idol Max Schmeling, wasn't worried. They cheered as the rockets were lit and, with a deafening explosion, the RAK-2 shot away, leaving the spectators choking in a cloud of white smoke. Each time von Opel stepped on the "gas," two more rockets ignited until he finally reached full strength and full speed: 143.75 mph. Crowds farther down the line reported that when the RAK-2 went by, its front wheels were completely off the ground. "I stopped thinking!" an ecstatic von Opel gushed when he stepped from the car. "I was acting on instinct alone, with uncontrollable forces raging behind me."

With that triumph under their belt, von Opel, Valier, and Sander wanted to try another run, this time on a railroad track, so they wouldn't have to worry about steering. On its first run in June 1928, the RAK-3 reached 158.75 mph, exceeding the RAK-2's record. They increased the charge to the equivalent of 825 pounds of dynamite for the next run. Moments before blastoff, von Opel decided the car should go driverless. The "pilot" sitting in the driver's seat was his unfortunate cat, who was killed when the car exploded three yards from the start.

THE SKY'S THE LIMIT

Von Opel moved on to his dream project: rocket-powered flight. Valier grafted rockets onto a airplane's fuselage, making sure the tail would be out of the way of the burning powder. On September 30, 1929, the rocket plane, with von Opel at the controls, was launched along 50 yards of track. It leaped into the air as if shot from a slingshot and flew for 2½ miles with an average speed of 93.75 mph before running out of fuel. There were no wheels on the plane, just sled runners, and it crashed to the ground in a mess of splinters. "Rocket Fritz," as he was now called in the press, survived the crash, having become the first person to fly a rocket.

* * *

THE GREAT NORDIC BIKER WAR

In 1980 a Danish biker named Jørn Nielson started a Hells Angels chapter in Copenhagen. From the start, his gang clashed with rival motorcycle clubs. But things really got out of hand in 1993 when a gang called the Undertakers allied with the only European chapter of the Angels' traditional stateside nemesis, the Bandidos, setting the stage for a biker war of international proportions.

When the Bandidos launched an anti-tank rocket into the Hells Angels' clubhouse, they retaliated by shooting the president of the Bandidos' Finland chapter. By 1995 the war had moved to Norway with another shootout in Oslo. And when the president of the Bandidos' Swedish chapter was assassinated in July, Bandidos stole some anti-tank weapons from a Swedish Army base and blew up Hells Angels–allied clubs in Helsinki and Helsingborg.

The war was now raging in four countries, with attacks and reprisals bouncing back and forth for the next two years. A car bomb outside a Bandidos clubhouse in Drammen, Norway, killed the only "civilian" in the war, Irene Baeddevold, who was unlucky enough to be driving by at the time. By 1997, 11 bikers were dead and 96 wounded. Eleven were doing time in prison, some for life. Both sides decided that they'd had enough. "Big" Jim Tinndahn, president of the Bandidos, shook hands with Hells Angels president Bent "Blondie" Nielson and called a truce, declaring that neither band would open any new chapters in Scandinavia. The event was carried live on Danish TV.

By the end of the decade, both sides had already violated the treaty.

HAUNTED CARS

Nothing sends a chill up Uncle John's spine faster than a story about things that go bump in the night—except maybe a story about things that go "Vroom!" in the night.

BETTER LATE THAN NEVER

On December 11, 2002, British police received several reports of a bad auto accident near Guildford, Surrey. A car, its headlights blinding oncoming drivers, had abruptly swerved off the A3 motorway and crashed into a ditch. But authorities arriving at the scene had trouble locating the car. Finally they found a wrecked Vauxhall Astra buried deep in the undergrowth. The driver was long dead, his badly decomposed body virtually a skeleton. A police spokesman said, "We believe the car left the road and ended up in the ditch during July. It doesn't appear that any other vehicles were involved. The car was discovered as a result of a report from members of the public who thought they saw a car's headlights veering off the road." The dead driver was identified as 21-year-old Christopher Chandler. Wanted by police for an alleged robbery, Chandler had been reported missing by his brother several months earlier. Investigators found that the car's headlights had been set on high beam at the time of the accident.

GHOST BUS OF LADBROKE GROVE

In London during the mid-1930s, motorists near the junction of St. Mark's Road and Cambridge Gardens in Kensington reported being terrorized by a red double-decker bus that had neither passengers nor a driver. Late at night, long after regular bus service had ended for the day, witnesses said a phantom bus emblazoned with route number 7 would mysteriously appear on a blind corner, forcing drivers to swerve to avoid it. It would then vanish without a trace. As the accident reports piled up, police officers scratched their heads. A typical report read:

> I was turning the corner and saw a bus tearing towards me. The lights of the top and bottom decks and the headlights were full on but I could see no crew or passengers. I yanked my steering

wheel hard over and mounted the pavement, scraping the roadside wall. The bus just vanished.

Police could find no physical evidence of a bus at the scene of the accidents. When witnesses declared the bus to be the phantom cause of a fatal crash in June 1934, the coroner publicly expressed his skepticism, prompting hundreds of people to send him and the local newspapers their own accounts of what was by then known as "the Ghost Bus." When a transport worker claimed to see the bus pull up to a depot and then disappear into thin air, officials decided to take action. They ordered the blind corner at St. Mark's and Cambridge Gardens straightened to provide better visibility for drivers. The move had a dual effect: Accidents were greatly reduced, and the ghost bus of Ladbroke Grove was never seen again.

HIGHWAY TO HELL

U.S. Route 491 cuts through the Four Corners region of the Southwest, heading south from Gallup, New Mexico, going through Colorado, and ending high in the Abajo Mountains of Utah. The highway has a long and storied history of ghost sightings, haunted vehicles, and more fatalities than normal for a relatively straight stretch of roadway. Over the years, drivers have reported seeing ghosts appear in their backseats, phantom animals such as crows and coyotes materializing out of nowhere in the middle of the road, and a female hitchhiker dressed in white who vanishes as soon as someone stops to pick her up.

And then there's the phantom truck. Several drivers along 491 have claimed that a large semi with flames shooting from its smokestack has suddenly appeared and tried to run them off the road. The truck reportedly accelerates until it is right on a car's bumper, sometimes at speeds upwards of 130 mph, forcing drivers to dive off onto the narrow shoulder and hope for the best. Motorists say the ghost truck disappears in a ball of flame as soon as it passes, prompting some to refer to the road as the "Highway to Hell." Or maybe the nickname is the result of the highway's former number. In 2003 "Route 491" replaced the old name: Route 666.

Jay Leno's 17,000-square-foot garage includes a gourmet kitchen.

JET ENGINES

So you want to build a supersonic jet? You'll want to understand exactly how a jet engine works. Uncle John breaks it down for you.

SUCK, SQUEEZE, BANG, BLOW

A jet engine is a gas-powered internal-combustion turbine engine that sends a constant stream of airflow through four stages: induction, compression, ignition, and exhaust. Think of it as: *suck*, *squeeze*, *bang*, and *blow*. At the front of the engine, spinning intake blades suck air into the engine and send it through compressor blades, which pressurize (squeeze) it up to 600 psi. In the combustion chamber this high-pressure air, dense with oxygen, gets sprayed with jet fuel and ignited (bang!). The blast of superheated air out the exhaust nozzle (blow), pushing the plane forward. Gas turbines are efficient: The force of the exhaust also spins turbine blades attached to a crankshaft, which spins the intake fan at the front, which sucks in more air, continuing the cycle.

To work, the combustion process must be continuous—an engine can stall if any of the four stages stops working. A rapid reduction in throttle, for instance, can cause a compressor stall, in which air builds up in the compressor and can't flow into the combustion chamber. This pressure has to go somewhere, so it shoots out the front of the engine with a big bang. But with enough altitude, this loss of power is easy to recover, and since modern jet engines have digital controls that automatically adjust fuel flow, nozzle position, rpm, and so on, stalls are rare.

JET TERMINOLOGY

• **Afterburner:** Some of the air flows around the combustor to keep the engine cool. A pilot who needs to go extremely fast can mix this extra air with the exhaust in a second combustion chamber, called an afterburner. While some propeller planes can reach about Mach 0.8, or 600 mph, there are jets that can hit Mach 3, or 2,500 mph.

A jet engine combustion chamber can reach 2,700°F.

• **Turboprop:** This is a jet engine attached to a propeller. Air is sucked in, compressed, and ignited, but instead of shooting out the back of the engine, the force turns a crankshaft, which spins the propeller.

• **Turboshaft:** The same thing, except the jet force spins a helicopter rotor instead of a propeller.

• **Turbofans:** Sound-dampening engines in which most of the air in the engine bypasses the combustor and acts as a muffler for the exhaust.

• **Scramjet:** A *s*upersonic *c*ombustion *ram*jet, it is the simplest of all jet engines: it has no spinning parts. Since there are no intake fans, a scramjet relies on forward motion to suck air into the funnel-shaped compressor. Scramjets are very efficient above Mach 5, but need help to get there. They are used mostly in guided-missile systems and space vehicles.

THE FIRST JET ENGINE?

A Greek philosopher, mathematician, general, and pal of Plato named Archytas is said to have built the world's first heavier-than-air self-propelled flying craft around 400 B.C. "The Dove" was a bird-shaped model made of wood powered by "hidden and enclosed air." Archytas might have been describing a steam-powered glider, which would mean he invented the jet engine 2,300 years before the Wright brothers made their first flight. The Dove reportedly flew 600 feet.

*   *   *

COMIC CAR COLLECTOR

Jerry Seinfeld is a Porsche guy, so much so that he spent two years and $1.4 million building a 20-car garage/gallery in Manhattan to house his collection of 47 vintage Porsches. Favorites include a 1959 straight-16 GT speedster, a Porsche 911S, and a 1955 Spyder 550—the same pearl-grey version that actor James Dean was driving when he crashed and died in 1957. The crown jewel? A $700,000 Porsche 959, one of only 200 ever built. Unfortunately, Seinfeld can only sit in it because Porsche never allowed it to be crash-tested to pass U.S. safety regulations. When Seinfeld married in 1999, he gave his wife a 1958 1600 Speedster.

HISTORY OF AIRSHIPS, PART II

The first two decades of the 20th century saw the golden age of dirigibles. (Part I starts on page 68.)

HARD BODIES

The first rigid dirigible was the invention of a Croatian named David Schwarz (1852–97). He built it completely out of aluminum, including the envelope. The first attempt to fly his design in 1893 was a disaster: fatal engineering flaws caused the envelope to implode when it was filled with hydrogen gas. Schwarz died 10 months before his redesigned ship lifted off at Tempelhof, outside Berlin. It rose quickly to 1,600 feet, but the ability to steer the craft was lost when power to both propellers failed during the ascent. The mechanic piloting the ship opened the gas release valve, returned the craft to the ground, and got out safely. Moments later the ship turned over and collapsed on itself. That marked the end of experiments with all-metal dirigibles.

"Z" FOR ZEPPELIN

The name most often identified with dirigibles belongs to the German Count Ferdinand von Zeppelin (1838–1917), so much so that, like Xerox for copies or Kleenex for tissues, the name is often used to refer to any airship. As early as 1874, Zeppelin made design entries in his diary for a rigid-framed, steerable airship containing individual gas cells. Twenty-six years later, he flew his first rigid ship, the Luftschiff *Zeppelin 1*, a flight lasting 18 minutes over about 3½ miles of Lake Constance in Germany.

The airship was built right on the lake in a floating shed. Its envelope was massive but pencil-thin (a shape that proved to have inherent flaws): 420 feet long and only 38½ feet in diameter, holding 399,000 cubic feet of hydrogen in 17 rubberized-cotton gas cells. Two metal gondolas hung fore and aft, each with a four-cylinder, water-cooled Daimler gasoline engine producing about 14 hp. Each motor powered two outrigger propellers bracketed to

...was an Australian production car, the Ford XB Falcon Coupe.

either side of the gondolas. Nonetheless, the LZ-1 was so underpowered that it was barely steerable.

By the time he launched the LZ-4, Zeppelin had worked out most of the bugs, resulting in a record-breaking 12-hour flight over Switzerland in 1908. A month later, while attempting a 24-hour endurance flight to win government funding for his Zeppelins, LZ-4 was pulled free of its moorings by a storm during an emergency overnight stop. The airship crashed in a fireball of exploding hydrogen gas. However, the German public rallied to Zeppelin's support by raising six million marks to build a new airship, allowing the count to create the Luftschiffbau Zeppelin (Zeppelin Airship Construction Company).

Another company, the Luftschiffbau Schütte-Lanz, built and flew 20 rigid airships from 1911 until 1917, all of them in military service. The company pioneered one lasting design innovation—the cruciform, a tail configuration with a horizontal stabilizer and elevator and a vertical stabilizer and rudder.

GERMAN AIRSHIPS

By 1914 all the elements of the German rigid airship were established: an interior, metal alloy frame of rings and longitudinal girders supporting interior gas cells filled with hydrogen, giving the airship its long, tapered, cylindrical shape with a cruciform tail piece. Multiple internal combustion engines were housed in engine cars, or *nacelles*, arranged in various configurations off the main frame. Passengers and crew were carried in gondolas attached under the frame, although more crew space was available within the frame.

Gas cells used an interior lining made of the most gas-impervious material known at the time: cow or ox intestines. The outer membrane of a large intestine was scraped clean of fat and dirt, and then soaked in water and glycerine. The prepared skins, called goldbeater's skins, after a parchment used in gold leafing, were stacked in layers that dried into an almost impermeable sheet. By 1914 demand for goldbeater's skin to make gas bags for rigid airships had exhausted the available supply. A typical World War I Zeppelin used about 200,000 sheets. A postwar report by a French officer noted, "In 1918, there was being made in Germany, many thousand square meters per day of goldbeater's skin fabric, the

The first successful two-stroke engine was invented by Scottish engineer Sir Dugald Clerk, in 1876.

tightness of which was practically perfect." He added that one animal furnished only one skin, and 15 were required to prepare one square meter of fabric.

GASSY MATTERS

The extremely flammable hydrogen gas used to inflate the envelope was always the Achilles' heel of dirigibles. So why did airship makers in Germany and elsewhere persist in using it? Hydrogen is the most abundant element in the universe, and easy and cheap to manufacture. It also has better lifting capabilities than other gases, including the second most abundant element in the universe, helium. However, helium is nonflammable—in fact, it acts as a flame retardant—and is only 5% less buoyant than hydrogen. But usable quantities of it are available only by fractional distillation from natural gas, which contains up to 7% helium, making it more expensive to make and subject to the marketing whims of those with the most natural gas resources. The United States cornered the global market for helium and held onto it for decades. So hydrogen remained the go-to gas for airship developers in the rest of the world.

Many people assume that airships are vulnerable to punctures to the gas envelope. But lighter-than-air ships stay afloat from the lifting quality and volume of the gas, not the inflation pressure of the gas inside the envelope. When the envelope is fully inflated, gas pressure inside it is about equal to that of the air pressure around it. So if the envelope is punctured, the gas doesn't blow out fast like an over-inflated party balloon but leaks out slowly. The big ships could sustain hundreds of holes and still stay afloat for hours.

A bigger problem with dirigibles was how to handle them once they were earth-bound. Many were wrenched from the hands of ground crews or blown away from their mooring masts by winds or storms, and badly damaged while being buffeted aloft or destroyed when they crashed. The floating behemoths regularly suffered severe structural damage just being moved in and out of their sheds by ground crews. Once aloft, the ships were also susceptible to catastrophic damage in storms. Nonetheless, in the early days of aviation, airships for all their faults were more reliable and safer than airplanes, and the European powers, led by Germany, continued to aggressively develop them.

The 1976 christening of NASA's space shuttle *Enterprise* was attended by the cast of *Star Trek*.

The world's first passenger airline, Deutsche Luftschiffahrts-Aktiengesellschaft, or German Airship Transportation Corporation, Ltd., was established in 1909 as an offshoot of the Zeppelin Company. Most of those early flights were sightseeing trips, but in 1919 a DELAG zeppelin began regularly scheduled flights between Berlin and Friedrichshafen, 370 miles to the south. The flights took 4 to 9 hours, compared to 18 to 24 by rail. In 1912 DELAG hired the world's first flight attendant, Heinrich Kubis, to provide service for the 23 passengers onboard. Also in that year, DELAG's airship *LZ-13 Hansa* made the first international passenger flight, a round trip between Berlin and Copenhagen. Between 1910 and the outbreak of war in 1914, DELAG zeppelins carried 34,000 passengers on roughly 1,500 flights, without a single injury.

AIRSHIPS AT WAR

The outbreak of World War I saw dirigibles pressed into military service as scouts, bombers, aerial gunships, and counter-submarine measures for both sides. Early on it became evident that their slow speed, lack of maneuverability, relative fragility, and low operating ceiling made them unusable over battlefields. The Germans used zeppelins to bomb London, but bad weather hampered their effectiveness. One zeppelin commander later wrote, "More often it was nothing but a stiff wind riding through a moonlit night that kept the ships away from England." British air defenses were provided with incendiary ammunition, so the Germans redesigned the airships to fly at higher altitudes, which made them even less accurate. As a result, zeppelin bombing was minimal, although it was still a propaganda tool for the German forces. The 51 zeppelin raids against England resulted in 557 deaths. Of the 84 German dirigibles used in the war, 60 were lost to accident or enemy action.

For more on dirigibles, turn to page 323.

* * *

EARLY NAMES FOR THE HELICOPTER

Instrument, screw, aerodynamic, pterophore, automoteur, aeroveliero, convertiplane, spiralifere, aerial carriage, helicoptere, aerial screw, stropheor

The subway in Copenhagen, Denmark, uses computerized, driverless trains.

READ MY BUMPER

LOL stickers seen on cars.

If you don't like the way I'm driving, you come and get these handcuffs off!

Pluto 2006. Running as an Independent Planet.

GIVE ME COFFEE AND NO ONE GETS HURT.

This would really be funny if it weren't happening to me.

I got this motorhome for my wife. Best deal I ever made.

Boldly Going Nowhere.

JESUS SAVES... He passes it to Gretzky... Gretzky shoots... He scores!

The face is familiar, but I can't quite remember my name.

Metaphors be with you.

When the chips are down, the buffalo is empty.

What's another word for thesaurus?

ZERO TO SIXTY IN 15 MINUTES.

Why is the alphabet in that order? Is it because of that song?

All those who believe in psychokinesis, raise my hand.

I've got a perfect body. Unfortunately, it's in the trunk and starting to smell.

Sorry for driving so close in front of you.

ELVIS HAS LEFT THE PLANET.

If this sticker gets smaller, the light is probably green.

THERE ARE 2 TYPES OF PEDESTRIANS: THE QUICK AND THE DEAD.

Beauty is in the eye of the beer holder.

Always remember you are unique, just like everyone else.

There are 3 kinds of people: those who can count and those who can't.

It is illegal to run out of gas on the German autobahn.

INDY PACE CARS: A SELECTED HISTORY

Since 1911, pace cars have always been chosen to represent American auto production at its best, and the competition each year among carmakers is fierce. As for the driver, that can be almost anybody in the news that year.

BACKGROUND

Indy 500 founder Carl Fisher is credited with devising the rolling start used at Indy and other races worldwide. Racers line up in rows according to the rank they qualified and are led around the track by a pace car for one to three laps before the green flag is lowered and the official race begins. Some notable cars and drivers over the years:

Driver: Eddie Rickenbacker (1925)

Car: Rickenbacker "8"

Story: This WWI American "Ace of Aces" shot down 26 planes in 1918. A renowned racecar driver before the war, Rickenbacker bought the Indy track in 1927 for $750,000. He sold it for the same amount 18 years later.

Driver: Wade Morton (1930)

Car: Cord L-29

Story: Morton was assigned to drive the pace car, but track legend has it that auto designer E. L. Cord drove the blue-and-white roadster himself.

Driver: Tommy Milton (1936)

Car: Packard "120"

Story: The first multiple Indy 500 winner (1921 and 1923), Milton suggested that race officials award the pace car itself to the winning driver. That year Louis Meyer won the race and took home the Packard that Milton drove. Today three cars are handed out: one to the winner, one to the pace car driver, and one to the Hall of Fame Museum in Indianapolis.

Driver: Wilbur Shaw (1949)

Car: Oldsmobile 88, 135-hp 303ci V-8

Story: Speedway President Shaw had won the Indy 500 three times (1937, 1939, and 1940) as a driver, and drove a Chevrolet Stylemaster Six-Series pace car in 1948. In 1949 he "drove" the pace car again but this time facing backward and waving to the crowd (a passenger steered).

Driver: Sam Hanks (1961)

Car: Ford Thunderbird, 300-hp 390ci V-8

Story: Hanks was the 1957 Indy 500 winner. A. J. Foyt saw his mother admiring Hanks's golden convertible pace car before the race and told her he'd win it for her. And he did.

Driver: Eldon Palmer (1971)

Car: Dodge Challenger, 300-hp 383ci V-8

Story: While driving down Pit Lane with astronaut John Glenn in the passenger seat, local car dealer Palmer crashed into the press stand in the only pace car accident in Indy history, injuring photographer Russ Lake.

Driver: James Garner (1975)

Car: Buick Century Custom, 325-hp 350ci V-8

Story: The legendary TV star is no stranger to auto racing. He got the racing bug after starring in the 1966 film *Grand Prix*, and raced and owned cars that ran at Daytona, Sebring, and the grueling Baja 500. Garner drove the pace car again in 1977 and 1985.

Driver: Marty Robbins (1976)

Car: Buick Century, 306-hp turbo V-6

Story: The great country-western singer and avid pro racer (his

...the first land vehicle to break the sound barrier.

best finish was 5th at the Michigan Motorstate 400 in 1974) introduced the first V-6 pace car to the Indy 500.

Driver: Chuck Yeager (1986)

Car: Chevrolet Corvette 230-hp 350ci V-8

Story: The yellow street-legal Corvette, the second of 10 that paced from 1978 to 2010, was probably the slowest speedster that sound-barrier-breaker Yeager ever piloted.

Driver: Jay Leno (1999)

Car: Chevrolet Monte Carlo, 215-hp 3.4L V-6

Story: The *Tonight Show* host is an avid collector and keeps over 300 classic cars in his 17,000-square-foot Big Dog Garage in Los Angeles.

Driver: Elaine Irwin-Mellencamp (2001)

Car: Oldsmobile Bravada, 270-hp Inline V-6 SUV

Story: The ex-Mrs. John Cougar and Victoria's Secret model was the first woman pace car driver. She later attended the 2004 Democratic National Convention as a delegate from Indiana.

Driver: Morgan Freeman (2004)

Car: Chevrolet Corvette C5, 345-hp 5.7L V-8

Story: The Oscar-winning actor said, "Right next to acting, my childhood dream was to drive on a Speedway track."

Driver: Colin Powell (2005)

Car: Chevrolet Corvette C6, 400-hp 6L V-8

Story: Like all pace car drivers, the Gulf War commander and former Secretary of State got to keep the C6 pace car. It matched the '05 Corvette coupe he already owned.

Driver: Lance Armstrong (2006)

Car: Chevrolet Corvette Z06, 505-hp 7L V-8

Story: The seven-time winner of the Tour de France knows a bit about racing…

The BMW logo was based on an aircraft propeller.

ICEBREAKERS: A TIMELINE

These ships are made to rip through ice-choked waters. They're rough, they're tough, and they go where other vessels don't dare.

BREAKING THE ICE

11th century: Russian traders build the earliest form of icebreaker, called a *koch* or *pomor*. The hulls on these one- or two-masted sailing ships are protected by a curved belt of oak or larch planking at the waterline. If a pomor is being crushed by ice fields, the surrounding pressure will push the rounded hull up and onto the ice with little or no damage to the ship.

1837: A wooden paddle steamer built to keep shipping channels in local rivers open during the winter is launched in Philadelphia. The prosaically named *City Ice Boat*'s paddles, powered by two steam engines, are armored with iron covers to chop ice.

1864: A modified tugboat, the Pilot, is built by Mikhail Britnev of Russia. Considered the first true icebreaker, it's based on the pomor boats, with an angled bow that enables it to ride up and over ice before smashing the ice with its weight.

1893–1912: Norwegian polar explorers utilize icebreakers like the *Fram* to open routes for expeditions to the Arctic and Antarctic. Perhaps the strongest wooden ship ever built, this vessel has unique features like a rudder and propeller that retract into the hull for protection.

1957: The Russian-built 16,000-ton icebreaker *NS Lenin* is the world's first nuclear-powered surface ship.

1977: The NS *Arktika* makes history when it becomes the first surface vessel to reach the North Pole. Its unique "air bubbling system" breaks ice by blasting air jets below the water line.

PARTY "ON THE ROCKS"

The oddest use of an icebreaker was a publicity stunt sponsored by Canadian brewery Molson. In 1995 the beer company reportedly rented an icebreaker to ferry 75 contest winners to the North Pole for a live show by Metallica. The weather didn't cooperate, so the "Polar Beach Party" was moved to a hangar in Canada.

"HOUSTON, WE HAVE A PROBLEM..."

In 40 years, NASA has lost 17 astronauts in three devastating incidents. Here's what went wrong, and what's done differently now.

APOLLO I (January 27, 1967)

Story: During a prelaunch test at the Kennedy Space Center in Florida, a fire started in the cabin of the *Apollo I* Command Module as it sat atop its Saturn I rocket. The fire killed astronauts Roger Chaffee, Virgil Grissom, and Edward White.

Probable Cause: Investigators never found the fire's original source but concluded that faulty wiring of the environmental control systems was the likely problem. The fire burned for 25.5 seconds before depleting the oxygen in the module. The escape hatch took a full 90 seconds to open because NASA had thought a quicker-acting hatch would increase the risk of accidental release in space.

Lessons Learned: The escape hatch was redesigned to have a faster release time. NASA also determined that the prelaunch test itself was inherently dangerous because the cabin atmosphere was highly flammable—100 percent oxygen. Following the accident, NASA appointed an Aerospace Safety Advisory Panel and created the Flight Safety Panel to monitor procedures.

SPACE SHUTTLE *CHALLENGER* (January 28, 1986)

Story: Seventy-three seconds after takeoff, the Space Shuttle *Challenger* exploded, killing all seven astronauts aboard, including the only civilian, schoolteacher Christa McAuliffe, as well as astronauts Gregory Jarvis, Ronald McNair, Ellison Onizuka, Judith Resnick, Michael Smith, and Commander Richard Scobee.

Probable Cause: Outside air temperatures had fallen into the low 20s while the *Challenger* sat overnight on its pad before takeoff. When Flight Control gave the go-ahead, the temperature was

Gus Grissom logged 4,600 hours piloting aircraft and 15 minutes 37 seconds piloting spacecraft.

still only 36°F, and Richard Scobee's wife asked if they would still launch even though there were icicles on the shuttle. NASA investigators concluded that the cold weather caused the rubber O-rings on the right solid rocket motor to not seal properly, allowing hot exhaust gas to escape and melt the skin of the launch vehicle.

Lessons Learned: NASA technicians redesigned the O-rings to withstand a wider range of temperatures.

SPACE SHUTTLE *COLUMBIA* (February 1, 2003)

Story: The Space Shuttle *Columbia* disintegrated on re-entry at an altitude of 203,000 feet and a speed of Mach 18, or 12,500 mph. NASA lost seven astronauts: Michael Anderson, David Brown, Kalpana Chawla, Laurel Clark, Rick Husband, William McCool, and Ilan Ramon. In addition, two members of the debris search team were later killed in a helicopter accident.

Probable Cause: The incident that doomed *Columbia* happened at liftoff 16 days earlier. Just 81.7 seconds after launch, a piece of insulating foam detached from the External Tank and damaged the Thermal Protection System on the front of the craft's left wing. During re-entry, when temperatures exceed 3,000°F, this breach allowed superheated air to enter the left wing and melt the aluminum supports, causing the ship to lose aerodynamic control and ultimately break apart. The *Columbia* Accident Investigation Board also blamed what they termed a "complacent and unsafe NASA organizational structure" for the tragedy. Restricted budgets and shifting priorities, among other institutional failures, had resulted in a space program without a "safety culture."

Lessons Learned: The investigating board concluded that despite the structural failure, *Columbia* itself was not unsafe. Subsequently, NASA implemented mechanical fixes such as stronger debris protection and sturdier insulation, but these efforts were overshadowed by the board's recommendation that NASA re-evaluate the entire Space Shuttle program. Top concerns were a breakdown of information sharing between divisions and a command structure that operated outside of Flight Safety Regulations. In 2010 President Obama announced that the Shuttle program would be discontinued in 2011.

First car to include anti-lock brakes: the 1966 Jensen FF.

FIRST MOTORCYCLE

Which came first, the American steam velocipede or the French vélocipède vapeur? *The jury's still out on who won the race to invent the motorbike.*

REPRESENTING THE USA

Sylvester Roper was a precocious young man. Born in 1823 in Francestown, New Hampshire, he had constructed a small stationary engine by the age of 12 and a locomotive engine by the age of 14. He'd never seen either mechanism before building one. Roper settled in the Boston area in 1854, working as a machinist. In his lifetime he invented the hand-stitch sewing machine, repeating shotgun, shotgun choke, various types of hot air engine, furnaces, screw-making equipment, bicycles, a steam-powered carriage and many other useful devices, including a "pocket fire escape" for traveling salesmen. But it was his steam-powered velocipede that made history.

"FAST FOOT"

Sometime between 1867 and 1969, Roper attached a twin-cylinder steam engine to a hickory-framed bicycle called a *vélocipède* (French for "fast foot"). He designed a rectangular firebox that he suspended between the saddle and the handlebars. Coal was shoveled in at the bottom and lit. Water was poured into the reservoir in the seat. The fire heated the water to boiling, and the resulting steam created pressure to turn the engine. A short chimney protruded from the back of the bike seat. Bike collector Pete Gagan describes riding the Steam Velocipede as "straddling a barbecue with an explosive device underneath."

There was a pressure gauge on top of the steam engine, with release valves on the sides. Roper controlled the steam throttle by twisting a cable attached to the handlebars. The bicycle had a spoon brake—basically, a piece of metal that put pressure on the iron-shod wooden wheels when a hand brake was squeezed. This method was useless in bad weather when the wet wheels slid past the metal spoon.

LOUD CONTRAPTION

In 1869 Roper premiered his steam-powered bicycle in Roxbury, Massachusetts. The bike was a hit with the public at fairs and circuses across New England, but his neighbors were not impressed. They complained that Roper's contraption spooked their horses, was annoyingly loud, and gave off a foul odor. After continued prodding from townsfolk, Roxbury police arrested Roper on one of his jaunts around town but had to release him when they discovered he had broken no laws.

It took more than 20 years for Roper to generate any business interest in his invention. Then in 1895 Pope Mfg., makers of the Columbia safety bicycle (one of the first bicycles to have same-size wheels and a chain-driven rear wheel) asked Roper to build them an improved version of his steam-powered bicycle. The company had visions of creating a new line of steam-powered personal transport, apparently unaware that gas-powered engines were about to make steam a technological afterthought. Nonetheless, the 70-year-old Roper built Pope a more streamlined and lightweight steam bicycle that carried a one-gallon reservoir and weighed 150 pounds.

GOING, GOING...GONE

In 1896 Roper took his Columbia steam bicycle to the Charles River bicycle track in Boston for a test run. He took a few exhibition laps around the wooden track, with bicyclists following him. During his first pass he reached a speed of nearly 40 mph. Ecstatic, Roper decided to make another pass and shoot for an even higher speed. As he hit 60 mph, spectators saw Roper's face turn pale. The steam bicycle lost power, the wheels wobbled, and he crashed to the ground, dead of a heart attack. Doctors determined that the heart attack had caused the crash, not vice versa. Newspapers reported that Sylvester Roper, the inventor of the first self-propelled two-wheeled machine in America, had "died in the saddle."

REPRESENTING FRANCE

Most historians agree that blacksmith Pierre Michaud and his son, Ernest, were among the first, if not the first, inventors of the modern pedal-powered bicycle. The two ran a carriage-making company in Paris, where they developed their velocipede, which was propelled like a tricycle with its pedals and crank attached to an over large front wheel. The rigid frame was made of iron and the wooden wheels rolled on iron tires. Despite being nicknamed the "boneshaker" by cyclists who experienced some pretty jarring rides on the rough roads of France, it was an instant success. Records show that Michaud's company manufactured a good number of velocipedes in 1864, but a year later, in 1865, the number hit 400, making it the biggest bicycle manufacturer in Europe.

Sometime between 1867 and 1869, engineer Louis-Guillaume Perreaux invented a steam-powered velocipede. Perreaux had much in common with Sylvester Roper. By the age of 12, he had invented the cane gun, a walking stick with a gun concealed inside. At 25, he was working on designs for a circular power saw, a multichambered gun, a lock mechanism, and a small steam-powered engine. It is this brass-plated, single-cylinder engine that Perreaux attached to a boneshaker to create France's first *vélocipède vapeur*.

STEAM DREAMS

Whereas Roper's engine and boiler hung between the bicyclist's legs, Perreaux tucked the engine—with boiler, firebox, and water tank—under the seat. It resembled a small keg of beer with multiple brass compartments and attachments. The rider got the motorcycle rolling with the pedals and then applied steam to the cylinder with a hand control. A steam pressure gauge was mounted in the rider's view above the front wheel. The *vélocipède vapeur* had a top speed of nine mph. If riders wanted to stop, they were out of luck: There were no brakes. Perreaux patented his steam velocipede on March 16, 1869, and a tricycle version in 1884.

AND THE WINNER IS...?

Although Roper never patented his steam velocipede, it was already being exhibited in 1869, the same year Perreaux's *vélocipède vapeur* was patented. So historians have declared a tie. But some sticklers define a motorcycle as a two-wheeled vehicle powered by a *gas* engine, which would effectively eliminate Roper and Perreaux. The title would then go to Gottlieb Daimler of Germany, who attached an internal combustion engine to his bonecrusher 16 years later, in 1885.

FAMOUS CARS: BAD-GUY EDITION

Fascist dictators, genocidal madmen, and hardened criminals all have one thing in common: They like to ride in style.

IL DUCE'S 1939 LANCIA

Details: Benito Mussolini, the dictator who ruled Italy from 1922 to 1943, understandably had a preference for Italian cars. He bought Alfa-Romeos to help the company stay afloat during the Great Depression, but for less sporty occasions Il Duce preferred a luxurious red Lancia Astura V-8 convertible.

Where is it now? At Wayne Lensing's Historic Auto Attractions Museum in Roscoe, Illinois, right between a German WWII motorcycle and a Horch Cabriolet used by Hitler's right-hand man, Heinrich Himmler.

DILLINGER'S GETAWAY CAR

Details: In 1934 the infamous Depression Era bank robber John Dillinger (1903–34) bought a 1933 Essex Terraplane. On April 31, he crashed it in a Minnesota farm field while escaping from a shootout with police. Dillinger was shot in the left leg, and the car still has two slugs embedded in the front panel. On July 22, 1934, Dillinger was shot and killed by FBI agents as he left the Biograph movie theater in Chicago.

Where is it now? At the National Museum of Crime and Punishment in Washington, D.C.

HITLER'S AND FRANCO'S 1939 MERCEDES-BENZ G4 SIX-WHEELERS

Details: Only 57 of these cars were made, and Der Führer had eight of them, which he used to tour cities his armies had just conquered. To power the four-ton off-roader, Daimler-Benz installed an M24-series air-cooled inline-8 with 5.0 (or 5.4) liter capacity, delivering 110 hp and a top speed of 40 mph. Generalissimo Francisco Franco received a G4 as a gift from Hitler.

In the US, 60% of new cars are purchased by women.

Where are they now? There are less than five genuine G4s left in the world. One of Hitler's is at Lensing's Historic Auto Attractions Museum in Illinois. In 2004 the Mercedes-Benz Classic Center in Fellbach, Germany, completed a full restoration of Franco's G4, which is now owned by the Spanish royal family. It is 100% roadworthy and sits in Madrid as part of the Royal Fleet.

KHRUSHCHEV'S 1962 CHAIKA

Details: Russian automaker GAZ made two of these custom four-door convertible V-8s for Soviet premier Nikita Khrushchev (1894–1971). The Communist leader gave one as a gift to cosmonaut Yuri Gagarin and kept the other Chaika (Russian for "seagull") for himself.

Where is it now? In 1968, after Khrushchev and Gagarin had died, the Soviet government gave both Chaikas to Hungarian dictator Janos Kadar. After the fall of Communism in 1989, Wayne Lensing bought them for his auto museum in Illinois.

BONNIE AND CLYDE'S LAST RIDE

Details: On April 29, 1934, bank robbers Bonnie Parker and Clyde Barrow stole a brand-new Ford V-8 out of Jesse and Ruth Warren's driveway in Topeka, Kansas. When the Warrens got it back three months later, the car had 2,500 miles on it, blood-stained upholstery, and 167 bullet holes. A posse of Texas lawmen had ambushed the bank robbers in west Dallas, emptying their Browning Automatic Rifles into the bodies of Parker, Barrow, and the '34 Ford.

Where is it now? The Warrens sold the car not long after the shootout. A mainstay of sideshows and special exhibits for decades, it ended up at Whiskey Pete's Resort and Casino 30 minutes south of Las Vegas, where it remains on display. Added attraction: the shirt Clyde was wearing during the ambush, complete with bullet holes.

* * *

"There are two kinds of pedestrians: the quick and the dead."

—Lord Thomas Robert Dewar (1930)

AROUND WE GO!

Roundabouts have been...well...around for over 100 years. So why do American drivers find them so baffling?

TRAFFIC FLOW, EURO-STYLE

There's a scene in the movie *National Lampoon's European Vacation* in which Chevy Chase's character, Clark Griswold, is driving through London with his family. When he enters the Lambeth Bridge *roundabout* (a traffic circle), he finds that he can't merge into the left lane. He gets stuck in the inner circle, going around for hours, declaring over and over, "Look kids, there's Big Ben! There's Parliament!" Darkness sets in and, his family asleep, Clark disintegrates into fits of hysterical laughter while muttering, "Big Ben! Parliament!" and, "I can't seem to get left." To quote Homer Simpson, "It's funny because it's true."

Many Americans can relate to Griswold's frustration and confusion the first time they find themselves entering one of these oddly foreign traffic-control intersections. Long a mainstay of European roads, the roundabout lost out to signalled intersections over a half century ago in the United States. But today it's slowly making a comeback.

CIRCULAR LOGIC

According to the experts, modern roundabouts are safer, they speed up commutes, and they're better for the environment when compared to intersections with signals. This wasn't always the case. The reason roundabouts fell out of favor in the U.S. was because in the early days, vehicles entering a roundabout had the right of way, which tended to clog up the circle. Traffic signals both outside and inside the roundabout further snarled traffic. Nearly parallel, or tangential, arteries allowed cars to plow into the circle at high speeds, causing accidents. Some early roundabouts even allowed two-way traffic inside the circle.

WHAT GOES AROUND

None of these conditions apply to modern roundabouts. New regulations, including a "yield-at-entry" policy that gives cars inside

Fastest trains currently in service: China's high-speed rail lines. They regularly reach 217 mph.

the circle the right of way, have made them safer and easier to use. In 2007 the Insurance Institute for Highway Safety published a study that tracked community reaction to roundabouts before and after construction. No one was surprised when researchers found that only 34 percent of motorists surveyed supported a roundabout before its construction. Shortly after the roundabout was in place, however, that number jumped to 57 percent. A year later, a full 69 percent liked them. It's a good thing, too, because traffic circles aren't going to go away anytime soon.

As of 2010, there were 2,000 roundabouts in the U.S., with more being built every day. Community planners use them in part because they're less expensive to build and maintain than intersections controlled by traffic lights.

DRIVING IN CIRCLES

• **Country with the most roundabouts:** France—which has over 30,000, more than half of all the roundabouts in the world.

• **City with the most roundabouts per square mile:** Milton Keynes, U.K. This English town has 130 traffic circles, an average of 3.82 per square mile.

• **First roundabout in the U.S.:** Columbus Circle in New York City, built in 1905.

• **World's largest roundabout:** Queen's Park Savannah in Port of Spain, Trinidad. It spreads over 260 acres, with a perimeter of 2.2 miles.

• **Most confusing roundabout:** Topping the polls is a series of five mini-roundabouts arranged in a circle in Swindon, England. Amazingly, it works.

• **Most dangerous roundabout:** The ten-lane Place Charles de Gaulle, which encircles l'Arc de Triomphe in Paris. An old-style "nonconforming" roundabout, it's fed from 12 avenues and triggers one accident every 11 minutes.

*   *   *

The term "aeroplane" was coined in 1842 by Frederick Marriott, the publicist for aviation pioneers William Henson and John Stringfellow.

WRONG PLACE, WRONG TIME

Car accidents claim tens of thousands of lives every year. As these celebrities found out, you don't have to be in a car to be killed by one.

• In 1949 Margaret Mitchell, author of *Gone With the Wind*, died in Georgia after being struck by a drunk driver. She was 48.

• In 1964 Percy Kilbride, who played Pa in the popular Ma and Pa Kettle movies of the 1930s and 1940s, was run down by a car near his home on Hollywood Boulevard. He was 76.

• In 1973 Clarence White, lead guitarist for the seminal folk-rock band the Byrds, was loading instruments into the band's van when he was struck and killed by a drunk driver. He was 29.

• In 1994 Jerry Rubin, co-founder of the Yippies and one of the infamous Chicago Seven, jaywalked into three lanes of traffic on Wilshire Boulevard in Los Angeles. One car swerved and missed; the car behind it killed him. He was 56.

• In 1999 singing cowboy star Rex Allen Sr. collapsed in his driveway from a heart attack. Not knowing he was there, his caretaker ran over Allen while backing out, killing him.

• In 2002 animator William "Tex" Henson, who drew Rocky and Bullwinkle and Chip 'n' Dale, died in Dallas after a pickup truck hit him. He was 78.

• Harvard professor and UFO expert John E. Mack, age 75, was walking home after dinner with friends in London when he was hit and killed by a drunk driver.

CLOSE CALLS

• In 1931 Winston Churchill was struck by a car while crossing a New York City street (being English, he'd looked the wrong way). He suffered head injuries and broken ribs.

• In 1982 actress Eileen Brennan was blindsided by a car outside an L.A. restaurant. Her legs were shattered and every bone on the left side of her face broken. It took her three years to recover.

The Chicago Post Office at 433 West Van Buren is the world's only drive-thru post office.

THE NEWMAN BUG

In 2011 a 1963 red convertible Volkswagen Beetle was offered for sale. The price? $250,000. Here's the story.

BITTEN BY THE BUG

In 1963 actor Paul Newman bought a new car. The superstar could have picked any of the great luxury or sports cars of the era but instead bought a little red Volkswagen convertible. Newman even posed with it in a few magazine ads. That in itself would make Newman's Volkswagen special to a future collector, but even more value was added in 1969 when Newman took his VW Bug to legendary Indy race car builder Jerry Eisert for a "mechanical upgrade."

Newman had just finished playing a race car driver in the film *Winning* and had developed a real craving for speed. And while he liked his VW, apparently he did not like the teasing he received from his Porsche-driving friend Robert Redford, who'd starred with him in *Butch Cassidy and the Sundance Kid* that same year. Newman's plan was to make his mouse into a monster that could smoke Redford's Porsche.

COOL HAND BUG

To transform the stock Beetle into the Newman Bug, Eisert removed the standard 40-hp engine and installed a 300-hp 351-cubic-inch Ford "Windsor" V8. The engine took up the entire backseat. It was the automotive equivalent of putting a rocket on a tricycle. Eisert also installed a five-speed ZF transmission, racing suspension, and radiators under the front and back hoods. The result? A "sleeper" (a car that looks slow but is a real beast under the hood) that was a cross between Herbie the Love Bug and Speed Racer's Mach 5.

Legend has it that Newman immediately took what he called his "Indy VW" out to Mulholland Drive for some heated street racing with film industry pals. He also hit the local racetracks to challenge all comers. The souped-up VW created a sensation at the track. When *Hot Rod* and *Speed Age* magazines decided to run features on it, Newman insisted they not mention him by name. He didn't want to lose the advantage of surprise when challenging unsuspecting muscle-car street racers at stoplights or on canyon runs.

BYE-BYE LOVEBUG

In the early 1970s, Newman's agents, managers, and family were urging him to get rid of his screamin' VW before he seriously hurt himself or someone else. He donated it to the auto engineering program at Chaffey College in Rancho Cucamonga, California, where students proudly repainted it in the school colors.

But giving up his Indy VW did not keep Newman off the racetrack. Racing had in fact become a second career that he pursued for 15 more years, arranging his shooting schedule to keep April to September open so he could race on the Sportscar Club of America circuit. Throughout those years, Newman donated many of his cars to the Chaffey College Auto Shop. When the head of the auto shop, Sam Contino, finally retired, the department presented Newman's legendary Indy VW to him as a retirement gift.

After Newman died in 2008 at age 83, Contino restored the VW to its original state. He offered the Newman Bug for sale in May 2011 at an asking price of $250,000. As of press time, it is still available.

* * *

PRANKSTERS

Paul Newman loved auto racing, and loved to talk about it. Eventually his pal Robert Redford grew tired of listening to the actor tell stories about his racing career and decided to do something about it.

On Newman's 50th birthday, Redford had a wrecked Porsche, minus its engine, dropped off in Newman's driveway with a big blue ribbon wrapped around it.

A short time later, Redford found a box sitting in his living room. It was so heavy, it had dented the floor. Newman had compacted the Porsche and sent it back to Redford in a crate.

Redford then turned the twisted block of metal into an ugly sculpture and dropped it off in Newman's garden.

The two of them never spoke of it.

LIGHTNING EXPRESS

In one of the great publicity stunts of the 19th century, the first "bullet train" in history sped coast-to-coast and captured the imagination of the nation.

THERE'S NO BUSINESS LIKE SHOW BUSINESS

In 1876 theatrical producers Henry C. Jarrett and Harry Palmer had a problem: Their hit production of Shakespeare's *Henry V* was scheduled to open in San Francisco on June 4...but their cast was still in New York. Traveling across the continent by train—the fastest transport then available—took seven days. Somehow, the cast had to cover the distance in four days, or the producers would lose their shirts. So how did these canny promoters solve their dilemma? They announced to the world that they would hire a special train and attempt the impossible: to cross the continent in only four days. And they got newspapers and private investors, anxious to be a part of history, to underwrite the scheme. The five major railroad companies agreed to clear their tracks from the Atlantic to the Pacific, arrangements were made for refueling stops along the way, and a train was readied.

HOT TICKET

Once the public heard that the cast of *Henry V* would be boarding a high-speed train just hours after closing their show in New York, tickets to the San Francisco play sold like hotcakes. Newspapers on both coasts gave daily updates about the play, its promoters, and the eagerly anticipated train trip. A luxurious top-of-the-line Pullman Palace hotel car was outfitted for the cast and crew, along with 16 special guests, including reporters from the *New York Herald* and *The Times* of London. Other guests booked seats at the exorbitant cost of $500 each (about $10,000 today), and train tickets were delivered to the lucky few in silver presentation cases. Some cautious passengers purchased life insurance before they set off on their 3,000-mile adventure.

Finally, on the morning of June 1, 1876, the Transcontinental Express, as it was officially called, pulled out of the Pennsylvania Railroad's Jersey City Station, heading west. The train had a

The world's first car ferry began operating in Minnesota in 1905. It could carry 6 cars.

mammoth task: cross three mountain ranges (the Appalachians, the Rockies, and the Sierra Nevada), two plains (the Great Plains and the Great Salt Desert), and two major rivers (the Mississippi and the Missouri) in 96 hours. The "Lightning Express," as the press took to calling it, sped across America, sometimes reaching speeds of a mile a minute.

PRECISION TIMING

All along the line, water, coal, and food supplies stood at the ready for quick loading. Crews of engineers, firemen, brakemen, and conductors took only minutes to hop on and off for new shifts. Engine changes were made in record time. Towns along the way rang church bells to let people know when the train was about to pass through, and crowds lit bonfires and cheered the speeding Lightning Express. As the train bulleted past town after town, telegraph operators spread the word: "The Lightning Express is on the way!"

For three days, all eyes were on Jarrett and Palmer's train, and everyone wanted to jump on the publicity bandwagon. The *New York Times* sent its June 1 edition on the train to Chicago so subscribers could have the paper on the same day it was printed. The post office placed mail bound for India and Southeast Asia on the Lightning Express for speedy delivery. Wells Fargo Bank loaded a safe full of money onto the baggage car in Omaha. The train even had own postmark, "Jarrett & Palmer Fast Transcontinental Express," for passengers who wanted to mail letters while on the journey.

ANOTHER OPENING, ANOTHER SHOW!

Three days, 11 hours, and 39 minutes after leaving New Jersey, the Lightning Express pulled into the station in Oakland, California, and the passengers disembarked to greet an enthusiastic crowd. Despite mechanical difficulties, a washed-out track in Utah—which required teams of Irish and Chinese laborers working around the clock to repair it—and brake failure coming down the Sierra Nevada, the Express beat its own estimated arrival time by nearly 12 hours.

On June 4, *Henry V* opened in San Francisco on schedule, to a sold-out house.

World's largest building: Boeing's Everett, WA, assembly plant, at 4.3 million square feet.

IMPOSSIBLE!

They said it couldn't be done…

BY STEAMSHIP

"How, sir, would you make a ship sail against the wind and currents by lighting a bonfire under her deck? I pray you, excuse me, I have not the time to listen to such nonsense."

—Napoleon Bonaparte, when told of Robert Fulton's steamboat (c. 1807)

BY TRAIN

"What can be more palpably absurd than the prospect held out of locomotives traveling twice as fast as stagecoaches?"

—*The Quarterly Review,* 1825

BY AIRPLANE

"Flight by machines heavier than air is unpractical [*sic*] and insignificant, if not utterly impossible.…No possible combination of known substances, known forms of machinery, and known forms of force, can be united in a practical machine by which man shall fly long distances through the air…"

—Simon Newcomb, astronomer-director of U.S. Naval Observatory, 1902

BY AUTOMOBILE

"The horse is here to stay, but the automobile is only a novelty, a fad."

—President of Michigan Savings Bank to Henry Ford's lawyer Horace Rackham, who ignored the advice and bought $5,000 in Ford stock in 1903, later selling it for $12.5 million

BY SUBMARINE

"I must confess that my imagination refuses to see any sort of submarine doing anything but suffocating its crew and floundering at sea."

—H. G. Wells (c. 1901)

BY SPACESHIP

"A rocket will never be able to leave the Earth's atmosphere."

—*The New York Times* (1936)

"Space travel is utter bilge."

—Dr. Richard van der Reit Woolley, Astronomer-Royal (c. 1956)

"Space travel is bunk."

—Sir Harold Spencer Jones, Woolley's replacement (c. 1955)

QUEST FOR SPEED, PART I

"Speed provides the one genuine modern pleasure." —Aldous Huxley

TOP OF THE HEAP

To hold the world land speed record is to reign supreme as the driver of the fastest vehicle on Earth, a title that has drawn hundreds of aspirants over the past century. For those who don't need to be the single fastest in the world but only the fastest in what they like to drive, there are dozens of sanctioned categories, groups, and classes in which to compete for national and international speed records.

ELECTRIC CAR DUELS

The first recognized land speed record was set on December 18, 1898, in Achéres, France, by Gaston de Chasseloup-Laubat. He drove a Jeantaud Duc electric car to 39.24 mph over a specially marked two-kilometer stretch of road. The event didn't create much of a stir, as the electric car was slower than the fastest bicycle (60 mph) or train (112 mph) of the day.

A month later, Belgian racer Camille Jenatzy (nicknamed "Red Devil" for the color of his beard) hit 41.42 mph over the same distance, only to be bested by Chasseloup-Laubat later the same day. Jenatzy regained the record on January 27 (49.93 mph), only to have it broken yet again by Chasseloup-Laubat. Jenatzy replied with his third and final land speed record on April 29, 1899, reaching 65.79 mph in the twin electric motor *La Jamais Contente*, the first car to go over 100 kilometers per hour (60 mph).

The brief land speed record dominance of the electric car came to an end on April 13, 1902, when Leon Serpollet drove his egg-shaped steamcar *Oeuf de Pâques* (Easter Egg) to 75.06 mph in Nice, France.

AUTO CLUB DUELS

On January 12, 1904, the first American took the record when a young Henry Ford drove a specially built car—actually, a gasoline engine attached to a bare chassis with no bodyworks, no rear sus-

The car-making material carbon fiber is as strong as steel but up to 60% lighter.

pension, and only a metal pivoting bar for steering—across the frozen surface of Lake St. Clair in Michigan. The "999" (named after a speed record–holding steam locomotive) reached a top speed of 91.37 mph.

But because the timing had been carried out by the American Automobile Association, the Automobile Club de France refused to recognize the record attempt. A record attempt overseen by the Automobile Club of Great Britain had suffered a similar fate a year earlier. This marked the beginning of decades of haggling between national automobile associations over who would be the "decider" when it came to determining a legitimate land speed record. As for Ford, he didn't care what the French association thought. The publicity he received from attempting the record helped him raise money for his newly formed Ford Motor Company.

BREAKING 100 MPH

The 100-mph barrier was breached on July 21, 1904, when Louis Rigolly pushed his Gobron-Brillié and its massive 12-liter engine to 103.56 mph (166.66 kph) down a beach road near Ostend, Belgium. However, the big news occurred on January 29, 1906, when Fred Marriott drove a steam-powered Stanley Rocket Racer to 127.66 mph. The Rocket Racer was the first automobile to beat the rail speed record of 112 mph. The Stanley Rocket Racer marked the end of the steamcar's reign as the king of speed; from then on, internal combustion engines would rule. *Trivia note:* Incredibly, that 1906 Rocket Racer record would stand for over a century, until the British steamcar Inspiration, dubbed "the world's fastest kettle," broke it on August 25, 2009, with an average speed of 139.8 mph.

NEW RULES

In early November 1909, the Blitzen Benz (Lightning Benz), driven by Frenchman Victor Hémery at Brooklands, England, set a record of 125 mph. The press trumpeted that the Blitzen Benz was "faster than any plane, train, or automobile." Hémery's record attempt was the first recognized land speed record to use electronic timing and the last to run in only one direction.

In March 1910, new rules established by the internationally recognized Association Internationale des Automobile Clubs

Reconnus would require runs to be made over a measured one-mile distance in opposite directions, with the two times being averaged for the record. To negate any effects of wind or slope, the two passes had to be made in 30 minutes. (Now one hour between passes is allowed).

Americans were still miffed at the French for their refusal to accept the AAA as an officially sanctioned timing organization on the Ford run, so the new rules were promptly ignored by American racers. This would be a source of confusion and conflicting record claims for decades. But the upshot of the change in rules was that the next sanctioned record was actually slower than the previous one. On June 24, 1914, Englishman L. G. "Cupid" Hornsted took his Blitzen Benz down the course at Brooklands under the two-way AIACR rules, for an average speed of 124.09 mph.

BREAKING 200 MPH

Up until WWI, land speed records were in general held by Europeans. The British dominated, and one family in particular—the Campbells—ruled for decades. Sir Malcolm Campbell set the world land speed record four times between 1924 and 1928, his fastest time coming in 1927 at Pendine Sands, Wales—174.88 mph.

The next notable attack on the record came March 29, 1927, when the 200-mph barrier was decisively shattered by Sir Henry Segrave at Daytona Beach, Florida. His Sunbeam 1000 HP Mystery (known affectionately as the "The Slug") was powered by two massive Matabele 12-cylinder airplane engines mounted one in front of the other. Fifteen thousand spectators lined the beach to watch the tall Englishman roar past at a new world record 203.79 mph. The trial almost ended in disaster. The Sunbeam's brakes overheated while Segrave tried to slow down, and he was forced to drive into the surf to bring the car to a halt.

Segrave's run at Daytona was the first by a European on American soil, but it started a trend. As cars got bigger, heavier, and faster, they needed more room for accelerating into and slowing out of the measured mile. The United States had the wide open spaces necessary—particularly at the Bonneville salt flats of western Utah. By 1935 Bonneville had become the preferred place to attempt land speed records.

...because the "outlaw lifestyle" of the movie would tarnish their image.

BREAKING 300 MPH

On September 3, 1935, eight years after Segrave's monumental run, Sir Malcolm Campbell took his Campbell-Railton-Rolls Royce "Bluebird" to 301.129 mph, his last land record attempt. After that he would turn his attention to the water. He ended up holding nine land speed records and four water speed records. His son, Donald Malcolm Campbell, followed in his footsteps in the '50s and '60s. Between them, they set 11 speed records on water and 10 on land. Donald would eventually hold seven world water speed records, and be the only person to hold the water and land speed record in the same year, 1964. He died on January 4, 1967, while attempting to break his own existing water record of 276 mph. He was going 320 mph when his boat, Bluebird K7, became airborne, and then broke apart after splashing down and cartwheeling across the water.

BREAKING 400 MPH

On the eve of WWII, a seesaw battle broke out on the flats between Englishmen Capt. George Eyston's eight-wheeled Thunderbolt and John Cobb's futuristic-looking, teardrop-shaped Railton Mobil Special. It was Eyston who had finally broken Campbell's record streak in mid-November 1937 in his Thunderbird, and he would stack two more records on top of that. Cobb topped Eyston's record on September 15, 1938, lost it back to his rival the next day, and then regained it on August 23, 1939, with a record of 369.70 mph that stood for the duration of the war.

In 1947 Cobb returned to Bonneville and bumped his record to 394.196 mph. Before 1947 the world land speed record had fallen as often as two to three times a year. Now it would stay unbroken for 16 years. Racers and mechanics began to wonder if the 400 mph barrier was unbreakable.

In 1963 the rules were changed by the FIA (Fédération Internationale de l'Automobile, which had superceded the old AIACR in 1947) to include "vehicles on at least four wheels which are propelled otherwise than through their wheels." That decision belatedly recognized what land speed racers already knew: The jet age had come to the ground.

Quest for Speed, Part II, starts on page 303.

The first rear-view cameras were used on construction vehicles in the 1970s.

THE FIRST STEWARDESS

In the early days of commercial aviation, one woman put together a team of skilled nurses to become the original flight attendants.

PLANE SCARED

Air travel in the 1920s was a brand-new way to see the world. It was modern, glamorous, and, to much of the public, terrifying. Even though passenger numbers increased every year, airlines were anxious to find a way to calm the public's fear of flying and attract more people onboard. Enter Ellen Church, a registered nurse from Cresco, Iowa. Church was also a licensed pilot and had originally approached Steve Stimpson, head of Boeing Air Transport, for a job at the controls but was turned down. She came back to him with a novel idea: Why not place nurses onboard planes to calm the passengers? Stimpson agreed, and on May 15, 1930, Ellen Church became the world's very first airline stewardess, flying Boeing's San Francisco-to-Chicago route. The flight took 20 hours and made 13 stops.

SKY GIRLS

Church recruited seven other nurses to become Boeing Sky Girls, and the "Original 8," as they became known, were an instant success. Within three years, all of the airlines had hired stewardesses. To become one, a woman had to be single, under 25, shorter than 5'4", weigh less than 115 pounds, and be a registered nurse. Some airlines required them to pledge not to get married for at least 18 months. Today flight attendants are responsible solely for passenger safety and comfort. In the 1930s, they were expected to fuel the plane, handle luggage, screw down loose seats, and help the pilot push the plane into the hangar. They made $125 a month.

A car accident grounded Ellen Church 18 months after her historic first flight. But she returned to the skies as a captain in the Army nurse corps during World War II, and was honored with an Air Medal for her work evacuating wounded soldiers from Africa, Italy, and France. Ever the sportswoman, Church died in a horseback riding accident in 1965, at the age of 60. The airport in her hometown was named Ellen Church Field in her honor.

In Kansas, it is illegal to screech your tires.

MY YACHT'S BIGGER THAN YOURS

Already own a 10,000-square-foot mansion? Drive a $2 million Bugatti? Fly to Aspen and Martha's Vineyard for the weekend? It may be time to consider buying the ultimate status symbol—a megayacht.

TOO MUCH IS NEVER ENOUGH

Nothing says, "I have an obscene amount of money" quite like an opulent, oversized boat. In 1985 there were only 300 private yachts that were more than 100 feet in length. Today any one of those would be shorter than any of the top 100 largest yachts in the world. *El Horriya* (478 feet) is one of the largest and is the oldest megayacht. Built in London in 1865 for the King of Egypt, it is now a training ship for the Egyptian navy. The 408-foot *Savarona* (named for a type of African swan) ruled the seas for decades. Built in 1931 for American heiress Emily Roebling Cadwallader, this yacht features a 282-foot gold-trimmed staircase and movie theater. The ship's library takes up an entire deck. Since 2003, however, seven yachts have eclipsed *Savarona* in size:

• The monstrous 538-foot *Eclipse* was built in 2010 for Russian oligarch Roman Abramovich for $1 billion, give or take a couple of hundred million. *Eclipse* has 24 guest cabins, a disco hall, multiple hot tubs, two helicopter pads, a mini "escape" submarine, a missile defense system, a laser-controlled anti-paparazzi "shield," a pair of swimming pools, and a crew of 70. It is one of four yachts the investment tycoon owns.

• The 531-foot *Dubai* was originally commissioned by Prince Jefri of Brunei in 1996 and later picked up for $300 million by the ruler of Dubai, Sheikh Mohammed bin Rashid Al Maktoum.

• Measuring 508 feet, *Al Said* is currently owned by Sultan Qaboos of Oman. Its six decks include a concert hall that can hold a 50-piece orchestra.

• The 482-foot *Prince Abdelaziz* was built in Denmark in 1984 for King Abdullah of Saudi Arabia.

• *Al Salamah* (456 feet), owned by Saudi Defense Minister Prince Sultan bin Abdul Aziz, was built in 1999 and has 60 state rooms and a glass-roofed indoor swimming pool.

• *Rising Sun* (454 feet), built in 2004 and owned by media tycoon David Geffen (see page 455 for details)

• *Serene* (439 feet), the largest yacht ever built in Italy, was built in 2010 and features two helipads, a submarine, and an indoor saltwater pool that can double as a moorage for the ship's tender.

• *Al Mirqab* (436 feet), owned by the Emir of Qatar and constructed in 2008, has five electro-diesel motors, each with a power output of 28,000 kw. (A Porsche 911 Turbo has an output of 353 kw.)

LESSONS IN EXCESS

Not everyone can own the biggest yacht, so when a person is trying to keep up with the Joneses (or, in this case, the Rothschilds), sometimes it's not size alone that makes the person. For example, when Russian banker Andrey Melnichenko was outfitting his $300 million, 394-foot, 23,600-square-foot megayacht, the *A*, he focused on the little things—like bath knobs that cost $40,000 each, a spiral staircase with a $60,000 banister, and a lounge decorated with white stingray-hide wallpaper and chairs made of alligator skins and kudu horns. A veritable floating fortress, it is outfitted to match, with 44 security cameras with motion detection and infrared night-vision, fingerprint-only access to the 2,583-square-foot master bedroom, and 44-mm bombproof glass throughout.

Some people prefer the more traditional sailing yacht to the diesel-power found on most of today's floating mansions. Compared to the *Dubai*—which has four 9,625-hp MTU engines, a 277,410-gallon fuel tank, and a top speed of 26 knots (30 mph)—hedge-fund manager Elena Ambrosiadou's *Maltese Falcon* is a quaint little sailboat. The 289-foot yacht's DynaRig sailing system features 25,791 square feet of computer-operated sails for optimum efficiency. The *Maltese Falcon* can cross the Atlantic in only

Traffic accidents are the number-one killer of Americans under the age of 34.

10 days on wind power alone. Other touches include three decks with transparent floors and a saloon featuring a life-size Bugatti made of porcelain.

WHY BUY?

Owning a megayacht isn't for everyone. Besides the high purchase price, the costs of maintaining and outfitting it can run into six figures per month. However, budget-conscious celebrities and socialites can still have all of the perks of an ocean-going palace without breaking the bank: by chartering one. There is a megayacht-for-hire to fit nearly every lifestyle and personality. For example, rapper/producer Sean "P. Diddy" Combs recently chartered *Solemates*, a 197-foot luxury yacht loaded with the latest in touch screen technology. Passengers control entertainment, climate systems, lighting, and blinds from 14 iPads installed around the boat. Other amenities include a gym that converts into a disco with an $80,000 light-and-sound system, an inflatable floating trampoline, and three remote-control racing sloops. Rental: $850,000 per week. Other celebrities who rent instead of buy: Jonas Brothers, Jon Bon Jovi, Mariah Carey, Robert DeNiro, John Travolta, and Russell Crowe, who chose the 110-foot yacht *Mustique* for a honeymoon cruise in 2003. Megayachting is a life fit for a king—or a queen: Just ask Queen Latifah, another frequent megayachter.

*   *   *

I LOVE MY MERCEDES

Emil Jellenik was certainly fond of his daughter, Mercedes. Even before he became one of the top dealers and promoters of Daimler cars in Europe, he competed in racing events under the pseudonym "Monsieur Mercedes." In 1900, as part of an agreement to sell more cars, he talked the company into naming the engine in their newest and fastest model the "Daimler-Mercedes," after his daughter. The new car was a sensation on the race circuit and soon became known only as the Mercedes. In 1903 Jellinek legally changed his name to Jellinek-Mercedes. By then the name Mercedes was a legally protected trademark belonging to Daimler-Benz, so he had to ask permission from the board of directors.

Video game designer Kazunori Yamauchi (*Gran Turismo*) helped develop the Nissan GT-R supercar.

THE GULLWING

From Le Mans to Rodeo Drive, the Mercedes 300SL "Gullwing" was one of the fastest, coolest production sports cars of the 1950s.

SPORTS CAR OF THE CENTURY

Designed by Rudolf Uhlenhaut in 1952, the original racing version of the Mercedes 300SL was all function. The form, it turned out, was a happy accident. In order to give the car an aerodynamic low profile, the engine was slanted 50 degrees to the left. The body was handcrafted around a tubular frame to save weight. Aluminum was used in the doors, hood, and deck lid in order to shave off even more pounds.

And it had double-curved doors that lifted up instead of out. When both doors were up and open, the car looked like a seagull in flight—hence the nickname. Critics considered the 175-hp single overhead cam straight-six engine underpowered for the endurance races the car was designed to compete in, but Mercedes-Benz had learned a thing or two about fuel injection while designing aircraft for the German Luftwaffe during World War II. Mercedes engineers injected fuel directly into the Gullwing's cylinders, boosting the car's top speed to 161 mph. That trick, combined with its light weight and low profile, made the 300SL one of the fastest cars in racing. The Gullwing took first place that year in three prestigious races 24 Hours of Le Mans, Nurburgring, and Carrera Panamerica in Mexico.

The car transformed Mercedes's reputation as a maker of reliable but staid sedans to that of a prestigious maker of high-performance sports cars. (In 1999 a panel of legendary racers declared the 300SL Gullwing the "Sports Car of the Century.")

RARE BIRD

The handcrafted 300SL racer was never meant to be a production car, but United States automobile importer Max Hoffman had other ideas for it. He badgered Mercedes management until they gave in and shipped 1,000 Gullwings to the U.S. Other than switching the steering from right- to left-hand drive and adding stylish flashes like slatted vents on the front fenders, eyebrow

The wall of cloth strips hanging down in a car wash is called the "mitter curtain."

moldings over the wheel-well arches, and chromed bumpers, the production W198 300SL was kept just like its racing cousin, right down to the aluminum. Only 1,400 of the two-seaters were built between 1954 and 1957, and they are now sought-after cult cars.

SAFETY FIRST

In 1957 Mercedes introduced the more sedate 300SL roadster to replace the Gullwing coupe. Gone were the famous winged doors, replaced by a standard front-hinged design. The carmaker insisted it was merely responding to requests for more comfort, but consumer satisfaction probably wasn't the only reason Mercedes discontinued the Gullwing. At Le Mans in 1955, a Mercedes 300 SLR, which looked like an open-cockpit version of a Gullwing, was being driven by Pierre Levegh when it spun off the track and crashed spectacularly into the grandstands. The driver and 86 spectators were killed. The resultant uproar over racing safety prompted Mercedes to quit the sport for the next 25 years. Mercedes never explained why they dropped the Gullwing from their lineup, but some industry experts speculate that they wanted to disassociate themselves from racing in general, and sportscars in particular.

THE GULLWING TODAY

Today the Gullwing is poised for a renaissance. In 2009 Mercedes-Benz introduced the SLS AMG, which has similar doors and is touted as "the spiritual successor to the Gullwing." A 525-hp all-electric version is due out in 2013.

*   *   *

BARNYARD BALLOONISTS

The first living creatures to fly in a hot-air balloon were a rooster, a sheep, and a duck. The three animals went up in a cloth-and-paper balloon built by Joseph and Étienne Montgolfier in 1673 at Versailles, France. The brothers had intended the flight crew to be humans, but King Louis XVI insisted that animals be used to test the effects of high-altitude travel. The flight, which was observed by a crowd of 130,000, lasted 8 minutes, reached a height of 1,500 feet, and landed the animal aviators safely on the ground 2 miles from the palace.

PHILLIPS 66

A look at an iconic American brand of gasoline.

PHILL 'ER UP

• **1905.** Oil wildcatters Frank Phillips and his brother Lee Eldas hit the first of 81 straight gushers.

• **1917.** The Phillips brothers start Phillips Petroleum in Bartlesville, Oklahoma. For the rest of his long career as an oil mogul, Frank Phillips insists he is just a "humble banker" with a side interest in oil.

• **1927.** How the brothers choose the company name is a story of synchronicity. The number 66 keeps popping up all through the deliberation process. Their new gasoline's gravity rating is 66. Their refinery is just off Route 66. Then a company executive recounts how, while road testing Phillips gasoline the day before, he'd remarked, "This car goes like 60 with our new gas." His driver checked the speedometer and said, "Sixty, nothing! We're doing 66." When asked where this took place, the executive says, "Highway 66." That cinches it. Phillips 66 is made the official name by a unanimous vote.

• **November 19, 1927.** The first Phillips 66 gas station opens in Wichita, Kansas. Customers who "Phill up with Phillips" get the first five gallons free. Phillips gas stations are built to look like cottages so that they will blend in with neighborhoods. They are always set close to railroads for easy delivery from tank cars.

• **1930.** Phillips 66 introduces the now-famous black-and-orange shield logo, designed to remind drivers of the company's enduring connection to the "Mother Road," Route 66.

• **Late 1930s to '60s.** Registered nurses are hired as "Highway Hostesses" to make random inspections of all Phillips 66 service stations within their region. Bathrooms must be sparkling clean and well stocked to receive a Highway Hostess seal of approval. The hostesses advise motorists where to find nearby dining and lodging. No reason is given as to why they have to be registered nurses.

• **1951.** Phillips 66 chemists Robert Banks and J. Paul Hogan create a milky-white oil-derived plastic they name Marlex. The company makes enough to fill several warehouses, but no one can figure out what to do with the stuff. Then a toy company named Wham-O! uses Marlex to make its greatest success: the Hula Hoop. Today Marlex, the trademarked name for HDPE plastic, is used to make baby bottles, milk jugs, detergent containers, and other household products.

• **1954.** With the introduction of TropArtic, Phillips 66 becomes the first oil company to offer an all-weather motor oil.

• **1959.** The Phillips 66 shield logo gets a makeover: The orange-and-black color scheme goes to red, white, and black, which it remains to this day.

• **1966.** Advent of the company's slogan "The Gasoline That Won the West." Phillips 66's longest-running slogan was "The Performance Company" (1973–2002). The current slogan is "Experts in Gas Since 1927."

• **1967.** Phillips 66 opens a gas station in Anchorage, Alaska, making it one of only two oil companies to have gas stations in all 50 states and Washington, D.C. (Texaco is the other.)

*   *   *

MAY WE QUOTE YOU ON THAT?

"The dangers are obvious. Stores of gasoline in the hands of people interested primarily in profit would constitute a fire and explosive hazard of the first rank. Horseless carriages propelled by gasoline might attain speeds of 14 or even 20 miles per hour. The menace to our people of vehicles of this type hurtling through our streets and along our roads and poisoning the atmosphere would call for prompt legislative action even if the military and economic implications were not so overwhelming…the cost of producting gas is far beyond the financial capacity of private industry.…In addition, the development of this new power may displace the use of horses, which would wreck our agriculture."

—U.S. Congressional Record, 1875

Before air traffic control towers, pilots avoided other aircraft by the "see and be seen" method.

MOCK WON!

Everyone knows about Amelia Earhart's attempt to be the first woman to fly solo around the world, but do you know who actually did it? Meet Jerrie Mock.

THE WRIGHT STUFF

Geraldine Frederitz had her first airplane ride in 1932, on a Ford TriMotor with her parents. It took only 15 minutes, but the exhilaration the seven-year-old felt as she flew above the earth lasted a lifetime. Afterward, little Jerrie told anyone who'd listen that she was going to be a pilot when she grew up. After all, she was from Ohio and her mother's maiden name was Wright, so flying was in her blood, right? Jerrie stayed true to her word, and when she got to high school she enrolled in a pre-flight training course. She was the only girl in the class. Later, at Ohio State University, she was the only woman in the aeronautical engineering program. Her flight plans got sidetracked in 1945 when she married Russell Mock, but three kids and 11 years later, Jerrie Mock was ready to return to her dream.

UP IN THE AIR, JUNIOR BIRD GIRL!

Mock took her first flying lesson in 1956 and soloed after just nine and a quarter hours of instruction. By 1958 she was flying complicated routes using only landmark recognition. In 1961 Mock became the manager of Price Field in Columbus, Ohio, the first woman to run an airport. Sundays she worked the airfield alone, refueling planes, tying them down, even making coffee for the pilots (her least favorite job). When her neighbor, an Air Force pilot, gave her an outdated collection of world airways charts, Mock papered her basement walls with them and plotted routes across the ocean. "I really had no intentions of being first at anything when this all began," Mock recalled. "I just wanted to see the world. But when I found out from the National Aeronautic Association (NAA) that a woman had never soloed around the world, it sounded like a fun thing to try."

CHARTING A COURSE

In 1962 Jerrie Mock began preparing for a solo flight around the world. Her husband, also a pilot, used his advertising background to line up financial support from the *Columbus Daily Dispatch* and airplane parts manufacturers, while she worked out the logistical details. According to Jerrie, "Nobody in Columbus knew a thing about flying over oceans or long-range navigation because nothing like this had been done before. I planned every mile of the flight myself, in my basement."

But before she could start the journey, she had to get air clearance from each country she would fly over. She went to Washington, D.C., and trekked from embassy to embassy, securing the necessary permits. She also arranged with the NAA to have observers and timers at each stop to document her landings and takeoffs for the official record. Mock remembered later, "The actual flying was a lot less complicated than putting together all these little details."

THE FLYING HOUSEWIFE

As preparations intensified, Jerrie was seldom at home, which ruffled feathers in her suburban neighborhood. In 1964 the prevailing attitude in American society was that a "good" mother stayed home with her kids. The fact that Jerrie's mother-in-law was taking care of hers while she flew back and forth to Washington, Wichita, and Fort Lauderdale provoked sharp criticism from the locals in Bexley, Ohio. She became known as "the Flying Housewife," which wasn't meant as a compliment.

But Mock stayed on task, modifying her 1953 Cessna 180 for the flight. She took out unnecessary seats, lined the cockpit with extra fuel tanks, and installed up-to-date avionics. She dubbed her plane *The Spirit of Columbus* and nicknamed it "Charlie."

AROUND THE WORLD IN 30 DAYS

Mock was shooting for an April 1 departure when she got word that Joan Merriam Smith of Long Beach, California, was planning to start her own round-the-world solo flight two weeks earlier, on March 17. In an instant, Mock's "see the world, set a record" adventure turned into a contest. Mock skipped some final modifications to her plane and moved her start date to March 19. Smith took off from California as scheduled in her Piper Apache, *The Spirit of Long Beach*, and, following Amelia Earhart's route, flew eastward.

In 1976 a Lockheed SR-71A Blackbird aircraft reached 2,913 mph,...

Mock left Columbus two days later, also heading east but following a shorter route. She lost her brakes landing in Bermuda and went into a series of 360-degree spins down the runway. She faced severe icing over the Atlantic, sand in her engine over the Sahara, and chronic malfunctioning of her long-range radio antenna. In Cairo, she mistakenly landed at a military base, and her plane was immediately surrounded by a squad of armed soldiers who were shocked to see a woman step out of the cockpit. Even though she was in an unofficial race, Mock managed to squeeze in some sightseeing on a few of her 21 stops, her favorite being a camel ride in the Sahara. Her rival, Smith, suffered mechanical problems and had fallen 25 days behind by the time Mock crossed the Pacific Ocean.

When "Charlie's" wheels finally touched down again in Columbus on April 17, 1964, Jerrie Mock was given a hero's welcome by local and state dignitaries, including Governor James A. Rhodes, who dubbed her "Ohio's Golden Eagle." The 38-year-old mother of three had completed her historic round-the-world solo flight in 29 days, 11 hours, and 59 minutes. When asked why she had made the flight, Mock replied, "I did it to give confidence to the little pilot who is being left in the jet stream of the space age." In 1970 Mock published a memoir about her historic adventure, *Three-Eight Charlie*, and *The Spirit of Columbus* remains on permanent display at the Smithsonian Air and Space Museum.

FOOTNOTE

Four years before Jerrie Mock's solo trip around the world, another Jerrie was chosen to be America's first female astronaut. Geraldyn "Jerrie" Cobb helped assemble a team of 12 other women pilots who became the first lady astronaut trainees, or the "Mercury 13." Although Cobb and her fellow trainees passed the same physical and psychological fitness tests as the male astronauts, none of them was allowed to go into space. What kept Cobb's crew grounded? Old-fashioned sexism. Here's John Glenn's answer when he was asked to explain the decision before Congress in 1963: "Men go off and fight the wars and fly the airplanes. Women are not astronauts because of our social order."

A few months later, Valentina Tereshkova of the Soviet Union became the first woman in space.

MOVIE QUOTE QUIZ

Each of these memorable quotes comes from a Vroom-themed movie. Can you name the movies? (Answers are on page 460.)

1. "Flying a plane is no different than riding a bicycle, just a lot harder to put baseball cards in the spokes."

2. "Hey, you know a guy around here with a piss-yellow deuce coupe, supposed to be hot stuff?"

3. "No, there is no terrible way to win. There is only winning."

4. "Mama, cars don't behave. They are behaved upon. Fact is, you demolished that Chrysler all by yourself."

5. "Your theory's fine, but you get this, Mister...that engine's rated at 2,000 horsepower and if I was ever fool enough to let it get started up it'd shake your patched-up pile of junk into a thousand pieces, and cut us up into mincemeat with the propeller."

6. "It's 106 miles to Chicago, we got a full tank of gas, half a pack of cigarettes, it's dark, and we're wearing sunglasses."

7. "Request permission to relieve bladder."

8. "You see, Mr. Scott? In the water, I'm a very skinny lady."

9. "I know I've made some very poor decisions recently, but I can give you my complete assurance that my work will be back to normal. I've still got the greatest enthusiasm and confidence in the mission. And I want to help you."

10. "Here's the first of the day, fellas! To old D. H. Lawrence."

11. "I'm a precision instrument of speed and aerodynamics."

12. "The chain in those handcuffs is high-tensile steel. It'd take you ten minutes to hack through it with this. Now, if you're lucky, you could hack through your ankle in five minutes. Go."

13. "What is this?" "I don't know, I think...I think it's the vast Grand Canyon!"

HONEY, I SHRUNK THE CAR

Art Ingels was just messing around with some spare parts and an old lawnmower. How could he know that he was about to invent the go-kart, a form of racing that kids of all ages could enjoy?

ON YOUR MARK

The post–World War II economic boom brought Formula One auto racing to the United States. But as the popularity of grand prix racing took off, so did the costs of entry. Many aspiring U.S. drivers and designers found themselves sidelined as European makers such as Alfa Romeo, Ferrari, and Maserati dominated the sport. Soaring ticket prices kept many fans estranged from their newfound love as well. Art Ingels saw that the average American's need for speed wasn't being met. As someone who worked as a race car designer for famed Indy Car builder Kurtis Kraft, he was in a unique position to do something about it.

GET SET

In 1956 Ingels spent most of his free time out in the garage of his suburban Echo Park, California, home with friend and fellow car enthusiast Lou Borelli. Their intent was to build a new competition race car. Instead they cobbled together an invention that would change the face of motorsports. Using the same steel tubing that went into his race cars, Ingels welded together a miniature frame consisting of two straight side rails with a single axle in front and a pair of rear stub axles. The pair added a rudimentary steering and seat hoop, a three-spoke steering wheel, and a couple of drag links. Then Borelli welded on the pièce de résistance—a two-stroke 2.5-hp West Bend 750 engine pirated from an old lawn mower. The gas tank sat high on the seat back, and an accelerator pedal activated a gravity feed to carry fuel to the rear-mounted motor that, in turn, powered the left rear wheel using a simple countershaft. There was no brake pedal. Instead,

Go-karts and minibikes are considered toys and don't require registration.

pulling a handle located on the right side of the frame jammed a brake pad against a disc welded to the right rear wheel. It was the world's first go-kart.

GO!

Ingels and Borelli took their new kart to nearby Baxter Street for its inaugural run. The street was a 100-yard straightaway culminating in a steep climb with a sharp turn to the left. Borelli zipped up the hill with ease, but the lawn mower engine had trouble getting Ingels's 210 pounds up the incline. Borelli, a maintenance engineer for Standard Oil, removed the motor and took it home to his workshop. After a few weeks of tweaking, he returned with a much improved engine that easily moved his friend's extra heft.

EVERYONE GETS IN THE GAME

Later that month, Ingels showed off the kart while working the pits at Pomona Raceway, where it was spotted by race car enthusiast and entrepreneur Duffy Livingstone. Seeing the commercial possibilities of the invention, Livingstone founded Go Kart Mfg. Co. in 1958. Livingstone was so successful that he eventually became known as the "Father of Karting."

Not to be left behind, Ingels tried to convince his boss, Frank Kurtis, to invest in a new kart manufacturing venture. Kurtis declined, so Ingels quit his job and, with Borelli, founded Caretta Works to build karts full-time. In addition to selling their very first go-kart, the two built and sold five more in time for Christmas in 1958.

Having missed his first opportunity, Kurtis got into the game in 1959, marketing the Kurtis Kart, complete with four-wheel torsion bar suspension. In a surprising twist of fate, a decade after its creation, Ingels's and Borelli's first kart came back to them as a partial trade-in on a new Caretta Kart in 1966. The inventors donated it to England's *Karting Magazine* in 1968, where it still graces the publication's offices.

DO-IT-YOURSELF RACING

Kart racing, or "karting," became a quickly expanding sport as hobbyists by the thousands built karts in their garages. For less

World's fastest lawnmower: Bob Cleveland's modified Snapper. In 2006 it hit about 80 mph.

than $200, an enthusiast could assemble a kart, purchase a helmet and a spare tire, pay the entry fee, and still have money left over for a burger and soda after the race. In the decades since 1957, the number of karts has swelled from fewer than a dozen to more than 100,000, in the following classifications:

• **Sprint Karting.** The original and most popular form of karting. Sprints take place on closed asphalt tracks that vary in distance between ¼ and ¾ of a mile (although some races are run on city streets). Classes include two-cycle and four-cycle single-cylinder engines between 50cc and 125cc, with top speeds exceeding 60 mph. Over 95 percent of professional race car drivers got their start in a sprint kart, including NASCAR champions Kyle Petty and Darryl Waltrip, and Formula One legend Michael Schumacher.

• **Speedway or Oval Track.** Karts with full wings and fairings zip around a short oval between ⅒ and ⅕ of a mile in length. Tracks vary from dirt to asphalt, while the two- and four-cycle karts have a special "off-set" design that allows them to hold a circle. A used speedway kart costs around $1,500.

• **Indoor Karting.** There are more than 130 indoor karting tracks in the United States alone. The karts are similar to outdoor sprint karts but include extra bumpers and other safety features. Gas or electric carts travel at speeds upwards of 40 mph. It is estimated that 1.5 million people participate in indoor karting every year.

• **Enduro Racing.** This is the karting world's version of Daytona and Laguna Seca. Enduro karts are built for speeds up to 90 mph, with the drivers lying nearly flat on their backs to decrease wind resistance and increase lap times. Races take place on professional tracks and last anywhere from 30 minutes to one hour. An entry-level kart can start at $2,000; but dual-engine or 125cc "shifter" motor-equipped karts are much more expensive, and much faster—a top-of-the-line shifter cart can go 160 mph!

• **Off-road.** The fastest-selling and newest vehicles in the sport. Similar to four-wheel ATVs, they offer single and dual seat designs. Races take place on marked dirt courses and trails.

• **Jr. Dragster.** Half-scale versions of Top Fuel dragsters with four-

In 2008 stuntman Liu Suozhu drove across a river by balancing the car on two steel cables.

stroke, single-cylinder, 5-hp engines and steel tube chassis propel kids 8 to 17 years old down an ⅛-mile track at speeds of up to 85 mph. Over 5,000 youngsters compete annually on 140 NHRA member tracks. Nearly 35 percent of the racers are girls.

• **Karting World Championship.** The championship is overseen annually by the Commission Internationale de Karting (CIK). Each year, kart racers from around the world show off their racing skills and test their mettle against competitors in five rounds, each held in a different country. Beginning in 2007, 100cc water-cooled Formula A karts were replaced by 125cc Touch-and-Go (TaG) KF-type karts.

* * *

THE GOLDEN RECORD

In 1977 NASA launched the Voyager space probes to explore not only Jupiter and Saturn but the outer solar system and beyond. Placed inside each craft was a 12-inch gold-plated copper phonograph record containing sounds and images from Earth. Famed astrophysicist and popular science writer Carl Sagan chaired the committee that chose what would go into, as he put it, "a message in a bottle tossed into the cosmic sea."

The golden record has people saying hello in 55 different languages, from extinct Sumerian to modern Chinese Wu. There are 115 sounds from nature: animals, birds, humpback whales, wind, surf, and thunder. Musical selections from different cultures include a Zairean pygmy initiation song, Peruvian panpipes, Beethoven's Fifth Symphony and Chuck Berry's "Johnny B. Goode." The record is encased in an aluminum jacket and includes a needle and cartridge with instructive pictures showing how to play it. Said Sagan, "A billion years from now, when everything on Earth we've ever made has crumbled into dust, when the continents have changed beyond recognition and our species is unimaginably altered or extinct, the Voyager record will speak for us."

Voyager II is presently 8.85 billion miles away from Earth, traveling into the universe at 50,000 mph. It and sister probe *Voyager I* are still transmitting data back to Earth.

By 1930 most of the technology used in automobiles today had already been invented.

NASCAR TROPHIES

What do you get when you win a NASCAR race? Well, it depends on the track.

TRACK: Martinsville Speedway

TROPHY: Grandfather clock

TALE: In 1964 racetrack founder Clay Earles got the idea of presenting winners with a grandfather clock. As he said, "Very few people have them and everyone wants one." Along with telling time, these unique clocks play "God Bless America" and "America the Beautiful." Richard "The King" Petty won his first in 1967 and loved it so much that he ordered several more of the $11,000 clocks for relatives and friends. Little did Petty know that he would go on to win 15 more.

TRACK: Memphis International Speedway

TROPHY: Elvis statue

TALE: Memphis, home to Graceland and all that is Elvis, proudly presents its race winners with a 27-inch-tall, 60-pound bronze statue of the King performing on a checkerboard stage. It's a replica of a statue on Beale Street, the only carved image of Elvis approved by the Presley estate.

TRACK: Nashville Superspeedway

TROPHY: Gibson Les Paul guitar

TALE: This electric guitar is covered with racing images hand-painted by NASCAR's official artist, Sam Bass. In 2009, when notorious bad boy Kyle Busch sailed into the victory lane after winning the Federated Auto Parts 300 NASCAR Nationwide Series, he made like a rock star and smashed his Les Paul trophy to smithereens in front of a horrified crowd. No one was amused, least of all Sam Bass.

TRACK: Las Vegas Motor Speedway

TROPHY: Jewel-encrusted belt

TALE: This enormous championship belt featuring a gold crest encrusted with rubies and diamonds is big and sparkly enough to be envied by any pro wrestler or boxer. Estimated value: $3,000.

TRACK: Daytona International Speedway
TROPHY: Harley J. Earl trophy
TALE: Winning the Daytona 500 is a career-making achievement, so it makes sense that the trophy, named after General Motors designer Harley J. Earl, is one of the most sought-after in racing. It's a miniature replica of a 1954 Firebird One on a black base shaped like Daytona's famous two-and-a-half-mile tri-oval.

TRACK: Dover International Speedway
TROPHY: Miles the Monster
TALE: Dover is known as the "Monster Mile," so it's only fitting that its trophy should be a 30-inch-tall Hulk-like sandstone statue clenching its ham-sized fists and glaring with glowing red eyes.

TRACK: Texas Motor Speedway
TROPHY: Beretta Jubilee 12-gauge shotgun
TALE: The top qualifier at each of the Lone Star State races walks away with this hand-carved firearm worth a whopping $65,000. Ladies and gents, start your engines—and duck!

TRACK: Atlanta Motor Speedway
TROPHY: Giant wildlife sculptures
TALE: Although Bass Pro Shops no longer sponsors a NASCAR event in Atlanta, its huge wildlife trophies are legendary. Each year a life-size statue of a grizzly bear (10 feet tall, 600 pounds), a pair of bald eagles, or a big-mouth bass perched on a four-foot-tall wood block would be presented to the winner, who must have accepted it with one thought running through his head: "Where am I going to put this thing?"

* * *

SHIP OR FLOATING CITY?

Some modern battleships require a crew of 6,000 to go to sea and weigh as much as 1,000 jumbo jets.

OKLAHOMA BIG 10

When it comes to matters of "vroom," the Sooner State has a surprising number of firsts to its credit.

• Oklahoma has produced more astronauts than any other state: eight.

• The world's first parking meter was installed in Oklahoma City on July 16, 1935.

• The biggest oil storage depot in the world is in Cushing. The 46.3 million barrels stored here will make enough gasoline to fill up half the cars in the United States.

• Oklahoma City's airports are named for two famous Oklahomans who died in the same airplane crash. Entertainer Will Rogers and aviator Wiley Post were attempting a flight around the world when their plane went down in Alaska in 1935.

• On July 5, 1943, a B-17 from a nearby army base dropped six practice bombs on Boise City, making it the only city in the lower 48 to be bombed during World War II. The pilot mistook the city lights for the target.

• The first yield sign was installed in Tulsa in 1950.

• Television's first Doppler radar tornado warning was issued from Elmore in 1982.

• Oklahoma has more miles of drivable road on old Route 66 than any other state.

• Burns Flat is home of the Oklahoma Spaceport, America's first inland launch pad for horizontal takeoffs and landings of vehicles like the space shuttle.

• There is an operating oil well on the state capitol lawn. It's called Capitol Site No. 1.

...that potential buyers must pass a background check.

CAR FINS

During the jet age, auto buyers wanted their cars to break the style barrier just like jets were breaking the sound barrier overhead.

LIGHTNING STRIKES

On a spring morning in 1941, Harley Earl and three designers from the Art & Color Section of General Motors went to Selfridge Field outside Detroit to take a look at a top-secret fighter plane. The Lockheed P-38 Lightning was a brand-new, ultra-modern twin tailed aircraft. Senior designer Bill Mitchell said they were particularly struck by the way the lines of the twin tail booms carried through from nose to tail. The designers also took note of the air intakes on the sides of each boom, as well as the stubby, vertical fins. They spent the next few months drawing sleek-looking new automobiles inspired by the P-38. But business as usual at GM came to a halt on December 7, 1941, when the Japanese bombed Pearl Harbor. Every GM division redirected its focus to supplying tanks and other vehicles for the war effort.

FARM TEAM

Fast-forward to 1944, when Frank Hershey returned from the war and became the senior designer under Harley Earl in the Cadillac division. Hershey submitted several design concepts that incorporated tail fins inspired by the P-38, but Earl found the fins too extreme. Just before Thanksgiving 1945, the United Auto Workers went on strike. Since the Cadillac design team couldn't go in to work at headquarters due to the lockout, Hershey invited them to Winkler Mill, his 60-acre farm. Out in the country, without corporate suits hovering over them, the designers created the Cadillac they wanted to build—a super-modern, jet-age-inspired ride with fins. Of course, it still had all the things that said "Cadillac"—the name in script along the front body, the goddess embossed on the hood, V emblem with crest up front, egg-crate grille, and massive "sombrero" wheel covers. Nonetheless, it was something new and wondrous. They sculpted a full-size clay model of their vision and invited Harley Earl and Cadillac general manager Nicholas Dreystadt to take a look at it.

Only Canadian to win a NASCAR Cup race: Earl Ross, in 1974.

FINTASTIC!

Earl had three words for Hershey when he saw the fins: "Take them off." Hershey started working on the front-end alterations first. When Earl returned two days later and saw the fins still there, he told Hershey that if he didn't remove them immediately, he would be fired. Once again Hershey hesitated—luckily, because it turned out that GM president Charlie Wilson and chairman Alfred P. Sloan liked the fins. Sloan was convinced the fins would become an effective stylistic trademark for Cadillac—and he was right.

When the 1948 Cadillac premiered, it caused a sensation in the auto industry. Packard, Chrysler, Ford, and others instantly started designing their own finned cars. The new look became such a craze that mail-order houses began selling fins that could be mounted on the rear fenders of older Fords and Chevys.

LOOK OF THE '50s

Throughout the 1950s, fins were the rage. By 1959 every major automobile manufacturer in the world had released at least one car with fins. Even staid Mercedes-Benz offered fins on its 1959 Heckflosse ("Fintail") sedans. As for Cadillac, its fins grew bigger and bigger. They reached their apogee in 1959 with the chrome-covered, low-bodied Coupe de Ville sedan and the Eldorado Biarritz convertible. Cadillac's extremely long and knife-sharp tailfins housed what became known as double-bullet taillights, giving the cars a rocket-powered look that moved the brand out of the jet age into the space age.

After 1960, however, the craze died out. Fins on most automobiles, with the exception of diehards Plymouth and DeSoto, started diminishing in size. By 1965 the excessive chrome, the double-bullet taillights, and the sweeping fins were all gone, yielding to a sleeker, more streamlined fashion throughout the industry. Cadillac's domination of the luxury-car market faded along with its fins.

* * *

THE MACH SYSTEM...

...was devised in 1877 by Austrian physicist Ernst Mach.

"Jam jar" and "La-Di-Dah" are Cockney rhyming slang for "car."

GRAPES AND ORDIES

A guide to who's who on the flight deck of an aircraft carrier.

CONTROLLED CHAOS

More than 200 people work the flight deck of an aircraft carrier. It's one of the few workplaces in the world where being blown overboard or sucked into a jet engine is a real possibility. To control the chaos, the crew members wear different colored "cranials": ball-shaped crash helmets that tell everyone who they are and what their job is.

YELLOW: Aircraft Handling Officers, Plane Directors.

"Yellows" are the only people authorized to control the movement of airplanes aboard a carrier, and they communicate mostly through hand and body signals. They are "valet parkers," and use a scale model of the flight deck to keep track of the 80-plus aircraft, 20 of which might be in motion at any given time.

RED: Explosive Ordnance Controllers, Crash and Salvage crews. Sometimes called "Ordies".

Life on a carrier deck is like a ballet, except that some dancers maneuver hoses full of jet fuel around speeding aircraft, and others carry live bombs. A typical carrier can hold 4,000 bombs and missiles in its "bomb-farm."

BLUE: Elevator Operators, Tractor Drivers, Messengers.

"Blues" put out the wheel chocks that keep planes from rolling around on deck. They also tow planes to and from the four 4,000-square-foot elevators connecting the flight deck and hangar bay. The elevators can move two planes at a time in about 15 seconds.

GREEN: Helicopter Support, Cat/Arrest Crew, Cargo Handlers.

"Greenies" run the Cat-Shot, a pressurized steam-catapult that can take a jet from 0 to 150 mph in 1.5 seconds. They also operate the wire-arrest landing system, a series of four braided steel cables that puts them just yards from a jet's afterburners. On-deck helicopter teams also wear green, and so do invited media and photographers.

First haircut in space? *Skylab 2* astronaut Paul Weitz got a trim from Pete Conrad in 1973.

WHITE: Plane Inspectors, Liquid Oxygen Crew, Medical Staff.
These crew members control all safety issues onboard, from medical emergencies to landing procedures with the "meatball," a setup of lights and mirrors that show a pilot when he's on the right approach to land.

PURPLE: Aviation Fuel Handlers.
A carrier can hold up to 3 million pounds of jet fuel, and "Grapes" refuel and defuel planes using gas pumps set above and below the deck. All the fuel lines are also purple. In addition, Grapes keep towing tractors gassed up and the launch catapult well greased.

BROWN: Air Wing Plane Captains, Air Wing Line Leading Petty Officers.
These are the mechanics and plane inspectors who do quality control to make sure a squadron's planes are always ready to fly.

WHO'S IN CHARGE?
Five officers command the flight deck:

- **Air Boss:** This officer, usually a commander, heads up the control tower. He's on the radio, in charge of everything that happens on the flight deck.
- **Mini-Boss:** The Air Boss's assistant.
- **Handler:** Controls the parade of aircraft in and out of the hangar bay. Yellows work for the Handler.
- **Air Bos'n:** Supervises crash-response teams and other aircraft-emergency responders.
- **Landing Signal Officer (LSO):** The LSO directs the final approach and landing of every plane on a carrier. This is the officer who tells each incoming pilot, "Call the ball"—meaning, "Make sure you can see the landing-light system."

* * *

"How better can I describe a cat-shot (catapult-shot off a carrier deck) than saying that it's like going from 0 to 130 in 1.5 seconds?"

—Lt. Matt Powers, USN

HOVERCRAFT

The dream of levitating in our own personal cars hasn't come true yet, but some handy uses have been found for air-cushioned rides.

BLOWING AIR

Like many modern marvels, the hovercraft was an idea that had to wait for technology to catch up with it. The "ground effect" principle—that trapping air between the ground and a vehicle creates a cushion of air that floats the vehicle, making it easier to propel forward—has been understood for centuries. In 1716, Swedish scientist Emmanuel Swedenborg drew plans for an air-cushioned vehicle that resembled an upside-down boat with a cockpit in its center. Oar-like scoops would push air under the boat on each downward stroke to raise the hull out of the water and let it ride on the compressed air being generated by the scoops. But there was no way a human being could row the scoops fast enough to make it work.

The first boat incorporating air-cushion technology was launched in 1915 by Austrian engineer Dagobert Müller von Thomamühl. With a top speed of 32 knots, the airfoil-shaped *Versuchsgleitboot* was to become a fast torpedo boat for the Austro-Hungarian navy. An aircraft engine blew lifting air under the bow while four others turned two submerged marine screws to move it forward. The craft was tested but never saw action in World War I.

Finnish engineer Toivo J. Kaario is credited with building the first true hovercraft in 1937, the *Pintaliitäjä* (Surface Soarer). For lack of funding, it never got beyond the prototype stage. It was Englishman Sir Christopher Cockerell who proved that a practical hovercraft could be made when he patented his design in 1952.

MOMENTUM CURTAIN

To demonstrate how his hovercraft would work, Cockerell used an air blower, a couple of tin cans (one smaller than the other), and a scale. Cockerell slipped the smaller can inside the larger one, leaving a space between the cans. He cut a hole in the top of the big can, attached the air blower and pointed the open ends at the scale. Air flowed over the top of the inside can and down the

According to the Rubber Manufacturers' Association...

space between the cans onto the scale. Cockerell's measurements showed that by channeling the air into a narrow stream, three times the pressure was created than by blowing a wide, unfocused blast of air. Plus, the ring of high pressure acted like a barrier between the air inside and outside of the ring. He called this effect the "momentum curtain." Applied to a hovercraft, it would keep high-pressure air trapped beneath it, providing a lot more lifting power with greater efficiency.

HOVER-WHATSIS?

Cockerell promptly took his newly patented prototype to the British government, which took one look and immediately classified it top secret. But no one seemed to know what to do with it. "The Navy said it was a plane, not a boat," Cockerell recalled. "The Air Force said it was a boat, not a plane. And the Army were plain not interested."

So Cockerell went commercial and built the Saunders Roe Nautical 1, which crossed the English Channel in two hours on July 25, 1959. The SR.N1 looked like an elongated Frisbee, 31 feet long by 25 feet wide, with a 10-foot-diameter air-intake and engine housing sitting amidships. Cruising speed was 18 to 20 knots.

Within three years, other British manufacturers had licensed Cockerell's patent and were turning out a dizzying variety of commercial and recreational hovercraft. The British have dominated the industry ever since. In 1962 the Vickers VA-3 became the first passenger (and mail) hovercraft, when it began service across the River Dee in Wales. The 24-seater was 56 feet long, with two turbine engines that made it skim along at 60 knots.

SKIRTING THE ISSUE

Both the SR.N1 and the Vickers VA-3 rode a mere 9 inches above the surface of the water. More vertical lift was achieved by dropping a double-walled, flexible rubber skirt (invented by American Norman McCreary for a vehicle called the Glidemobile) down from the hull to channel the airstream blowing from the hull vents. The 4-foot-tall skirts running beneath the hull did a better job of maintaining a good seal with the ground or water. Now a hovercraft could climb over obstacles almost as high as its skirts, whether on waves or on uneven terrain.

...more than 85% of drivers don't know how to check their tire pressure.

That skirt led to another innovation, the bag skirt. The skirts were replaced by a tube, much like a bicycle tire inner tube, that ran underneath the hull. Vents were cut into the tube to direct pressurized air underneath the hull for lift. Multiple, smaller finger skirts, like air-filled ruffles, were added to the bottom of the main bag skirt, with air blowing between the two skirt systems. The individual finger sections quickly adjusted to surface changes, providing an even smoother ride over uneven surfaces.

HOVER FERRIES

By the mid-1960s, hovercraft ferries like the "Mountbatten"-class *Princess Anne* and *Princess Margaret*, at 185 feet the world's largest civilian hovercraft, were hauling 418 passengers and 60 cars across the English Channel at over 65 knots. However, in a world of ever-rising oil prices, more fuel-efficient high-speed catamaran ferries crowded out the hovercraft, and they were all retired by 2000.

Except one. The world's longest-running hovercraft service still crosses the Solent Strait between Portsmouth and Ryde, on the Isle of Wight. The Solent's low tides take the sea too far out for a ship to moor near roads or bus routes. But a hovercraft can easily glide over the exposed flats at low tide and "dock" at the hoverport launch ramp, within walking distance to town. Over 26 million people have used the service since 1965.

THE ULTIMATE ATV

Hovercraft excel at moving large loads over rough terrain like swamps, mud, or ice. They are used by coast guards around the world because they are so adaptable to shifting tides and coastlines. Cargo hovercraft can haul up to 350 tons; non-propelled hover barges, up to 2,500 tons. Despite their massive size, they are gentle on the surface beneath them. While hovering, the barges exert a mere 1 psi of ground pressure. (By comparison, the average human footprint is 8 psi.) This makes them a good choice for hauling cargo to sensitive environments, such as the Alaskan pipeline or oil-drilling platforms on wetlands. Since 1998 the U.S. Postal Service has been using a hovercraft to deliver mail in snowbound areas of northern Alaska. And hovercraft are especially well suited to flood rescue operations and relief missions to regions, such as Sudan, that have few usable roads.

Legendary football coach Knute Rockne died in a Fokker Trimotor plane crash in Kansas (1931).

SPACE BUGGY

Three unusual vehicles have been parked on the moon for 20 years, abandoned and neglected—but not forgotten.

GIMME A LIFT

It was *Apollo 14* astronaut Alan Shepard who convinced NASA that if men were going to work on the moon, they needed the lunar equivalent of a pickup truck. As part of their assigned tasks, Shepard and Edgar Mitchell were required to lug scientific equipment a mile across the lunar surface, and they had to climb 400 feet up the rim of Cone Crater in the process. After two hours and 10 minutes, the astronauts were still huffing and puffing up the side of the crater. They were forced to turn back the mission when ground control grew alarmed at the spike in their heart rates from the exertion. It became clear that some kind of vehicle was required to increase the range of their surface explorations and make those forays safer.

MOON RIDE

NASA decided to have a vehicle available for the next Apollo mission, scheduled for July 1971. The $19 million contract (which would swell to $38 million with overruns) to develop and build four Lunar Roving Vehicles was awarded to Boeing. The project presented unique challenges. First of all, since flight space on the Apollo spacecraft was at a premium, the rover had to be ultra-light and capable of folding up like a portable bicycle. Since gravity on the moon is only one-sixth that of Earth, the rover needed only to be strong enough to bear one-sixth the weight of the astronauts and their gear—but this meant it couldn't be tested on Earth. So no one could really know if the vehicle could do what it was supposed to do until Apollo astronauts set it up on the moon, clambered onboard, and flipped the Go switch.

It took Boeing engineers 17 months. What they came up with was a 10-foot vehicle that weighed a mere 460 pounds but could bear 1,080 pounds. Each of its four wheels was powered by a ¼-hp electric motor linked to two 36-volt battery systems. If one of these broke down, the remaining battery had enough juice to return the rover to base. Front and rear wheels were steered by a T-shaped controller set in the middle of the console between the two astronauts. To go forward, the controller was pushed forward; toggling it to either side turned it left or right. Pulling back on the controller put on the brakes. The lunar rover had a top speed of 10 mph and a battery range of 78 hours. It could go up 20-degree hills and climb over obstacles and small crevasses. There were seatbelts, a radio, and TV cameras to send info back to Mission Control, and an onboard navigation system that took continual readings off the sun to tell riders exactly how to get back to the lunar module.

ON THE MOON

• **Apollo 15.** When David Scott and James Irwin landed the Lunar Module near Hadley Rille on July 30, 1971, and deployed the Lunar Roving Vehicle, they found that they could steer with only the rear wheels. Even so, they were able to drive 2½ miles down the Rille (a long groove in the lunar surface) collecting rock samples. The ride was so bumpy that they would have been thrown from the rover without the weight of the rocks. When they left the moon, they pointed the rover, with its TV camera on, at the Lunar Module so it could transmit the sight of the astronauts lifting off.

• **Apollo 16.** Rover #2 was brought up in April 1972. There was no way to reuse a rover from the previous mission because missions landed hundreds of miles apart. Upon arriving at Cayley Basin, astronaut John Young spun the rover in tight circles to "test the wheel grip." The rear mudguard fell off, covering the riders with a cloud of moon dust.

• **Apollo 17.** On the last manned mission to the moon, Rover #3 performed flawlessly, covering 22 miles and hauling 250 pounds of lunar rock back to the spaceship. Along the way, Commander Cernan set a moon land speed record of 11.3 mph. Cernan and Harrison Schmitt parked their LRV-3 and lifted off in the Lunar Module on December 19, 1972.

* * *

Karl Benz (1844–1929), founder of Mercedes-Benz, was against all forms of auto racing.

Mr. Toad, in Kenneth Grahame's *The Wind in the Willows*, manages to smash up seven cars.

THE STALL OF FAME

One of Uncle John's mottos: "When you gotta go, you gotta go—unless you're on a train."

NO FLUSHING!

In the early 1930s, William O. Douglas and his fellow law-school professor Thurman Arnold were riding on the New Haven Railroad when Douglas went to use the restroom. While there, he saw the advisory sign that every railroad commuter knew by heart: "Passengers will please refrain from flushing toilets while the train is standing in or passing through the station." At the time, train toilets flushed directly onto the tracks, which was fine way out in the country but pretty disgusting in a station.

Tickled by the musicality of the phrase, Douglas decided to put it to music. Arnold suggested a silly tune used in cartoons, Dvořák's "Humoresque Number 7." So the duo improvised a goofy love-song spoof that became a surprising hit. Soon everyone was singing it, adding their own, often bawdy, lyrics. But Douglas swore in his autobiography, *Go East, Young Man*, that he and Arnold were the original authors. Of course, we believe him. After all, he was the longest-sitting Supreme Court Justice.

Passengers will please refrain from flushing toilets while the train
Is in the station. Darling, I love you!
We encourage constipation while the train is in the station,
Moonlight always makes me think of you.
If you wish to pass some water, kindly call the Pullman porter,
He'll place a vessel in the vestibule.
If the porter isn't here, try the platform in the rear—
The one in front is likely to be full.
If the ladies' room be taken, never feel the least forsaken,
Never show a sign of sad defeat.
Try the men's room in the hall, and if some man has had the call,
He'll courteously relinquish you his seat.
If these efforts are in vain, then simply break a window pane—
A novel method used by very few.
My occupation after dark is goosing statues in the park,
If Sherman's horse can take it, why can't you?

Are you flying at "nose-picking speed"? In Navy lingo, you're going pointlessly slow.

MR. MOTOR RACING

Considered the greatest driver to never win a World Championship, at 81 years old, Stirling Moss remains the epitome of class in the sport of motor racing.

ROAD WARRIOR

British driver Stirling Crauford Moss (b. 1929) won over 200 international races, 16 of them Grand Prix events, in a career stretching from 1948 to 1962. Unlike some modern racers and many American drivers, who stick to Formula One or NASCAR "stocks" exclusively, Moss raced all kinds of cars on all kinds of tracks, from sports car endurance rallies like Le Mans or the Targa Florio to the elite Formula One events like the Grand Prix de Monte Carlo. At times it seemed as if he didn't care what he was driving or where—he just loved to race.

Moss came to racing cars naturally. Both parents were avid amateur racers, his mother in rallies and trials, his dad even going so far as to race in the 1924 Indy 500. (Alfred Moss was attending the Indian Dental School, making him the first and so far only dentist to race in the Indy 500. He placed a respectable 12th.) Moss fell in love with Cooper cars as a teen and talked his parents into helping him buy a Cooper 500 as his first racer; he maintained an association with Cooper throughout his career.

When he turned professional at 18, Moss's success with the Cooper 500 drew the attention of racing teams across Europe, and by the time the Formula One World Championship began in 1950 he was contracted to drive for the famed Scuderia Ferrari. Just before his first race at Bari, his car was given to another driver. Although Ferrari realized later they'd made a mistake and tried to recruit him again, he never forgave them for their cavalier treatment, making a point of racing only for other, preferably British, teams. But his stubborn refusal to race for the team with the best cars would come back to haunt Moss.

TAKING THE CHALLENGE

In the early 1950s, Moss racked up wins with Maserati, Cooper,

Porsche, Jaguar, and Mercedes. His win at the 1955 Mille Miglia was as historic as it was record-breaking. One of the greatest races, the Mille Miglia was a single lap 1,000 miles long, beginning and ending in Brescia, Italy. Drivers always rode with a co-driver, who served as navigator and mechanic, ready to change a tire or wheel when necessary since support teams were usually far behind.

It was a consummate test of driver and machine. When Juan Fangio finished second in 1953, he was steering his Alfa with one wheel, the track rod for the other having broken. The course was full of blind corners and other traffic hazards that made finishing at all a dubious proposition. A huge advantage fell to drivers who knew the route, which automatically gave Italian drivers the edge since they could train on the course.

SECRET WEAPON

Moss decided that the only way he could beat the Italians was to "know" the course better than they did—which he accomplished by having co-driver Denis Jenkinson take copious notes of every bend, dip, blind curve, and potential obstacle as they drove the course ahead of time. Although this practice is common in rally racing today, no one had ever thought of it before. As a result of his planning, when Moss and Jenkinson left the start in their Mercedes 300 SLR, Moss could focus all of his skill on driving and not worry about what might be coming up. Jenkinson would tell him, "You can take this curve at full speed, but ease off coming off the 'S' in the village, there's a dip," and so forth, and Moss would floor it, hitting 170 mph on the straights and barrelling through the curves.

As the hours clicked by, they passed more and more cars and realized their plan was working. Jenkinson later wrote, "Moss was driving right on the limit of adhesion all the time, sometimes over the limit, driving in that awe-inspiring narrow margin that you enter just before you have a crash—unless you have the Moss skill." When they came across the finish line, the great Juan Manuel Fangio was a half hour behind them. They'd won in 10 hours, 7 minutes, and 48 seconds, a record that was never beaten. As the first Britons to win the Mille Miglia, they became national heroes. Mercedes commemorated the victory by naming the ultimate edition of the Mercedes 300 SLR number "722"—Moss's number in the race.

GOOD SPORT

Ironically, it was a supreme act of sportsmanship that earned Moss the nickname "Mr. Motor Racing." In the 1958 Grand Prix of Portugal, Moss was dueling with fellow Briton Mike Hawthorn not only for that race but for the World Championship. During the race, Moss saw Hawthorn spin out and then recover his car and continue the race. Moss went on to win, while Hawthorn took second. Then race officials accused Hawthorn of cheating by restarting his car incorrectly and threatened to strip him of the precious seven World Championship points he'd won. Moss came to Hawthorn's defense, and the challenge was denied. At the season's end, Hawthorn nipped the championship from Moss by a single point. Had Moss let the challenge stand, he would have had his World Championship. Moss always insisted that it was more important to win by the rules than simply to win.

GRAND OLD MAN

That was the closest Moss came to taking a World Championship, although he finished second four times. He continued to race, with less and less success due to the weaker, mostly British cars he felt compelled to support. He did score exciting wins at Nurburgring and Monte Carlo in 1961, but later that year he suffered a bad crash at Greenwood that left him in a coma for a month. When he came back to the track, the old magic wasn't there and Moss decided to retire from professional racing. He was only 33.

He didn't quit, though. Moss remains one of the most popular and best-loved figures in racing, appearing up until the age of 81 in historic car rallies and races. His books became best sellers, and he traveled the world as a goodwill ambassador for motor sports. Although he supports making cars and courses safe, he's admitted to a nostalgia for the wilder, less regulated days.

"To race a car through a turn at maximum speed is difficult," Moss says, "but to race a car at maximum speed through that same turn when there is a brick wall on one side and a precipice on the other....Ah, that's an achievement."

In *The Big Lebowski*, The Dude's car—stolen, trashed, set afire—is a 1973 Ford Gran Torino.

THE CAR THAT SAVED A CITY

Akron, Ohio, is so associated with tires that it's been called the "Rubber Capital of the World" But it was once in danger...

TIRE CITY

In 1925 the business of Akron was rubber. The industrial city of 208,000 was home to four of the biggest tire makers in the world: Goodyear, B.F. Goodrich, Firestone, and General Tire. Business was booming, especially in the new balloon tires that B.F. Goodrich touted as the best way to "cushion yourself against rough travel." When Cap dePaolo won the 1925 Indy 500 using Firestone balloon tires, sales of the tires went up for all four manufacturers. Factories were working overtime, and it seemed the good times would last forever.

In 1928, however, a lawsuit was filed by the Steel Wheel Corp. of Detroit against Goodrich, demanding that the Ohio tire maker stop making its popular Silvertown balloon tire. A Michigan inventor, Alden L. Putnam, had received a patent in 1925 for the balloon tire. In 1928 Steel Wheel gained control of the patent and set out to squash the competition. "Should the court ruling favor the Steel Wheel firm," the *Detroit Free Press* reported, "millions of dollars in damages will be involved." Executives at Goodyear, Firestone, and General Tire knew that if Steel Wheel Corp. won its lawsuit against Goodrich, they would be next in line. The tire industry, Akron's single largest employer, would be wiped out in a matter of months.

SMILING RALPH

Salvation came in the form of a former race car driver and neophyte carmaker, Ralph K. Mulford, known as "Smiling Ralph." Born in Brooklyn in 1884, Mulford rose quickly to the ranks of top drivers in the early years of racing, taking national driving championships in 1911 and 1918. He was best known for placing second at the controversial second running of the Indy 500 in 1911. Some sportswriters and fans claimed that bad officiating had robbed Mulford of the victory when he received the checkered flag ahead of rival Ray Harroun but was then instructed to take three "safety" laps. When he pulled into the pits, Harroun was already being congratulated by the crowd.

Mulford took the setback in stride and turned his focus to carmaking. In 1917 he built a 10-foot, two-seat runabout called the Mulford Special Roadster. And it was this little car that saved the city of Akron.

TELL IT TO THE JUDGE

Judge Arthur Tuttle presided over "Steel Wheel Corp. vs. B.F. Goodrich Tire Company" in federal court in Detroit. Mulford came to Michigan to testify on behalf of the Ohio tire maker, and told this story: In 1919 Mulford had brought his Special Roadster to the B.F. Goodrich plant in Akron to have it fitted for a pair of the new tires the company was starting to sell—balloon tires. He had seen a similar style at the Goodyear plant the year before, and had even told company officials, "Since there's no name for a tire like these, I'm going to suggest we call them balloon tires." The name stuck.

All of this had taken place six years before Putnam filed for his patent. As proof, Mulford presented a postmarked letter he'd written to his wife shortly after his 1919 visit to Akron that confirmed his story. Judge Tuttle ruled in favor of Goodrich, and thousands of tire workers in Ohio breathed a collective sigh of relief. After reading the verdict, the judge went for a celebratory ride in the Special Roadster with Mulford—a photo of the two men sitting in the roadster grinning at the camera made the front page in the *Detroit Free Press* and other newspapers the next day.

AFTERWORD

Mulford went home to New Jersey and went into the auto repair business. He was inducted into the Indianapolis Motor Speedway Hall of Fame in 1953 and died at age 88 in 1973. The Mulford Special Roadster vanished until 1953, when Goodrich workers preparing to demolish a warehouse found it stored in the building. They were about to throw it away when Rex T. Brown, a former Goodrich employee, recognized it as the car from the famous trial. Todays it's owned by a private collector.

In the United States, only 12.4% of stolen car cases are closed each year.

DICTIONARY OF DRAG

Want to sound like a seasoned drag-racing fan? Here are a few terms to throw around next time you're at the track.

Drag racing: In the 19th century, the main street of a town (often the widest street) was called the "main drag" because horses used to "drag" wagons and carts down it. Drag racing started on city streets before it moved to country roads and finally to specially built drag strips. A drag race is a contest of speed between two vehicles from a standing start over a measured distance. An electronic timing system determines the winner.

Drag strip: A straight racetrack that is usually a quarter of a mile long. The earliest official drag strip, Santa Ana Drags, began running races on an old airfield in 1950.

Dragster: The first dragsters were street cars with bodies "chopped" down (cut away) to reduce weight. Soon dragsters were built specifically for racing, using exotic fuels like nitromethane and methanol, and engines were moved from front to back.

Burnout: Before each race, the driver revs the engine while pressing the brake and "lays rubber," i.e., spins the tires without moving the car forward. This process heats the tires to improve their traction.

Staging: After the burnout, the driver lines up, or "stages," at the starting line.

Christmas tree: A pole holding two columns of lights, one for each racer. At the top, two small amber lights light up when the racer has properly staged. Below these are three large amber lights that illuminate in a countdown sequence, followed by a green light that starts the race.

Red-lighting: If the driver breaks the starting light beam before the green "Go" signal, the red light flashes and that driver is disqualified.

Race format: The loser of a race is eliminated. The winner goes on to challenge other winners until only one champion is left.

Shutdown area: A dragster traveling at 333 mph needs a long track to slow down. Shutdown areas that are too short have been responsible for catastrophic accidents, prompting calls from safety advocates for a 1,000-foot track instead of the traditional ¼-mile (1,320-foot) strip.

National Hot Rod Association: The NHRA was formed in 1951 by Wally Parks. It oversees most of the drag racing events in North America and has 80,000 members, 140 member tracks, 35,000 licensed competitors, and 5,000 events annually.

DRAG RACING CLASSES

Each of the hundreds of classes in drag racing is determined by weight, engine size, fuel, body style, modifications, and other factors. There is even a Junior Dragster class for younger racers. But there are only four professional categories of drag racing:

1. Top Fuel

The fastest accelerating vehicles in the world. The 7,000-hp dragsters are 25-foot-long open-wheeled missiles built out of chromoly (chromium and molybdenum alloy) steel tubing and carbon-fiber composite. They have oversized slick tires in the rear and small tires in front to maximize their straight-line speed. At race-ready trim they weigh about 2,250 pounds. Top Fuel dragsters accelerate to 100 mph in .7 seconds, reaching an average speed of 333 mph, and run the quartermile in less than 4.4 seconds. They're fueled by a mix of 90% nitromethane and 10% methanol, also called racing alcohol. At full throttle, the dragsters consume 1.5 gallons of fuel per second, the same as a fully loaded Boeing 747. Runs cost $1,000 per second. Top Fuel dragsters leave the starting line at five times the force of gravity, the same Gs as a space shuttle launch, and accelerate faster than a fighter jet.

2. Funny Car

They loosely resemble a production-made automobile, but are built out of carbon-fiber composite. Each is a super-charged, fuel-injected, nitromethane-burning machine that is only slightly slower than a Top Fuel dragster. Funny Cars typically cover the quartermile in 4.7 seconds at speeds of up to 330 mph. Like Top Fuel dragsters, they can travel the length of four football fields in less than five seconds. The 17-inch rear tires used for both classes wear out after four to six runs (about 2 miles). At the end of a race, a Funny Car deploys two parachutes to slow down. They create a reverse force seven times greater than gravity.

3. Pro Stock

They are often called "factory hot rods" because they look so much like street cars—but looks can be deceiving. Pro Stocks are some of the most technologically advanced machines in drag racing. They undergo extensive modifications to the cylinder heads, manifold, chassis, and rear suspension. Sometimes called "all-motor" cars because they cannot use turbo-chargers, superchargers, or nitrous oxide, they are carbureted, gas-burning vehicles. A top Pro Stock car can run the quartermile in 6.6 seconds at speeds of more than 208 mph.

4. Pro Stock Motorcycle

The two-wheeled equivalent of Pro Stock cars, these highly modified motorcycles eat up the quartermile in less than 7 seconds at over 195 mph. Each chromoly steel chassis is "skinned" (covered) in a lightweight aerodynamically enhanced replica of the original motorcycle body. The class features a wide variety of makes and models. Engines include the 2-valve, 4-valve, and Harley V-Twin.

* * *

I'LL TAKE IT FROM HERE

Captain: "Got any ideas?"

First Officer: "Actually…not. "

(Cockpit exchange between Captain "Sully" Sullenberger III and First Officer Jeff Skiles on January 15, 2009, after hitting a flock of birds that knocked out both engines shortly after takeoff from La Guardia airport in New York City. Sullenberger guided the disabled jet in a perfect glide onto the Hudson River with no loss of life.)

Controls on exhaust emissions were first introduced 1965, in California.

SELF-FLYING "FORTRESS"

From the wartime archives, here's a strange story.

GHOST RIDERS IN THE SKY

On November 23, 1944, a British anti-aircraft unit in Cortonburg, Belgium, watched a westbound American B-17 "Flying Fortress" bomber pass overhead and make an emergency landing in a nearby plowed field. The crippled plane bounced to a stop with one wingtip dug into the dirt and three of its four engines still running. The men on the ground waited for the pilot and crew to come out, but no one appeared. When they boarded the bomber, they were stunned to find it empty. Fur-lined flight jackets had been left in the cabin, along with half-eaten chocolate bars. A flight log on the navigator's table had the words "Bad Flak" written in it below an entry indicating that the plane had actually returned to England. Strangest of all were a half-dozen parachutes, still onboard and neatly wrapped, ready for use. So what had happened to the crew?

KEEP CALM, CARRY ON

The 8th Air Force Service Command of Belgium sent a team to investigate. The plane's serial number led them to the 91st Bomb Group based in England and the stunning news that the crew was back on base, safe and sound. Apparently, while on a mission to bomb the Merseburg oil refinery in Germany, the plane had developed engine trouble. Then enemy flak knocked out the #3 engine and penetrated the bomb bay, without exploding the bombs. When he realized the ship wasn't going to make it, pilot Lt. Harold R. DeBolt set the plane on auto-pilot heading toward Brussels. The crew dumped everything they could off the plane to lighten it and bailed out, using other parachutes. The B-17's engines corrected themselves, and the *Phantom Fortress* set itself down, with minimal damage, in Belgium.

During the war, there were many stories of a B-17—a superbly designed and very stable plane—flying pilotless long after the crew died or bailed out, but this was the only time a Flying Fortress ever landed itself.

Seattle reporter Richard William coined the name "Flying Fortress" for the Boeing B-17.

A BRIEF HISTORY OF THE POPEMOBILE

When the Holy Father goes for a ride, he goes in (ultraprotected) style.

POPES IN MOTION

Before the invention of the automobile, the pope traveled like most other heads of state—in a horse-drawn carriage. At home in Rome, a ceremonial sedan chair called the *sedia gestatoria* was the pontiff's favored mode of getting around Vatican City. Twelve red-suited footmen called *palafrenieri* carried him on their shoulders to and from papal ceremonies in St. Peter's Basilica. Today that lavish lift is used only to usher a new pope to his coronation.

In 1930 Daimler Benz AG gave Pope Pius XI his first set of papal wheels: a black Mercedes-Benz Nürburg 460 sedan, complete with its own custom throne-chair. Powered by an eight-cylinder in-line engine, the Nürburg 460 had a top speed of 60 mph. The plush throne-chair was covered in fine silk brocade and air-cushioned to soothe the papal tush. The interior paneling was richly carved in burr walnut, and the ceiling was hand-embroidered by Benedictine nuns with an elaborate dove. There was even a push-button communication system that allowed the pope to tell the driver what to do, with instructions that read like an opera score: *sinestra* (left), *destro* (right), *presto* (faster), *adagio* (slower), *volta* (turn), *casa* (home), and *alt* (stop). Known inside the Vatican as the Rome Vehicle, the Nürburg 460 weighed more than two tons and is considered the first Popemobile. For the next 50 years, Pius and his successors were ferried about their papal business in a succession of mostly Mercedes-Benz limousines and sedans designed for comfort and visibility.

Then, on May 13, 1981, everything changed.

PONTIFF PROTECTION

On that Wednesday, Pope John Paul II's windowless white Fiat Campagnola was inching through a throng of worshippers in St.

Peter's Square when a Turkish assassin named Mehmet Ali Agca shot the pope four times with a Browning Hi-Power semiautomatic pistol. The pope survived the attack, but his days of riding in straightforward luxury were over. From then on, the operative word in papal transportation was *protection*.

Understandably, John Paul II took a personal interest in all future Popemobile designs. When he toured Great Britain a year after the assassination attempt, he rode in a 21-ton, 10-wheeled behemoth built by British Leyland. Sheathed in bomb-proof armor, the Leyland Constructor 24-15 was the first papal vehicle to use bulletproof glass. The Holy Father could sit above the roofline of the truck, completely visible to the crowd, and still be fully enclosed. All subsequent Popemobiles have continued or improved upon the features of the Leyland Constructor: three-inch explosive-grade protective glass, a half-inch-thick steel undercarriage, air filters to guard against chemical and biological attacks, and cabins lined with military-grade Kevlar armor.

RIDE, *EL PAPA*, RIDE!

The Popemobile continues to be among the most customized cars on earth. It's one of the only vehicles designed expressly to exhibit the passenger while completely isolating him. Each sparsely decorated vehicle (official color: mystic-white mother-of-pearl) is fitted with an elevated glass bubble with a seat for the pope, and most have extra seats for papal aides and security. The only markings are a small papal crest and the manufacturer's emblem. Pope Benedict's current Mercedes-Benz M-Class SUV has religious imagery of the Madonna and Child on the wall above his seat.

The pope keeps two Popemobiles at the Holy See in Rome; others are scattered throughout the world for use when traveling. The host country chooses the driver, but this position is not honorary: In an emergency, the driver must be able to shuttle the pope at high speed through thick crowds in a heavy vehicle that was not built for speed or handling. Although seldom required to go more than 10 mph, some Popemobiles, like the 2006 VW Phaeton, can hit 150 mph and go 0 to 60 in less than eight seconds.

First time the military F-22 and CV-22 planes were allowed to be filmed:...

IF ONLY CHRIST COULD SEE THIS

There is no official name for the pope's vehicle, but one thing all Popemobiles have in common is their license plate: SCV-1. This is short for *Stato della Citta del Vaticano*, meaning "Vatican City State." The joke around Rome is that SCV really stands for *Se Cristo Vedesse*, "If only Christ could see this." The term *Popemobile* didn't become common until John Paul II's trip to Poland in 1979. Although the pontiff made a personal request to the media in 2002 to stop using what he considered an undignified term, the name stuck, and as recently as 2006, the Vatican itself used the term in its press releases.

Most Popemobiles are gifts from the manufacturer, so they cost the Catholic Church nothing. Mercedes-Benz estimates that if the pope had to pick up the tab himself, a new Popemobile today would set him back over $300,000. How about resale? In 2006 the 21-ton Leyland Popemobile was sold at auction for $70,000—not much, considering that Popemobiles are always kept in pristine condition and are driven less than 400 miles per year.

QUIS TUNC? ("WHAT NEXT?")

Since becoming pope in 2005, Benedict XVI has urged the Vatican to become a sustainable-energy user. Photovoltaic cells and solar cooling units have been installed on Vatican buildings, and Benedict has let it be known that he wants his next Popemobile to be solar-powered. To date no carmaker has figured out a way to build an extremely top-heavy vehicle powered by solar cells that still can accelerate quickly in an emergency. So for now, the pope will continue to rely on gasoline, the Lord, and his custom-built Mercedes-Benz G500 SUV.

CLASSIC PAPAL RIDES

• **1960 Mercedes-Benz 300D Landaulet.** The Landaulet replaced the original Nürburg 460. It had modern amenities such as air-conditioning and a two-way radio so the pope could talk directly to the driver.

• **1964 Lincoln Continental Executive Limousine.** This 20-foot limo was specially fitted for Pope Paul VI's 1965 visit to New York. It had a bullet-resistant Plexiglas windshield, platforms for security officers, and a hand-crank that raised the pope's seat 12 inches higher to make him more visible to the crowd.

• **1979 FCS Star.** Karol Józef Wojtyła was born in Poland in 1920. When he returned in 1979 as Pope John Paul II, he rode in this Polish-built truck originally used for firefighting. The top of the truck was turned into an open platform shaded by an awning under which the pope could stand and wave.

• **1980 Mercedes-Benz 230 G.** Used for John Paul II's 1980 visit to Germany, this SUV-style vehicle set the standard for subsequent papal vehicles with its transparent glass structure and raised seats, which ensured that the pope was visible to his followers.

• **1982 SEAT *Papamóvil.*** Tricked out for John Paul II's visit to Spain, this tiny open-air economy sedan was the smallest Popemobile ever made.

• **1999 City Bus.** In 1999 John Paul II rode in a glass-walled city bus through enormous crowds in Mexico City. After his death, it was put on display at the city's Basilica de Guadalupe and has become a popular destination for Catholic pilgrims.

* * *

HOT SEAT

In 1963 a test pilot was in a Lockheed F-104 Starfighter at 104,000 feet when it began to spin wildly and fall toward the ground. The pilot tried to regain control but finally had to bail out. As he ejected from the plane, he was hit in the face by the detached seat, red-hot from the ejection rocket blast. The seat caught the rubber seal of his pressurized helmet on fire, and the oxygen-rich interior of his helmet went up like a blow torch. When the pilot tried to remove his helmet and turn off the oxygen, his glove caught fire. By the time he put out the fire, he had parachuted down—and hit the ground hard. Amazingly, the test pilot not only lived to tell the story but became the first pilot to break the sound barrier. His name: Chuck Yeager.

DANICA PATRICK 101

A hard-driving speed freak, Danica Patrick has broken barriers for women racecar drivers since her debut in 2005.

DANICA DATA

Born: March 25, 1982.

Hometown: Roscoe, Illinois.

Home base: Scottsdale, Arizona.

Identifying mark: Tattoo on lower back of a checkered American flag with wings and stars.

Lucky number: 7.

Favorite racing movie: *Days of Thunder.*

Racing pedigree: Her father, T. J. Patrick, raced motocross, snowmobiles, and midgets; mother Bev was a snowmobile mechanic. Danica started go-karting in 1992, age 10.

Education: Canada's Formula Ford Racing School, Class of 1998, age 16.

First car: Mustang Cobra. Burned through three sets of brakes in first 8,000 miles.

Sponsor: Godaddy.com, the world's largest Internet-domain registrar. In exchange, she became a company spokesperson, or "Godaddy Girl."

What's in her garage: Mercedes-Benz ML 63AMG; Lamborghini Gallardo.

Current Indy car: #7 Godaddy.com Honda/Dallura for Andretti Autosport.

Current NASCAR Nationwide Series car: #7 Goddaddy.com Chevrolet Impala for JR Motorsports.

DANICA FIRSTS

Championship: 1994 World Karting Association, age 12.

"Rookie of the Year": 2005 Indy 500; 2005 IndyCar Series Season.

IndyCar: Winner, 2008 Japan 300, the first woman to win an IndyCar race.

Indy 500: Placed third in the 2009 Indy 500, the highest finish ever by a woman.

Cover star: In 2005, became the first Indy 500 driver in 20 years to make the cover of *Sports Illustrated.* (The previous was Danny Sullivan.)

NASCAR: First woman to lead a lap at Daytona International Speedway, 2011 NASCAR Nationwide Series.

RANDOM FACTS

Most popular: Voted the IndyCar series "Most Popular Driver," 2005–2010.

Commercial success: According to TiVo, the most watched Super Bowl commercial of 2009 was her Go Daddy "Enhancement" commercial.

Swimsuit model: Featured in four-page spread of *Sports Illustrated* Swimsuit Issue (February 15, 2008).

Acting: Guest-starred on *CSI: NY* episode title "The Formula" in 2010, playing a (wait for it!) racecar driver.

Video game star: Appears in Activision's "Powered-up Racing Game," *Blur.*

Music video: Co-stars in Jay-Z's "Show Me What You Got."

Author: Autobiography, *Danica: Crossing the Line* (2006).

Selected quote: "I need to beat them, belittle them, and make them feel small. Trying to run them off the road at 170 mph isn't sweet and kind."

* * *

GOOD ANSWER

When asked whether his tires played an important part in his winning race, 1980 Formula One World Champion Alan Jones replied "Oh, absolutely. You see, they keep the wheels from touching the ground."

World's fastest standard train: The French TGV reaches a record 357.2 mph.

THE SIDECAR: A TIME LINE

These days we don't see many motorcycle sidecars other than in reruns of Two Fat Ladies *and Marx Brothers movies. But the funny little seat with a wheel of its own has a long and colorful past. Here are a few highlights.*

1900

The first attempt to add a passenger to a motorcycle is the fore-car, made by H. Adams in England. It replaces the front tire with a wicker seat and a pair of bicycle tires. Although the design will be improved by Birmingham's Garrard Manufacturing Company in 1904, the fore-car has a serious design flaw—the passenger is seated directly in front of the driver, obscuring the view.

1902

The rear-car is developed by the Cygnet Rear Car Company in Buffalo, New York. It is a three-wheeled contraption with its own differential that places the passenger behind the "motor-bicycle"—facing backward. Unfortunately, the rear-car has the tendency to flip over while going uphill.

1903

The first workable sidecar design is inspired by an editorial cartoon by George Moore in the British magazine *Motor Cycle*. The cartoon, lampooning the challenges involved in accommodating passengers on motorcycles, shows a wicker trailer with three wheels, bolted to the side of a motorcycle. Three weeks after the magazine appears, the Graham Brothers of Enfield, England, copy cartoonist Moore's design and shortly thereafter sell their patent to Components Ltd., the parent company of Ariel Motorcycles. The first sidecars are called "sociable attachments" or simply "sociables" because, unlike their predecessors, they allow driver and passenger to converse while traveling. By World War I, the sidecar is a ubiquitous part of motorcycling.

Audi, Lincoln, Hyundai, and BMW all offer a factory-produced civilian armored car model.

1913

American inventor Hugo Young solves the problem of instability that sidecars have, especially at high speeds and during turns. He develops a flexible connection between motorcycle and sidecar that allows the bike to remain balanced even at high speeds. Young's Flexible Sidecar Company becomes the largest sidecar manufacturer in the world. The sport of sidecar racing soon becomes hugely popular on both sides of the Atlantic. Sidecar racers adopt separate steering, flat platforms for prone passengers, and other innovations to increase speed. Backyard inventors begin tweaking the designs—leaning the bike toward the sidecar and angling the sidecar's wheel slightly toward the bike—to gain a speed advantage. These innovations will serve the sidecar well in its next incarnation—as a dog of war.

1914–18

During World War I, Dutch-made Excelsior motorcycles equipped with sidecars shuttle medical supplies to Allied troops on the front lines and haul wounded soldiers back to base. The Patent Collapsible Sidecar Company (later Watsonian Folding Sidecars) of Great Britain makes sidecars that can be stowed out of the way while navigating obstacles in the field. Clyno of England builds the first sidecar with a machine gun mounted on it in 1914 (the 750cc V-twin cycle is picked by Winston Churchill), and soon German manufacturers like Steib are building similar sidecars for the other side. In 1917 and 1918, the U.S. military employs about 20,000 gun-mounted sidecars from motorcycle manufacturers such as Indian and Harley-Davidson in the war effort.

1939–45

BMW makes 600-cc sidecars with an axle connecting the motorcycle's rear wheel to the sidecar's wheel. The extra traction combined with an onboard machine gun mount turns the German bikes into hell on wheels. The Afrika Corps uses three-wheeled warmobiles to terrorize Allied troop convoys in hornet-like hit-and-run raids. The success of the Axis tactics prompts the United States to order 500 of its own driveshaft-enabled sidecars from Harley-Davidson and Indian. However, the war ends before they can be tested in battle.

Sidecars are also called hacks, side-hacks, chairs, platforms,...

1950s

After World War II, the sidecar motorcycle rapidly falls out of favor with consumers. Though a sidecar-equipped motorcycle can get double or even triple the gas mileage of most automobiles, motorists opt for the comfort and convenience of cars. Manufacturers like Swallow of England notice the trend and turn their attention to automaking. (Swallow is better known today for making Jaguar sports cars.) The arrival of affordable, fuel-efficient cars like the Austin Mini leads to the demise of all but one British sidecar manufacturer, Watsonian.

1970s

A brief surge in sales occurs during the gas crisis.

2010

Harley-Davidson, the last major U.S. maker, rolls out its last sidecar.

TODAY

The sidecar persists, with companies like the Russian Ural continuing to sell them throughout the world. Manufacturers like Krauser Domani are replacing the sidecar with BMW-powered vehicles in which the passenger compartment is folded into a sleek aerodynamic cowl with the motorcycle. Sidecar racing continues to attract fans. No other form of road racing relies so much on teamwork. Modern racers bear little resemblance to street models: The driver's seat has been removed, and driver and passenger kneel on a platform. The engine is at the rear of the vehicle, lowering the center of gravity and lifting a sidecar's speed to 160 mph.

* * *

HERE'S TO ME!

"I'm sure we would not have had men on the Moon if it had not been for Wells and Verne and the people who write about this and made people think about it. I'm rather proud of the fact that I know several astronauts who became astronauts through reading my books."

—Arthur C. Clarke, sci-fi author

TOTAL RECALL

All carmakers produce a really bad car now and then (Toyota's recent recall troubles come to mind). But the Ford Motor Company may hold the dubious title of Top Lemon Maker in the industry.

WORST CAR EVER MADE?

Car: Ford Pinto (1970–80), recalled 1978

Details: The Pinto went on sale in the fall of 1970, and almost immediately consumers began complaining. According to critics, the problem with the Pinto was its fuel tank or, more precisely, where it was located—between the rear bumper and rear axle, right next to four large bolts jutting out of the differential housing. A minor rear-end collision at low speed would collapse the tank like an accordion, causing gas to gush out and resulting in an explosion. Ford insisted the car was fine. Not to rush things, the National Highway Traffic Safety Administration opened an investigation into the Pinto's safety four years later.

In 1977 *Mother Jones* magazine printed a scathing exposé. "For seven years," the article began, "the Ford Motor Company sold cars in which it knew hundreds of people would needlessly burn to death." *Mother Jones* claimed to have uncovered an in-house memo proving Ford president Lee Iacocca and top management had known about the exploding gas tank danger *before* the car went into production. Ford designers had offered ways to correct the problem, but the company refused to spend the $11 per car that it would cost, figuring it would be cheaper to pay the injury and death settlements resulting from possible lawsuits. The company lobbied hard to prevent a law—Federal Motor Vehicle Safety Standard 301—that would force them to redesign the car.

As the death toll from gas-tank-related Pinto accidents mounted into the hundreds, "Lee's car," as disgruntled Ford workers came to refer to the Pinto, became a symbol of corporate greed to angry consumers. In 1977, a court in Orange County, California, awarded $125 million in damages to Richard Grimshaw for injuries he

Largest-ever single-model vehicle recall: 12 million Ford Super Duty trucks (2008)...

sustained when the Pinto he was in (he was 13) burst into flames in a low-speed accident. That amount exceeded all profits Ford had made on the car. A lengthy appeals process reduced the penalty to $6.6 million but the point had been made. In 1978, 2.2 million Pintos (and Mercury Bobcats) were recalled to have plastic shields, at a cost of $1 each, installed to protect the gas tanks. According to *Forbes*, since 1971 Ford has paid out millions in Pinto claims.

"THE EXPLODER"

Car: Ford Explorer (1991–2001), recalled 2001

Details: The Explorer was the top-selling SUV in the world for a decade, even though it had two major problems: 1) In an emergency road-handling situation, the top-heavy Explorer tended to flip, and 2) The standard-issue Firestone Wilderness A/T tires had a tread separation flaw that caused them to blow out. Put tires that explode on an SUV that rolls, and you've got one killer combination. In 2000, Bridgestone/Firestone recalled more than 6.5 million Wilderness A/T tires, but reports of fatalities kept rising. The *Wall Street Journal* reported in 2001 that more than 200 deaths were directly attributable to Explorers with those tires. The same year, Ford recalled the 1991–2001 Explorers, or "Exploders" as they were derisively nicknamed by mechanics across the country, and replaced the defective tires. In 2009, the federal Cash for Clunkers program reported that 6 out of 10 vehicles traded in were Ford Explorers.

WINNER: LARGEST RECALL EVER

Cars: Almost all Ford, Lincoln, and Mercury cars, SUVs, pickups, minivans, motor homes, and sedans (1992–2004). Total of 8 recalls, 1999–2009

Details: Ford's problem with switch fires began in 1996, when the automaker recalled 7.9 million vehicles because of an overheating ignition switch in their Aerostar, Bronco, Crown Victoria, Mustang, Thunderbird, and three other models. But that recall was nothing compared to what followed. Most Ford models built from 1992 to 2004 came with a $20 cruise control switch designed by Texas Instruments. The device was designed to shut off the cruise control whenever the driver stepped firmly on the brakes. But the switch had a design flaw: It drew current from the car battery even when the engine was off. According to the NHTSA, "The faulty switch could leak hydraulic fluid, overheat, smoke and then burn, and sometimes caused a fire even when the ignition was turned off, parked and unattended." As of 2000, the NHTSA had received reports of more than 1,500 fires caused by the switch. Many had started in a parked car in a garage long after the driver had gone to bed. In 1999, Ford began recalling 16 *million* vehicles. The recalls were completed in 2009.

* * *

TRAVEL VAC

The train of the future may well be a VacTrain, a *mag-lev* (magnetic levitation) train that, theoretically, will travel at extremely high speeds through vacuum tunnels. Engineers are currently looking at the VacTrain as the basis of creating a global subway network between continents and even under the oceans. According to the Discovery Channel's Extreme Engineering program *Transatlantic Tunnel*, the lack of air resistance in a vacuum tunnel would allow a VacTrain to reach speeds between 4,000 to 5,000 mph (5 or 6 times the speed of sound at sea level). A passenger could make the 3,100 mile trip from New York to London in 54 minutes.

The concept of transcontinental tunnel travel is not new: Jules Verne's son Michel wrote about one in an 1888 story titled *Un Express de l'Avenir* ("An Express of the Future"). Robert Goddard, the father of American rocketry, was issued two of his 214 patents for work on vac-train technology. Arthur C. Clarke described them in his 1956 novel *The City and the Stars*, and Harry Harrison's 1975 novel *Tunnel Through the Deeps* detailed a mag-lev tunnel system on the ocean floor.

In the 1970s, Dr. Robert M. Salter of the RAND think tank proposed a VacTrain route down the northeast corridor of the United States, but the estimated $1 trillion price tag killed the project. Tunnel-boring technology has improved dramatically since then, and the project is back on the desks of engineers in China, the U.S., and England. Today the cost of a transatlantic tunnel is thought to be closer to $175 billion, which seems—almost—affordable.

In the "24 Hours of LeMons" race, the cars are lemons—any costing over $500 are penalized.

VROOM COUNTDOWN

5, 4, 3, 2, 1... a miscellany of Vroom-ish factoids, by the numbers.

5 MONSTER TRUCK MOVIES

1. *Maximum Overdrive* (1986). AC/DC soundtrack accompanies Stephen King tale of alien-controlled big rigs that trap people in a truck stop, demanding blood and servitude. King's only directorial effort, to which he later admitted to being coked out of his mind throughout. Starring: Emilio Estevez.

2. *Take This Job and Shove It* (1981). Based on the hit song, the film introduced Bob Chandler's "Bigfoot" Ford F-250 to the world, ushering in the age of monster pickup trucks. Starring: Robert Hays.

3. *Duel* (1971). Steven Spielberg's first full-length film features an innocent driver menaced by a Peterbilt. Starring: Dennis Weaver.

4. *Killdozer* (1974). Construction workers building an airstrip on a Pacific island in WWII encounter an ancient temple-dwelling life form that commandeers their earth-moving equipment. Starring: Clint Walker.

5. *Jeepers Creepers* (2001). Siblings on spring break are stalked by a demon that drives an old truck and stashes bodies in an old church. And they keep hearing this funny old song on the radio. Starring: Gina Philips.

4 MAGIC KINGDOM FACTS

1. Fastest speed reached on Space Mountain: 30.3 mph.

2. The Disneyland Railroad circling the park travels 20,000 miles per year.

3. In the Rivers of America, the sailing ship *Columbia*, meant to be a replica of the first American ship to circumnavigate the world, is really a replica of the *Bounty* (of *Mutiny on the Bounty* fame) built from Captain Bligh's detailed diaries.

4. The Disneyland Marching Band has quick-stepped more than 3,500 miles since opening day in 1955.

What were *buckets, crates, flivvers,* and *heaps*? 1920s slang terms for cars.

3 HOT NASCAR FACTS

1. During a race, temperatures can top 100°F inside a car.

2. The floorboard temperature can hit 170°F.

3. A typical driver loses 10 pounds of sweat during a race.

2 RULES FOR NASA'S DEHYDRATED BEEF SANDWICHES

1. The coating shall not chip or flake and it must not break when handled.

2. There shall be no damp or soggy areas and no rancid or foreign odor.

1 WEIRD COINCIDENCE

1. In 1991, 19-year-old Cristina Vernoni was struck and killed by a train as she drove her car across an unguarded railroad track in Reggio Emilia, Italy. Four years later, her father lost his life crossing the very same tracks. Even more bizarre? Engineer Domenico Serafino was the driver of both trains.

* * *

AIRPLANE FEVER

Some people collect cars or motorcycles. Actor John Travolta collects planes and flies them. Travolota's obsession began as a youngster when he hung dozens of model airplanes from the ceiling of his room. When he became a father, he named his first son Jett. He owns five aircraft and hangars them at his $4.9 million estate in the fly-in community of Jumbolair in Ocala, Florida. A private runway leads from Greystone Airport to Travolta's front door. The plane collection parked on his property includes three Gulfstreams and a Lear Jet, as well as a $3 million customized 707 that he bought from Qantas Airlines, making him the only private citizen to own a former commercial airliner. He named it *Jett Clipper Ella* after his first two children. Travolta employs a cockpit crew of six, who, along with Travolta, wear navy-blue uniforms and white caps. According to Jumbolair developer Terri Jones, "Travolta uses the 707 as the family van, and the Gulfstream as his sports car."

What were the Satan, the Snob, and the Silver Pigeon? Defunct motorcycle brand names.

LITTLE DEUCE COUPE

In the 1960s, the Beach Boys waxed poetical over a hot rod in a song that took them to the top of the charts. But what exactly were they talking about? Uncle John deconstructs the lyrics of this classic car tune.

BACKGROUND

The Beach Boys' "Little Deuce Coupe," which went to #4 on the 1963 Billboard Top 100, is a paean to a heavily modified version of the original 1932 Ford Model B Coupe (three- or five-window), which was itself an updated version of the Model A. Priced at $490 (the equivalent of $7,700 today), the car was a phenomenal sales success in the '30s—which meant that 20 years later there were a lot of them still around for teenagers to pick up on the cheap. But it wasn't just any old car, as the Beach Boys' gearhead lyrics, written by Roger Christian, prove.

"Just a little Deuce coupe with a flathead mill..."

What made the new car especially exciting was the introduction of its flathead V-8 engine (nicknamed the "mill"), a first for its time. And hot-rodders loved to strip down and soup up old Deuces (the "deuce" referred to the "2" in "'32"). They would "cherry" a Deuce by removing the fenders, running boards, and hood, lowering the body on the frame (channeling) or the roof height (chopping), adding lots of flashing chrome and eye-poppingly imaginative paint jobs.

"...but she'll walk a Thunderbird like it's standin' still."

The Deuce's standard V-8 was powerful for its day—1930s gangsters loved it—but later hot-rodders squeezed even more horsepower out of it.

"She's ported and relieved and she's stroked and bored."

"Porting and relieving" was one souping-up trick: the process of grinding and polishing the engine block to reshape and smooth the passages around the valves and exhaust ports to increase air intake and outflow of exhaust gases.

Another was "stroking and boring": machine work done to increase engine displacement, usually listed in cubic inches or cubic centimeters. "Stroking" increases the length the piston can travel inside the cylinder, while "boring" widens the cylinder diameter to accept larger pistons.

To handle the pumped-up horsepower and avoid a blown engine, a hot-rodder would install a beefier clutch and a four-speed stick-shift transmission. Then it was time for the Deuce to hit the street…or lake bed.

"She'll do a hundred and forty with the top end floored."
Southern California hot-rodders preferred to hold their races on dry lake beds such as El Mirage and Muroc. With so much power running through a stripped-down, lightweight machine, it was easy to lose traction in the rear wheels and burn rubber shifting through all four gears, leaving telltale scorch marks behind. With the rear end hopping and fishtailing around, it also required considerable skill to keep a Deuce moving straight down the course—or street—at high speed.

"She's my little Deuce coupe, you don't know what I got."
Running through a street-legal muffled exhaust, the Deuce would have purred like a kitten, but uncapping the pipes for racing allowed the exhaust to blow straight through an alternative set of unmuffled pipes. And the so-called "lake pipes" would roar! Some 'rodders even installed a lever in the cab that connected to a cable which ran to the cutouts on the lake pipes. So a Deuce driver could be idling at a red light, then flip the lever to open up the lake pipes and give the street a blast of the power tucked away in that flathead mill.

NOT SO LITTLE

As for that original stock '32 Ford coupe that sold for a crowd-pleasing $490? Fully cherried out, that little Deuce coupe today would set you back at least 25 grand.

* * *

TOUGH BRAKE

A Formula 1 car takes 45 seconds to go from 186 mph to a stop.

ADVANCED FLYING

You mastered flight basics on page 116. Now it's time for some hair-raising acrobatic aerial maneuvers.

BARREL ROLL

Often confused with an aileron roll (see page 116), a barrel roll starts as a loop with the nose about 45 degrees above the horizon. Then the pilot starts a coordinated roll, finishing up straight and level, on the same heading where the plane started. Like many aerial maneuvers, the barrel roll was born in air-to-air combat during World War I. Pilots on the defensive found that the roll helped them avoid bullets and shake the "bogies" off their tails. When on attack, it helped them stay behind the enemy by maintaining superior airspeed without flying past the target. Modern fighter pilots still do barrel rolls to avoid bullets and missiles, but this maneuver is considered an entry-level maneuver for a combat aviator.

IMMELMAN TURN

Used in dogfights during World War I by the first fighter planes, the Immelman starts as a loop to gain altitude. When the plane is upside down, the pilot performs a half-aileron roll to regain normal, level flight. Pilots use this turn to quickly change direction. The maneuver is named for Max Immelmann, Germany's first flying ace, who is thought to have invented it. He is credited with at least 15 "kills" of Allied planes from 1915 to 1916 until he was shot down on January 12, 1916, by British pilot George McCubbin.

SPLIT-S

This advanced maneuver is a reverse Immelman, with the roll first followed by a downward loop. To perform a split-S in the EA-6B Prowler, the Navy's primary carrier defender, the pilot flies on a straight and level flight path at 350 knots (400 mph), then noses up about 10 degrees and does a barrel roll until he's upside down, (or, as Tom Cruise said in *Top Gun*, "inverted"). Pulling the stick

A 5-star safety rating on a vehicle means a 10% or less chance of serious injury in a crash.

back at this point aims the jet toward the ground, then curves the plane back to straight and level flight, but in the opposite direction, 9,000 feet lower. The advantage: If a combat plane isn't designed for air-to-air combat, its best maneuver isn't an attack; it's an escape. With a split-S, it can change direction quickly and head for the ground.

SPIRAL DIVE

Also known as the "death dive," the spiral dive isn't so much a maneuver done on purpose; it's a problem that pilots face now and again. This high-g trap happens when the physics of flight work against you: At level flight, the plane's *lift vector*—the direction that the lift force exerts on the wings, relative to the ground—points straight up. At a 30-degree bank, the lift force points 30 degrees from vertical. But if a high bank angle in a turn isn't corrected quickly enough, the plane will turn progressively tighter as the nose dives. Even worse, since the outside wing is traveling farther, and therefore faster, it is generating more lift than the inside wing. All of this combines to turn the plane even more tightly into a death spiral. This maneuver is dangerous for pilots who don't understand it, since their instincts lead them to pull back on the yoke, which only makes the spiral tighter. Experts say the correct solution is to level off the wings first, then begin to regain horizontal flight.

FORMATION FLYING

This air-show attraction is often called "fingertip flying" because several planes fly so close to each other that from the ground it looks like someone moving his fingertips through the air. The specialty of the Air Force Thunderbirds and the Navy Blue Angels, formation flying consists of hundreds of formations, including classics such as the Diamond, the Delta Roll, and the Missing Man, a symmetrical formation with one plane missing, flown on solemn occasions. Formation flying is often performed over sporting events, preferably right over the stadium, so the rear-pilot, or "slot," can extend his speed specialized brakes, or "boards," and hit the thruster to make as much noise as possible. As a rule, formation flying is a bad combat choice since it allows the enemy to hone in, or "tally," on multiple aircraft at once.

Combat pilots typically fly a few miles apart so they can see more of the sky, and watch each other's backs. Outside of combat, planes fly in formation to stay close to each other, to keep visual contact in bad weather, or while transferring fuel from a flying gas station.

CUBAN-8

If you were to trace this maneuver through the air, you'd see the plane perform one full loop followed by another to make a sideways figure eight. The plane ends up at its original altitude and direction. On the descending parts of the loops, the pilot executes a half roll so that there are no "outside loops," which is an easy way to pull negative gs and make the blood rush to your head. It's not only painful but can cause a blackout. The Cuban-8 is one of the hardest maneuvers to learn. But since it incorporates every angle and direction, it's a great way to learn how to fly an airplane. Best of all, it's fun.

For even more advanced combat maneuvers, go to page 365.

* * *

FIRST DRIVE-THRU

Harry Snyder, founder of In-N-Out Burger, is credited with opening the first modern drive-thru in Baldwin Park, California, in 1948. (The idea actually dates back to 1931, when a California restaurant called the Pig Stand came up with the concept but never built the drive-thru.) Snyder installed two-way speaker boxes outside the In-N-Out so customers could place orders in the drive-thru line and pick up their food at a special window, a concept largely unchanged to this day. Snyder's first In-N-Out was strictly drive-thru or walk-up—there was no indoor seating. Surprisingly, it would be nearly 30 years before McDonald's installed its first drive-thru window in 1975 near a military base in Sierra Vista, Arizona. Today drive-thrus are synonymous with fast food.

...a record 220,000 Mustangs on its first day on the market in 1964.

BEAUTIFUL SPEED

Before Bugatti, cars were functional. But this eccentric Italian changed all that, building superfast cars that remain stunning works of art today.

GOING IN STYLE

Ettore Arco Isidoro Bugatti was born into an artistic family in Milan, Italy, in 1881. His grandfather was a notable sculptor and architect, and Bugatti grew up in a home filled with the Art Nouveau creations of his father Carlo, a prominent furniture and jewelry designer. He brought this legacy with him as he began a career as an engineer in 1898. Working for several automotive pioneers, Bugatti quickly earned a reputation for innovative design, winning a gold medal at the 1901 Milan Trade Fair for a car that he built himself.

That prize-winning design caught the eye of industrialist Baron de Dietrich, who brought Bugatti to Alsace to create a series of De Dietrich-Bugatti cars (the underage Bugatti had to get permission from his father). In 1910 Bugatti formed his own company in Molsheim, France, where his initial creations combined progressive engineering with eye-catching style. At a time when cars tended to be built like tanks, Bugatti constructed one of the world's first compacts. Light in weight but strong in performance, the 1,400-cc, four-cylinder vehicle was a sensation when it debuted at the 1910 Paris Automobile Show.

BACK TO THE DRAWING BOARD

Bugatti's ambitious dreams were put on hold by World War I, during which he drafted designs for aircraft engines. Soon after the Armistice in 1918, he turned his attention back to designing cars—specifically, race cars.

The decision proved lucrative. At the 1921 Voiturette Grand Prix, Bugatti's cars took the first four places, leading to a rush of orders for his Brescia model. This initial success was short-lived—his cars were soon left in the dust by "supercharged" models from competitors like Fiat. So he went back to the drawing board and came up with a design that would make history: the Bugatti Type 35.

A CAR FOR THE AGES

The Type 35 became the most successful racing car of all time, netting 1,850 wins in the years following its debut. Bugatti spared no expense in his pursuit of winning, and the Type 35 was the perfect expression of his obsession. Its camshaft, built from a composite of nine separate pieces, was said to cost as much as the rest of the car. The running gear and body were just as refined as the engine. To keep the center of gravity low, the two-seater rode on an underslung chassis, and the drum brakes were finned for cooling, with extra cooling obtained from a fan effect created by the open wheels. The aluminum body was formed by hand, with a tapered tail that anticipated aerodynamic race car design by decades.

A 35B won the first Monaco Grand Prix in 1929. Driver Jean-Pierre Wimille also scored wins at the 24 Hours of Le Mans in 1937 and 1939. A refined model, the Bugatti Veyron, had a top speed of 250 mph, an amazing feat for automobiles of the time.

RAGING GENIUS

Bugatti's overweening ego and short temper came to light during this period. A dandy who loved fine suits and elegant living, Bugatti didn't fit the down-to-earth image of most carmakers. His bold appearance and astronomical self-confidence led colleagues and employees to call him *Il Patron* ("The Boss"). The huge popularity of his well-designed, gorgeous cars lulled him into resting on his laurels while other manufacturers continued to innovate.

It was said that one could not simply purchase a Bugatti: you had to prove you were worthy of one. When a customer complained that the cable brakes on his 35B were not as reliable as the newer hydraulic brakes starting to appear on other automobiles, Bugatti reportedly snapped, "I make my cars to go, not to stop." When another client brought his car back to the factory three times for adjustments, Bugatti purportedly stormed out of his office and yelled, "Do not let it happen again!"

New models like the Type 46 Touring Car and the Type 55 Roadster continued to draw accolades, but Bugatti's visionary designs and lofty standards were too exacting to be profitable. His cars were almost entirely handmade, with an attention to detail that few, if any, automakers have come close to matching. Engine blocks were delicately scraped to make certain that they were

In 2007 the Bugatti Veyron Pur Sang's limited run of five cars sold out in less than 24 hours.

smooth and flat enough to not need to be sealed with gaskets. Safety wires were meticulously threaded in intricate patterns. Spring axles were delicately manufactured and passed through carefully crafted openings. A passionate fan of horse racing, Bugatti called his beloved metal babies *Pur Sang* ("thoroughbreds").

ROYAL BUST

In 1929 a wealthy Englishwoman told *Il Patron* that his cars reminded her of Rolls-Royces. She meant it as a compliment, but the remark cut Bugatti to the quick. He considered the lumbering Rolls-Royce déclassé and immediately set out to build his conception of the most luxurious car in the world.

His prototype contained one of the largest automobile engines ever built. Originally designed for airplane use, its eight cylinders and near 15-liter capacity could produce almost 300 hp. Elegant touches included a steering wheel made out of walnut and interior knobs covered in whalebone. His brother Rembrandt, a prominent sculptor, designed the radiator cap, which featured a silver elephant standing on its hind legs, triumphantly raising its trunk in the air.

The Bugatti Royale was designed—literally—for royalty. Bugatti hoped to sell the initial run of 25 to monarchs across Europe. But the car went into production just as the Great Depression devastated the world economy. In the end, only six of his masterpieces were sold.

REBIRTH

Bugatti survived the Depression by building airplane engines and repurposing the massive Royale engine for the French railway. After Bugatti died in 1947, the company quit making cars and focused on its aircraft business.

In 1987 an Italian named Romano Artioli bought the name and hired former Lamborghini designers to bring new Bugatti sports cars to the market. With its 1,184-hp engine and a top speed of 267.85 mph, the 2011 Bugatti Veyron EB 16.4 Super Sport is the fastest street-legal car in the world, and at $2.78 million, is priced in the royal tradition of the Bugatti Royale of long ago. And what happened to Ettore Bugatti's six original Royales? Today they're among the rarest and most valuable cars in the world. In 1990 a Japanese firm bought one for $15.7 million dollars.

During its 50-year life time, a subway car will go through 48 wheels, 24 motors, and 24 axles.

SCREW-MOBILES: A TIMELINE

There's no question that the invention of the wheel changed human history, but they tend to get stuck in mud and snow. One solution for all-terrain driving: "driving a screw."

1899. Swiss-born American inventor and farmer Jacob Morath comes up with a screw-propelled vehicle. Instead of wheels or tracks, it has huge pontoons that work like a drill against the ground, pulling the vehicle forward. The screws counter-rotate (one turns clockwise, the other counter-clockwise) to keep in a straight line. To turn, the driver locks one screw in place and lets the other move the vehicle in the appropriate direction. Morath's intent is to make a new kind of plow—not a bad idea, since one of the side effects of a screw-driven vehicle is that it chews up the ground—but apparently no one uses his design to do that.

1907. However, his work inspires the Peavey brothers of Maine to build a screw-driven tractor to work their back-country logging operations. Their design proves to be a bust: the driving screws work fine in muddy and hard snow conditions but are too small to bite effectively in soft powder snow.

1920. It isn't until the Ford Motor Company gets into the act that a workable screw-driven tractor is built. A 1926 newsreel shows remarkable footage of the Fordson Snow-Motor easily navigating four-foot-deep snow in rural Michigan, and pulling 20 tons of logs. A conventional tractor engine and body are mounted on a pair of augur-pontoons driven with bicycle-like chains. Separate clutches allow the driver to deliver power to each pontoon separately, making the vehicle very maneuverable. An alternative version has a Chevrolet sedan body mounted on the pontoons to carry passengers. The January 1926 issue of *Time* magazine reports that the Fordson Snow-Motor is ferrying passengers across the snowbound McKenzie Pass in Oregon. The vehicles are also shipped to snowy nations like Norway, Sweden, and Canada.

1940s. World War II sees renewed interest in screw-mobiles, espe-

In 1938 Route 66 became the first American highway to be fully paved.

cially as potential amphibious troop carriers, with attempts made by all sides of the conflict to develop workable military prototypes. Even though marsh screws (as they were also called) move well through bogs, swamps, snow, slush, and ice, they are limited to those conditions. On regular roads they are a disaster, trailing deep scars behind them. Only the Russians, faced with the necessity of mining and logging vast tracts of permanently snowbound forests in Siberia, press on.

1960s. The Russian work pays off with the ZIL-2906, known as the "Cosmonaut's Blue Bird," which is designed specifically to retrieve cosmonauts from their otherwise inaccessible landing sites in Central Asia.

One of the most successful all-terrain screw-driven vehicles is built in 1960 by Dutchman Joseph Jean de Bakker, owner of a machine shop in Hulst and an avid fisherman. Annoyed at having to wait for the tide to go out or in to reach his favorite fishing area, he builds an amphibious marsh screw-driven vehicle. It's engineered so both screws can rotate in the same direction. The result is that the Amphirol can go sideways as well as forward and backward, at speeds up to 35 mph, through any terrain, including water.

2002. A British team led by Steve Brooks builds the Snowbird 6, which combines track and screw attributes. Brooks and his team intend to drive it across the Bering Strait between Russia and the United States, a feat that has never been done, and the Snowbird 6 needs to float, move through crushed ice and over icebergs, and climb out of the water onto pack ice. To make it, they take a Bombardier tracked vehicle used to groom ski trails and fit two pontoon screws to retractable arms connected to either side of its body. The idea is that the pontoon screws will both float and drive the craft through water or icy slush but can be raised to let the tracks take over on solid ice. Snowbird 6 is powered by a six-cylinder, 16-hp Perkins 1000 series diesel engine, with a combination of Sunstrand hydraulic pumps and Hagglund hydraulic motors working the tracks and screws. In 2002 Brooks and his co-driver Graham Stafford drive onto the pack ice off the coast of Alaska and arrive two days later in Big Diomedes, Russia. Snowbird 6 has traveled the 24 miles of open ice and frozen water flawlessly. The toughest obstacle is the two hours it takes each morning to get the engine started, due to the –30°F temperatures.

Only person to set both world land and water speed records in the same year:...

TOLL TRIVIA

Roads cost money to build and maintain, and making travelers pay to use them is as old as recorded history.

• An Assyrian king named Ashurbanipal collected tolls on the Susa-Babylon highway 2,700 years ago.

• In 400 B.C., philosopher Aristotle complained about being gouged for tolls while traveling in Arabia and Asia.

• In the 1500s, turnpikes were gates for animals, consisting of horizontal wooden barriers that turned on a center pin. Over time the meaning shifted to "a barrier where a toll is paid." By 1750 the word referred to the road itself.

• In 1800 a new highway cost $9,000 per mile to make ($110,000 today), so toll booths were placed every few miles to pay for each section.

• Early American toll roads had primitive roadside ATMs in the form of horse-drawn carriage-bankers.

• A stretch of I-80 and I-90 in Indiana called the "Skyway" will be operated as a toll road by an Australian-Spanish company for the next 75 years.

• In 1833 the Louisville-Nashville Turnpike (part of I-65 today) had five toll booths per mile. The 175-mile trip cost $12 ($267 today).

• In 1845 the 249-mile trip from Nashville to Atlanta cost 10 cents a mile, or $24.90 ($575.73 today).

• In 2011 a trip from Philadelphia to Pittsburgh on I-76 cost $24.50 for a passenger car, $60 for a truck.

• Longest toll road in the U.S.: Gov. Thomas E. Dewey Thruway, New York to Pennsylvania, 496 miles, $21.75.

• Most expensive U.S. state turnpike over 100 miles long: Pennsylvania Turnpike, 8.5 cents per mile.

• Most expensive U.S. state turnpike, period: Delaware Turnpike, 11.4 miles long, 26.8 cents per mile.

• Most expensive toll in the world: Confederation Bridge, Nova Scotia to Prince Edward Island, $40.50 Canadian ($40.64 U.S.).

CAR STARS

Put the pedal to the metal with these cinematic joy rides by matching each synopsis with a title. *(Answers are on page 460.)*

1. Young stock car driver must learn to channel his talents with help from his pit crew, his 1990 Chevy Lumina, and his post-crash female brain specialist.

2. New York detective on narcotics detail targets drug kingpin and tails elevated train in ground-breaking high-speed chase in his 1971 Pontiac LeMans.

3. Master car thief reluctantly agrees to scheme to steal 50 luxury cars, including a 1967 Shelby Mustang GT, during one night. Rival gang tries the same stunt simultaneously; cops have their hands full.

4. Undercover cop infiltrates the subculture of L.A. street racers in his Mitsubishi Eclipse RS-T.

5. Race-car driver finances a new engine for his 1964 Elva Mk. VI and an entry into the Las Vegas Grand Prix by taking a job as a singing casino waiter. He also chases girls.

6. The winning streak of a Chevy Monte Carlo-driving NASCAR speed-demon is broken by a gay French Formula One driver. His wife takes his fortune, his best friend takes his wife, and he's back with the parents.

7. Southern matron and the black chauffeur of her 1948 Hudson Commodore develop an unusual friendship that spans 25 years.

8. Assigned to protect a mob informant, tough-guy detective gets ambushed, after which he and his '68 Ford Mustang GT Fastback take to the streets of San Francisco to hunt down the hit men.

A. *Bullitt*

B. *Talledega Nights: The Ballad of Ricky Bobby*

C. *Days of Thunder*

D. *The French Connection*

E. *Gone in Sixty Seconds*

F. *Driving Miss Daisy*

G. *The Fast and the Furious*

H. *Viva Las Vegas*

HANS AND FRANZ

What vehicle has a top speed of 2 mph and burns 150 gallons of fuel per mile? Hint: NASA has two of 'em.

WAKE UP AND SMELL THE MUSCLES

Imagine a 20-foot-tall platform the size of a baseball diamond, mounted on caterpillar treads. Called a Crawler-Transporter, it's the massive vehicle NASA uses to move spacecraft from the Vehicle Assembly Building (VAB) to the launch pad at the Kennedy Space Center in Florida. This six-million-pound diesel-guzzler is the largest self-propelled land vehicle on Earth, and NASA has two of them—nicknamed Hans and Franz after the 1980s *Saturday Night Live* musclemen. Each one is large enough to block a four-lane highway in both directions.

BORN TO RUN—NOT!

Hans and Franz are outfitted with Mobile Launch Platforms that adjust to different spacecraft. A Crawler's engines are capable of moving the vehicle's 3,000-ton mass, as well as a fully loaded 2,300-ton Space Shuttle. Onboard leveling systems keep the nose of the Shuttle, 200 feet above, vertical to within the width of a basketball. While carrying a rocket on the four-mile trip from the VAB to the launch pad, the Crawlers average 1 mph, but they still have speedometers. To date the Crawlers have racked up more than 2,500 miles, about as far as a round trip from Kennedy Space Center to the South Milwaukee, Wisconsin, headquarters of Bucyrus International, which built the machines for NASA in 1965. At top speed, the trip to Wisconsin and back would take seven weeks and the 5,000-gallon fuel tanks would have to be filled more than 60 times.

SCHWARZENEGGERAN STRENGTH

Each Crawler-Transporter has two 2,750-horsepower Alco diesel engines that drive four 1,000-kilowatt generators, which in turn power 16 traction motors. Two other engines run the steering, lighting, ventilation, and leveling mechanisms, for a total horsepower of over 7,500. Seventy-five-horsepower electric motors pump fuel to the engines, which burn a gallon of diesel every 42 feet (0.008 mpg). Each one of the six mufflers weighs 3,000 pounds. The entire package rests on eight treads, which have 456 one-ton "shoes," 57 on each track. Each shoe bears a weight of 125,400 pounds, not counting the Crawler itself or the fully fueled Space Shuttle sitting on top of it.

WE WILL PUMP (CLAP) YOU UP!

A Mobile Launch Platform (MLP), one of NASA's three customizable docking stations, rides on top of the Crawler. The MLP is a two-story steel structure carrying umbilical connections to all of the rocket's liquid and electrical systems. Sixteen jacking cylinders can tilt the Crawler-MLP-Shuttle assembly up to five degrees. The route to the launch pad has a five percent vertical rise, requiring the Crawler to keep the platform perfectly level at all times. Leveling systems and positioning software guided by laser sensors keep the nose of the rocket within 10 arc minutes of vertical and can position the entire Crawler as little as one-eighth inch horizontally.

With nearly 20 million pounds riding on their shoulders, Hans and Franz handle "slow," according to Bob Myers, who's driven the C-Ts for two decades. "It takes some time to learn how to get out on the Crawlerway and learn how to anticipate a turn and learn how it's going to accelerate, decelerate, and stop." The Crawlerway is Hans and Franz's private 130-foot-wide roadway made of eight inches of smooth river rocks over seven and a half feet of fill and gravel. Once the MLP and rocket are docked at the launchpad, Hans (or Franz) is backed out and returned to the VAB. There's a cab at each end, so Myers doesn't have to look over his shoulder.

HEAR ME NOW AND BELIEVE ME LATER

NASA plans to keep Hans and Franz as long as their "pumpitude" lasts. So far, they show no signs of wearing out. So before any more space programs get off the ground, they will start with a very slow trip to the launchpad aboard the world's strongest muscle cars.

Between 1981 and 2003, the average horsepower of cars sold in the United States rose 93%.

LIFE'S A FITCH

John Fitch is a nonagenarian Formula One racer, race car designer, and safety innovator who shows no signs of slowing down.

GULLWING AT TWILIGHT

In 2003 race car driver John Fitch took friend Bob Sirna's 1955 Mercedes-Benz 300 SL "Gullwing" to the Bonneville Salt Flats in Utah to attempt a new land speed record. He was 87. Fitch was the ideal driver for the attempt—after all, he had raced the car successfully when it was brand-new. In 1955 Fitch drove a stock Gullwing coupe past a field of 600 cars to take first-in-class in Italy's famed Mille Miglia endurance race. When the 2003 speed attempt failed due to a faulty fuel-injection pump, Fitch joked that he had driven the same car faster 50 years before "in the rain, at night, on a road with 60 other cars."

GAME CHANGER

Born August 4, 1917, in Indianapolis, Fitch went to Europe in 1949 and became the first American to race successfully on the Continent. He drove his modified Ford flathead-engine Fiat 1100—nicknamed the "Fitch Model B"—to several wins in 1950 and in 1951 sped to victory at the 24 Hours of Le Mans with co-driver Phil Walters. He went on to be the first Sports Car Club of America national champion in 1951. Two years later, Fitch and Walters won at Sebring and won first-in-class at Le Mans despite a spectacular crash that sent Fitch's car flipping end over end at 140 mph when the left rear wheel sheared off of the car.

The crew chief had insisted that Fitch wear a five-point harness during the race—a safety precaution unheard of in an era when the sum of a driver's safety gear was usually a leather helmet and goggles. Many drivers even refused to wear seat belts, reasoning that it was better to be thrown clear of an accident than possibly be trapped inside a burning car. The harness undoubtedly saved Fitch's life. It was that crash, and another in the same race two years later, that reset the course of his life.

TERROR AT LE MANS

After Fitch was named Sports Car Driver of the Year by *Speed Age* magazine in 1953, an offer came to drive for legendary Mercedes-Benz. Fitch became Mercedes' first and only American driver. Many consider that team—which included the likes of Juan Manuel Fangio, Karl Kling and Stirling Moss—to be the most formidable racing lineup in the history of motorsports.

Unfortunately, Mercedes' domination of racing came to an abrupt and deadly end at the 1955 24 Hours of Le Mans. Fitch was paired with French driver Pierre Levegh. While Fitch watched from the pits waiting for his turn to drive, several cars braked suddenly in front of co-driver Levegh, forcing him to make an abrupt correction in his Mercedes 300 SLR. The car clipped the rear tire of an Austin-Healy driven by Lance Macklin at 150 mph. Levegh lost control and smashed into an earthen embankment—the only thing separating the track from the spectators. Pieces of the car, including the hood and axle, went tearing into the crowd. Levegh was killed instantly, along with 86 fans—many of whom were decapitated by metal debris. More than 100 others were injured in what remains the worst accident in the history of racing.

Devastated, Fitch suggested to the officials that Mercedes withdraw from the race, despite a sure win. He felt that a German carmaker shouldn't be associated with a victory achieved under such horrific circumstances, especially with memories of World War II so fresh. Mercedes agreed and pulled their racing team. The automaker wouldn't field another one for 25 years.

SAFETY FIRST

Fitch continued to race, but his new obsession became safety. He began developing safety devices, and one of his inventions—the Fitch Compression Barrier—is now found on oval race tracks around the world. Hollow cylinders between the guardrail and the wall absorb a crashing vehicle's energy without allowing it to bounce back onto the track. Another of his inventions, the Fitch Displaceable Guardrail, is mounted on skids so that it slides with the car upon impact—again absorbing the car's energy.

Fitch's safety concerns extended beyond the racetrack to every-

The Yosemite Valley Railroad (1907–45) never entered Yosemite Valley. It ended at...

day drivers. Those yellow sand-filled plastic barrels seen at freeway off-ramps are called Fitch Barriers.

In 1998 he was awarded the Kenneth Stonex Award from the National Academy of Sciences for his contributions to road-traffic safety. The commendation:

> "John Fitch's achievements in road safety throughout the world have spanned four and one-half decades. His lifetime contributions have covered the full spectrum of highway safety—the roadside, the vehicle and the driver. All have resulted in significant reductions in injuries and fatalities on the motorways of the world."

DESIGNING MAN

As he worked to transform highway and racetrack safety, Fitch never stopped tinkering with cars. While managing the Corvette team, Fitch became interested in the Chevy Corvair because of its superior track-handling abilities. He fiddled with its engine to bring it up to 155 hp to compete with faster Mustangs, tightened up the steering ratio, and added alloy wheels and metallic brake linings. The *pièce de résistance* was a fiberglass "Ventop" overlay that improved aerodynamics and gave the car its signature "flying buttress" profile. He added a wood-rimmed steering wheel and christened his creation the Fitch Sprint. It remains a popular collector's car. In 1966 Fitch again used the Corvair as the basis for his most famous creation, the street-legal Fitch Phoenix. The 175-hp, steel-bodied Phoenix looked like a smaller, low-cost version of the Mako Shark Corvette, and Fitch thought he'd make a fortune with it. Ironically, the project died when Chevy decided to discontinue the Corvair because of safety issues.

AUTO SAGE

At 94 Fitch is still inventing and still driving. He continues to tout his safety equipment at auto shows and share tales of his storied career with fans who line up for a photo-op.

Perhaps it's time for Fitch to write an autobiography. That is, another autobiography. He wrote his first one, *Adventure on Wheels*, more than 50 years ago—in 1960, when he was just a green 43-year-old.

...the park boundary. Construction of railroads is prohibited in US National Parks.

WANT FRIES WITH THAT?

Biodiesel is a vegetable-based, clean-burning alternative to diesel made easily from waste products like fast food cooking oil. And that is exactly what many communities are doing.

BUCKFRY

When the OPEC oil embargo of 1973 shut down filling stations across the United States, the fuel shortage inspired faculty and students at the Mechanical Engineering department of Ohio State University to find an alternative way to run their cars and buses. Students collected used cooking oil from the cafeteria, filtered out the leftover bits of burgers and fries, and came up with a new fuel they called Buckfry, named for the Buckeye State. Soon OSU students were hopping aboard a "French Fry" bus powered by Buckfry. When the embargo ended in 1974, gas prices dropped and OSU, along with the rest of the country, reverted to its gas-guzzling ways. Buckfry, and biodiesel in general, was set aside.

GREASED LIGHTNING

As the world has grown more environmentally conscious and oil prices have risen again, biofuel has made a comeback.

• In 1999 five engineering students from the University of Colorado built a biodiesel processor on campus, which fuels 13 buses to this day.

• About the same time, chemistry students at the University of Montana approporiated a school bus, nicknamed it the Bio Bus, and converted it to biodiesel made from recycled cooking oil left over from campus dining halls.

• Purdue, Dartmouth, the University of Rochester, and the University of Texas are some of the many other colleges that power buses with biodiesel.

• Popular music stars like Willie Nelson and Sheryl Crow tour in French fry–powered buses.

• Every city bus in Halifax, Nova Scotia, has been running on biodiesel since 2004.

The Bell 222 helicopter used on *Airwolf* was later used as an air-rescue ambulance.

• The train used by England's royal family and entourage has been biodiesel-powered since 2007.

• Disneyland runs its famous monorail and other trains on biodiesel made from leftover grease from Magic Kingdom restaurants.

• In 2008 Green Flight International became the first airline to fly a jet aircraft, an Aero L-29 Delfin, on 100% biodiesel fuel.

FUEL FOR THOUGHT

• Any diesel engine can run on biofuel.

• The basic ingredients of biofuel are vegetable oils derived from crops like soybeans, animal fats such as lard, waste cooking oil, and even certain kinds of algae, combined with methanol and lye in a process called *transesterification* that removes the glycerin from the oil, making it combustible in a diesel engine. (Note that, unless you are a professional chemist, we don't recommend trying this at home. Handled improperly, lye can cause severe burns, and methanol can flat-out kill you.)

• Some drivers swear biodiesel smells just like McDonald's French fries, while others say its aroma is closer to popcorn. Andy Pag, a British environmental campaigner who's been traveling the world since 2008 in a biodiesel-powered bus, puts it this way: "It's noisy, uncomfortable, slow, and it smells like a bus driver's armpit. But when you are using rubbish, you can't expect too much."

• To find places to fill up with biodiesel while you're on the road, go to the online resource Sustainable Biodiesel Alliance.

*　　*　　*

MOTHER LOAD

Remember how people use to try and see how many people could be stuffed into a VW Bug? Imagine breaking the Earth into small pieces and stuffing them into 20-ton railroad cars. Now imagine those cars passing by at a railroad crossing at the rate of one per second. How long would it take for the train to go by? 100 million years—which means you would have had to start watching that train when the first mammals appeared on Earth.

FAMOUS CARS: THE KENNEDY COLLECTION

The images of President Kennedy's motorcade driving through Dallas on November 22, 1963, are an indelible part of American history. Here's what happened to the black convertible limousine that will always be associated with his death, along with the other cars millions saw in the days to come.

X-100 LIMOUSINE

John F. Kennedy rode to his 1961 inauguration in President Eisenhower's 1950 Lincoln Cosmopolitan "Bubbletop," since his own 1961 Lincoln Continental convertible was still being modified. Ford extended the factory model by three feet, lengthened the wheelbase to 156 inches and added removable steel roof panels, hydraulic rear seats (to make the president more visible), retractable steps near the wheel wells for Secret Service Agents, auxiliary jump seats, and two more steps on the rear bumper. These modifications added 2,600 pounds to the limo, which already weighed 2.5 tons.

The massive vehicle was powered by a stock 430-cubic-inch V-8. The "X-100," as it came to be known, was leased to the government for $500 per year, and arrived at the White House in June 1961. Kennedy brought the X-100 to Dallas for the specific purpose of making himself more visible. Texas looked to be a key state in the 1964 election, and Kennedy thought a series of open motorcades would endear him to the historically conservative voters. Ford had designed a protective plexiglass top for the limousine, but despite rain on the morning of November 22, Kennedy opted to forgo it.

After the assassination, the X-100 was given a massive security overhaul at Ford's Cincinnati plant. The frame was reinforced to support the weight of 13 new bullet-resistant glass panels, armored top, bomb-proof floor armor, titanium steel body armor, and hand-built engine. The X-100 served the White House until 1977, when it was retired and moved to the Henry Ford Museum in Dearborn, Michigan.

In the *Peanuts* comic strips, the plane that Snoopy "flew" was a Sopwith Camel.

PRESIDENTIAL HEARSE

Kennedy was pronounced dead on November 22, 1963, at Parkland Hospital in Dallas. A hearse was sent by the O'Neal Funeral Home to transport the president's body to the airport. The white 1964 Cadillac limousine had been outfitted as a hearse by Miller-Meteor of Piqua, Ohio. Jackie Kennedy rode with her husband's body in the hearse, the curtains drawn, to Love Field, where Air Force One sat on the tarmac. After Secret Service agents placed the bronze casket on the plane, Mrs. Kennedy and Vice President Lyndon Johnson climbed aboard. Minutes later, a Texas judge delivered the oath of office, and Johnson became the 36th president of the United States. O'Neal Funeral Home sold the hearse to Arrdeen Vaughan, a local dealer who had lived in the O'Neal Funeral Home while attending mortuary school. He kept the hearse next to a Jeep used by fellow Texan LBJ. In 2010 Randy Koeppel bought it from Vaughan's dealership. (He was told that Vaughan had passed away, but when contacted by Uncle John, Arrdeen Vaughan reported that he is still very much alive.) The 1964 Cadillac hearse remains on display at his dealership in Mesa, Arizona.

PRESIDENTIAL AMBULANCE

When Air Force One landed in Washington, D.C., the ambulance that took the president's body to the National Naval Medical Center in Bethesda, Maryland, was a gray 1963 Pontiac Bonneville owned by the U.S. Navy. It was rumored that the Kennedy family had the ambulance destroyed in the 1980s, but in 2011 it—or a facsimile—was sold by a private owner at Barrett-Jackson Auto Auctions in Scottsdale, Arizona. The auction house confirmed the vehicle's authenticity…sort of. The ambulance was without a doubt a gray 1963 Pontiac Bonneville like those used by the Navy but, after thorough research, the auction house declared they "do not believe there is a person alive who can answer" whether this is the specific vehicle that carried President Kennedy. Nonetheless, the ambulance sold for $132,000 to Addison Brown of Paradise Valley, Arizona. She's convinced it's the real deal, and she said she "wanted a piece of history." For now it's in her private collection, but she intends to donate it to the Smithsonian Institution.

World speed record for trains: The Japanese experimental MLX01 reached 361 mph in trials.

ASSASSIN'S AMBULANCE

Two days after JFK's death, his accused assassin, Lee Harvey Oswald, was himself infamously shot by local nightclub owner Jack Ruby in the basement of the Dallas police station. Police rushed Oswald to Parkland Hospital in a white 1962 Ford ambulance (also owned by the O'Neal Funeral Home). There he was pronounced dead, two days and seven minutes after the president. The ambulance is displayed today at the Historic Auto Attractions Museum in Roscoe, Illinois, right next to an actual window from the Texas School Book Depository building, from which Oswald allegedly shot the president. Museum owner Wayne Lensing is a short-track chassis manufacturer, history buff, and memorabilia collector.

* * *

WILD RIDE

At 3:30 p.m. on June 6, 2007, the police dispatcher in Paw Paw, Michigan, received an unusual call. "You are not going to believe this," the caller said. "There's a semi truck pushing a guy in a wheelchair on Red Arrow Highway." At first, authorities wondered if it was a prank, but more calls confirmed that a man in a wheelchair was definitely attached to the grille of a semi traveling 50 mph down the highway. Two undercover officers spotted the truck, made a quick U-turn, and caught up with it, with wheelchair still attached, as it pulled into its home base. When the driver asked what was wrong, the cops told him to look at the front of his truck. He nearly fainted.

It seems that 21-year-old Ben Carpenter, who has muscular dystrophy, was in the process of crossing the highway in his motorized wheelchair when the light turned green. The driver of the semi didn't see Carpenter, who was just in front of the truck's hood. When the wheelchair got sideswiped by the truck, it spun around 90 degrees until it was facing forward, and its handles lodged in the truck's grille. Thus began Carpenter's wild ride. The truck pushed Carpenter, who was seat-belted into his chair and clutching a soft drink, for nearly four miles. The wheelchair tires lost most of their rubber, but miraculously, Carpenter was unharmed. (He did, however, spill his soda pop.)

The fuel pump used to fill race cars could fill the tank of an average car in 4 seconds.

HOG WILD

What made Milwaukee really *famous was an iconic motorcycle built and perfected by childhood chums Bill Harley and the Davidson boys.*

D-I-Y MOTOR-BICYCLE

When they were young men, Walter, Arthur, and William Davidson of Milwaukee, Wisconsin, loved nothing better than to go fishing with their best buddy, William Harley. They'd hop on their bikes after work or on weekends and ride out to Lake Michigan. It occurred to the boys that if they could put motors on those bicycles, they'd get to the lake a lot sooner.

In 1901, word that the Wolfmüller Brothers of Germany were making and selling motorcycles reached Milwaukee. Bill Harley and Art Davidson thought they'd try making one of their own. Both worked at an engineering firm, Harley as a draftsman and Davidson as a pattern maker for metal casting. After Harley drew up a blueprint of an engine designed to fit into a bicycle, he and Art Davidson set out to build it in the 10- by 15-foot shed in Davidson's backyard. Company legend has it that the one cylinder 400-cc engine was made out of household castoffs, including a carburetor made from a tomato can. Walt Davidson, who worked as a mechanic for a railroad, stepped in and helped them complete their first motor-bicycle. Unfortunately, it didn't have enough power to go uphill without pedaling, so they wrote it off as a good first try.

IF WE BUILD IT, THEY WILL BUY

In 1903—the same year the Wright Brothers made their famous flight at Kitty Hawk and Henry Ford founded Ford Motor Company—Harley and Art and Walt Davidson launched the Harley-Davidson Motor Company. They built a stronger frame to support a more powerful engine (with a little help on the carburetor from mechanical wiz Ole Evinrude, soon to be famous for outboard motors). That lifted their work out of the "motorized bicycle" category into the full-fledged motorcycle realm. That first year, they sold a total of three motorcycles. A man named H.D. Lang bought one and was so impressed he decided to open the first Harley-Davidson dealership, in Chicago. Bill Harley figured the fledgling company could use a little more mechanical expertise, so he enrolled in the engineering department at the University of Wisconsin.

By 1906 they'd moved from the backyard shed into their own factory on what is now Juneau Avenue in Milwaukee, had six full-time employees, and had advanced to a 50-motorcycle production run. They also had a catalog and a hip name for their newest motorcycle: the Silent Grey Fellow. Silent, because its efficient muffler gave a quiet ride. Grey, because of the paint color. And Fellow, because the bike was a reliable, trusted companion on the road. It sold for $200 ($4,800 today).

THE H-D VISION

With each passing year, the company added more improvements and innovations to create the unique Harley-Davison motorcycle we know today:

- The signature Harley engine sound: 2 "pops" and a pause, caused by the way the pistons connect to the crankshaft (1907)
- The 45-degree V-twin motor (1909)
- The "Bar and Shield" logo (1910)
- The signature tear-drop shaped gas tank (1920s)
- The eagle painted on the gas tank (1930s)

OVER THE DECADES

In the Army Now. When the United States entered WWI, the military bought one out of every two Harley-Davidsons sold. By 1918, 20,000 of the bikes were in Europe. Solo and sidecar machines were used by dispatch riders, and combat rigs were equipped with machine gun mounts. The first Allied soldier to enter Germany was dispatch rider Corporal Roy Holtz, who rode across the border on a Harley-Davidson.

The Roaring Twenties. This was the decade of the sidecar, or "chummy car," for Harley-Davidson. The company shipped more sidecars, sidevans, and parcel cars than ever before. They also targeted a whole new market: liberated women. Women had recently won the right to vote, so company advertising urged women to "celebrate the freedom and control that comes from taking to the open road on a 1920 Harley-Davidson Sport motorcycle, the "Woman's Out-Door Companion."

The Great Depression. The 1930s saw the release of the most influential motorcycle in Harley-Davidson history: the 1936 "Knucklehead" 61 E, so-called because its engine looked like the back of a clenched fist. With its rounded tank, curving fenders, and instrument panel, the 61 E established the look for future Harleys. It was the first motorcycle to use overhead valves and a recirculating lubrication system.

World War II. In 1941 the United States was back fighting in another world war. This time the company supplied more than 90,000 motorcycles for the war effort and introduced many more young soldiers to the thrill of riding a Harley, which had a lasting impact on the company. After the war, many of the soldiers came home and bought Harleys for themselves, forming motorcycle clubs that became the basis of Harley culture of today. When some of those clubs turned into less than savory associations like the Hells Angels, the company tried to disassociate itself from them, at one point offering to donate Hondas to the clubs so that they wouldn't buy Harleys. The ploy didn't work, so the company countered the association by linking its motorcycles to a nostalgic patriotism.

HARLEY WRECKING CREW

Early on, Harley-Davidson focused on making sturdy, reliable rides and didn't immediately address motorcycle racing. Company president Walter Davidson was the best rider and most aggressive of the founding four, so he was chosen to test the racing waters. In 1908, he entered the Long Island Reliability Run and received a perfect score on the first day and the second day. The next week he won an economy run, posting a top mark of 188 mpg.

That was enough encouragement to start a Racing Division at Harley-Davidson. They brought in William Ottaway as racing director in 1913, and over the course of the next year he helped develop bikes and assemble a team of top-notch riders that were dubbed the "Harley Wrecking Crew." For years, the Wrecking Crew entered all kinds of racing events, from board tracks to road races to cross country, and triumphed. Today, Japanese bikes dominate most forms of racing, but on dirt tracks the Harley is still "top hog."

Country with the most railroad stations: India, with 7,083.

ENTER THE HOG

In 1920 a winning team of Wisconsin farm boys racing Harley-Davidsons attracted notice. They were known as the Hog Boys because of their team mascot, a live hog. After a win, the driver would set the hog on the gas tank of his Harley and make a victory lap. Soon riders began referring to their Harleys as "hogs." In 1983, capitalizing on the "hog" moniker, the Harley-Davidson Motor Company formed a motorcycle club and called it the Harley Owners Group, or H.O.G. They also changed their initials on the New York Stock Exchange from HDI to HOG. There's even a radio station in Milwaukee with the call letters WHOG.

THE EAGLE SOARS ALONE!

Harley-Davidson has always been a family-owned company, which has helped it weather the ups and downs of the market. During the Depression, publicly owned motorcyle makers like Indian were forced to keep making new (and not always the best) product to appease shareholders, and it ultimately wiped them out. By the end of the Depression, Harley-Davidson was one of only two American motorcycle manufacturers still in business.

By 1950 the original founding four had died and the next generation took over. William H. Davidson, William A.'s son, became president and held the position for 29 years. His son, Willie G. became director of styling and helped revolutionize the Harley-Davidson image by utilizing design ideas from customizers. There were missteps: in 1969, the company was strapped for cash and decided to merge with American Machine and Foundry Company. Product quality suffered and many devoted fans turned away, convinced that Harley-Davidson had lost its mojo. The influx of flashy new Japanese models made the brand look dated.

The second-generation of leadership got the message. In 1981, Harley-Davidson bought back all of its shares from AMF and made a renewed commitment to product quality, with the rallying cry "The eagle soars alone!" They made tradition and the American way the core of their advertising and consciously made the new Harleys echo the glory days of the past. Sales soared. At Harley-Davidson's 100th anniversary in 2003 more than 10,000 fans showed up in Milwaukee to form the biggest motorcycle parade in history.

AUTO INNOVATIONS

It's hard to imagine a car without basic features like windshield wipers or seat belts. But all those inventions had to come from somewhere. Here's a brief history of the things we now take for granted.

Windshield wiper (1903). An inventor from Alabama named Mary Anderson patents this simple device that became standard on most cars by 1916.

Electric headlights (1912). Cadillac owners are delighted by the new headlamps, which replaced existing systems like Ham's Auto Inspector-and-Tail Lamp: "Guaranteed to light on just one match!"

Rearview mirror (1911). Ray Harroun, engineer and driver for the Marmon Motor Company, installs one on his #32 Marmon "Wasp" and wins the first Indy 500.

Electric starter (1912). Inventor Charles Kettering eliminates the hand crank starter forever...and goes on to become head of research for General Motors.

Power door locks (1914). These first appear on the ultraluxurious Scripps-Booth Roadster. An ad for the car reads "Worth is not figured by dollar-cost units."

Four-wheel braking system (1924). Buick makes it a standard feature.

Chrome (1926). Oldsmobile adds a little "bling" to its radiators.

Tilt-steering column (1928). Another first from Buick.

Shatter-resistant glass (1929). Cadillac makes it standard.

V-16 engine (1930). In 1926 engineer Owen Nacker connected two Buick straight-8s to a common crankshaft. Cadillac refines the design and incorporates it into the 1930 Madame X Landaulet, which establishes Cadillac's reputation for luxury cars.

No-draft ventilation (1933). Fisher Body of Detroit debuts this feature on all General Motors cars—it circulates fresh air without creating a draft. It would become popular with cigarette smokers.

Automatic transmission (1940). The new line of Oldsmobiles features "Hydra-

Matic" drive, the first fully automatic transmission, for $57 ($876 today).

Air conditioning (1940). This Packard option costs an additional $274 ($4,200 today).

Tail fins (1948). Inspired by the flowing lines of the P-38 fighter plane, designer Franklin Q. Hershey adds fins to the 1948 Cadillac, creating an instant classic.

Power steering (1952). Offered as standard on Buicks, Cadillacs, and Oldsmobiles.

Automatic headlamp dimming (1952). Offered by Oldsmobile.

Power brakes (1953). Another first from Buick.

Seat belts (1958). Long offered as a (seldom-used) option, seat belts became standard equipment after the Saab GT-750 introduced them at a car show.

Cruise control (1959). A special feature in the Chrysler Imperial.

Front-wheel drive (1966). The Oldsmobile Toronado is the first commercial car to offer it.

Traction control (1971). From Buick, for safety.

Anti-lock brakes (1971). Buick, Cadillac, Chrysler, and Nissan all introduced them this year.

Onboard navigation system (1995). General Motors debuts Guidestar. Drivers must tell the device "Next" for it to move on to the next instruction.

Night vision (1999). On the Cadillac DeVille Concours, the system locates obstacles like animals and pedestrians in the dark before the driver can see them.

Onboard entertainment system (1999). Oldsmobile's system includes an LCD monitor, headphone jacks, and remote control.

"Quadrasteer" (2002). Chevrolet and GMC introduce this four-wheel turning system, which enables a full-size pickup to turn as nimbly as a small car.

Automatic parallel parking (2004). Prius debuts this feature in Japan and Great Britain. Drivers can take their hands off the wheel and let the car park itself.

Wi-fi (2011). The newest Fords allow drivers to connect to the Internet.

LOONY LAWS

Planning a road trip? You'd best be aware of these quirks of state jurisprudence.

• In Florida, the fee to hitch an elephant to a parking meter is the same as for a parked car.

• It's against the law to drive around California in a housecoat.

• You may not cross the Minnesota state line with a duck on your head.

• Illinois law requires a car to be driven with a steering wheel.

• Kentucky means business: no female may appear on a highway in a swimsuit unless escorted by at least two officers, or armed with a club.

• It's illegal for a cab driver to have sex in the front seat while on duty in Louisiana.

• No gorilla may ride in the backseat of any car in Massachusetts.

• Shaving in the middle of Main Street in Oxford, Mississippi, will get you arrested.

• It's illegal in North Carolina to drive through a cemetery for pleasure.

• It is illegal to drive blindfolded in the state of Alabama.

• If driving on the sidewalk in Oregon, give pedestrians the right of way.

• Any motorist driving along a country road at night in Pennsylvania must stop every mile, send up a flare, and wait 10 minutes for the road to clear of livestock.

• A couple may not engage in a sexual act in a car at lunchtime in Carlsbad, New Mexico—unless the car has curtains.

• In Rhode Island, when passing a car on the left, you must make a loud noise.

• Any motorist in Washington with criminal intentions must stop at the city limits and telephone the chief of police to inform him that he's coming to town.

• When a woman drives in Tennessee, a man must walk in front of the car and warn other motorists. Also, it is illegal to drive while asleep.

World water speed record: 317.58 mph, by the *Spirit of Australia* hydroplane in 1978.

ISN'T THAT SPECIAL?

Sometimes carmakers look to an outside partner to provide extra marketing power—called co-branding. Here are some hits and misses.

Eddie Bauer Explorer and Bronco (1984). Ford's partnering with the legendary outdoor recreation retailer to create special editions was a million-dollar stroke of genius that continues to pay dividends.

Gucci Hornet Sportabout (1972). The AMC Hornet was a compact introduced under the slogan "The little rich car." Sticking with the "rolling in dough on a budget" theme, AMC had the clever idea to offer a luxury trim package for their Hornet Sportabout wagon by Italian fashion designer Aldo Gucci, whose name alone connoted extravagance. It featured the famous green, red, and buff striping on thickly padded upholstery and Gucci emblems on the door panels. The Gucci Hornet Sportabout was a resounding success; more than 5,000 were sold in the two years it was offered. This inspired AMC to continue the designer label concept by offering the (Pierre) **Cardin Javelin** in 1973 and the (Oleg) **Cassini Matador** in 1974.

Levi's Gremlin (1973). The subcompact Gremlin was AMC's response to the gas crisis of the 1970s. In 1973 the automaker partnered with Levi-Strauss to create "the economy car that wears the pants." The interior featured denim-colored side panels and seats with copper rivets, classic orange-thread stitching, and, of course, a red Levi's tag. The concept worked so well that AMC expanded the trim line to its Jeep CJ-5 and CJ-7 models.

Sinatra Imperial (1982). In 1981 Chrysler was on the verge of bankruptcy. To reassure consumers that the company was solvent, they brought back their Imperial luxury car line. President Lee Iacocca enlisted the help of his friend Frank Sinatra to appear in ads and sing the theme song, "It's time for Imperial!" With Sinatra promoting the line, Chrysler offered a limited-edition "fs" Imperial: painted "Frank Sinatra Glacier Blue" (to match his eyes), with deep blue Mark Cross leather seats and a leather case containing

Race car drivers consider it bad luck to enter and exit from the same side of the car.

16 Sinatra music cassettes. The cost: $23,000 (about $52,000 today). The "fs" edition was dropped in 1983; Chrysler had sold only 12,385 out of a projected 25,000 cars. Sinatra, however, got to keep his personal "fs" Imperial stretch limo—a gift from pal Iacocca.

Snoopy Mitsubishi Pajero Mini (2000). The 50th anniversary of the *Peanuts* comic strip in 2000 gave Mitsubishi the idea to plaster images of Snoopy as a WWI flying ace all over its Pajero Mini. Snoopy's face was on the spare tire cover, speedometer, tachometer, and hubcap, and the rear mud flaps had his paw prints. *Peanuts* creator Charles Shulz's signature was painted on the left rear quarter panel of the mini SUV. The promotion was successful enough that the Snoopy special edition was brought back the next year.

Harley-Davidson Ford F-150 Super Cab (2000). "Harley-Davidson" evokes images of rugged individualists clad in black leather jackets astride rumbling hogs. Basically, Harleys ain't for sissies, and Ford latched onto that idea when it offered the Harley-Davidson Edition of its F-150 Super Cab pickup. It's adorned with the famous Harley insignia on the side and back panels, and upholstered in black leather. The F-150 is offered only in the two Harley colors, Tuxedo Black and Ingot Silver. Various H-D models released since 2000 have had sales of over 75,000. The 2011 model features "Harley-Davidson" spelled out in satin chrome along the top of the bed, and ultra-hot red-and-white detailing across the hood and down the sides of the truck.

Superman Toyota Yaris (2006). The term "Limited Edition" really applies to Toyota's Superman Yaris, which was offered exclusively in Indonesia. Painted "Superman Blue," the subcompact Yaris 1.5 is basically a bulletin board featuring the iconic DC comic hero. The famous "S" shield is emblazoned on the hood, leather seats, steering wheel, gearshift, parking brake, floor mats—even the tissue box. And of course, it wouldn't be a Superman car without the Man of Steel himself flying across the entire side of the car. The edition was unsuccessful. Even before its release, fans in both the auto and comic book worlds were asking, "Why does Batman get the ultra-cool Batmobile and Superman get the teeny-weeny Yaris?"

Aptly named: The HMS *Inflexible* (1876) had the thickest armor of any battleship—42 inches.

BARNSTORMERS

Barnstorm: (of a pilot) to give exhibitions of stunt flying, participate in airplane races, etc., in the course of touring country towns and rural areas. —Dictionary.com

FLYING DAREDEVILS

A glut of leftover Curtiss JN-4 "Jenny" biplanes, former World War I flyboys looking to make a fast buck, and a notable lack of regulations conspired to make barnstorming a booming business in 1920s America. The most–popular shows drew tens of thousands of fans to county fairs and rural airstrips across the country. Admission was 25 to 50 cents, and a little more bought a joy ride with the pilot in his biplane. No stunt was out of the question as daredevil pilots looped-the-loop and barrel-rolled above swarms of thrill-seeking spectators.

As pilots tried to one-up each other with ever more death-defying tricks—such as midair transfers, wing-walking (and dancing), and stunt parachuting—casualties and property damages mounted, prompting Congress to clamp down with civil air regulations. The Air Commerce Act of 1926, which, in part, regulated "stunt flying," was the death-knell for barnstorming…but it was sure fun while it lasted. Here are some of the daredevils who took to the air.

FLYIN' WITH A LION

Roscoe Turner (1895–1970) was as well known for his looks and showmanship as for his flying ability. A tall, strapping man with a waxed mustache, sky-blue jacket, tan whipcord breeches, black riding boots, and officer's cap, Turner epitomized the image many had of the daring adventurer. He started out as a wing walker and stunt jumper with pilot Harry Runser. When Runser quit the team, Turner took the controls and started Roscoe Turner's Flying Circus. By the end of the 1920s, Turner was flying stunts in Hollywood, most memorably in Howard Hughes's epic *Hell's Angels*. In 1930, he teamed up with his most famous co-pilot, a lion cub named Gilmore, who joined him on two record-setting transcontinental flights. Turner became known as the "pilot with the lion."

When Gilmore died in 1952, Turner had the lion stuffed and kept it in his home until his own death in 1970. (Gilmore is currently in cold storage at the Smithsonian Institute.)

"UPSIDE-DOWN" PANGBORN

Like many other barnstormers, Clyde Pangborn (1895–1958) learned to fly as a pilot in World War I. Unlike some of his contemporaries, however, his military career was unexceptional—save for a little trick he learned while serving as a flight instructor at Ellington Field in Houston. While teaching cadets how to fly, Pangborn taught himself to "slow-roll" his Jenny biplane onto its back. That earned him his nickname, "Upside-down," and helped launch his career as an aerial showman after the war. Along with business partner Ivan Gates, Pangborn founded Gates Flying Circus, one of the most popular aerial troupes of the Roaring '20s. In an early stunt, Pangborn attempted to mount a flying plane from a moving car. He slipped from the rope ladder, dislocating three vertebra and sustaining strains and bruises—the only serious injury of his illustrious career. His most popular trick was to change planes in mid-flight. In 1924, "Upside-down" Pangborn garnered even more fame for his mid-air rescue of a stuntwoman whose parachute had become entangled in the landing gear of a plane at an air show.

While he attempted the world's first trans-Pacific flight from Japan to Washington State in 1931 (along with co-pilot Hugh Herndon Jr.), Pangborn's barnstorming experience proved extremely useful. When a new piece of equipment failed early in the flight, Pangborn was forced to perform repairs on the wing of the Bellanca Skyrocket, barefoot, at 14,000 feet. The pair completed the historic flight with a successful belly landing in Wenatchee, Washington—4,500 miles and 41 hours, 15 minutes, away from their takeoff in Samishiro Beach, Japan.

QUEEN BESS

When Bessie Coleman (1892–1926) couldn't find a flight school in the United States willing to accept an African-American woman, she went to France and got her pilot's license there. Upon her return to the States, no one would hire her as a commercial pilot, so she went back to Europe and learned how to stunt fly. Her first show on September 3, 1922, at Glenn Curtiss Field in Garden City, New

...Technically, it's still legal above that height.

York, made her an instant celebrity. Black, beautiful, and fearless, she defied convention even as she drew record crowds. She traveled around the country, performing and giving lectures encouraging women and African-Americans to take up flying. In her home state of Texas, she fought segregation by insisting on a single entry gate at her air shows for both whites and blacks (although seating in the arena was still segregated).

Tragically, Coleman was killed in 1926 while scouting parachute landing sites for an air show in Jacksonville, Florida. With her mechanic William Wills at the controls, her Jenny biplane suffered a mechanical failure and spun into a steep nosedive. Coleman wasn't belted in and was thrown from the plane at 500 feet. She died on impact. Wills was killed moments later when the plane crashed.

PANCHO BARNES

Florence Lowe (1901–75) was a wealthy tomboy from Pasadena, California, who preferred dirty jokes to debutante balls. The 19-year-old bride's restless nature challenged her marriage to Episcopal priest C. Rankin Barnes, and in 1925 she left her husband and young son and ran off to Mexico. Watching her ride a donkey prompted a friend to quip that she looked like Don Quixote's sidekick, "Pancho" (mistaking the name Sancho Panza). After four months, Pancho Barnes returned home and resumed her former life. She fell in love with airplanes and made her first solo flight after six hours of instruction. She promptly purchased a Travel Air biplane and began buzzing her husband's Sunday church services. Soon after, she formed her own air show, Pancho Barnes Flying Mystery School, with a young parachutist named Slim. Their signature stunt was to pull a young woman from the audience under the pretext of taking her for a joyride. Instead, once airborne, Slim would push the woman out of the plane and pull the ripcord on her parachute. Luckily, nobody was ever injured. After her show was grounded for legal reasons, Barnes moved on to airplane racing, breaking Amelia Earhart's speed record by more than 10 mph with a blistering 196.19 mph. Unlike many of her contemporaries, Barnes survived her barnstorming endeavors. She helped found the Hollywood stunt pilots union and became close friends with test pilots Chuck Yeager and Buzz Aldrin.

BMW stands for Bayerische Motoren Werke (Bavarian Motor Works).

AHEAD OF THEIR TIME

Some brilliant ideas for cars that were too advanced for their day.

IDEA: Gas/electric hybrid

CAR: Lohner-Porsche Mixte (1899)

STORY: A century before the Toyota Prius made its debut, Ferdinand Porsche, a 24-year-old engineer at Jacob Lohner and Company, built the world's first hybrid car. The Lohner-Porsche Mixte internal combustion engine charged a bank of batteries that fed current to electric motors located in the front wheel hubs, resulting in an ultra-efficient hybrid that dispensed with the need for a transmission or clutch. It created a sensation at the World Exhibition of Paris in 1900 and made an automotive superstar of the young Dr. Porsche. The car never became more than a novelty, and only 300 Mixtes were built between 1900 and 1905. Porsche went on to design the sports car that bears his name, as well as the innovative Mercedes-Benz SSK and the Volkswagen Beetle.

IDEA: Unibody construction

CAR: Lancia Lambda (1922)

STORY: Each year from 1922 to 1932, Italian automaker Lancia produced a new version of its groundbreaking model. Before the Lambda, most automobiles were built like carriages, with a wooden frame covered by wooden or metal panels. The Lambda was the first to utilize *monocoque*, or unibody construction, which meant the exterior supported the load rather than a frame. The result was a lighter, more fuel-efficient vehicle. Today, most hybrids and virtually all race and high-performance cars feature unibody construction. Eventually, all cars will probably utilize the lighter, stronger body type pioneered nine decades ago.

IDEA: Flying automobile

CAR: Aerocar (1949)

STORY: Seventy-five patents have been filed over the years for

If the temperature goes below –40°F, tires will freeze flat.

flying cars but only one has taken off—kind of. Unlike previous attempts at a flying car, Mo Taylor's Aerocar had foldable wings, so the pilot/driver could stow them after landing and tow them behind the vehicle. Unfortunately, the Aerocar was neither road-worthy (due to its necessarily lightweight construction) nor particularly airworthy. Only five Aerocars were ever built—which may have been for the best. Imagine escaping traffic gridlock by taking to the skies, only to face the much more serious consequences of road rage at 10,000 feet.

IDEA: Fiber optics
CAR: Chevrolet Chevelle (1967)
STORY: The Vigilite Monitoring System—a fiber-optics device that monitored a car's exterior lights and alerted the driver to any burned-out bulbs or other malfunctions—was available as a $26.35 add-on to the Chevelle. Most customers were unconvinced they needed it, and only 117 were sold the first year. The system did better on the following year's Camaro—1,755 were installed in the classic muscle car. The system declined in popularity after that, though, and Chevy dropped it as an option for all but its highest-priced cars in 1970. In 1975, the fiber-optic system made a comeback as a standard feature on new Cadillacs. Although a common feature now, the cars with the original system have become collectors' items and sell for more than $1,000 today.

IDEA: Door stretcher
CAR: Imperial Crown Convertible (1967)
STORY: The Imperial Crown two-door convertible came with a standard "door stretcher," a device Chrysler was so proud of that it featured it prominently in ads to promote the luxury car—even above the car's six-way power seats and nylon "fur" trim. "Door stretcher" was a bit of a misnomer—it was simply a motor in the front seat that allowed a passenger in the rear seat to move the seat forward and out of the way by touching the seat back. The space-age gadget didn't save the car from bad reviews. *Popular Mechanics* listed "water leaks, drafts, spotty paint jobs, sloppy trim and upholstery fit" among the car's faults. Sales were so slow that only 474 Imperial Crown Convertibles were made the following year, and the line was then dropped.

The 1st manned helicopter flight (1907) got 12 inches off the ground and lasted about 30 sec.

IDEA: Quick-defrost glass

CARS: Ford Thunderbird and Continental Mark IV (1974)

STORY: Ford introduced this option on its luxury Thunderbirds and Continental Mark IV models. Using the same technology found on Boeing 747s, it consisted of transparent metallic film sandwiched between layers of polyvinyl butyral and glass. The car required a second alternator to send heat to the film, which Ford claimed would melt frost and ice five times faster than standard grid-type defrosters. There were a few drawbacks: From inside, the glass appeared clear, but viewed from outside, it had a yellowish tinge. The glass was also expensive—$360 for a replacement windshield ($1,400 today). Ford soon discontinued the product.

TO THE FUTURE

Within the next few years, automakers will be introducing a slew of gadgets we didn't know we could live without. Some are already in development:

• Mercedes Benz is working on *adaptive brake lights* that get progressively brighter or dimmer depending on how hard the pedal is pushed.

• Already available on some models is a *collision mitigation* system that automatically applies the brakes and tightens seat belts when it senses an accident is about to occur.

• Audi and Volvo have been experimenting with *blind spot detection* systems to alert drivers to cars in adjacent lanes that they can't see in their side mirrors.

• Nissan has already developed an elastic resin topcoat that helps to prevent scratches, but future cars may incorporate *self-repairing paint* to fix damage.

• *Self-parking* cars and *electric window tinting* are already on the horizon too.

• *Active tires* that adapt to different road conditions and even *autopilot systems* that guide commuters to their destinations are poised to appear within the next 20 years.

NASCAR engines burn 110-octane leaded gasoline; Indy cars burn pure methanol.

ATTENTION, PLEASE!

Given half a chance, flight attendants can be pretty funny. Here are the best one-liners heard on some recent flights.

"People, people! We're not picking out furniture here. Find a seat and get in it!"

"At the pointy end of the plane is our captain."

"We'll be coming through the cabin to make sure your seat-belts are fastened and your shoes match your outfit."

"Ladies and gentlemen, if you wish to smoke, the smoking section on this airplane is on the wing. If you can light 'em, you can smoke 'em."

"In the event of a sudden loss of cabin pressure, oxygen masks will descend from the ceiling. Stop screaming, grab the mask, and pull it over your face. If you have a small child traveling with you, secure your mask before assisting with theirs. If you are traveling with two small children, decide now which one you love more."

"Welcome to Amarillo. Please remain in your seats with your seat belts fastened while the captain taxis what's left of our airplane to the gate."

"Ladies and gentlemen, we will be turning down the cabin lights. This is for your comfort and to enhance the appearance of your flight attendants."

"The yellow button above your head is the reading light; the orange button releases the hounds."

"This aircraft is equipped with a video surveillance system that monitors the cabin during taxiing. Any passengers not remaining in their seats until the aircraft comes to a full and complete stop at the gate will be strip-searched as they leave the aircraft."

"Sit back and relax, or lean forward all twisted up; the choice is yours."

"Please remain in your seats until Captain Crash and the crew have brought the aircraft to a screeching halt up against the gate. And once the tire smoke has cleared and the warning bells are silenced, we'll open the door and you can pick your way through the wreckage to the terminal."

THREE FOR THE ROAD

What has three wheels and goes like a bat out of hell? If it's not the neighbor kid on a trike, it's probably a Morgan. This British company began hand-crafting three-wheelers more than a century ago.

THREE BEATS FOUR

British engineer Henry Frederick Stanley Morgan (1881–1959) built his first three-wheeled car in 1909. The Morgan Runabout featured a pair of independent suspension front wheels, a stiff wooden frame, and a single rear wheel powered by a 7-hp Peugeot engine. The Runabout's power-to-weight ratio of 90 hp per ton made it one of the fastest cars on the road at the time. It was also a head turner. Everywhere H.F.S. (as he liked to be called) went, people asked where they could buy one. He'd only intended to use the Runabout for personal use, but the interest convinced him to turn his invention into a business. And thus the Morgan Motor Company was born in 1910 in Malvern, England.

WINNING GOLD FROM THE GET-GO

In 1910 Morgan premiered a pair of Runabouts at the Olympia Auto Show in London. The first three-wheelers (one 8-hp and one 4-hp model) were well received but didn't attract many orders due to one major limitation: Each had only a single seat. But the new Runabouts showed their mettle when it came to racing. H.F.S. entered one in the London-to-Exeter Time Trial and cruised to a gold medal. In 1912, a Morgan Runabout broke the one-hour world record in the 1100cc class at Brooklands (the world's first motorsport circuit in Surrey, England), zipping along at just under 60 mph. Dorothy Morgan raced her brother's car in rallies and reliability trials all over Europe, where she rarely finished less than first. In 1913 a Runabout driven by W. D. South rocketed up the prestigious Shelsey Walsh Hill Climb at a world-record average speed of 22 mph. That same year *Cyclecar* magazine editor Gordon McMinnies raced another Runabout to victory in the *Cyclecar* Grand Prix in Amiens, France. By the end of 1913, the Runabout had won more awards for speed and reliability than any other light car on the road.

VICTIM OF ITS OWN SUCCESS

The Morgan Motor Company was on a roll. After test driving a Runabout, famed World War I flying ace Albert Ball called it "the nearest thing to flying on the ground" and promptly bought one. Sales skyrocketed. Morgan introduced two- and four-seat versions of the car, which was now dubbed the "Three-wheeler." By 1918 Morgan was producing 50 cars a week at a new factory, nicknamed "The Works," and had become one of Britain's most successful car manufacturers.

But four-wheeled competitors were getting irritated with the speedy upstart. At Brooklands, the speedy Morgans were required to start a lap behind their four-wheeled counterparts to even the odds. Then in 1924, during a Junior Car Club 200-mile race, a three-wheeler crashed when the tread came off its rear tire just as it was crushing its rivals. Although the driver and mechanic survived, race organizers seized the opportunity to ban three-wheelers from future JCC events. Although it continued to win races elsewhere in Europe (recording time trial speeds of 100-plus mph), the Morgan's lowered visibility in England resulted in fewer sales. In 1936 Morgan Motor Company began producing four-wheeled cars like everybody else, and quit making three-wheelers altogether in 1952.

ROARING BACK

The company survived by handcrafting sporty four-wheel roadsters in the spirit of classic MGs and Triumphs. Over the years, "Moogies" (as the cars are called by enthusiasts) attracted wealthy collectors like Ralph Lauren and Mick Jagger, who could afford the $300,000 sticker cost.

In 2011, in honor of its 100th anniversary, the company reintroduced an updated three-wheeler at a more user-friendly price. The new five-speed Morgan 3 Wheeler comes equipped with a Harley Davidson-style V-twin fuel-injected motorcycle engine that propels the car from 0 to 60 mph in 4.5 seconds, with a price tag of less than $40,000. Said one bemused reviewer, "You're basically strapping yourself to an engine." A company spokeperson quipped that Morgan didn't know whether to call its new throwback "a pod racer, fighter plane, speeding bullet, or car."

Wold's oldest train station still in use: the Wylam, Northumberland, UK station, built in 1835.

GHOST TRAINS

These trains really put the "boo" in caboose.

ONLY THE DEAD GET OFF AT KYMLINGE

Just outside of Stockholm, Sweden, there's an abandoned metro station on Line 11 known as Kymlinge. Construction on the stop was halted in 1976 when the town decided to turn the area above it into a nature preserve. In the years since, Kymlinge has become associated with its own ghost train. The *Silverpilen*, or "Silver Arrow," was built in the mid-1960s as a test model for the Stockholm underground and was the only train in the metro system to retain its silver color—all subsequent trains were green. Until it was scrapped in 1996, the *Silverpilen* was used only as a backup, and it was an unusual sight for passengers expecting to catch the usual green train.

But what's more shocking is that people continued to see the silver train long *after* it was scrapped: Witnesses have reported spotting the train, often late at night, in the abandoned tunnels. Sometimes the cars are empty, while other times ghostly passengers occupy *Silverpilen*'s spectral seats. Local legend claims that a few real commuters have inadvertently boarded the ghost train, where they disappeared for weeks or months at a time, only to return with no memory of where they'd been. Some were never heard from again, prompting the locals to say, "Only the dead get off at Kymlinge."

TRACK LIGHTING

Over the years, hundreds of people have reported seeing unusual lights along an abandoned rail line in St. Louis, Saskatchewan, despite the fact that the tracks themselves have long since been removed. Several years ago, Serge and Gail Gareau decided to entertain a couple of out-of-town guests by taking them to the spot where the lights had been most often seen. The foursome parked beside the former site of the tracks and waited. Suddenly a bright yellow light appeared in the distance with a smaller reddish glow beneath it. The lights hovered above the old track bed.

When the friends drove in that direction, the lights vanished, only to reappear right behind them. Unnerved, the couples beat a hasty retreat.

The mayor of St. Louis, Emile Lussier, says the story of the lights dates back to an incident in the 1920s when late one night, while performing a routine check of the track, a Canadian National Railway engineer was struck and decapitated by his own train. The small reddish glow is said to be from the dead engineer's lantern as he searches for his missing head. The big white light is, of course, from the steam engine that killed him.

LINCOLN'S DEATH TRAIN

After Abraham Lincoln was assassinated in April 1865, a funeral train delivered his body from Washington, D.C., to its final resting place in Springfield, Illinois. Frequent stops were made along the way to allow mourners to pay their respects. At each halt clocks were stopped to commemorate the event. Several years later, a rail worker on the line between New York City and Albany (part of the death train's route) was clearing brush late one night in April when he reported a chilly wind, "like just before a thunderstorm," sweeping over the tracks. A "huge blanket of utter darkness" rolled over the man, snuffing out his lantern. Then a blue glow enveloped the tracks, followed by the bright headlight of a train.

The man cowered against a tree as a steam engine covered in black crepe emerged out of the darkness. A skeletal orchestra, led by a spectral conductor, played a dirge from a flat car behind the crewless engine. An identical train followed the first, except this time, in place of the phantom musicians, there was a single black crepe-covered coffin. Ghostly soldiers wearing blue Union uniforms stood at attention along the track and saluted the casket as it passed. The worker fled back to the Hudson Division station to find that the clocks were all running six minutes late. Ever since, every April brings reports of people hearing unexplained steam whistles, seeing mysterious plumes of smoke, and feeling chilly winds along the route of the train. To this day, some claim that watches and clocks still stop wherever it goes.

City with the most Rolls Royces per capita: Hong Kong.

PADDLES & MEATBALLS

Landing a jet on an aircraft carrier is one of the hardest things a navy pilot does. Lt. Matt Powers, USN, who's landed 200 times in the S-3 Viking and the EA-6B Prowler, tells how it's done.

STACK AND LAND

At its busiest, an aircraft carrier can launch two aircraft and land one every 37 seconds. Every licenced pilot can land a plane, but only naval aviators do it on a ship moving at 40 mph. "Each day during a case-1 (high visibility) pattern," says Lt. Powers, "over a dozen jets will be in the same small slice of sky at the same time, maintaining separation and landing on a moving boat at constant intervals, all without saying a word over the radio." In case-2 and -3 conditions, visibility is lower and fewer planes occupy the same airspace.

Aboard the carrier, the Air Boss (the officer in charge of all operations involving aircraft) decides which planes will land first, based on damage and fuel levels. The rest "stack up" around the carrier in a circular holding pattern. When it's his turn to come in for "recovery," or landing, the pilot performs a "break turn"—a screaming, high-G turn—ending up behind the carrier and in line with the runway.

PADDLES AND THE MEATBALL

Powers says, "To increase morale and give a thrill to our maintainers (crew members who service and maintain the aircraft) who've been sweating on the flight-deck for hours, we'd try to rip-off a perfect break-turn just beyond the bow so the troops could literally watch their hard work in action." Then the jets circle behind the stern of the ship and line up with the runway, which is pointed 14 degrees away from the direction the ship is moving. Inside the plane, explains Powers, "The instrument panel provides lineup and altitude corrections, as does the Naval flight officer (that's me). My job is to help the pilot without overwhelming his already busy senses."

Outside the plane, the pilot takes visual cues from an array of lights and mirrors, and audio cues from radio signals by the land signals officer, nicknamed "Paddles." During the 1920s, the early days of aircraft carrier aviation, landing signal officers waved pilots in with large flags, but they later switched to colored handheld paddles. Today the "paddles" are an optical display called the IFLOLS (the Improved Fresnel Lens Optical Landing System). Pilots call this lighting display "the Meatball," because as they approach, it looks like a large red circle. Horizontal green lights flank it. When the Meatball lines up with the green lights, pilots know they're on the right approach path, or "glide slope."

The final leg of a daytime carrier landing begins three-quarters of a mile from the stern of the ship. That's when the LSO says, "Three-quarters of a mile, call the ball," to which the pilot replies, "Roger, Maverick has the ball."

EASING HER IN

While maneuvering the jet into position, "adjustments must be slight and immediate," says Lt. Powers. "Too much correction could cause you to lose altitude, which means you have to increase your airspeed to get back on glide slope. You must catch these fixes like you catch an egg. Otherwise you create a yo-yo effect, either side-to-side or up-and-down."

Pilots landing on *any* runway want to be flying straight with their wings level, but it's even more important to be accurate when trying to land on a runway that's only 1,000 feet long; 252 feet wide; lined on each side with expensive aircraft, explosive fuel tanks, and sailors…and is moving.

Even the best pilots in the best aircraft with the best crew can still have an accident. The Navy doesn't take a break when the seas get rough. If a wave hits the ship at the wrong moment, it can raise or lower the runway so quickly that no pilot can react in time. If the runway is too high, the plane might crash into the stern, sending sheared metal and flaming jet fuel across the flight deck at 100 mph. If the crew is lucky, they'll be able to eject.

PERFECT LANDING

On a successful recovery, the pilot hits one of four arresting wires, held taut by hydraulics, that are strung across the runway about 50 feet apart. The pilot must catch at least one of the cables with the tailhook, a metal hook attached to an eight-foot rod under the tail of the plane. The wires can slow a 54,000-pound aircraft from 150 mph to 0 mph in the length of a football field. Pilots never aim for the first wire, since it's the closest to the edge of the ship. It's safe to land with any of the four wires, but to advance, Naval aviators have to consistently grab the third.

DON'T SINK IN THE DRINK

When the wheels hit the runway, the pilot fires the engines to full power. This seems counter-intuitive, but should the pilot decide to "bolter" (abort the landing), the plane needs to get back in the air immediately. There's no room to taxi to a stop like on a regular runway, which can be a mile long. If a pilot lets his plane taxi too far, he falls off the front of the ship. The Navy hates that.

The LSO grades every landing, regardless of the pilot's experience. Pilots who are new to carrier landings have to complete 12 daytime landings before they're awarded Carrier Qualification. They must qualify again to land at night. In the end, a Naval aviator always has to get it right on his first real-world attempt. There's no one else who can fly the plane. This is what makes landing on an aircraft carrier, as Lt. Powers says, "The single most professional and impressive aspect of a Naval aviator's career." And he or she does it every day.

*   *   *

INDY 500 SNAKE PIT

In the 1970s and 1980s, the southeast corner of the Indy 500 oval, just inside the first turn, was known as the "Snake Pit"—a hardcore party spot for local college students, rednecks, and bikers. Flashing, streaking, fighting, and heavy intoxication used to fuel the party, but Indy 500 management eventually built bleachers there to limit the rowdiness. That worked for a while, until the party moved to Turn 4 and became Snake Pit II. The rowdiness ramped up again, and Indy management clamped down once more, sending in roving patrols of police, sometimes on horseback, to calm the crowd. In 2010 the Snake Pit moved again, to infield turn #3, this time under official Indy 500 sanction.

...built by Ohio State University students in 2010, reached 271.7 mph.

TV SPY RIDES: A QUIZ

James Bond isn't the only spy with a cool car. These small-screen operatives have their own tricked-out rides. See if you can match the series with its signature vehicle. *(Answers and trivia are on page 461.)*

SERIES	VEHICLE
1. *The Man from U.N.C.L.E.* (1964–68)	**a.** Sunbeam Tiger roadster
2. *Mission: Impossible* (1966–73)	**b.** GMC Vandura G-1500
3. *The Prisoner* (1968)	**c.** Volvo P1800
4. *The A-Team* (1983–87)	**d.** Chrysler Crown Imperial
5. *The Green Hornet* (1966–67)	**e.** Ford F-1 panel van
6. *Get Smart* (1965–70)	**f.** AMT Piranha
7. *The Saint* (1962–69)	**g.** Bentley Speed Six
8. *The Avengers* (1961–69)	**h.** Lotus Seven S2

QUEST FOR SPEED, PART II

In the 1950s, it was possible to buy a surplus fighter jet engine for as little as $500. The engines would power wheeled vehicles to unprecedented speed. *(Part I is on page 201.)*

GOING WITH THE FLOW

Simply put, a turbine is a rotary engine that extracts energy from a fluid flow and converts it into useful work. Hero of Alexandria defined the concept in A.D. 150, but aside from paddle-wheel boats, turbine technology wasn't used in transportation until the early decades of the 20th century, when a flurry of patents resulted in the first gas turbines designed for jet propulsion. It was only a matter of time before automakers looked for ways to use this powerful new technology. Chrysler built 50 production model turbine-powered sedans for consumer testing and put them on the American roads in 1963, but by 1979 the program had fizzled out as too expensive an alternative to combustion engine cars.

Firestone partnered with the U.S. Air Force to create the SAC Fireboid, a Boeing 175-hp gas turbine fitted to an auto chassis. The Fireboid competed at the 1955 National Drag Meet and made a demonstration run at the Indy 500 that year. Turbine cars with smaller marine or helicopter turbine engines started competing at Indy in 1962, but six years later public reaction against the new technology resulted in restrictive rules that eliminated them from racing. A similar fate befell turbo cars in Formula 1 racing in 1989. It has been left to dragsters and land speed record chasers to see just how fast a turbo engine can power a car.

MORE RULES AND REGULATIONS

No less than five turbojet cars showed up at Bonneville in 1962, most of them powered with the GE J47 engine used in the USAF F-86 Sabre fighter. While they all showed promise, none distinguished itself and at least one proved disastrous: On its second test run, the Infinity crashed at 250 mph, killing driver Glenn Leasher.

The following year, 26-year-old Craig Breedlove drove Spirit of America, a three-wheeled, turbojet thrust-propelled vehicle, to what should have been the new land speed record—408.312 mph—but the FIA refused to recognize it. Why? Spirit of America had only three wheels, not the required minimum of four, and none of the wheels was driven by the engine. However, the Fédération Internationale Motorcycliste *did* recognize the vehicle, classifying it as "a motorcycle and sidecar," and created a new non-motor-driven class to accommodate the new racer. So the fastest land vehicle was now a motorcycle, and John Cobb's 1947 speed of 394.196 mph was still the FIA-recognized record.

Cobb's record fell officially on July 27, 1964, when Donald Campbell drove his Bluebird CN7 to 403.10 mph on Lake Eyre, Australia. Like Spirit of America, Bluebird was powered by a turbine engine—but one connected to a drive shaft that powered its four wheels. FIA thereby recognized Campbell's time as the new official world record. However, Campbell was disappointed not to have beaten Breedlove outright; he had designed Bluebird to go 500 mph. Breedlove's record remained the one to beat.

BREAKING 500 MPH

That set the stage for an astonishing month of trials at Bonneville in October 1964. The record was reset five times by three different drivers. As the winter rains descended, showering the flats and ending the competition, Art Arfons's Green Monster was on top at 536.71 mph, beating Breedlove's best run of 526.28 mph, the first to cross the 500-mph barrier. Recognizing the inevitable, the FIA and the FIM met in December in Paris and agreed to recognize as an absolute land speed record the higher speed recorded by either body, by any vehicle running on wheels, whether wheel-driven or not. Breedlove's previous records were officially acknowledged retroactively.

BREAKING 600 MPH

For a two-week period that October, Breedlove held the World Land Speed Record and the Guinness World Record for the longest set of skid marks ever made. Coming out of the measured-

Longest train journey: the Transsiberian Express from Moscow to Vladivostok. It takes 8 days.

mile portion of the run on its return pass, the Spirit of America lost its parachute brakes and hurtled out of control for 5 miles across the salt flats, taking out a line of telephone poles before crashing into a pond at 200 mph. Breedlove swam ashore and quipped, "And for my next trick, I'll set myself on fire."

Breedlove decided to take no chances with the FIA's rules. He came back the following year with a four-wheel Spirit of America to recapture the record with a 600.601-mph run. That feat made him the first person in history to go more than 400, 500, and 600 mph in a land-based vehicle. His record would stand for five years.

It would take the Blue Flame, a liquid-fuel rocket car driven by Gary Gabelich, to break Breedlove's record. Fueled by a combination of hydrogen peroxide and liquified natural gas pressurized by helium gas, the Blue Flame scorched the salt flats on October 23, 1970, with a speed of 630.388 mph.

BREAKING 700 MPH

There have been four subsequent land speed records set since the Blue Flame's. Today the record stands at 763.035 mph, or Mach 1.03—faster than the speed of sound. The new mark was set on October 15, 1997, by RAF pilot Andy Green in the British-made Thrust SSC II, powered by two Rolls Royce jet engines.

Such high speeds beg the question—when does a car become a plane? Before his death in 1952, Cobb said, "A jet-propelled car would not be a motorcar; it would be a sort of aeroplane dragging its wheels along the course."

For traditionalists, a car must have an internal combustion piston engine powering the wheels. For them, the FIA land speed record stands at 415.896 mph, set on September 26, 2008, by Tom Burkland in the Burkland Streamliner. That car is 24 feet long, 38 inches wide, and 41 inches tall, powered by two 450-plus ci supercharged, alcohol-fueled engines with the crankshafts bolted together nose-to-nose. It's not the family car, but it is unmistakably an automobile.

For Part III, go to page 396.

GIMME A BRAKE!

Early automaking focused on making vehicles go. Making them stop was an afterthought.

SOLE POWER

In 1885 Carl Benz gave the first demonstration of his gasoline-powered tricycle to a gathering of curious spectators outside his Mannheim, Germany, workshop. As Benz and his wife, Bertha, rode his new invention around in circles, the crowd marveled at all the technological wonders the tricycle had: electrical ignition, carburetor, water cooling system, rack-and-pinion steering, and rear springs. What it didn't have was brakes. Benz lost control of the vehicle and plowed into a brick wall. Both riders were uninjured in what may well have been the first automobile accident.

Henry Ford's first horseless carriage, the Quadricycle, didn't have brakes, either. The two-speed automobile, introduced in 1896, featured a wooden frame, a single seat, and four bicycle tires. The two-cylinder engine had a top speed of nearly 18 mph. When Ford wanted to stop his car, he had to put it in neutral and rub the sole of his shoe against the rear tire, Fred Flintstone style.

PULL THE LEVER

Brakes were soon standard equipment on new cars, but automakers relied on systems like those used on horse-drawn carriages. Most incorporated a lever that, when pulled, jammed a pad against the solid rubber tire. The heat from the friction quickly ground tires down to the rim. In 1899 Gottlieb Daimler came up with a rudimentary drum brake. He strapped a cable to the chassis and wound the other end around a drum on the rear axle. As the vehicle moved forward, the cable tightened, making it easier for the driver to pull the lever when it came time to engage the brakes. That same year the Columbia Automobile Company introduced a dual rear braking system, complete with a bell that rang when the vehicle came to a full stop. None of these efforts could disguise the fact that these brake systems were scant improvement over Henry Ford's shoe.

Longest ownership of a new vehicle: Carl T. Keller bought a new Packard in 1951...

DRUMROLL, PLEASE

In 1902 Louis Renault came up with the idea of using a lever-activated brake pad (or shoe), which would press against a wheel-mounted drum to stop the vehicle. The modern brake was born! Later that year, American automaker Ransom E. Olds decided to test his own new external braking system against a Columbia Victoria car with the Renault-style drum brakes and a horse-drawn carriage with the old-fashioned tire brake. The brake on the Olds consisted of a single flexible stainless-steel band wrapped around a drum on the rear axle. When pressure was applied with a pedal, the band contracted around the drum, causing the vehicle to stop.

In the test, Olds's car went from 14 mph to a stop in 21.5 feet. It took the Victoria with the Renault brakes 37 feet to achieve the same results. As for the carriage, it took the driver 77.5 feet to come to a halt. Olds's design had its drawbacks, though. When stopped on a hill, the band tended to unwind, causing the vehicle to roll backward, so drivers had to carry wheel chocks. Also, since the system was exposed to the elements, it rusted out quickly, requiring a brake overhaul every 200 to 300 miles.

DEADLY DISCS

Over in Great Britain, F. W. Lanchester patented a spot disc braking system in 1902 quite similar to those in use today. However, when the copper brake linings came in contact with the metal discs, they made a piercing squeal that annoyed people for blocks around. Another Englishman, Herbert Frood, solved the metal-to-metal problem of Lanchester's disc brakes in 1907 by replacing the copper linings with asbestos pads. Asbestos was strong, sound absorbent, and heat resistant. Now motorists could drive 10,000 miles between brake jobs.

Automakers and motorists were delighted. Unfortunately, asbestos was later found to be a carcinogen responsible for several diseases including lung cancer. Despite this, it wasn't until 1988 that asbestos brake pads were phased out in favor of Kevlar and other modern materials.

FLUID MECHANICS

Shortly after the end of World War I in 1918, Malcolm Lockheed (then Lougheed) became the first person to adapt hydraulics to brakes. When the pedal was pushed, fluid pressure was transferred from a cylinder through a tube to the shoes, which in turn pushed against brake drums. Hydraulic brakes removed the effort often associated with braking, making them easier to use for a fast-growing part of the new automobile market—women. In 1921 the Duesenberg Model A became the first passenger car to be equipped with four-wheel hydraulic brakes. It took another full decade for other manufacturers to get onboard with the new technology, which has changed little over the years. In 1939 Ford became the last major manufacturer to switch over to the superior hydraulic brakes.

BRAKE INNOVATION TIMELINE

• The 1950s brought more braking innovations, including vacuum assist (power) brakes, self-adjusting drum brakes, and brake booster disc brakes.

• In 1962 the Studebaker Avanti became the first American car to exclusively feature disc brakes, although they had been popular for years in Europe.

• In 1966, an anti-lock (anti-skid) braking system (ABS), first developed by Great Britain's Road Research Laboratories in 1958, was used in a production car for the first time—a Jensen FF sports sedan. The system used a series of valves to control how much pressure each brake received from the master cylinder, and when. A new and improved ABS, including electronic sensors, became standard on most cars in the 1990s.

* * *

ENTRANCE REDESIGN, PLEASE

In 2007 a woman in Dusseldorf, Germany, mistook a subway entrance for the opening to an underground parking garage and got halfway down the stairs before realizing her mistake. By then, her Volkswagen Cabrio was stuck and had to be extracted by a tow truck. This wasn't the first time that this had happened. Four years before, a man performed the same driving maneuver for the same reason, with the same result.

In England, an automobile muffler is called a *silencer*.

HAUNTED HIGHWAYS

Driving these roads can be hazardous to your sanity.

GHOST ROAD

The A-75 Kinmont Straight in southwest Scotland is known by locals as the Ghost Road. On this 1.5-mile stretch from Annan to Gretna Green, wraithlike figures have been known to hurl themselves in front of passing cars on a regular basis. Since 1957 drivers traveling it at night have reported seeing human specters of different ages and time periods, plus various ghostly animals. "It was in July when I was driving back from my mother's house in Eastriggs around 10 p.m. on a clear, well-lit night," reported Donna Maxwell from New Path. "All of a sudden a man appeared in front of my car and just stood there, looking sad. I was doing around 50 mph and I slammed on the brakes. I was convinced I hit him but I couldn't see anyone."

Maxwell's story is not unusual. In 1962 Derek and Norman Ferguson were driving on the A75 late one night when a large hen flew into their windshield, vanishing on impact. The hen was followed by an old woman, waving her arms, followed by a screaming man with long hair, who himself was followed by more animals. All of the apparitions ran toward the car, then vanished into thin air. In 1995 Garson and Monica Miller struck a man in a red sweater and dark trousers near Annan, but when they stopped the car, there was no sign of a body.

SATAN'S ALLEY

A 10-mile stretch of rural Clinton Road between Newfoundland and Upper Greenwood Lake in Passaic County, New Jersey, is rumored to be the site of satanic gatherings and sacrifices. Strange creatures, including red-eyed hounds, monkeys, and mysterious hybrid animals, have been spotted along this two-lane road, along with a ghostly girl driving a ghostly Camaro. But seeing a "ghost boy at the bridge" is the tale most often told about Clinton Road. Apparently, if you throw a penny over the bridge at Clinton Brook late at night, within a minute the spirit of a boy who drowned in the water below will toss it back at you.

In military air lingo, "angels fifteen" means 15,000 feet above sea level.

TUEN MUN ROAD

Built in 1977, Tuen Mun Road is one of Hong Kong's oldest motorways and is notable for its narrow carriageway and many blind spots. The high accident rate is officially blamed on heavy traffic, but locals and tourists swear it's something else. Many tell of spooky apparitions that pop up out of nowhere. Startled drivers swerve to miss the phantoms and smash into real cars. The theory is that the ghostly jaywalkers are specters of past crash victims.

BLOODSPOINT ROAD

Tales of ghastly doings along this stretch of country road in Cherry Valley, Illinois, date back to its 19th-century namesake, Arthur Blood. A spate of unexplained cattle deaths, followed by a series of fires that burned houses and fields, left the locals panicked. When the rumor spread that Blood's children had befriended a witch, the neighbors turned on the family in a fury. Arthur went insane and hung his children in the barn. Ever since, the road has been thought cursed. A bus full of children coming home from a party went off the railroad bridge and crashed on the tracks below. Local legend says that if you drive onto the bridge, stop, and put your car in neutral, a mysterious force will push your vehicle the rest of the way across the bridge. As you pass, spectral children will appear on the road and leave handprints on the sides of your car. Some drivers have reported a black phantom truck that tried to run them off the bridge, while others have said they were chased by a demonic hound.

* * *

HOVER-HOOVER

When hovercraft "air cushion" technology became all the rage in the '50s, the Hoover Company came out with a wheel-less hovercraft vacuum cleaner. The dome-topped Constellation rode along on its exhaust. That line was discontinued in 1975 but in 1973 Hoover came out with the low-profile, flying saucer-shaped Hoover Celebrity canister model. After a brief run as an hovercraft vacuum, they added wheels. Working versions of both models are now collector's items.

THE FLYING PANCAKE

The Zimmer Skimmer plane had an unorthodox and ugly design, but it could do something other planes couldn't—it could take off and land like a helicopter.

BACKGROUND

In 1933 Charlie Zimmerman was one of a handful of engineers working for the National Advisory Committee on Aeronautics at Langley Memorial Aeronautical Research Laboratory in Virginia. Zimmerman, whose actual area of expertise was electrical engineering, had quickly become the in-house expert on theoretical aerodynamics. So when NACA challenged its engineers to design the ultimate safe airplane—i.e., one that wouldn't stall—Zimmerman was ready.

FLYING DINNER PLATE

Zimmerman knew that the surest way to make an airplane stall-proof was to lower the aspect ratio of its wings. Mathematically, the aspect ratio is the square of the wingspan divided by the wing area, which means that the broader the wing, the lower the aspect ratio. He took a regular wingspan and shortened it until it was almost a square. Then he curved the wingtips until he had something that looked like a stretched-out circle. The wing and fuselage were now fused into one seamless curved edge. When he showed his design to his fellow engineers, one cracked that he'd designed an aerodynamically correct dinner plate.

Zimmerman saw much more than that. His calculations showed that his odd circular wing might really do the job. The unorthodox shape of the wing meant his craft would generate more lift than a conventional wing. Such a high angle of attack meant that it could land at very low speed. "I began to realize," Zimmerman wrote later, "that I would have an airplane that could actually take off and land almost vertically without stalling." In other words, a plane that had all the advantages of a helicopter but would be far simpler and safer to operate.

There was a glitch, however. The unorthodox wing shape created a lot of drag. Wind tunnel tests showed that the low-aspect wing generated little tornado-like whirlwinds off its wingtips that hurt the wing's efficiency. Zimmerman's solution was simple: He set his propellers in line on the outer edge of the wing and made them turn in the opposite direction of the vortices, to neutralize their effect. Problem solved, he submitted his design and waited to hear from the judges at NACA.

IN THE NAVY

NACA loved his concept, so much so that he won the competition. But they declined to sponsor his design because they thought it was too unconventional. Instead they took the two runner-up ideas and greenlighted them for development into prototypes.

It was a crushing disappointment, but Zimmerman refused to give up. For two years he worked nights and weekends with two colleagues to build a one-man wooden model with a seven-foot wingspan, powered by two 25hp Cleone engines. It never flew: He couldn't get the engines to synchronize correctly. So in 1936 Zimmerman junked the larger model for a smaller-scale version only 20 inches long—and this one flew beautifully. He filmed the mini-model in flight, and the footage so impressed executives with United Aircraft in Connecticut that they provided Zimmerman with the facilities and resources to build his plane.

A demonstration of an electric remote-controlled version called the V-162 piqued the Navy's interest in 1939, especially the plane's almost vertical takeoff and landing capability, which made it very attractive to a naval air force that was growing more and more reliant on aircraft carriers. The green light was given to build a full-size version, to be named the V-173.

ZIMMER SKIMMER

Nicknames given to Zimmerman's plane by skeptics at the Pentagon included "the Zimmer Skimmer" and "the Flying Pancake"—both were fairly accurate descriptions of the craft under construction. At 23 feet wide and 26 feet long, the V-173 sat 12 feet off the ground with its nose in the air at an improbably steep 22-degree angle. The nonretractable landing gear jutted out from the lower fuselage like two sets of beanpoles. A pair of 80hp Continental engines powered the 16-foot-diameter three-bladed wooden propellers. To save weight and money, the airplane was framed out of wood and covered with fabric. Fully fueled, the plane weighed 3,000 pounds.

CHARLIE, SHE FLIES! SHE FLIES!

By 1941 the V-173 had passed its static wind tunnel tests, and it was time to take it up in the air for a real test drive. On November 23, 1942, pilot Boone T. Guyton climbed into the cockpit of the V-173 and received his last instructions from an understandably nervous Zimmerman. Aside from a few small-scale models this plane had flown only in theory. Guyton gave Zimmerman a thumbs-up, secured the canopy, and taxied onto the runway. As predicted, the V-173 took off after a very short takeoff run, and minutes later the Flying Pancake was several hundred feet above the steel gray waters of Long Island Sound. Guyton turned the stick to the left to veer north—and that's when he discovered he couldn't turn the airplane.

Eventually Guyton was able to edge the plane around by literally wrestling the stick repeatedly, each time easing the plane a few more degrees in the right direction. There was clearly a major flaw in the guidance system, but once he had gotten the craft going in the right direction, everything else worked perfectly. Years later, Guyton recalled thinking to himself, *Charlie, she flies. She flies!*

Guyton later described the landing as "sensational, unlike any other I've ever made." Once over the runway, he pulled the stick all the way back and hit the throttle. The airplane hovered just above the tarmac, then sank gently onto the runway. Charlie Zimmerman's "Flying Pancake" had completed its first manned flight.

END OF THE LINE

Over the next few years, the guidance issues were straightened out, and more powerful engines were added to the plane to give it greater stability. But for all practical purposes, that was the end of the line for the Flying Pancake. The Navy hurried a larger, more powerful version into production called the XF5U-1. Nine feet wider, two feet longer and higher, the new version was to be the world's fastest yet slowest fighter plane. Engineers predicted that it would fly up to 400 mph but land at 40. By 1947 the XF5U-1 was

...was powered by a 2-cylinder, 4 horsepower engine.

ready for flight trial and Guyton was to be her test pilot. But on March 17, the Navy pulled the plug on the project. All work and testing stopped, and all prototypes were scrapped.

Zimmerman never received an official explanation as to why the Navy so abruptly tossed aside 15 years of work. By all accounts he took it stoically, even offering a possible explanation: "I saw a legitimate reason for the cancellation. The jets were here, and they promised better speed." He went back to work with NACA, which later morphed into NASA, from which he retired in 1967.

The XF5U-1 was destroyed as ordered. The Flying Pancake, however, suffered a kinder fate. It was placed in storage at the Norfolk Naval Air Station in 1949 and later moved to the National Air and Space Museum, where it remains today.

* * *

FLIGHT TRAINING TIPS

Basic Flying 101

1. Try to stay in the middle of the air.

2. Do not go near the edges of it.

3. The edges of the air can be recognized by the appearance of ground, buildings, sea, trees, and interstellar space. It is much more difficult to fly there.

—from a note posted at Vance Air Force Base, Enid, Oklahoma

"The only time an aircraft has too much fuel onboard is when it is on fire."

—Charles Kingsford-Smith, Australian aviation pioneer

"What is the cause of accidents? Usually it is because someone does too much too soon, followed very quickly by too little too late."

—Steve Wilson, investigator, National Transportation & Safety Board

"Nobody who gets too damned relaxed builds up much flying time."

—Ernest K. Gann, aviation writer

The Chinese began to make kites—the first form of glider—around 350 B.C.

GAME PLAY

A quick guide to six hot virtual driver games.

DiRT 3

Platforms: PS3, Xbox 360, PC GFWL

Review: "*DiRT 3* sees the return of classic modes: Rally, Trail Blazer, Head 2 Head, Land Rush and Rally Cross, and adds new ones which can all be grouped together under the title of Gymkhana; events that are all about performing 'tricks' and stunts. An addictive mix of simulation and arcade racing styles that's both enjoyable and challenging.... The graphics are exceptional.... Landscapes are lush, all of the tracks absolutely beautiful and stunningly lit, and the plethora of weather settings—snowy, windy, dusty, rainy, sunny—are a sight to behold."

—Craig Snow, gamrReview

GRAN TURISMO 5

Platform: PS3

Review: "*GT5* is without a doubt the most complex and complete commercial-racing experience available. It features over 1,000 real-world cars, a huge roster of real-world tracks...and a vast number of racing options.... There are License Tests to help you improve your skills and a variety of practice modes, including free and timed runs, and even a drift mode. *GT5* is an amazingly deep racing game that offers an almost mind-boggling amount of racing challenges, cars, tracks and features and a superb Online Mode that gives the game incredible longevity."

—Jaz Rignall, GamePro.com

NEED FOR SPEED: HOT PURSUIT

Platforms: Xbox 360, PC, PS3, Wii

Review: "*Need for Speed: Hot Pursuit* completely embraces that spirit of adolescent madness and just runs with it. There is no wedged-in storyline here. You can play as a cop or a racer, and you increase your rank or wanted level as you run people off the road, drift around corners, drive into oncoming traffic (as a racer), and

Built in 1922, Oregon's Columbia River Highway was America's first planned scenic roadway.

generally behave like a motoring maniac....The more you drive, crash, smash and win, the more cool stuff you get. It's simple, and it works."

—Ryan Geddes, IGN

MARIO KART WII

Platforms: Nintendo Wii

Review: *Mario Kart Wii* offers varied multiplayer and thoroughly integrated online modes that will keep you coming back for more. *Mario Kart Wii* added motorcycles and dirt bikes to the weapons-based go-kart racing. The extensive multiplayer options, deeply integrated online functionality, multitude of controller schemes available, and simple gameplay makes *Mario Kart* great fun and quite possibly the most accessible...ever."

—Lark Anderson, CNET.com

REAL RACING 2 HD

Platforms: iOS

Review: "Racing iOS devices (iPhone, iPad) just got a heck of a lot better with *Real Racing 2*. The game offers realistic a racing experience complete with 16-car races, fantastic online multiplayer integration, and a career mode that take you through beautifully rendered versions of some of the biggest racetracks in the world....If you're after a solid racing title for your favorite super-sized touchscreen device, there's no substitute for *Real Racing 2*."

—Game Pro, *Ultimate Games Guide*

ATV WILD RIDE

Platforms: Nintendo DS; supports local multiplayer

Review: "Behind the wheel of an ATV, fans of arcade-style racing will feel right at home....[The game comes loaded with an] impressive amount of game content...including a World Tour mode that spans more than 20 tracks across a variety of exotic locations...unlockables, varied racers and ATVs to put to the test. [W]here others have tried and failed, Renegade Kid succeeds in building a solid portable DS racer with *ATV Wild Ride*."

—Nick Chester, Destructoid.com

Neiman Marcus sells an electric car shaped like a big cupcake.

WILD KINGDOM

When carmakers search for the perfect name, they often find inspiration in nature.

MAMMALS

Stutz Bearcat (1912–34)
Jaguar (1945–)
Singer Gazelle (1956–67)
Chevrolet Impala (1958–)
Buick Wildcat (1962–70)
Chevrolet Cheetah (1963–65)
Ford Mustang (1964–)
Ford Bronco (1966–96)
Mercury Cougar (1967–2002)
Triumph Stag (1970–78)
Ford Pinto (1971–80)
Audi Fox (1973–79)
VW Rabbit (1974–)
Mercury Bobcat (1975–80)
Chevrolet Bison (1977–80)
Dodge Ram (1981–)
Mercury Sable (1986–2005)

FISH

Corvette Stingray (1963–76)
Plymouth Barracuda (1964–74)
AMC Marlin (1965–67)

BUGS

Volkswagen Beetle (1938–)
Hudson Wasp (1952–54)
Dodge Super Bee (1968–71)
Datsun Honey Bee (1973–78)

BIRDS

Kissel White Eagle Sportster (1927)
Buick Skylark (1953–97)
Doretti Swallow (1954–55)
Studebaker Hawk (1957–61)
Datsun Bluebird (1959–2005)
Studebaker Lark (1959–66)
Ford Falcon (1960–70)
Pontiac Firebird (1967–2002)
Plymouth Road Runner (1968–80)
Stutz Blackhawk (1971–87)
Pontiac Sunbird (1975–94)
AMC Eagle (1979–87)

SNAKES

Shelby Cobra (1961–67)
Dodge Viper (1991–)
Dodge Copperhead (1997)
Python Amphibious Vehicle (2009)
Ford Mustang Shelby GT640 Golden Snake (2011)

WORLD'S FASTEST GRANDPA

The true story of a 68-year-old who rode his Indian motorcycle into the record books.

HARD-RIDING KIWI

In 1920 a 20-year-old New Zealander named Herbert James ("Burt") Munro bought a new motorcycle, an American-made Indian Scout. The cycle was powered by a 600cc, 55-hp engine, with a top speed of 55 mph. Munro had no way of knowing at the time that he and his motorcycle would be inextricably linked for the rest of his life, on a quest for speed that would take them all the way to the salt flats of Bonneville and a world record that remains unbeaten.

By his mid-20s, Munro and his Indian Scout were a fixture at speed events around New Zealand. He worked as a motorcycle salesman and mechanic to support his racing habit, even finding the time to marry and to father four children. But as he wrote years later in a letter to a friend, life for him had become, and would remain for decades, "weekends and nights getting ready for hill-climbs, trials, and standing ¼ and flying ¼ mile events, and 1-mile dirt sidecar races." In 1940 he set the New Zealand Open Road speed record at 120.8 mph, his first major record and one that stood for 12 years. But Munro was convinced that his Indian could go much faster.

ULTIMATE CUSTOMIZATION

Munro began transforming his motorcycle into the Munro Special, a never-ending process of design and fabrication that lasted 40 years. His engineering skills were completely self-taught. He worked out designs in his head, and used cast-off tools and materials that he scavenged or persuaded supporters to donate. Munro lengthened and lowered the Indian's frame, rebuilt the suspension, replaced the standard two-cam, push-rod setup with his own four-cam system, and converted the bike to run with overhead valves and his own lubrication system. He made cylinder sleeves from discarded municipal cast iron gas pipe, made connecting rods from a broken Ford truck axle, and casted and machined his own pistons, flywheels, cams, and followers. He even made his own racing slicks by carving the tread off normal tires with a knife. "I'll suddenly think of some new scheme to get more speed," he said. "Of course these brainwaves often made it slower or just more blown parts." He estimated that he had over 250 engines break down on him. As for safety, it was never a priority. As a result, Munro suffered some spectacular mishaps that resulted in broken bones, concussions, a brain hemorrhage, loss of teeth, severe burns, a torn up shoulder, and untold amounts of skin and flesh lost to gravel, sand, and salt.

OFFERINGS TO THE GOD OF SPEED

By the mid-1940s, Munro's marriage had fallen victim to his true passion. In 1948 the newly divorced Munro quit his job and decided to devote himself full-time to the pursuit of speed. He lived a monklike existence in a cinder block two-car garage that he built himself, sleeping on a single bed in the corner with suitcases stuffed beneath it to hold his clothes. One wall held shelves for parts (the motto "Offerings to the God of Speed" hand-painted on one of them). His work bench and lathe took up another wall, and a homemade motorcycle stand was in the center.

Writing to a friend in 1970, Munro said, "For one stretch of 10 years I put in 16 hours every day, but on Christmas Day took the afternoon off." When his doctor advised him to take it easier due to angina, he cut back to 10-hour days.

Munro decided to build a streamliner, an aluminum shell that would fit around the bike for better aerodynamics. Inspired by his observation of goldfish at a local botanical garden, he spent five years hammering out and welding together the shell. It almost killed him on a test run at the 1960 Canterbury Speed Trials. Once he got up to speed, he found that the shell fit too snugly for him to weight-shift for control or to reach the gear shift by his right leg. It also generated so much turbulence that the Indian began to swing wildly out of control. At 150 mph something broke in the engine, sending the bike into a 500-foot skid.

First animals in space? Fruit flies, on a US-launched V2 rocket on Feb. 20, 1947.

Undaunted, he scrapped the streamliner but used it as a mold to build modified, fiberglass versions.

FAST ON THE FLATS

Munro had set numerous records in New Zealand and Australia, but his ultimate goal was to run the Munro Special over 200 mph. To do that, he'd require bigger tracks than either country could provide. In August 1962, at the age of 63, Munro traveled with his Indian for the first time to the Bonneville Salt Flats in Utah for Speed Week. Over the next five years, he would make nine attempts to break the American Motorcycle Association world records in the Flying One Mile-Class S. It became the hardest, most dangerous challenge of his life.

"I had some of the worst out of control rides on record," he wrote later. "At the Salt in 1967 we were going like a bomb. Then she got the wobbles just over half way through the [nine mile] run. I sat up, the wind tore my goggles off and the blast forced my eyeballs back into my head—I couldn't see a thing. We were so far off the black line that we missed a steel marker stake by inches. I put her down—a few scratches all round but nothing much else." He was traveling at close to 200 mph.

LEGACY

Munro broke his first record in 1962 (178.97 mph with an 850cc engine). He followed that with another in 1966 (168.066 mph, under-1000cc). But the run that cemented his place in motorcycle racing legend occurred on August 26, 1967, when he set an under-1000cc world record of 183.586 mph. Munro clocked 190.07 mph in qualifying, the fastest-ever officially recorded speed on an Indian motorcycle. He was 68, and a grandfather. His motorcycle was 47. His record still stands.

Bad health kept Munro from competing at Bonneville again, and from reaching his elusive 200-mph goal. He died on January 6, 1978. In 2005 the movie *The World's Fastest Indian*, starring Anthony Hopkins, introduced Burt Munro to the world outside racing. Munro was inducted into the AMA Motorcycle Hall of Fame in 2006. He summed up his passion memorably, "You can live more in five minutes on a motorcycle in some of these events I've been in than some people do in a lifetime."

BRICKYARD TRADITIONS

After a century, "The Greatest Spectacle in Racing"—the Indianapolis 500— is bound to have a few time-honored (not to mention quirky) traditions all its own.

"GENTLEMEN, START YOUR ENGINES!"
Ever since two-time winner turned speedway president Wilbur Shaw called out the famous catchphrase for the first time in the early 1950s, 400,000 fans gather every year to hear 33 of the world's fastest cars roar to life in unison. When Janet Guthrie became the first woman to race in the 500 in 1977, owner Tony Hulman declared, "In company with the first lady ever to qualify at Indianapolis, gentlemen, start your engines!" Since there's usually more than one woman in the race today, the current starter, Hulman's daughter Mari, says, "Ladies and gentlemen, start your engines!"

CARB DAY
The Thursday before the race used to be called Carburetion Day: the last day teams could adjust their car's carburetor to "race day trim" from the less fuel-efficient configuration used for speed trials. The term's a bit of a misnomer now, since modern race cars don't use carburetors—they're fuel-injected. The last time carburetors were used at the 500 was in 1963, when Jim Clark and Dan Gurney drove stock-block Ford-powered Lotuses to second and seventh places, respectively. Carb Day remains the last day spectators can watch the drivers practice, and the only time other than the race itself when all 33 cars are on the track at the same time.

11th ROW CHARITY BALL
The Friday before the race, the pavilion at the Brickyard Crossing Golf Course (four of its holes lie inside the track oval) hosts a charity dinner honoring the three slowest qualifiers, whose times have put them in the 11th (and last) starting row. Since 1973, local comedians and racing celebrities have roasted past honorees, including Mario Andretti, Johnny Rutherford, Tom Sneva, and Al Unser, who are also given bonus checks based on their starting

positions: 31, 32, or 33 cents (before taxes). By the way, no driver has ever come from the last row to win the race.

BOMBS AWAY

Spectators at the two-and-a-half mile oval track at Indy can be a mile away from each other—and that's just in the grandstands. In the days before public address systems, track officials detonated a small bomb the morning of race day as a signal to fans that the entrance gates were open. Over the years other bombs have signaled various events throughout the day, but this is the only one that survives. Slugabeds, be warned: The gates open at 6:00 a.m.

SING IT AGAIN, JIM

Legend holds that a brass band played "Back Home Again in Indiana" during the final lap of Indiana-born Howdy Wilcox's 1919 win. What's beyond dispute is that the song has been sung prior to every race since 1946. That year James Melton of the New York Metropolitan Opera sang it, backed by the Purdue Marching Band. Over the years, the band has accompanied entertainers such as Mel Tormé, Vic Damone, and Dinah Shore. Since 1972 the honor has gone to actor Jim Nabors, TV's Gomer Pyle. The finishing touch? On the last line of the song, speedway workers release a giant batch of helium balloons into the air.

GOT MILK?

One of the first things the winner does in Victory Lane after the race is take a long pull from a chilled bottle of milk. Originally, that quaff was buttermilk. Louis Meyer won the 500 in 1928 and 1933, so when he qualified for the race in 1936, he knew how thirsty he'd be at the end. His mom reminded him how refreshing buttermilk was on a hot day, so he told a crew member to have a cold bottle waiting for him after the race—which he won. Later, a dairy industry executive spotted a newspaper photo of Meyer drinking the buttermilk and saw a marketing opportunity. The next year, the dairy company offered a bottle of milk to the winner, and a tradition was born. The ritual was broken most famously in 1993 by Brazilian winner Emerson Fittipaldi. As the owner of an orange grove back home, he decided to drink a glass of OJ after his win to promote Brazilian oranges. (He later drank milk, too, but only after getting an earful from tradition-minded fans.)

It may be the shoulder (of the road) to you; to Brits, it's the *verge*.

HISTORY OF AIRSHIPS, PART III

In the years following World War I, airships were increasingly popular, with aeronauts setting records all over the globe. But it all came crashing down on May 6, 1937, in Lakehurst, New Jersey. *(Part II is on page 177.)*

RECORDS

The first airships built by England's Royal Navy were copies of a Zeppelin L33 shot down in Yorkshire in 1916, during the war. The L33 was a super-Zeppelin: 649 feet long, 78 feet in diameter, with a gas capacity of nearly two million cubic feet. The giant was powered by six Maybach 240-hp Hslu engines capable of pushing her to 59 mph, with an operational ceiling of 13,500 feet. The copies were completed a year after the war and were so successful that the British government decided to build a fleet of them to link the far-flung British Empire. A weak post-war economy later scuttled that idea.

A Zeppelin called R34 made the first east-to-west transatlantic flight in 1919, leaving Britain on July 2 and setting down on Long Island after 108 hours. The trip set another first when Major E. M. Pritchard parachuted down to show the American ground crew how to moor the airship. The jump made Pritchard the first person to reach American soil by air from Europe. Seven years later, *Norge*, a semi-rigid Italian-built airship, made the first flight over the North Pole. It was also the first aircraft to make a trans-polar flight between Europe and America.

THE *GRAF ZEPPELIN*

Germany returned to airship prominence in 1928 with the launch of the Zeppelin company's *Graf Zeppelin* (LZ-127). Count von Zeppelin had died in 1917, and the company was now headed by Dr. Hugo Eckener, who saw airships as vessels of peace rather than war. The *Graf Zeppelin* flew to Lakehurst, New Jersey, after which Eckener and crew received a ticker-tape parade in New York City and an invitation to the White House. The *Graf* toured Germany,

Italy, Palestine, and Spain. In August 1929 she set off to circumnavigate the globe. Onboard was Hearst Syndicate reporter Grace Marguerite Hay Drummond-Hay, who became the first woman to circumnavigate the globe by air.

After completing a successful round-trip crossing from Europe to Brazil in May 1930, the *Graf Zeppelin* began flying the first regular transatlantic airline route, carrying mail and passengers from Frankfurt to Recife in 68 hours, and later on to Rio de Janeiro.

NOT TO BE OUTDONE

The British hurried to finish the R101, a rigid airship destined for Imperial Airship service between England and India. It had 50 staterooms on two decks within the envelope. There was dining room for 60, two promenade decks, and an asbestos-lined smoking room for 24, as well as a grand 55,000-square-foot lounge on the upper deck. It crashed and burned on its maiden overseas voyage to France, in October 1930, killing 48 of the 55 passengers. That ended British attempts to build lighter-than-air ships and prompted Zeppelin's Eckener to announce that the new sister ship of the *Graf Zeppelin* would be filled instead with helium.

THE *HINDENBURG*

The *Hindenburg* was the largest airship ever built: 803 ¾ feet long with a gargantuan envelope volume of over 7 million cubic feet, with 112 tons of useful lift (minus the weight of the ship itself). This put her in the same class as a Boeing wide-body 747-400F cargo plane, one-third the length of the *Hindenburg*. The *Hindenburg*'s maiden flight was on March 4, 1936. However, despite Eckener's announcement, the envelope was full of hydrogen. The United States had embargoed its helium supplies. Given that the German company's airships had never lost a passenger, people presumed they had figured out how to make using hydrogen safe. The *Hindenburg* joined the *Graf Zeppelin* on the transatlantic line to Rio de Janeiro. Her 72 passengers traveled in style and luxury at 85 mph. A remarkable feature was the smoking lounge. Entry was restricted to a pressurized antechamber air lock designed to keep smoke or flames from escaping the lounge. The room was asbestos-lined, with a cigarette lighter attached by a cord to a table in the lounge. As passengers had to relinquish matches and lighters upon boarding, the lounge was the

Motto of anti-submarine-warfare pilots: "If you're gonna fly low, do not fly slow!"

only place where one could smoke during the trip. The vessel was said to be so stable that a pen or pencil could be stood on a table without falling. Often passengers had no idea they had lifted off until they looked out a window.

A transatlantic ticket was US$400 (about US$6,300 today), a considerable sum in the Depression '30s. The *Hindenburg* completed 17 round-trip transatlantic flights in 1936, her only full year of service—10 to the United States, 7 to Brazil—carrying 2,798 passengers.

DISASTER

The *Hindenburg* made a final South American flight in March 1937, and then left Frankfurt for Lakehurst, New Jersey, on May 3. Three days later, just after 7 p.m., the ship approached the mooring mast and dropped her landing lines. As the ground crew grabbed hold of the lines, the dirigible burst into flames and collapsed. In 37 seconds, 13 passengers, 22 crew members, and one linesman were dead. There were 62 survivors.

Exactly what caused the *Hindenburg* to explode is still undetermined, but the giant Zeppelin had so fascinated the public that the impact of the disaster was tremendous. The whole episode was caught on newsreels, and images of the burning ship with the stricken voice of eyewitness Herbert Morrison reporting from the scene, became etched in the collective memory.

Work had already begun before the crash to build the LZ-130. Eckener had visited President Roosevelt and secured from him an assurance that helium would be made available for peaceful purposes. But as the 1930s wore on, it became clear that the United States had no intention of giving Nazi Germany any helium. The LZ-130, christened the *Graf Zeppelin II* in 1938, made 30 cargo flights but was scrapped with the *Graf Zeppelin* in 1940 to provide metal for the Nazi war effort.

Amazingly, even after the *Hindenburg* crash, the public desire to travel by airship was such that 400 people bought tickets for the next scheduled flight. Their money was refunded in 1940. It was World War II, as much as anything, that brought an end to the passenger dirigible.

Turn to page 417 for Part IV.

Actual footage of the *Hindenburg* is shown in the 1937 film *Charlie Chan at the Olympics*.

BY THE NUMBERS

Lists of curious car facts.

3 BIGGEST LOADS OF CARS LOST AT SEA

1. Cargo ship *Cougar Ace* lost stability off the coast of Alaska on July 24, 2006, with 4,813 Mazdas valued at $96 million aboard. All of the cars were later scrapped.

2. Cargo ship MV *Hyundai 105* sank near Singapore on May 22, 2004, with 4,191 Hyundais and Kias valued at $40 million.

3. Cargo ship *Tricolor* sank in the English Channel on December 14, 2002, with 2,862 Volvos, Saabs, and BMWs valued at $45 million.

10 MOST EXPENSIVE CARS IN THE WORLD

1. Bugatti Veyron, $1,700,000, top speed: 267 mph

2. Lamborghini Reventon, $1,600,000, top speed: 211 mph

3. McLaren F1, $970,000, top speed: 240 mph

4. Ferrari Enzo, $670,000, top speed: 217 mph

5. Pagani Zonda C12 F, $667,321, top speed: 215 mph

6. SS C Ultimate Aero, $664,400, top speed: 257 mph

7. Saleen S7 Twin Turbo, $555,000, top speed: 247 mph

8. Koenigsegg CCX, $545,568, top speed: 245 mph

9. Mercedes-Benz McLaren Roadster, $495,000, top speed: 206 mph

10. Porsche Carrera GT, $440,000, top speed: 205 mph

7 CARS WITH 2 NAMES

1. Audi 5000 (U.S.), Audi 100 (world)

2. Fiat Strada (U.S.), Fiat Ritmo (world)

3. Isuzu Rodeo (U.S.), Isuzu MU (world)

4. Jaguar XKE (U.S.), Jaguar E-type (world)

5. Mitsubishi Montero (U.S.), Mitsubishi Pajero (world)

6. Suzuki Sidekick (U.S.), Suzuki Vitara (world)

7. Volkswagen Rabbit (U.S.), Volkwagen Golf MK1 (world)

In 1968 the Russian Tu-144 became the first commercial airplane...

SPACE SHUTTLE R.I.P. 1981–2011

After 500 million miles traveled, the longest-lasting program in U.S. space aviation has come to an end. Here's a timeline of the 30-year adventures of the Enterprise, Columbia, Challenger, Discovery, Atlantis, *and* Endeavour.

1977: Test-shuttle *Enterprise* makes its first flight on August 12. Originally named *Constitution*, but a write-in campaign from *Star Trek* fans made NASA rechristen it.

1981: On April 12, *Columbia* blasts off from Launch Pad 39A at Kennedy Space Center in Florida. *Columbia* orbits Earth 37 times before landing at Edwards Air Force Base in California.

1983: *Columbia* becomes the first shuttle to put parts of Spacelab into orbit. Spacelab is billed as "science around the world and around the clock."

1984: On February 7, Bruce McCandless II makes the first untethered spacewalk as he floats around *Challenger* on its fourth mission.

1985: *Atlantis* debuts October 3 on a classified mission, one of 10 commandeered by the Pentagon to conduct military research.

1986: An O-ring fails at liftoff, and *Challenger* explodes 72 seconds later, killing all seven onboard, including the shuttle's first civilian astronaut, teacher Christa McAuliffe.

1989: After a 13-month grounding to address safety issues, *Atlantis* sends the Magellan probe on its way to map Venus. Five months later *Atlantis* sends the probe Galileo on its way to Jupiter.

1990: *Discovery* puts the Hubble Space Telescope into orbit in April.

1992: On its debut mission, *Endeavour* serves as home base to the first three-person spacewalk. Pierre Thuot, Richard Hieb, and Thomas Akers retrieve the Intelsat VI (F-3) satellite.

...to exceed Mach 2 (twice the speed of sound).

1993: On September 22, *Discovery* touches down at Kennedy Space Center at 3:56 a.m. iinthe first shuttle night landing.

1995: On June 29, *Atlantis* is the first American shuttle to dock with the Russian space station *Mir*. It is the 100th manned spaceflight controlled from Cape Canaveral.

1997: In May *Atlantis* brings Michael Foale up to the *Mir* station and Jerry Linenger back down, completing the first of many missions to exchange space station crew.

1998: *Columbia* pulls away from Spacelab for the last time, completing the 20th and final Spacelab mission. Parts of it are used to build the International Space Station (ISS).

1998: *Endeavour* brings up NASA's Unity connecting module and links it to the Russian Zayra command module already in orbit. Unity and Zayra are still part of the ISS.

1999: On May 29, *Discovery* becomes the first shuttle to dock with the ISS.

2003: During liftoff on January 16, *Columbia* has a malfunction with its foam insulation, which causes the shuttle to break apart on re-entry 16 days later. All seven astronauts are killed.

2007: After sitting idle for five years, *Endeavour* is sent aloft to bring supplies and structural pieces to the ISS.

2008: The Space Station becomes even more international when *Endeavour*, *Atlantis*, and *Discovery* add sections made by space programs in Canada, Japan, and Europe.

2009: *Atlantis* completes the last of four shuttle missions to fix the Hubble Space Telescope. NASA declares the repairs a success.

2011: After 39 missions, *Discovery* retires in March; *Endeavour* follows in June after completing its 25th. *Atlantis* concludes its 33rd mission with a successful landing on July 21, 2011, marking the 135th shuttle mission and the end of NASA's Space Shuttle Program.

License plates predate cars. They were used on horse-drawn carriages first, in 1884.

INTERSTATES BY THE NUMBERS

Take this potpourri of notable interstate info down the road with you.

WHY I-5?

The interstate numbering system is organized and logical. Adopted by the Highway Administration in 1957, it mandates east-west interstates to have even numbers and north-south routes to have odd numbers. The lower-numbered roads are in the South and the West, and increase numerically as you move north and east. So I-5 and I-10 meet in Los Angeles, and I-90 intersects with I-95 in Boston. Major routes end in "0" and "5," like I-75 and I-80, which both span the country. Major arteries are always divisible by five.

"Circumferential highways" (beltways) and bypasses have three-digit numbers, with the last two digits being the major artery near the beltway. For instance, I-695 loops around Washington, DC, and connects to I-95, its "parent" road. If a beltway doesn't connect to its parent, the first digit is odd.

I-NOMALIES

• So I-50 should be a major east-west highway somewhere in the middle of the country, right? Well, yes, except for one problem—it doesn't exist. An interstate and a smaller route cannot have the same number in the same state.

• I-99 should be the easternmost road in the United States. Instead it runs through the Allegheny Mountains of Pennsylvania, almost 200 miles west of I-95. Its number should be something like I-280, but Representative Bud Shuster (R) didn't think those numbers were catchy enough, so he broke tradition (and some say the law) and named it "99," after a streetcar he remembered riding on as a child.

• Commerce has always been built around transportation routes. In the 18th century that meant navigable rivers, and railroads in the 19th century. Between 1980 and 1991, there were fifteen new automobile plants built in America. Thirteen were built along a single Midwest corridor close to I-65 and I-75.

SPEED LIMITS

Interstate speed limits are set by individual states. During the 1970s oil crisis, the federal government withheld funding if the limit exceeded 55 mph, and states quickly fell in line. When the restriction was lifted in 1995, Nevada was the first to set a 75-mph speed limit. Other states followed suit, but only Montana tried to get away with no limit, only a suggestion for drivers to be "reasonable and prudent." A federal court said no, and today Montana's limit is 75 mph.

EXIT SIGNS

All interstate exits are numbered, but states use one of two methods to choose the numbers. Most order their exits according to mileage. The first might be Exit 6 (six miles from the state border); the second, Exit 35 (35 miles from the border); and so on. As with interstate route numbers, exit numbers go up as you travel north and east.

Some states, however, number exits consecutively, regardless of the distance between them. This method is found mostly in the Northeast, and it's losing popularity. Pennsylvania switched to the mileage system in 2003, Maine in 2004.

Most exits are on the right, but there are some left-side exits. The exit number sits above the larger main sign—if it's on the left side, the exit is on the left.

MISCELLANY

• Interstates make up only 1% of public roads but carry 25% of passenger transport.

• As of 2011 there are 46,876 miles of interstate, enough to build a four-lane highway almost twice around the equator.

• The longest interstate highway is I-90, spanning the 3,020 miles from Seattle to Boston.

• In 1960 there were 200,000 miles of commercial railroads in the

The font used on interstate signs is Highway Gothic.

United States. By 2008 that number had dropped to 94,000 miles. Today 45% of all freight is carried over the interstates.

• I-95 connects Florida and Maine. Its 2,000-mile course passes through 15 states, including all 13 original colonies.

• The Lone Star State has 3,200 miles of interstate within its borders, the most of any state. New York has the most interstate routes—29. California ranks second in both categories: 25 interstates totaling 2,500 miles.

• The highest point in the interstate system is also the highest vehicular tunnel in the world—the Eisenhower/Johnson Memorial Tunnel (I-70) crosses the Continental Divide at 11,000 feet, 60 miles west of Denver.

• The lowest point in the system is also a tunnel, and one of the most heavily traveled sections of road in the country. Trucks going from most ports and warehouses on the East Coast use the Fort McHenry Tunnel (I-95), 107 feet below the surface of Baltimore Harbor.

• The interstate system has 55,000 bridges, not counting the local and state bridges that cross it.

• When the highway project started in the mid-1950s, there were 61 million vehicles on American roads. Today there are 250 million.

* * *

SIX NATIONAL RACING COLORS

For the 1900 Gordon Bennett Trophy Race in France, a color-coded system was devised to identify competing cars from different countries. The system has been used ever since. Here are the current colors for the six major racing nations:

• *France*—blue with white numbers

• *Germany*—silver (originally white) with red numbers

• *Great Britain*—dark green with white numbers

• *Italy*—red (originally black) with white numbers

• *Japan*—white with red circle on hood and black numbers

• *United States*—blue and white (originally red) with blue-on-white numbers

A hand with a pair of fives in Texas hold 'em poker is referred to as a "speed limit."

CACKLEFEST

A cacklefest is a gathering of cackle cars. What's a cackle car? Read on.

THAT'S SOME REUNION!

The idea for the Cacklefest began at the annual California Hot Rod Reunion in 2000. Held at the Auto Club Famosa Raceway in Bakersfield, this event is dedicated to honoring the legends of drag racing and hot-rodding. Several years before, Steve Gibbs, director of competion for the National Hot Rod Association, and Greg Sharp, curator of the NHRA Motorsport Museum, started bringing the vintage top fuel dragsters from the museum and put them on display on "Memory Lane" behind the pitside grandstands.

In 1999 reunion organizers inaugurated the Twilight Memorial, a ceremony during which the names of drag racers who died in the past year are read aloud to the crowd over the public address system. It was after that first Twilight Memorial that Gibbs got the idea to push-start a number of the vintage nitro-burning, front-engine Top Fuel dragsters in rapid-fire succession, just to pump up the crowd. As Gibbs recalled, "I told Greg that it looked like I could probably put six to eight cars on the track, cackling all at once. Then Greg said, 'We'll have a regular cacklefest.'"

And that's how the cacklefest got its name. After every Twilight Memorial, an array of vintage Top Fuel dragsters, or "cackle cars," are push-started at the starting line. The resultant noise from all of those gigantic engines roaring to life and revving all at once is a cacklefest of monster proportions. The cacklefest has become a much-loved and highly anticipated feature of drag-racing reunions across the United States and Canada, and in the United Kingdom.

CACKLE CAR, DEFINED

A cackle car is any dragster that was certified to run in the top Fuel or Funny Car class more than 20 years ago. Today these classic race cars can no longer compete legally in NHRA-sanctioned events but remain showpieces from a fabled era. Most are powered by 354- and 392-cubic-inch Chrysler Hemi engines.

What was a Go Devil? The nickname for the engines in World War II Jeeps.

THE BENTLEY BOYS

They were young, wealthy, and wild—and for half a decade they made a British luxury sedan the most exciting racing car in the world.

RELUCTANT RACER

Walter Owen Bentley (1888–1971) knew how to make luxury cars that were durable and powerful. His problem was getting the world to notice. In an upscale market dominated by brands like Mercedes-Benz and Rolls-Royce, Bentley's Motorworks was constantly struggling to stay afloat. A friend suggested that Bentley enter one of his cars in the recently inaugurated 24 Hours at Le Mans race in France, considered (like today) the greatest test of car and driver in the world. A good performance would raise the company's profile among the market demographic that really mattered—the very wealthy. Bentley had little interest in racing but agreed to check out the 1923 race. He came away smitten by the excitement and glamour of the event. When a privately entered Bentley driven by John Duff placed fourth, the autobuilder decided to put together his own racing stable of drivers and cars. Cars he had. But where to find drivers?

LIVE FAST, DRIVE FASTER

The solution came in the form of a playboy named Joel Woolf Barnato, who loved Bentley motorcars. So did his circle of friends, all racing enthusiasts and high-living bon vivants. Their names and bios read like characters in a P. G. Wodehouse novel:

- **Barnato**—Called "Babe" by his friends, scion of a South African diamond fortune
- **Sir Henry "Tim" Birkin**—Heir to a lacemaking company, notorious playboy, considered the best driver of his generation
- **Glen Kidston**—Drop-dead handsome, impeccably tailored, the richest of them all, a former submarine captain who had the dubious distinction of having been torpedoed twice on the same day
- **Dr. J. Dudley "Benjy" Benjafield**—Nicknamed "the Bald Chemist," a top bacteriologist when he wasn't setting speed records racing cars

• **Bernard Rubin**—Madcap Australian with a fearsome reputation behind the wheel, and a fortune that came from a string of pearl fisheries in the Orient

• **S. C. H. "Sammy" Davis**—Influential editor of *Autocar* magazine, wrote under the pseudonym Casque (French for "helmet").

Others in the core group of 12 included the Frenchman Jean Chassagne, Baron André d'Erlanger, auto engineer Clive Gallop, and steeplechase jockey George Duller.

What Barnato and his friends had in common was seemingly unlimited money and a furious passion for racing cars. Bentley made the young men an offer they couldn't refuse: unlimited access to his best and fastest cars to race whenever and wherever they wanted. Bentley would cover their expenses; all they had to do was win. The group of youngbloods soon became known as the Bentley Boys.

DOMINATING LE MANS

At Ardenrun, Barnato's lavish country estate in Surrey, England, the quarter-mile gravel drive was often turned into an impromptu speedway. Birkin, Kidston, and the rest would come roaring down from the city in their cars, girlfriends in tow, and spend the weekend racing each other, stopping in the "pits" for glasses of champagne served by waiters wearing linen helmets and racing goggles. Romance novelist Barbara Cartland, who had a longtime affair with Kidston, wrote years later that the boys "were great drivers and even better dancers."

Barnato and friends ate, drank, and slept cars, sometimes literally (Barnato created the Bentley Cocktail, a combination of Calvados and Dubonnet that became a staple at swank bars). But it was on the track that the Bentley Boys proved they had the right stuff, particularly at Le Mans. The races in 1925 and 1926 were disasters—none of the Bentleys that started made it to the finish line. But starting in 1927, Bentley motorcars driven by various combinations of Bentley Boys completely dominated the greatest event in auto racing, winning four years in succession. Benjafield and Davis kicked things off with a dramatic come-from-behind win in 1927. Then Barnato won the next three, teaming with Rubin, Birkin, and Kidston in succession. In 1929 the Bentley

World's largest naval hovercraft: The Russian Zubr. It's 187 feet long, 73 feet wide...

Boys ran the table, placing not only first but second, third, and fourth as well.

GREEN POWER

What made the Bentley cars—always painted English racing green—such a potent force in racing was the genius of W. O. Bentley himself. The cars themselves were boxy things that led Ettore Bugatti to sniff that Bentleys were "the world's fastest trucks." Bugatti's own cars were sleek and elegant but also maddeningly fickle to maintain and prone to breakdowns. What Bentley had created was an engine and chassis that could take everything the 24-hour endurance race at Le Mans dished out—and then some. Four models set the standard for racing in the 1920s:

• **3-liter:** The model that started it all. At two tons, it was heavy and a bit slow by sportscar standards of the day. (By contrast, its main competitor, the Bugatti Type 35, weighed less than a ton.) The car made up for its weight with strength and innovation. Its straight-4 cylinder engine was the first to use four valves and two spark plugs per cylinder. The engine block and cylinder head were cast as a single block for durability. Winner of Le Mans in 1924, and again in 1927.

• **4½-liter:** Dissatisfied with the 3-liter's lack of power, W. O. ramped up engine displacement from 182 ci to 268 ci, and 70 to 130 hp. The 4½-litre won the 1928 Le Mans outright and placed second, third, and fourth in 1929.

• **Speed Six:** The most successful of all Bentley racers, the Speed Six reflected W. O.'s never-ending quest for more power and speed through bigger engines. Its 6½-liter inline-six cylinder engine proved to be the right combination of power and durability, winning Le Mans in '29 and '30.

• **Bentley Blower:** A supercharged version of the Speed Six, put together by driver Tim Birkin over the objections of W. O., who thought using forced induction to increase power was a poor design (he preferred larger displacement). He may have been right; despite its quickness and power, the Blower never won a race, due to an un-Bentley-like tendency to break down. Both Blowers entered in the 1930 Le Mans failed to finish. Ironically, the Bentley Blower is the most loved of the Bentley line. Ian Fleming owned one and had his superspy James Bond drive one as well. The

...and can carry three battle tanks at speeds up to 69 mph.

Blower appeared again as the ride of John Steed in the classic '60s TV series *The Avengers*. Today a classic Bentley fetches $150,000 at auction; a Bentley Blower can go for more than $2 million.

LE TRAIN BLEU

In 1930 the Bentley was the hottest car in Europe, and the Bentley Boys, led by the irrepressible "Babe" Barnato, the toast of chic salons from Mayfair to the French Riviera. It was in Cannes, in the bar of the Carlton Hotel, that the last great exploit of the Bentley Boys began as a bar bet. Most fashionable socialites of the day took Le Train Bleu (the Blue Train) from Calais to Cannes. Barnato bet 100 pounds that his Bentley Speed Six coupe could not only cover the 750 miles to Calais ahead of the train but that he'd get across the Channel to his club in London before the train reached the dock.

The next day, March 13, 1930, the train pulled out of the Cannes station at 5:35 p.m., destination Calais. Alongside, accompanied by the cheers of his friends, was Barnato in his Bentley. He drove nonstop through the night, braving heavy rain and a flat tire, reached the coast at 10:30 a.m., boarded the ferry to Dover, and was sipping champagne in the Conservative Club in London by 3:20 p.m.—four minutes before Le Train Bleu pulled into Calais. The French police, however, were not amused. Barnato was fined far more than his winnings from the bet for racing on public roads.

LAST HURRAH

Sadly, the Bentley Boys barely survived the decade that spawned them. The win at Le Mans in 1930 proved to be their last. W. O. Bentley may have been an automotive genius, but he was a poor businessman. By 1925 Barnato had become the de facto chairman of the ailing company, pouring his own considerable fortune into it. But even his diamond millions weren't enough for Bentley Motors to survive the Depression that followed the market crash of 1929. In July 1931, Barnato pulled out, and Bentley was forced to sell his company to his fiercest rival, Rolls-Royce, which retired the brand. With no signature car to drive, the Bentley Boys went their separate ways. Kidston, Birkin, Rubin, and Barnato all died relatively young, flaring out as quickly as the flamboyant and daring era they had come to personify.

In the 1920s, a plane ticket cost about $5.

DANGER GIRLS

Here are the stories of the amazing women who risked life and limb to ride the Wall of Death (*see page 85*).

MILE-A-MINUTE GIRL

Margaret Gast was at one time the only female board-track motorcycle rider in the world. Born in Germany in 1877, she emigrated to America at 16 and began competing in long-distance bicycle races. Eight years later, she was the best women's cyclist in America, even beating the men's 2,000-mile record. Billing herself as "The Mile-a-Minute Girl," she turned to motorcycle racing and became a top attraction at carnivals and fairs, performing stunts and competing in races on a portable wooden track known as The Saucer. She went on to ride her Flying Merkel Special Racer motorcycle on the Wall of Death, or Motor Drome. "My hardest life was the eight years when I was doing Motor Drome work. I was carried away in ambulances several times. My worst accident was in Palm Beach. They carried me out as gone." As Gast saw other riders crippled, killed, and even burned to death, she realized it was only a matter of time before her number came up. So she quit and opened a health studio in Manhattan. She was still working as a massage therapist when she died at 84.

LILLIAN LAFRANCE

During the Roaring Twenties, Lillian LaFrance was a Wall of Death superstar. In her trademark outfit—goggles, jodhpurs, riding boots, and skull-and-crossbones T-shirt—she thrilled audiences with her femme fatale aura and reckless motorcycle skill. Little did her fans suspect that Mlle. LaFrance was actually little Agnes Micek from Atwood, Kansas. The second of nine girls raised in a strict Catholic family, Agnes was determined from an early age to not become a worn-out farmwife like her mother. As soon as she could escape, she ran off to join the carnival and ride the Motor Drome. "It was the thrill of risking my life that made me take to Drome riding," she explained. "I was the girl who flirts with death. From childhood I was inspired by wanderlust. I was always alone, dreaming of adventures—how to ride a pony out West, to follow my calling to fame. This was my secret. I shared it with no one." By the age of 30, LaFrance was known as "the premier motorcycle daredevil rider in the world." Not only did she ride the Wall of Death on her Indian Scout motorcycle, but she was equally skilled on her custom four-wheeled midget racer. She died in 1979 at age 85.

DYNAMITE DORIS

Doris Craven was a London teen working the cosmetics booth at the 1931 Olympia Fun Fair when she met "Tornado" Smith, a dashing man in a crisp shirt, tie, beret, and horn-rimmed glasses who was the premier daredevil motorcycle rider in England. The first Briton to ride the Wall of Death, he thought he'd impress young Doris by taking her for a spin on the Wall. Even though she passed out in his sidecar as they circled the Drome at 60 mph, Doris was bitten by the thrill bug and insisted on going again and again.

Tornado Smith was always looking for ways to spice up his act. He was the first to drive a car on the Wall of Death and was known for riding his motorcycle with a coffin sidecar, complete with a skeleton as passenger. Smith gave Craven a course in motorcycle stunt riding that winter, and by Easter she'd made her debut at Barry Island in Glamorgan as "Dynamite Doris." Doris morphed into "Marjorie Dare" and later Mrs. Tornado Smith, when she married Smith on Christmas Day 1934.

One of the couple's most popular acts had Dare sitting at the bottom of the Drome knitting while Smith whirled by in his Indian Scout inches from her head. Then she'd jump in the sidecar and continue her knitting. For the big finish, Dare would leap out of the car in a pair of roller skates and be towed around the wall before letting go and completing a circuit on her own. The couple had a lamb named Sparky and a lioness named Briton for pets. At first Briton rode the Wall on Smith's handlebars but as she grew larger, she was moved to the sidecar. After their retirement to Southend-on-Sea, it was a common sight to see Dare going for a swim with Sparky, or find the couple taking Briton for an evening stroll.

Early Harley-Davidsons were nicknamed the "silent grey fellows" for their quiet engines.

MORGAN STORM

Considered the last of the great female daredevils, Samantha Morgan ran away from a foster home at age 11. She was living on the street when she met Sonny Pelaquin, "The Mad Penguin," at the Dade County Youth Fair in Florida. After seeing him perform his Wall of Death show, Morgan was determined to ride the Wall herself. Only 15, she told him she was 18 so she could join his crew. Pelaquin became her mentor. He taught her how to ride a motorcycle sidesaddle, do an upward split, and perform a unique double trick ride with Russ Noel, his cousin. From the 1970s to 2006, beautiful blond Samantha Morgan rode the "Thrillarena," as it was called, under the name Morgan Storm. At the peak of her career, she did four shows an hour in a 16-hour day. When she wasn't performing, Morgan maintained her collection of vintage motorcycles.

Morgan was badly burned doing a double firewall stunt; she broke her back three times and nearly every other bone in her body (except her elbows) riding "Beth," her 1931 Indian Scout motorcycle. Despite the injuries, Morgan insisted, "When I am on the Wall I feel free and it's the only time when all my pains and the pains of this world go away." In 2008 her reckless lifestyle caught up with her. She died on her Florida ranch while recovering from injuries. She was 53.

* * *

WHO'S WRIGHT?

Alberto Santos-Dumont (1873-1932) of Brazil made the first publicly witnessed flight of a fixed-wing aircraft on October 23, 1906, in his *Oiseau de proie* ("Bird of Prey"), a biplane made of bamboo and silk wings. Powered by an Antoinette engine designed by Léon Levavasseur for boat racing, the airplane also had wheels that allowed it to take off under its own power. Since the Wright brothers' 1903 Flyer used skids that required their aircraft to be catapulted into the air, supporters of Santos maintain that his was the first successful unaided, fixed-winged aircraft flight. To this day, the country of Brazil recognizes Santos-Dumont as the father of aviation.

On average, 2004 car models were 6% less fuel efficient than 1987 cars.

BLACK-AND-WHITES

Johnny Law...rollers...the fuzz...the Man...
coppers....Here's what they drive.

ANATOMY OF A POLICE PURSUIT VEHICLE

The most common police car models in North America have been the Ford Crown Victoria, Dodge Charger, and Chevrolet Caprice. Most have V-8 engines and heavy-duty suspension. The bodies are built of high-strength steel and have energy-load paths for crash protection. Each police department has special needs and can upgrade its vehicles accordingly.

Following is a list of what a police department with mucho bucks can get in a fully tricked-out 2012 Chevrolet Caprice:

- **Engine.** The Caprice's 6.0-liter V-8 is rated at an estimated 355 hp with 384 pound-feet of torque. The six-speed automatic transmission is performance-calibrated for police duty and can accelerate from 0 to 60 mph in less than six seconds. A Performance Algorithm Liftfoot (PAL) calibration, within sport shift mode, lets the transmission understand driving conditions and select the required engine torque.
- **Lights.** Most police cars have a bar on top with a rotating strobe or halogen light that flashes blue, red, and white. Headlights can be made to flash, and strobes can be fitted in the headlights, tail lights, and indicator lights. Some newer cars are equipped with lighted message display boards.
- **Sirens.** These can be set on "wail" or "yelp." A new technology called the "rumbler" is being developed to cut through to drivers playing loud music.
- **Push bumper.** This allows the car to be used as a battering ram.
- **Forward Looking Infrared Camera (FLIC).** This unit is so sensitive it can track the footprints of a suspect in complete darkness.
- **Remote start with theft alert system.**
- **Front seats.** Bucket seats are molded to accommodate an officer's equipment belt with cutouts for handgun and radio. A center-mounted shifter gives the officer more elbow room.

During WWI, Ford had an airplane division. Its most successful aircraft:...

• **Air bags.** These are all about protecting the officer. The car is built to withstand a 75-mph rear-end collision. There are front air bags and front seat head curtain air bags that allow a full-width rear-seat barrier for greater officer safety.

• **Command center.** A 12-inch interactive touch screen controls lights, siren, gun lock, trunk opener, and rear door locks. It contains an advanced GPS system so HQ is always aware of the PPV's location. The screen is a mobile data terminal that lets police look up criminal records, incident reports, and immediate crime scene information.

• **Automatic license plate recognition (ALPR).** A camera system that instantly reads license plates as the PPV cruises the streets. It does an automatic trace, gives constant feedback on the touch screen, and alerts the officer of any potentially dangerous suspect vehicles nearby. The ALPR system is capable of reading 1,800 plates per minute.

• **Tetra Radio (Terrestrial Trunked Radio).** A high-speed, long-range four-channel system designed for government, military, emergency, and police use.

• **Runlock system.** Allows the engine to run without a key. The moment the parking brake is released, the engine turns off. This allows an officer to leave the vehicle running while investigating a crime scene and prevents anyone from making a quick getaway with the patrol car.

• **Blind-spot system.** Two radar sensors located in the rear quarter panels detect vehicles in surrounding lanes. If a car enters the driver's blind-spot zones, the system alerts the driver with a warning light in the side-view mirror.

• **Reverse-gear traffic alert.** This warns the officer of any oncoming traffic when the vehicle is backing up.

• **Interior lights.** They change from white to red for nighttime stops to help prevent night blindness.

• **Locking racks.** Shotguns and patrol rifles are stored here, usually behind the front seat.

• **Prisoner partition.** This separates the good guys from the potentially bad ones. It used to be an iron mesh gate or bullet-

...the 4AT Trimotor, called the "Tin Goose."

proof glass, or both. Now it is a seamless partition of bulletproof glass that curves around and behind the front seat, offering better visibility for the officer. Lest some knife-happy perp think he can stab the driver through the upholstery, there are steel plates on the back of the front seat.

• **Back seat.** This part of a cop car can be subject to a lot of bodily fluids, so first and foremost it must be washable. Seats are vinyl or hard plastic and are molded with cutouts to accommodate a handcuffed suspect. By design, there is very little leg or head room, making it nearly impossible for a suspect to hurl himself around or kick at the driver. Police also believe a cramped back seat gives them a psychological advantage over a prisoner. Rear windows are reinforced with wire mesh, and, of course, the back doors cannot be unlocked from the inside.

• **Trunk.** The onboard computer hard drive and wiring is stored in a pullout tray in the trunk, as are two batteries: one for the car, one to run extra equipment. The flat-bottomed trunk is roomy enough to accommodate bulletproof vests, a shotgun, first-aid kit, portable defibrillator, oxygen cylinder, cervical collar, fire extinguisher, floor jack, auxilliary battery, bolt cutters, scene tape, duct tape, several orange vests, portable breath test, print kit, biological specimen kit, plastic gloves, and any additional gear that might be specific to the officer's training and assignment.

* * *

REFUGEE, A TEDDY BEAR

When the Space Shuttle *Discovery* took off in 2006, Commander Mark Polansky wanted to honor his Jewish heritage. So he contacted the U.S. Holocaust Museum to see if there was an artifact he could carry on board. They gave him a replica of Refugee, the tiny teddy bear that Holocaust survivor Sophie Turner-Zaretzky had carried with her through her confinement in the Warsaw Ghetto and eventual escape from the Nazis. When Polansky came back from space, he sent Refugee to Turner-Zaretzky with a note that read, "Traveled 5,330,398 miles. In space for 12 days, 20 hours, 45 minutes. Not bad for a bear."

FILL 'ER UP!

Air-to-air refueling is the aviation equivalent of threading a needle...at 10,000 feet and 300 miles per hour.

BACKGROUND

The first fuel transfer between planes in midair was a publicity stunt. On November 12, 1921, wing-walker Wesley May strapped a gas can on his back, stepped off the wing of a Lincoln Standard biplane and onto that of the Curtiss JN-4 "Jenny" two-seater biplane flying beside him, opened up the Curtiss's gas tank, and poured.

The U.S. military's first attempt at air-to-air refueling was to dangle a 50-foot fuel hose with a shutoff valve from one biplane to another flying below. The passenger in the backseat of the lower plane had to grab the hose and hitch it to the fuel intake. By 1923 military fliers could keep their planes in the air for over 35 hours using this method, leading to the first non-stop circumnavigation of the globe. In 1949 the *Lucky Lady II*, a B-50A "Superfortress" bomber, refueled in the air four times during its 94-hour trip around the world.

The Air Force has more efficient methods today. Nonetheless, air-to-air refueling remains one of the trickiest and most dangerous maneuvers.

STEADY AS SHE GOES

The flying gas station that is an air tanker drags either a "flying boom"—a telescoping fuel pipe that hangs down like a bee's stinger behind the tanker—or a "probe and drogue," meaning the fuel hose has a small parachute, called a drogue, that keeps it from flapping around in the wind. A receiver plane flies in below and behind the tanker, guided by direction lights controlled by the boom operator on the tanker.

The drag from the extra equipment makes docking hard enough, but the midair interaction between two huge aircraft is much more difficult. Pilots have to compensate for the wake of

The New York City Police Department used bicycles to pursue speeding motorists in 1898.

the tail engine as well as for the turbulence created by the tanker aircraft itself. If the receiver aircraft approaches too quickly, it can find itself pushed up into the tail of the tanker. "These aircraft are not exactly nimble," says Lt. Col Kirk Reagan of the USAF. "It takes slow and steady movements and a lot of patience."

GASSED UP, GOOD TO GO

Modern refuelers like the KC-135 "Stratotanker" and HC-130P "Hercules" can hold up to 100 tons of jet fuel, twice the weight of the plane. They can pump that fuel into another jet at 5,000 pounds per minute, making a refuel of a fighter jet a matter of seconds, not minutes.

Air-to-air refueling becomes a lot harder flying at high altitude with what pilots call a "combat load-out." "Lots of bombs and missiles equals more drag," says F-16 pilot Maj. Rob Redmond, USAF. Plus, "it can be disorienting flying through weather off the tanker's wing while waiting for your turn to get gas, and also while 'on the boom.'" He adds, with typical pilot understatement, "It is also nice when they stay out of the clouds."

Carrier-based tanker pilots also have to know how to "hawk"—to set the tanker in a flight pattern behind and well above a jet on its landing approach to the flight deck. This happens when a jet returning from a sortie is low on fuel and may not be able to circle back and try landing again. "If the pilot were to 'bolter,' that is, not land that time around," says Lt. Matt Powers, who worked as a flight officer on a carrier-based S-3 Viking tanker, "all he had to do to find us is look up. It's all about customer service."

NKAWTG

Although air-to-air refueling is one of the most dangerous midair flight operations, tanker pilots don't get as much recognition for their flying skills as fighter pilots. "As far from the tip of the spear as we airborne tankers may be," says Lt. Powers, "nothing is quite as satisfying as when the pilot who borrowed a few thousand pounds of gas from you comes to thank you in the ready room after the flight."

As the air tanker motto goes, NKAWTG: Nobody Kicks Ass Without Tanker Gas.

Highest speed ever in a Formula 1 race: In 2004 Antonio Pizzonia reached 229.9 mph.

DEEP DIVE

Stardate: January 23, 1960. Aquanaut Jacques Piccard's mission? To go where no human has gone before: seven miles into deep ocean.

PROJECT: NEKTON

In the 1950s and '60s during the height of the Cold War between the United States and the Soviet Union, both countries raced to dominate every space on Earth: land, air, and sea. The deployment of nuclear submarines made the U.S. realize the strategic importance of developing extreme depth submersibles for both military and scientific purposes. In 1958 the U.S. Navy purchased the *Trieste*, a bathyscaphe built by Swiss scientist Auguste Piccard. The word *bathyscaphe* was coined by Piccard from the Greek words *bathos* ("deep") and *skaphos* ("ship"), literally meaning "ship of the deep." Piccard (1884–1962) was a respected physicist who'd worked with Albert Einstein and was the first human to travel to the earth's stratosphere and deep into its oceans. He and his son Jacques had taken the submersible 10,000 feet below the surface of the Mediterranean in 1953.

Under the code name Project Nekton, the Navy decided to send *Trieste* deeper than any manned vehicle had ever gone before.

OBJECTIVE: CHALLENGER DEEP

Picture a Grand Canyon 1,500 miles long carving out an arcing curve along the bottom of the western Pacific Ocean. This huge gash in the Earth's crust is called the Mariana Trench, which is part of the Ring of Fire that runs like a horseshoe from New Zealand to Alaska to the tip of South America.

The deepest spot in this chasm, the Challenger Deep, lies 35,000 feet (seven miles) below sea level. Consider that Mount Everest, by comparison, is 5½ miles (29,085 feet) above sea level. Add two more miles to Everest and you have the depth of the Challenger Deep. This depression, two miles off of Guam, was named for the British naval survey ship HMS *Challenger*, which first recorded its depth in 1875. Eighty-five years later, on January

23, 1960, Jacques Piccard and Don Walsh descended into the Challenger Deep to see for themselves what lay at the very bottom of the ocean.

PILOTS: PICCARD AND WALSH

Jacques Piccard (1922–2008) had worked closely with his father in the creation and operation of the *Trieste*, so when the U.S. Navy paid $250,000 for the bathyscaphe, the 38-year-old was brought along as advisor and pilot. The *Trieste*'s other pilot was Lt. Don Walsh (1931–), a U.S. Navy submarine officer. Walsh volunteered for Project Nekton in 1958 and was selected to lead the mission and serve as co-pilot on the Deep Dive.

SHIP: *TRIESTE*

Trieste had the railings and conning tower of a submarine, but it was really more of an underwater balloon. Its 50 feet of interconnected floats were filled not with air but with 22,500 gallons of gasoline. Gasoline was chosen because unlike air, which compresses under pressure, it's not affected by external pressure changes and, being lighter than water, it still retains buoyancy. Water ballast tanks were at the fore and aft of the float, along with chambers full of small iron pellets. Suspended below the giant float was a white metal sphere with five-inch-thick walls, just big enough to hold the two men. This pressurized chamber contained a rebreathing system like those used in spacesuits and spacecraft. *Trieste* descended by loading it with shotgun pellets and expelling enough gasoline to make the craft sink. When the bathyscaphe wanted to rise, pellets were dumped on the ocean floor and the remaining gasoline floated it to the top. Battery-run spotlights mounted on the vehicle lit up the sea floor.

MISSION: DEEP DIVE

In the early morning hours of January 23rd, the ocean-going tug *USS Wandank* towed the *Trieste* from Guam 200 miles through rough waters to a point in the ocean above the Challenger Deep. Piccard and Walsh were prevented from boarding for almost an hour by 20-foot waves battering the submersible. Once onboard, the two pilots discovered that the heavy seas had ripped away some hull sensors and other equipment. Piccard and Walsh decid-

Disney World monorails have traveled enough miles to drive to the moon and back 30 times.

ed to go ahead. The hatch was secured, and at 8 a.m., *Trieste* sank below the surface and began its slow descent into the Mariana Trench.

During the next five hours, *Trieste* passed out of the Sunlit (*Euphotic*) Zone (0–660 feet) through the Twilight (*Disphotic*) Zone (660–3,300 feet) that receives some sunlight but not enough for photosynthesis to occur, into the utter darkness of the Midnight (*Aphotic*) Zone. At 32,400 feet, an explosion like a small earthquake rocked the *Trieste*. Piccard anxiously checked the gauges to see if the float had been punctured or their sphere cracked. Nothing seemed amiss, and the mission continued. (They later found that the window in the bathyscaphe's entrance tunnel had cracked under the immense pressure but had not leaked.) Now *Trieste* was entering depths of the ocean where no human had ever ventured before.

HADAL ZONE

The term "hadal" comes from the Greek word *hades*, which means "the unknown." In this place of darkness, it is perpetually cold and any oxygen that filters down is centuries old. As the aquanauts entered this zone, they knew it would only be a short time before they reached the floor of the Challenger Deep. They had no idea what its geology would be like. Rocky or solid? Some scientists thought the floor was a thick ooze that could swallow the *Trieste* whole like quicksand. The pilots hoped they were wrong.

At 35,813 feet, the *Trieste* set down, raising a plume of pale silt. Piccard and Walsh were stunned to see an unfamiliar species of flatfish, like a flounder, scurry away. They also spied some shrimp. Both sea creatures were colorless. This was a stunning discovery. Here at the most inhospitable environment on Earth—no light, extremely cold temperatures, and bone-crushing pressures of 16,000 psi—vertebrate life could still exist! The two men were also happy to report that, although the ocean floor was covered with what appeared to be a thick layer of diatomaceous ooze, it did not swallow the *Trieste* as predicted.

MISSION ACCOMPLISHED

Piccard and Walsh discovered the cracked window while on the ocean floor and, worried that it might not hold, decided to cut

Oldest naval vessel still in service: The USS *Constitution*, commissioned in 1797.

short their time at the bottom. They spent 20 minutes gathering scientific data, ate chocolate bars for some quick energy, and then dumped 16 tons of lead BBs onto the ooze and began to rise toward the surface. The trip back took 3 hours and 15 minutes. *Trieste* broke the surface at 4:56 p.m., and when the aquanauts emerged into the afternoon light, they were greeted by a flyover of Navy jets dipping their wings in salute.

Since *Trieste*'s historic journey to the Challenger Deep, no human has returned there. Japanese researchers and the Woods Hole Oceanographic Institute have sent down unmanned vehicles, but so far Piccard and Walsh remain the first and only humans to see the bottom of the ocean firsthand.

THE NEXT GENERATION?

As of 2011, a new breed of aquanauts are busy making plans to take the seven-mile journey back to the bottom of the Mariana Trench. It is a club of billionaires, as it were. Each has built his own submersible and planned his own expedition to the Challenger Deep. The three aquanauts are Oscar-winning director James Cameron, whose films *Avatar*, *Titanic*, and *The Abyss* examine fantastical worlds under the sea and in space; Virgin Air mogul Richard Branson; and Google's executive chairman, Eric E. Schmidt. Each is a visionary in his own field; each one has very deep pockets—the cost of building a deep-dive mini-sub and its mother ship ranges from $20 to $40 million.

Branson, for one, plans to make his investment back by charging tourists $250,000 apiece to visit the Challenger Deep. His sub looks like a small underwater jet plane. Cameron's submersible is a one-man vehicle designed to allow him to personally explore the deepwater ocean trenches. Schmidt, founder of the Schmidt Ocean Institute, sees his three-person craft as "a world asset capable of providing scientists with unlimited access to the deep ocean."

* * *

A MOVING EXPERIENCE

When Harrods of London first installed escalators in 1889, an attendant was hired to offer brandy and smelling salts to terrified customers as they got off.

PRE-WRIGHT FLIGHT: MUSCLE POWER

"It is possible to fly without motors," said Wilbur Wright, "but not without knowledge and skill." And, as these early aviation pioneers found, a lot of elbow grease.

DEVICE: Ornithopter (1485)
INVENTOR: Leonardo Da Vinci (1452–1519)
DETAILS: When he wasn't busy painting the Mona Lisa; cataloging human anatomy; or designing bridges, cannons, catapults, paddleboats, odometers, armored cars, machine guns, and musical instruments, Da Vinci tried to figure out the secret of flight. His sketchbooks dating from 1485 to 1505 show drawings of winged aircraft meant to fly through the air just like birds. These "Ornithopters" were to be made of wood and stretched canvas, with a wingspan of about 10 feet. Some versions had flapping wings; some even had a rudder. To stay aloft, all of them used the muscle power of the operator, who was to lie horizontally in the middle of the device and move the wings by flapping his arms.

COULD IT FLY? According to legend, Da Vinci built a prototype Ornithopter and had a student test it (no record of how that turned out). It's unclear how many of the ideas made it further than sketches. Using modern materials and engines, replicas of some of Da Vinci 's designs have flown successfully, but even the fittest human wouldn't have the strength and endurance to keep an Ornithopter in the air.

DEVICE: Autogyro (1493)
INVENTOR: Leonardo Da Vinci (1452–1519)
DETAILS: Da Vinci understood that flying with the birds didn't mean that you had to fly *like* the birds. A proto-helicopter called the Autogyro was the result. One of his most famous sketches depicts a wooden contraption with a vertical spiral screw made of bamboo reeds, starched linen, and metal wiring. The spiral rested on top of a spinning circular platform, where two to four men turned a central crank, which turned the screw. Da Vinci believed

that when "turned swiftly, the said screw will make it spiral in the air and it will rise high."

COULD IT FLY? Nope.

DEVICE: Oscillating wings (1678)

INVENTOR: Besnier (17th century)

DETAILS: Not much is known about French locksmith Besnier, except that he put his keys and locks aside long enough to invent a flying contraption. His invention consisted of two long wooden rods fitted at each end with foldable kite-like sails. The rods pivoted over each shoulder, and Besnier, leaning forward and grasping each rod like a javelin, would alternately raise and lower them. On the down stroke, the wings would unfold and provide lift; on the up stroke, they would fold together to reduce drag.

COULD IT FLY? Believe it or not, it did. Besnier started by jumping from chairs and windowsills, and with practice became good enough to flap over rooftops (starting from higher rooftops, of course). As with all human-powered airplanes, the human was the weak link. Besnier tired too quickly for long-distance flights.

DEVICE: *Ptérophore* (1786)

INVENTOR: Alexis Paucton (1732–98)

DETAILS: In 1786 French inventor Alexis Paucton described an apparatus with two spinning airfoils, which he called *ptérophores*. In order to fly, the pilot would "give to the first *ptérophore* a suitable circular speed. This single *ptérophore* would lift him vertically, but in order to move horizontally he should be supplied with a tail in the shape of another *ptérophore*."

COULD IT FLY? No. Substitute the word "rotor" for *ptérophore*, and it sounds like Paucton was describing a helicopter. Unlike the modern design, Paucton's "main rotor" and "tail rotor" were simply attached to a chair, and the pilot "gave the revolving motion" by means of a hand crank. Paucton realized that human muscle power wouldn't be enough to get the chair off the ground, and it's likely that he never built a prototype.

DEVICE: Governable Parachute (1853)

INVENTOR: George Cayley (1773–1857)

Indian Railways, India's largest employer, has 1.6 million employees.

DETAILS: Cayley, an engineer and English nobleman, is considered the father of modern aviation. He was the first person to define the four principles of flight: lift, thrust, drag, and weight. The Governable Parachute (also called the Flyer) was Cayley's first great prototype success. It was a glider made of cloth, silk, and metal wires built around a wooden frame, with fixed wings and adjustable horizontal and vertical tail segments, including a movable rudder. The apparatus weighed about 150 pounds.

COULD IT FLY? It could, and did. In 1853 Cayley brought his invention to a high hill at Brompton Dale, near Scarborough, England. At 79 years of age, he was too frail to fly it himself, so he instructed his carriage driver to climb aboard and take it for a spin. After a controlled "flight" of about 900 feet, the Flyer crashed. The terrified coachman immediately quit his job, saying, "Sir, I was hired to drive and not to fly." Cayley knew that he was close to achieving real flight; he only lacked a way to generate more power than, as he phrased it, "the animal system of muscles." In 2003 Virgin Atlantic Airlines founder Richard Branson did find a way: Using modern materials and ultralight, high-powered engines, he flew a replica of the Flyer in Salina, Kansas.

* * *

THE MOD SQUAD

In 1965 Braniff Airlines announced "The End of the Plain Plane." As part of Braniff's makeover, the airline hired fashion designer Alexander Girard to oversee every aspect of design for the company. Girard came up with a multi-colored fleet of jets: orange, beige, lemon, turquoise, ochre, and two shades of blue. The complementary interiors had seven different color schemes, using 56 different Herman Miller fabrics in red, green, orange, blue, yellow, and grey. The flight crews' ultra-mod uniforms, designed by Emilio Pucci, were plum, lavender, and orange, complete with colorful boots. Flight attendants were even given clear plastic bubble helmets to protect their hair in case of rain. Two decades later, the crew uniforms on *Star Trek: The Next Generation* resembled the cut and style of the original Braniff designs.

Before wipers, people smeared a mixture of onions and carrots on windshields to repel water.

HUMAN METEOR

An Austrian daredevil is poised to test a high-altitude pressure suit in a dazzling free fall that, if successful, may ultimately save the lives of future astronauts.

SUPER SUIT, SUPER MAN?

Could an emergency escape in the upper atmosphere, at the edge of space, be survivable in the right suit? What if the *Challenger* crew had been wearing pressurized, oxygen-fed suits with helmets and parachutes when their shuttle exploded in 1986? What about the *Columbia* crew, who died on re-entry in 2003?

The David Clark Company of Worcester, Massachusetts, thinks the answer is yes. They've been making anti-g suits and pressurized uniforms since 1941. Now the company is building and testing a new "super" suit that may help future astronauts survive catastrophes. Funded by energy-drink maker Red Bull, the Stratos Mission intends to send 41-year-old Austrian parachutist Felix Baumgartner aloft in late 2011 to test the new suit. He'll ascend in a balloon to 120,000 feet, then dive headfirst 23 miles to Earth. Maintaining the right diving posture—arms angled down and out in a V—is critical. In such thin air, the body can start spinning, causing a "red-out," where blood spins into the brain so fast that it ruptures blood vessels, and the centrifugal force can even separate the brain from the spinal cord. (A test pilot lucky enough to survive such a spin was clocked at 143 rpm before his chute opened.)

In the 35 seconds it takes to fall from 120,000 to 100,000 feet, Baumgartner will break the sound barrier. The risk here is that while his head breaks the sound barrier and goes supersonic, his body is still subsonic. This could create a shock wave that rips him apart. Denser lower air will slow him to 160 mph, and after another six minutes of free fall, he'll open his chute and return to Earth.

Baumgartner has been prepping for the Stratos Mission since 2010, training in the Perris Skyventure vertical wind tunnel in California with altitude-record-setting parachutist Joe Kittinger while fine-tuning the supersonic space suit at the Dave Clark Company headquarters in New England. If successful, he will be the first person to fall from outer space to Earth—and survive.

DO YOU KNOW NASCAR?

Ladies and gentlemen, start your quizzes!
(Answers are on page 462.)

1. When former NASCAR driver and current TV commentator Darrell Waltrip announces, "Boogity, boogity, boogity! Let's go racing, boys!" what's he really saying?

a. Time for all drivers to get in their cars.

b. The starter has waved the green flag.

c. Spectators should take their seats; the race will begin shortly.

2. What is the Darlington Stripe?

a. The black stripe on the passenger door of a car at Darlington caused by scraping the outside wall of the track.

b. A yellow stripe painted on the back of a rookie's car at Darlington Raceway to let other drivers know that this is their first race on this track.

c. The green stripe that diehard Darlington Raceway fans paint on their faces.

3. Drivers who misbehave have to sit where?

a. The Principal's Office.

b. The Bad Boy Box.

c. The Big Red Trailer.

4. When drivers complain about a Stop 'n' Go, what are they talking about?

a. A penalty for driving too fast on the pit road.

b. Too many caution flags during a race.

c. The pit's convenience store isn't open for business.

5. A contact patch is:

a. A quick fix on a dent.

b. The part of the tire that touches the road.

c. Two cars running too close for comfort.

First sitting president to attend a NASCAR race: Ronald Reagan, at the 1984 Firecracker 400.

6. What's it called when a driver purposefully bumps a car that's in his way?

a. The NASCAR nudge.

b. Using the chrome horn.

c. Putting the metal to the metal.

7. What's the Big One?

a. A 10- to 15-car pile-up at Talladega or Daytona.

b. The nickname for the pace car.

c. The Firecracker 500.

8. If Kyle Busch radios his crew chief and tells him that his car is running like Jack the Bear, what's he saying?

a. Get ready to put on a new set of tires at the next pit stop.

b. He's had a sudden drop in oil pressure and is losing power.

c. The car is running beautifully; all systems are go.

9. What does it mean when a driver is called a sand bagger?

a. He held his car back during qualifying so he can surprise the field with a burst of speed during the race.

b. He's too inexperienced to handle his car without adding extra weight in the trunk for traction.

c. He pushes his car to the limit so often that he crashes into the protective barriers.

10. While officials are assessing the condition of the track, the term "bear grease" comes up. What are they talking about?

a. A car leaking oil has put a dangerous slick on the track.

b. A sudden downpour has made the track unsafe for racing.

c. They need patch material to fill holes and cracks in the track.

11. Around NASCAR, what's a fabricator?

a. A driver who lies about his racing skills.

b. A car seat upholsterer.

c. The worker who makes the sheet metal body of a stock car.

R.I.P. (RUST IN PEACE)

The obituaries of some notable companies in automotive history.

STUDEBAKER (1852–1967)

By the time Studebaker began making automobiles in 1902, it had already been in the wagon-building business for half a century. The very first Studebaker car, the Runabout, was an electric vehicle. Thomas Edison purchased the second Runabout that was built and drove it for 23 years. In 1904 Studebaker switched to internal combustion engines and by 1923, the company was selling 150,000 cars a year.

A decade later, during the Great Depression, the company was one of the few automakers that allowed the United Auto Workers to organize at its plants, touting the need for a well-paid, "content" workforce. During World War II, Studebaker made engines for the B-17 "Flying Fortress" bomber, as well as so many personnel carriers that the name Studebaker became synonymous for "truck" in Russia. After the war, the company went back to making cars and posted record profits.

By 1950 Studebaker was faced with the choice of modernizing its factories or maintaining the highest-paid workforce in the industry. It stuck by its workers and the decision proved fatal. Rivals like GM and Ford paid their workers less and used that financial advantage to undercut Studebaker cars in price. By 1953 Studebaker was losing millions of dollars a month. To stay in business, the automaker tried to merge with Packard, but the deal required Studebaker to cut wages and benefits, which infuriated Studebaker workers. In 1955 the UAW organized slowdowns, work stoppages, and a 36-day general strike at Studebaker. The company never recovered. It went under in 1967, at the age of 117.

HUDSON (1909–54)

Known for its innovations, the Hudson Motor Car Co. was the first automaker to put the steering wheel on the left side and an oil light on the dashboard (both in 1911), and the first to introduce dual brakes (1936). The company also broke new ground in 1939 by hiring the industry's first female automotive designer, Betty Thatcher Oros. At its peak in 1929, Hudson was selling 300,000 cars a year, making it the third largest automaker in the world behind Ford and Chevrolet. The company had just survived the Great Depression when World War II dealt another blow: Hudson was forced to close and retool its factories to make bombs and bullets for the war effort.

In an effort to revive its name and fortunes after the war, Hudson focused on racing. By the early 1950s, the low-slung, six-cylinder Hudson Hornet was beating rival V-8s in NASCAR races (many Hudson Hornet records, including continuous wins in a single season, still stand today). What the reborn Hudson wasn't doing was selling passenger cars. In order to keep up with the Big Three (GM, Ford, and Chrysler), the company tried to merge with rival Studebaker. When that deal fell through, Hudson was taken over by another competitor, Nash, in 1954. Together they formed American Motors Corporation (AMC). The Hudson name was retired for good in 1957.

CROSLEY (1939–52)

Radio pioneer Powel Crosley Jr. owned the Cincinnati Reds baseball team in the late 1930s, but his real dream was to build cars. In 1939, Crosley introduced a two-cylinder convertible that weighed less than 1,000 pounds, putting it at a marked disadvantage in an accident with the much heavier cars of the day. What the car lacked in power and safety, however, it made up in gas mileage. Gas rationing during World War II made consumers take another look at the $250, 50-mpg Crosley, and sales began to climb. It didn't hurt that most competing automakers had been forced to drop passenger production to retool for the war effort. By 1942 Crosley was the only civilian carmaker operating in the United States. This encouraged him to think he could single-handedly change the nation's automobile tastes. He remarked, "Why employ 3,000 pounds to carry a person around when 900 pounds will do as well?"

In 1949 he introduced the Hotshot, America's first postwar sports car. But the sheet-metal construction of its engine felt flim-

Was it a joke? The AMC Gremlin was introduced on April Fools Day, 1970.

sy to consumers used to more durable and reliable cast iron, and sales tanked. In an attempt to save itself, the automaker went in the opposite direction and produced a combination farm tractor/jeep it called the Farm-O-Road in 1950. It didn't work. In 1952—the year it shuttered its doors—the company sold only 1,522 vehicles. Over time the name Crosley became synonymous with "unsafe": the 1961 driver's-ed scare film *Mechanized Death* featured a mangled Crosley Hotshot on its posters. In 2001 *Time* magazine named the Hotshot one of the 50 worst cars of all time, calling it a "major hunk of junk."

EDSEL (1957–59)

On September 4, 1957, the Ford Motor Co. debuted its Edsel brand to much public anticipation and fanfare. When the curtains parted at dealerships to reveal the new car, eager consumers—many of whom had lined up for blocks to get a first peek—let out a collective gasp. The vehicle featured an oversized oval "horse-collar" grill that one reviewer said "resembled an Oldsmobile sucking a lemon."

There was even less public enthusiasm for the car's name. After thousands of names were considered, just ten—including Citation, Corsair, and Pacer—were presented to Ford's executive committee. Chairman of the Board Ernest Breech didn't like any of them. He insisted the car be named Edsel, after Henry Ford's late son and former president of the company. Upon hearing of the decision, the company's public relations manager, C. Gayle Warnock, sent a one-line memo to the head of the naming committee: "We have just lost 200,000 sales."

Its name was to create more problems for the Edsel: 1958 models were manufactured by UAW members who remembered the car's namesake as a union-busting tyrant. Cars showed up at dealers with mysteriously faulty brakes, oil pans that fell off, and doors that wouldn't close, often with notes on the steering wheel letting salesmen know specifically which parts were missing. Edsel became an acronym for "Every Day Something Else Leaks." Ford mercifully pulled the plug on the Edsel in 1959. It was the biggest debacle in automotive history, costing the auto company an inflation-adjusted $2 billion.

Every year in the US, some 650,000 tons of rubber is worn off of tires, becoming toxic dust.

GHOST PLANES

Some areas of the world account for more than their share of aircraft disappearances due to "causes or reasons unknown"...

BERMUDA TRIANGLE

• Flight 19, a squadron of U.S. Navy TBM Avenger torpedo bombers, disappeared during a mission on December 5, 1945. Two Navy PBM Mariner Seaplanes were sent to look for the lost patrol. One plane was never seen again. A passing tanker reported a huge fireball in the air near where the Mariner was last reported. An oil slick was all that was found of the missing plane.

• On December 28, 1948, a Douglas DC-3 with 32 on board disappeared on a flight from San Juan, Puerto Rico, to Miami. As with many unexplained disappearances in the area, the weather was "fine with high visibility." No debris from flight NC16002 was ever found.

• Two British South American Airways planes vanished one year apart in January 1948 and 1949. The first, G-AHNP Star Tiger, with 31 aboard, was headed to Bermuda from Santa Maria Island. It never arrived. The second, G-AGRE Star Ariel, with 20 aboard, was en route from Kindley Field, Bermuda, to Kingston, Jamaica, when it disappeared. Regarding the Star Tiger, the British Ministry of Civil Aviation issued a press release which read, "In closing this report it may truly be said that no more baffling problem has ever been presented for investigation. What happened in this case will never be known and the fate of Star Tiger must remain an unsolved mystery." A similar conclusion was reached in the case of the Star Ariel.

THE PEAKS

The Peak District stretches from northern Derbyshire to south Yorkshire in northern England. "The Peaks," as it is commonly known, was Britain's first national park. It consists of 555 square miles of moor land, odd landscapes, and bizarre-looking rock formations with names like Back Tor, Cakes of Bread, and Salt Cellar. It is also known as England's Bermuda Triangle.

• On July 22, 1954, two Sabre Jets were taking part in a military exercise over the Peaks. When radio contact was lost, the planes were reported missing and a search was organized. Hikers discovered the wreckage of the missing jets near Black Ashop Moor, where they'd plowed into the ground—50 miles off course.

• During World War II, scores of planes crashed and more than 300 airmen lost their lives in The Peaks. Over 60 crash sites have been preserved in the area. Many believe that some of the lost planes still make appearances to this day. Since the 1970s, dozens of witnesses have reported seeing (and hearing) a low-flying World War II–era Allied B-25 bomber near Denbigh Moor. In 1987 parents and children in the village of Llangernyw were forced to run for cover when a rusty Herculean Aeroplane banked so close to the school that witnesses were astonished it didn't smash into the building. The plane leveled off and disappeared over the moors. A check with nearby airfields revealed that no low-altitude flights had been authorized in the area. In subsequent sightings, the plane appeared suddenly and just as quickly disappeared.

• On May 18, 1945, RCAF Captain Anthony Sonny Clifford and a crew of five were on their final training mission over the Peaks. The Lancaster bomber, nicknamed "Vicky the Vicious Virgin," had survived 17 bombing runs against the Germans, including its final mission targeting Hitler's infamous Eagle's Nest hideaway at Berchtesgaden. The Lancaster smashed into Dark Peak between Sheffield and Manchester in bad weather. All six airmen were killed. In October 1982, a couple having a moonlight picnic near Ladybower Reservoir spotted a plane flying low over the water. As it came closer, they saw in the bright moonlight that it was a vintage World War II Lancaster bomber. It then vanished.

In March 1997, "Vicky" was spotted again by friends hoping to glimpse the Hale-Bopp comet, and a farmer who had to duck when the plane flew low over his head. A short time later, a gamekeeper and his wife watched the Lancaster disappear into the foothills, followed by an explosion and fireball that rocked the area. Two helicopters, a 141-person rescue team, and 100 police with dogs combed the area searching for a crash. The search was called off 15 hours later when no wreckage was found. No planes were reported missing in the area.

On Nov. 5, 1870, the Reno Bros. gang committed the 1st successful train robbery in the US.

• On July 24, 1946, USAF DC-3 Dakota transport commanded by Lt. George Johnson crashed into Dark Peak 100 yards from where "Vicky" had met her fate the year before. There were no survivors. Like the Lancaster, the Dakota makes repeat appearances, but unlike its noisy, explosive counterpart, the Dakota prefers to sneak up on witnesses. In 1995 postman Tom Ingle was walking his Golden Retriever in the moors. He was just 50 yards from where the Dakota had crashed 50 years earlier when he saw a transport struggling to stay aloft 60 feet above the hills. As the plane banked out of sight, Ingle was sure it would crash. But there was no sound. "Although I could see the propellers going round, there was just an eerie silence," he said later. Running to the "crash site," he found no wreckage—just sheep quietly grazing. To this day, his dog refuses to walk down the lane. Other witnesses have since reported seeing—but not hearing—the war plane.

* * *

BOAT QUOTES

"Driving a powerboat is a bit like having one person throw a bucket of water over you while another hits you with a baseball bat."

—Steve Curtis, eight-time world champion, offshore power boat racing

"Fortunately the boat we rented had a motor in it. You will definitely want this feature on your sailboat too, because if you put up the sails, the boat tips way over, and you could spill your beer."

—Dave Barry, humorist

"My mom said she learned how to swim when someone took her out in the lake and threw her off the boat. I said, "Mom, they weren't trying to teach you how to swim."

—Paula Poundstone, comedian

"There are a lot of mysterious things about boats, such as why anyone would get on one voluntarily."

—P. J. O'Rourke, humorist

Most-ticketed car model in America: Mercedes SL drivers get 400% more tickets than average.

THE CANNONBALL RUN

This outlaw road race spawned five movies, numerous books, and a swarm of imitators. And all because some guy refused to drive 55.

ONE BIG CRAZY IDEA

The executive editor of *Car and Driver* magazine, Brock Yates, was mad as hell. In the early 1970s, speed limits across the United States were being lowered to 55 mph as the result of lobbying by highway safety and oil-conservation activists. But Yates was having none of it. To protest what he felt was a gross infringement on personal liberty, he decided to promote a cross-continental car race that would prove that driving above the legal limit was not only fun but safe. The Cannonball Baker Sea-to-Shining-Sea Memorial Trophy Dash was born:

> All competitors will drive any vehicle of their choosing, over any route, at any speed they judge practical, between the starting point (New York City) and the final destination (Redondo Beach, California). The competitor finishing with the lowest elapsed time is the winner.

The trophy? A free-form sculpture made of wrenches, hammers, pliers, and other found objects.

THE ASSASSIN AND CANNONBALL BAKER

Automotive Magazine once called Yates "one of the Grand Pooh-Bahs of automotive Journalism," but the automaking world referred to him as "The Assassin." An opinionated, in-your-face motorhead, Yates spent five decades shaping the way several generations of readers viewed cars. Not only was he a magazine writer and editor, but he also penned two screenplays and several books and did color commentary on auto racing for CBS, TNN, and the Speed network. At heart, Yates was always an outlaw, bucking the establishment whenever he could and as loudly as he could. It was only natural that one of his heroes was a risk-taking speed freak.

Born in 1882, Erwin R. Baker was as much of an entertainer as he was a motorcycle and racecar driver. At an early age, he toured the vaudeville circuit as an acrobat. When he gave up showbiz for motorcycle racing, he didn't give up showmanship. One of his ear-

Two Detroit men opened the first car wash, the Automated Laundry, in 1914.

liest stunts was racing a passenger train from one town to the next. Over his lifetime, he set 143 point-to-point records totaling 555,000 miles. One of the most amazing was a 53-hour, 30-minute solo drive from coast to coast in 1933. He averaged 50 mph in his Graham-Paige Model 57 Blue Streak 8 at a time when there were no highways or freeways and few maintained roads of any sort. A New York reporter nicknamed him Cannonball after the famous Illinois Central Cannonball Express train. Baker was the first driver to win a race at the Indianapolis Speedway and the first commissioner of NASCAR. This motorcycle and automobile racing legend died in 1960.

THE FIRST DASH

Taking Edgar "Cannonball" Baker's many cross-continental road trips as his inspiration, Yates announced that the first Sea-to-Shining-Sea Memorial Trophy Dash, would commence at midnight on May 3, 1971 at the Red Ball Garage on 31st Street in New York City. Only one team showed up to race that year: Yates; his 14-year-old son, Brock Jr., as lookout for Smokey; *Car and Truck* editor Steve Smith; and staff writer Jim Williams. Their ride was a Dodge Custom Sportsman Van they dubbed "Moon Trash II."

Forty hours, 51 minutes later they reached the Portofino Inn, a racecar driver hangout owned by ex-racer Mary Davis, in Redondo Beach. Although their travel time was relatively slow, it provided lots of fodder for Brock Yates's column. His subsequent reports in *Car and Driver* of their "pedal-to-the-metal" adventure prompted eight teams to show up for the next race, in November 1971.

THE NEXT DASH

For the second Cannonball Run, Yates teamed with American racing legend Dan Gurney, who drove their Ferrari Daytona to a new record time of 35 hours, 54 minutes. As they accepted the coveted S-K Tools "Nutmaster" trophy, a reporter asked Gurney how fast they had to go. Gurney smiled and said, "At no time did we exceed 175 mph."

One accident was reported that year: Contestants racing a Travco Motorhome had a major lasagna spill inside the RV. They still finished the race in 57 hours.

OVER THE YEARS

• In 1972 an all-woman team led by "The Pink Lady," Donna Mae Mims, made the run in a Cadillac limousine. They flipped the limo somewhere near Amarillo, dousing themselves with the contents of their portable toilet. They reported one broken arm and three grossed-out crew members. The limo was totaled.

• In 1972 some guys hired to drive a Cadillac Coupe de Ville out to California entered the race and won (they delivered the Caddy six days ahead of schedule).

• In 1975 a team driving a GMC Dually pickup took a shortcut out of the Start parking lot right through a chain-link fence and directly onto the freeway. They came in second.

• That same year, three guys in a Mercedes-Benz decided to pose as priests, in hopes that highway cops might give a break to men of the cloth. They became known as the "The Flying Fathers."

• The final year of the race, 1979, saw more than 40 teams compete. A British couple rode in their chauffeur-driven Rolls Royce, and two guys on a motorcycle, one in drag, pretended to be newlyweds. Dave Heinz and Dave Yarborough set the all-time Cannonball Run record time of 32 hours, 51 minutes, which meant that their Jaguar XJS had maintained an average speed of 87 mph.

MEDICAL MAYHEM

As always, the biggest concern was how to avoid the inevitable costly speeding tickets along the way. One racer driving through Ohio in a Ferrari got five tickets in three miles. Yates's wife, Pamela, joined her husband for the final run with a clever ruse to avoid tickets—her team drove a Dodge Van ambulance with a monster engine custom-built by drag racer Dick Landy. With Pamela as the critically ill passenger, movie stuntman-director Hal Needham as the ambulance driver, and actual doctor Lyle Royer as the EMT, Yates and company flew down the highway with sirens blaring and lights flashing. The trick worked so well that they received a few police escorts along the way. Unfortunately, the ambulance went "Code Blue" about 50 miles from the finish line (engine failure).

...the 2-door Ford Bronco, replacing it with the 4-door Expedition.

HOORAY FOR HOLLYWOOD

Time magazine ran a feature story about the Cannonball Run in 1975, which piqued public interest so much that two movies appeared the following year: *Cannonball,* starring David Carradine, and *The Gumball Rally,* with Michael Sarrazin. In 1981 director Hal Needham, who had actually participated in the 1979 run as the ambulance driver, asked Yates to write a screenplay telling the real story behind the race.

Yates later said he wrote a more serious version of the screenplay for Steve McQueen, but Burt Reynolds was cast, along with Farrah Fawcett, Dom Deluise, Jackie Chan, Roger Moore, and a long list of other celebrities, and *The Cannonball Run* (and its sequel in 1984) became an over-the-top comedy.

THE RUN TODAY

The success of the Hollywood films has made the Cannonball Run a sporadic but ongoing tradition not only in the United States but also in countries around the world. The most famous race is the Gumball 3000, a 3,000-mile international rally that runs on public roads in a different locale every year.

As for Brock Yates, he figured he'd made his point and decided to stop racing before he got arrested. However, in 1984 he founded a new (and legal) closed-course rally called One Lap of America. The premise was simple: Driving teams circumnavigate the lower 48 states, starting and finishing in Darien, Connecticut. The team that "matches Brock's mileage" is declared the winner. The race was immediately popular and continues, in a modified format, to this day. It is now directed by that lookout from 40 years ago, Brock Yates Jr.

*   *   *

WHEELS UP!

An airplane design from 1876 by Alphonse Penaud of France included retractable landing gear, an innovation that did not appear on a working plane until 1917, over 40 years later.

Odds of your remote keyless-entry fob opening another car's doors: one in a billion.

COMBAT FLYING

Uncle John happens to know a few fighter pilots. Here are some of the fancy moves they do in their planes while defending the good ol' U.S. of A.

THIRTY-DEGREE DIVE

The pilot aims the nose of the plane 30 degrees below the horizon line. When the plane reaches a predetermined altitude, the bombardier releases the payload. If necessary, the pilot then begins a "safe escape maneuver." This dive gives a pilot on a bombing run a clear trajectory without exposing his plane to return fire any longer than necessary. In a T-45C training jet used by the Navy and the Marine Corps, a crew has only four seconds to release its bombs between a starting altitude of 4,500 feet and the hard deck at 3,000 feet. Civilian planes may also dive to avoid bad weather or other aircraft. Since a sustained dive can simulate weightlessness, NASA has a specially fitted turbojet that lets people experience this aspect of space flight. Nicknamed the "Vomit Comet," this plane executes a repeated series of steep dives and climbs, to the delight of passengers like physicist Stephen Hawking, who took a ride in 2007.

SAFE ESCAPE MANEUVER

Immediately following a low-altitude bomb release, the pilot executes a hard 5-g turn away from the target site. This is called a "turning maneuver level turn." Another method is the "climbing safe escape maneuver": the bomb fragments, or "frag," could damage the bomber itself, so the idea is to be far, far away when things explode. Believe it or not, weapon fragments can fly thousands of feet through the air.

LAG ROLL

This is one of many ways an attacker can reposition during an attack. If you're already behind your enemy, start a barrel roll and trace a circle around the enemy with your aircraft's nose. Once you've effectively slowed your overtake, get the enemy in your sights and attack. The roll keeps you right behind the enemy with his "6 o'clock" (tail) in your sights.

TURN-CIRCLE-ENTRY

During air-to-air combat, a pilot sometimes executes a tight, high-g turn, experiencing g-forces that make a 200-pound person feel like they weigh a ton. An attacker uses "turn-circle-entry" to get onto a turning defender's flight path (a circle in the air). This is critical in order to effect a stable, follow-on gun or missile attack. If the target aircraft is in a high-g turn, the attacker needs to pull high-gs to enter the turn circle, all while looking around to keep track of the enemy. These turns can result in neck and back problems for pilots.

RAMMING

In World War I, ramming was taught by both sides as an offensive option. When a pilot found himself out of weapons, fuel, and luck, he could choose to turn his plane—and himself—into a weapon. In World War II this strategy was made famous by the kamikaze suicide pilots. The U.S. military neither teaches nor encourages ramming. It costs the Air Force $1,500,000 to basic-train a pilot. A fighter plane may cost 10 times that amount. No one wants to throw away an investment like that on a heroic gesture.

It's a good bet, though, that if a U.S. pilot found himself as the last line of defense against an enemy plane aiming to drop a nuclear bomb on Hometown, USA.... Well, you get the picture.

OVERHEAD LANDING PATTERN

A combat pilot doesn't always follow the traditional "downwind-base-final" landing pattern. Sometimes a pilot will land by starting directly over the runway, then bank hard in a turn called the "break," which sends the plane hurtling toward the ground before banking into a full turn. The plane ends up directly over the runway and low enough to begin landing procedures. A civilian plane is not subjected to enemy missiles and bullets while landing, so the safest procedure is a long, steady, controlled approach. A combat plane needs to land in a quick, low-profile way. A fighter pilot can use this maneuver high up in the air as well, to deny an enemy a missile shot and complicate follow-on attacks.

Only two US states that don't require car insurance: Wisconsin and New Hampshire.

THE BEAST

No matter what you call it, the president's armored limousine is a tricked-out ride that even James Bond would envy.

TOP SECRET

On January 20, 2009, just in time for Barack Obama's inaugural parade, General Motors rolled out the toughest, most sophisticated mobile bunker of a First Limo ever made. The latest in a long line of Cadillacs that have joined the First Fleet, "The Beast," as it's been nicknamed, is one of the most closely guarded secrets in the Oval Office. Says Nicholas Trotta, assistant director for the Secret Service Office of Protective Operations, "Although many of the vehicle's security enhancements cannot be discussed, it is safe to say that this car's security and coded communications systems make it the most technologically advanced protection vehicle in the world." A GM spokesman added, "One of the specifications is we don't talk about the specifications."

That said, enough details about this über-limo are known to confirm that Caddy One is the road-going equivalent of Air Force One.

QUICK SPECS

Length: 18' 6½"

Height: 5' 10"

Weight: 7–8 tons

Engine: 6.5-liter diesel; 8 mpg

Top speed: 60 mph

Estimated cost: $300,000

OUTSIDE

Body: Titanium, dual hardness steel, aluminum, and ceramic to break up possible projectiles. A reinforced five-inch-thick plate covers the undercarriage to protect against bomb blasts.

Doors: Armor-plated, eight inches thick, and as heavy as the cabin door on a Boeing 757. It's been said the doors are "able to withstand a direct hit from an asteroid." The doors have no keyhole.

Secret Service agents are the only people who know the trick to gain access to the passenger area. In case of an emergency, the president's car can be locked up as tight as Fort Knox.

Windows: Ballistic glass five inches thick. Only the driver's window can be lowered, and then only three inches—enough for the driver to speak to a Secret Service agent.

Tires: Kevlar re-enforced, shred and puncture resistant, with steel rims that allow the limo to escape at full speed even if the rubber tires are destroyed.

Gas tank: Armor-plated, filled with a special foam that prevents the tank from exploding even after a direct hit.

INSIDE

Lighting and sound: A fluorescent halo lighting system installed in the headliner lights the interior. The thickness of the car body and windows makes it extremely quiet. If the president wants to hear a cheering crowd, he must do so through internal speakers.

Seats: Hand-sewn leather. Two front seats for the driver and the lead protective agent, three rear-facing seats in back, and two forward-facing, reclining seats for the president and a guest. Embroidered with presidential seal.

Driver's seat: Standard steering wheel. The dashboard contains a communication center and GPS tracking system. It also has an enhanced video system with bumper-mounted night vision cameras. The driver is CIA-trained to handle the most-difficult conditions. A glass partition separates the passengers from the driver. Only the president has a switch to lower the glass.

Presidential seat: Equipped with a fold-away laptop desk with computer and WiFi, a state-of-the-art satellite communication system with a direct line to the vice president and the Pentagon, and a panic button to summon help if needed.

OTHER SPECIAL FEATURES

Communications: A voice and data device links "Limo One" to the White House Communication Agency (WHCA) Roadrunner that travels at the rear of the motorcade.

Entertainment system: 10-disc CD player

Defense system: The Beast is equipped with night-vision cameras, pump action shotguns, and tear gas cannons that fire from the front bumper. The limo can also fire a multispectrum infrared smoke grenade to act as a visual obscurant to operator-guided missiles.

Medical supplies: Bottles of the president's blood are kept onboard in case he needs an immediate transfusion.

Limo transporter: When the president travels to state events, the limo is transported by a U.S. Air Force C-17 Globemaster III.

Trunk: Contains an oxygen tank and a fire-fighting system.

THE FLEET

The president travels with as many as 45 vehicles in his motorcade. The more potentially dangerous the situation, the larger the number of vehicles. In case of emergency, a group of eight vehicles called "the secure package" will split from the motorcade and move the president to a safe location. A typical motorcade consists of

- 11 local motorcycle officers
- 7 local patrol cars
- 4 limousines
- 2 vans for staffers
- 2 vans for the press pool
- 1 communications vehicle
- 1 van with medical team
- 1 ambulance
- 10 sport-utility vehicles carrying a bomb-sweep team, a counter-assault team, a local SWAT team, and Secret Service agents.

* * *

SUPERCHARGE ME

One of aviation's biggest innovations has been the supercharger, which makes flying at high altitude possible. The supercharger compresses the thin air above 10,000 feet into its sea level equivalent, which allows the plane's engines to work at full power at any altitude. Without the supercharger, no plane would be able to fly into the stratosphere.

PLANE FACTS

"If God had really intended man to fly, he'd make it easier to get to the airport," wrote George Winters. With that in mind, here are a few notions to contemplate as you fly the friendly skies.

• Air travel is the second-safest mode of transportation. The elevator/escalator is first.

• Airlines update the fares in their computers 250,000 times a day.

• The first airplane toilet was a hole in the fuselage through which a passenger could see the countryside passing below.

• Only 25% of the passengers in First Class pay full fare. The rest are upgrades, frequent fliers, and airline employees.

• Tolerance for alcohol drops by 30% at 30,000 feet—which explains the number of staggerers disembarking from flights.

• Between 1916 and 2000, more than 3,500 sightings of Unidentified Aerial Phenomena (UAP) were reported and documented by military, civilian, and commercial pilots and their flight crews.

• In 2009 the Civil Air Authority reported 3,520 cases of "air rage." The average perpetrator is 30 to 39 years old. A disproportionate number are seated in Business or First Class. Alcohol is usually involved.

• The Unclaimed Baggage Center in Scottsboro, Alabama, sells 10 million items of lost luggage every year.

• The biggest passenger plane in the world is the Airbus 380 superjumbo jet. It can carry 853 passengers and, if set upright, would rise 23 stories.

• A Boeing 747's wingspan (120 feet) is longer than the Wright brothers' first flight (112 feet).

• The longest commercial flight is the nonstop from New York to Hong Kong, traveling 8,439 miles over the North Pole in 15 hours, 40 minutes.

World's cheapest production car: the $2,500 Nano, made by India's Tata Motors (2008).

TWO BY FOUR

When it comes to winning world championships on both two and four wheels, John Surtees is all alone at the top.

FALSE START

John Surtees, born February 11, 1934, in Surrey, England, had a less than auspicious introduction to driving a car. As a teenager, he borrowed his mom's Morris Minor to take the driving exam. Halfway through the test, it ran out of gas. The instructor had to push the car (with the chagrined teenager behind the wheel) to the top of a hill so they could coast down to a gas station. Recalled Surtees, "I'm still amazed that I passed."

FIRST ON TWO WHEELS...

Motorcycles were another matter. His father, Jack, was a motorcycle dealer and weekend racer in south London. In 1949 Surtees rode to victory with his dad in a sidecar-equipped Vincent—until race officials discovered the junior Surtees was only 15, a year younger than the limit. He quit school the following year and went to work for Vincent HRD Motorcycle Works as an apprentice. He also began racing bikes. He won his first solo race at 17, then stunned the racing world by nearly upsetting Grand Prix champion Geoff "The Duke" Duke in an Auto-Cycle Union endurance race at the Thruxton Circuit near Hampshire.

In 1955 Norton Works chief Joe Craig signed Surtees for his team. It didn't take long for the 21-year-old to make good on Craig's faith in him. Of 76 races, Surtees won 68, including the 250cc class at the Ulster Grand Prix. Two of those wins came against world champion Duke. In 1956 Surtees jumped to the Italian MV Agusta team and won his first Fédération Internationale de Motocyclisme 500cc Endurance World Championship. He'd go on to win six more: three additional championships in the 500cc class and three in the 350cc class—in 1958, 1959, and 1960. When he was 26, he abruptly retired from motorcycle racing. He felt he'd gone as far as he could go on two wheels.

Earliest use of the word "truck": the 1600s. It referred to the wheels on a ship's cannons.

...THEN ON FOUR

As a motorcycle racer, Surtees liked to joke that the only reason he bought his first car—a used Jowett Jupiter for £250 in 1953—was to haul bike parts around. But he came to see automobiles in the context of racing. Fresh off a win at the 500cc Nations Grand Prix motorcycle race at Monza in 1960, Surtees switched to Formula One cars. He took second in the British Grand Prix later that year and won the pole postion in Portugal as the fastest qualifier. He raced with Cooper in 1961 and with Lola in '62, performing well enough to catch the eye of Enzo Ferrari, who offered Surtees the top slot with his team. Ferrari was confident that Surtees had the potential to become the first crossover champion, and he was right. Surtees won the German Grand Prix in 1963, then dominated the Formula One circuit in 1964 to take the world championship.

A LEGENDARY CAREER

Surtees left Ferrari to start his own team in 1965. While driving a Lola in a North American Can-Am series race, he suffered life-threatening injuries in a horrific crash. Race observers assumed he would retire. Not Surtees. He was back racing for Ferrari the following year in the season opener, the Belgian Grand Prix, and won. It was one of his most memorable victories, as he fought through blinding rain to take the checkered flag.

Surtees split with Ferrari for good the next year after falling out with team manager Eugenio Dragoni. It was a move both Surtees and Ferrari agreed later was disastrous for both sides. He had his moments, winning the final race of the 1966 season for Cooper and giving the brand-new Honda team its second victory by nipping Jack Brabham in 1967 Italian Grand Prix. But Surtees never again achieved the success he had had with Ferrari. In 1970, just before his 40th birthday, he quit racing.

Surtees managed his own team through the 1970s, but medical problems stemming from old injuries forced him to take it easy. He was inducted into the International Motorsports Hall of Fame in 1996 and was named a Grand Prix "Legend" by the International Motorcycling Federation in 2003. When asked how he was able to become world champion in two different sports, he smiled and said, "I was a bit nuts, really."

Longest solar-powered plane flight: 163 miles, by AeroVironment's *Solar Challenger* (1981).

ALTERNATIVE RIDES

There's more than one way to get from point A to point B.

TUK-TUK

Savvy tourists in the traffic-clogged capital of Thailand wisely avoid taxis for the convenience of a three-wheeled motorized rickshaw called a *tuk-tuk*—so named because of the distinctive sound of its two-stroke engine. As on a three-wheeled motorcycle, the driver sits over the front wheel and passengers ride on a bench seat between the rear wheels. Both driver and passengers are covered by an umbrella-like canopy, but otherwise the *tuk-tuk* is open-air. It can handle two to five passengers, depending on whether they are *farang* (westerners, 2), Thai (3), or children (5). With a top speed of 35 mph, *tuk-tuks* are not the fastest ride, but their scooter-like maneuverability lets them thread through spaces in traffic jams with great agility.

Although fuel efficient at 80 mpg, *tuk-tuks* by their sheer numbers have become a major source of air pollution throughout Asia. Travelers have discovered that a *tuk-tuk* ride can be an expensive proposition if the fare is not negotiated up front. Plus there's no guarantee passengers will reach their destination. Many drivers hail from rural areas and often don't know their way around the cites. Most have never passed a driving test. (*Travel tip*: When riding in a *tuk-tuk*, never rest your feet on the rail behind the driver's head—it's considered a sign of disrespect.)

BODA-BODA

The *boda-boda* (derived from the English word for "border") is simply a bicycle with a padded passenger seat installed behind the rider. In the 1960s and '70s, they were used to smuggle people and goods back and forth across the "no-man's-land" between Kenya and Uganda ("border-to-border"). Today *boda-bodas* shuttle passengers cheaply and efficiently around cities and remote areas all over East Africa, where the lack of paved roads can make travel difficult. In Kenya alone, over 200,000 young men make their liv-

Longest train bridge: China's Wuhu Yangtze River Bridge. (It's 6.5 miles long.)

ing operating *boda-bodas*. In a country where unemployment is high and those who do have jobs make an average of a dollar a day, a *boda-boda* driver can earn three times that amount. It's no walk in the park, however—the typical *boda-boda* operator pedals upwards of 30 miles each day. That's changing, too, as over a third of *boda-bodas* are now motorized.

MATATU

Nairobi, Kenya, is home to another inexpensive form of public transport: the *matatu*. The name for these privately owned minibuses is Swahili slang for the three 10-cent coins a fare used to cost. The once illegal "pirate taxis" were legalized in 1973 and quickly took over Kenya's roads. Today *matatus* are the only form of public transit left in Nairobi.

Residents and government officials have other names for them: "Messengers of Death" and "Killer Disease." Often garishly painted with names like "Aggression," "Upsetter," "Why Drive When You Can Fly?," and "Thug Couture," the buses—usually overflowing with riders standing shoulder-to-shoulder in the open sliding door—careen wildly down Kenya's potholed roads, which, according to the World Health Organization, are some of the most dangerous in the world. Although the Kenyan government has tried to crack down on *matatus*, requiring safety belts, speed limits, and stricter licensing, drivers continue to whip their minivans around Nairobi with hair-raising indifference to public safety.

MINI-MOKE

The Austin Mini-Moke looks like a kiddie-car version of a Jeep that's been stripped of its doors, windows, and every nonessential item. Its name comes from the Austin Mini parts it was originally made of, and "moke," an archaic English word for donkey. First released in 1964, this tough, tiny car was meant to be parachuted into remote areas to carry supplies and paratroopers for the British army. Unfortunately its low ground clearance and anemic (34-hp) engine often resulted in the opposite—a promotional film actually showed four soldiers on maneuvers getting out and carrying their Mini-Moke whenever they hit rough terrain.

A bust with the military, the Mini-Moke soared to cult status in Britain when it appeared on the 1967 TV series *The Prisoner*.

From there it spread to other Commonwealth countries, especially those with beaches, like Australia and New Zealand. It turned out that the Mini-Moke, though lousy in rough terrain, made an awesome dune buggy. Today Mini-Mokes are the rental of choice on islands like the Seychelles, Barbados, and Mauritius, and they're the official police car of Macau.

JEEPNEY

The end of WWII left the war-torn Philippines with an unexpected bounty: tens of thousands of American Jeeps left behind by the U.S. Army. Filipinos converted the Jeeps into small buses and used them to reestablish a public transportation system that had been destroyed during the Japanese occupation. The Jeeps were extended in length to add extra seats, metal roofs were welded on for sun protection, and every available surface was painted and decorated with elaborate designs. Over the years the jeepney (an amalgam of *Jeep* and *jitney*) has become an oft-mocked but much-loved hallmark of Filipino life and remains the most common form of public transport in the islands.

Jeepneys are always overcrowded, and it's not unusual to share a seat with a couple of chickens on their way to market. There's no conductor; drivers expect passengers at the rear to hand their fare to the person next to them, who passes it until it gets up front to the driver. It's an honor system that's rarely abused. Usually the driver paints the starting and ending destinations on the side of the vehicle but how the jeepney gets there is mostly improvised. There are no official stops—if someone needs to get off, they yell at the driver and he slows down long enough for them to hop off. Today the old army Jeeps are mostly gone. Local manufacturers have stepped in to build new versions with better engines and more comfortable seats without sacrificing the noise and crowding so beloved by traditionalists.

ZIP DRIVE

Car sharing is one of the newest ways travelers and urbanites can get around all over the world. Here's how it usually works: Members pay an application fee and a nominal annual fee (or a monthly fee for frequent drivers), plus an hourly or daily use charge. In return, they receive the use of a car that can be picked up at a

...and each car is inscribed with a personalized poem. Prices start at $660,000.

predetermined location using a smart card to unlock the doors. Gas, insurance, and a fixed number of miles are included in the price. It's often cheaper than a rental car and saves the driver the cost of maintaining a car of her own. A DePaul University study found that each shared car in use takes 9 to 13 privately owned vehicles off the road, reducing traffic congestion and pollution. Users of shared cars also drive 33–37 percent fewer miles than if they owned a car, which means they are walking, biking, or using public transportation the rest of the time. The U.S. has around 30 car-share companies, with over half a million members among them. The largest company is Zipcar, which operates a fleet of 8,000 vehicles in more than 50 cities in the United States, Canada, and the U.K.

* * *

REMEMBER THE *HUNLEY*!

In 1864 the Civil War had been raging for three years and the Northern blockade of Southern ports and harbors was slowly choking the life out of the Confederacy. Wealthy New Orleans lawyer Horace Hunley decided to take matters into his own hands and hired James McClintock and Baxter Watson to design a "fish-boat" that could cruise undetected *under* water and blow the Union ships to smithereens. The two engineers designed a bullet-shaped hull 3½ feet wide, 4 feet tall, and 41 feet long. It had stabilizer fins and was propelled through the water by a seven-man team working a handcrank to turn the propeller in the aft; an eighth man worked a ballast pump. The CSS *Hunley* worked, but it was fraught with problems. A few snorkel-like attachments that were supposed to pump in fresh oxygen malfunctioned, and the slightest move by any crewmember could flip the vessel. When General P.T. Beauregard got the idea to attach a spar torpedo to the bow, the *Hunley*'s fate was sealed. On February 17, 1864, the submarine snuck up on the Union ship USS *Housatonic* and rammed the torpedo spar into its side. The resulting explosion sank the Union ship in minutes. Unfortunately for the *Hunley*, the turbulence caused by the explosion swamped the sub, and it and its crew went to the bottom as well.

We say "vroom-vroom," but in Batak (Indonesia), it's *ngong-ngooongngng*.

THE AMAZON

In June 1901, green-eyed beauty Camille du Gast became the world's first female racecar driver. But that wasn't the only thing this wonder woman could do…

LIFE IN THE FAST LANE

By 1901 Camille du Gast had already been causing Parisian tongues to wag for years. She had posed naked for the French painter Henri Gervex and been squired by many lovers, including James Gordon Bennett, flamboyant owner of the New York *Herald* and an auto racing enthusiast. But it was du Gast's penchant for taking risks that set her apart from even other unconventional women of her day. The Paris public was scandalized by du Gast's exploits as a balloonist and parachutist (she was the first woman in history to do either). And they knew of her prowess in fencing, shooting, and mountaineering—hardly acceptable sports for a woman at the turn of the 20th century.

Du Gast had always been a daredevil. So it was fortunate that in 1890, the 22-year-old adventuress married wealthy Dufayel department store magnate Jules Crespin. He loved adventure too, and when his wife became interested in ballooning in 1895, Crespin purchased two gas balloons that they launched at fêtes and other public events to advertise the store. She excelled at ballooning, often working with well-known aeronaut Louis Capazza. In 1900, when her husband purchased a Peugeot and a Panhard-Levassor, du Gast soon got rid of her chauffeur and learned to drive them herself.

QUEEN OF THE ROAD

In June 1901, du Gast notched another first for women when she became the first to compete in an automobile race. She entered her 20-hp Panhard-Levassor in the great Paris-to-Berlin rally and finished a respectable 33rd out of 100. That inspired her to get a faster car and keep racing.

In 1903 she entered her De Dietrich racecar in the Paris-to-Madrid race, which was touted as the race of the century. Du Gast made a striking impression at the starting line, sitting ramrod-

Nickname of the Douglas C-47 Skytrain used by in Europe during WWII: the Gooney Bird.

straight behind the wheel in a corseted dress and a lady's cap modified with flaps to protect her from the wind and dust (most cars of the time had no windscreen). She started the race positioned 29th in a field of 275. As she drove off, a reporter for the British magazine *Autocar* reported, "the gallant Frenchmen applauded and raised their hats, but for ourselves we must confess to a feeling of doubt as to whether fierce long-distance racing is quite the thing for ladies."

From the start there were many accidents, many of them fatal. As for du Gast, she was making excellent time, moving up to eighth place in just 72 miles. As she overtook a racer named Salleron, Englishman Phil Stead accidentally bumped her. His car flipped off the road, trapping Stead beneath it. Du Gast gallantly gave up her chance of winning and stopped to help, staying with Stead until help arrived, then returning to the race. Fellow racer Charles Jarrott said later that if du Gast hadn't stopped, Stead would surely have died. Salleron drove on.

Alarmed at the carnage, race officials stopped the race at Bordeaux. "The Race of Death," as it came to be known, was du Gast's last. She'd more than proved herself, saving a man's life and then driving to a respectable finish, but authorities decided road racing was too dangerous for women. Although the press had dubbed her "The Valkyrie of the Motor Car," du Gast was barred from further competition "to avoid the risks of her feminine nervousness."

L'AMAZONE

Du Gast took the ban in stride. Barred from road racing, she took to the water and successfully raced her motorboat *Turquoise* in Monaco. Then came another catastrophic race: the Algiers-Toulon motorboat race across the Mediterranean. A violent storm disabled or sank six of the seven boats. Du Gast was pulled unconscious from the sea by a warship. However, she had come closest to reaching the finish in Toulon, so she was declared the winner. Her survival of two horrific competions earned du Gast the nickname *L'Amazone*.

Camille du Gast shifted her focus to charity work until her death in 1942. Her love of speed and racing, and her refusal to comply with societal expectations of women, opened the door for female racers of later generations.

The one working car in 1968's *Chitty Chitty Bang Bang* sold in 2011 for $805,000.

START YOUR PROPELLERS

Aircraft races have made headlines for over a century.

THE PRIX DE LAGATINERIE (May 23, 1909)

There's still a debate over what was truly the world's first "air race." That's because the most likely contender was pretty much a dud. The Prix de Lagatinerie was widely promoted across France as the first great air race, and 30,000 spectators journeyed to the Port-Aviation airport south of Paris expecting to see the continent's most famous pilots compete in a dazzling display of aeronautics. A 5,000-franc prize was set aside for the winner of a 10-lap main event.

Because of the limitations of the aircraft of the day, the task proved too difficult for the four entrants. Making matters worse, the race started hours late as a result of technical problems and wind delays. The restless crowd was kept entertained with an impromptu kite contest. Only two of the pilots managed to get their planes off the ground, but neither finished the race. The anointed winner, Léon Delagrange, logged five laps before his coolant tanks boiled over.

TRANSCONTINENTAL RELIABILITY AND ENDURANCE TEST (October 8–31, 1919)

World War I flying ace General Billy Mitchell organized this controversial race to promote U.S. military airpower to politicians and the public. He assembled 48 military planes to depart from two starting lines on opposite coasts. Half were to fly west from Long Island to San Francisco, then back again; the other group were to fly east from San Francisco and back. The *New York Times* trumpeted the event as "the greatest aerial race ever attempted."

However, by the halfway point, seven pilots were dead from crashes, prompting the *Chicago Tribune* to call the race an example of "rank stupidity." Undaunted, Mitchell refused to call it off. Two more pilots died before the event finally came to a close. Of the 48 planes that set out, only 8 finished the trip. A complete catastrophe, the race boomeranged on Mitchell: The negative publicity it generated delayed the creation of the U.S. Air Force for several years.

Most large American cities had one or more cable car lines by the year 1890.

NATIONAL AIR RACES (1920–49)

Established by media baron Ralph Pulitzer to promote his newspaper, the *New York World*, and the budding aviation industry, these events took place annually during the latter part of August at airfields around the country. The races not only provided an outlet for pilots to strut their stuff, they also helped promote innovation during the golden age of aviation. Events included cross-country races, glider demonstrations, and parachute-jumping contests in addition to the popular Thompson Trophy Race, in which pilots blazed around pylons set up at the corners of a polygonal course that varied from 5 to 10 miles in circumference, depending on the shape of the host airfield.

A massive crowd turned out for the inaugural air race at Mitchell Field, New York. The 37-plane race had a staggered start of two minutes apart. For the majority of the three-lap race, all of the planes were buzzing around the course at the same time, creating an awesome spectacle for the crowd. Pilots tried to shave their turns as close to the pylons as possible, giving rise to the new sport of "pylon-polishing." The winner that year was Corliss C. Mosley, flying a Verville-Packard biplane.

The inaugural Thompson Trophy race of 1929 shook up the air racing community. Up to this point air racing had been dominated by military planes. The Thompson Trophy, however, was open to all comers, and the very first trophy was won by civilian pilot Douglas Davis in his Travel Air "Mystery" plane. The mystery referred to Davis's daring use of a Whirlwind engine, very powerful but considered too bulky for racing—until he proved otherwise with his win. It was the first, but not last, time a civilian plane would beat a military plane in the air races.

More than 500,000 tickets were sold to the 1929 air races. That same year, the NAR's Women's Air Derby, nicknamed the "Powder Puff Derby," became the first women-only air race. Amelia Earhart came in third that year, behind fellow air legends Gladys O'Donnell and winner Louise Thaden.

The 1931 competition saw the introduction of one of the weirdest aircraft ever to fly. The Gee Bee (named for its makers, the Granville Brothers of Springfield, Massachusetts) was designed by a man who'd never made a racing plane. When Bob Hall submitted his initial drawings, someone asked if he'd forgotten to

Alexander Graham Bell helped design several airplanes and held five patents in aeronatuics.

draw in the rear half. Derisively called the "Flying Silo," the Gee Bee looked out of proportion: stubby wings stuck onto a squat fuselage stuffed with a gigantic Pratt & Whitney Wasp engine. The cockpit was at the back of the plane, almost parallel with the rear stabilizers. Yet the Gee Bee was a rocket in the air, winning the Thompson Trophy two years in a row. Its unorthodox shape made it inherently unstable and hard to fly, and every Gee Bee that was built crashed sooner or later.

Suspended during World War II, the NAR resumed in 1946, only to be canceled permanently three years later when Bill Odom, fresh off his world record for fastest solo flight around the world, lost control of his P-51 Mustang and crashed into a house, killing himself and the two people inside.

Reno National Championship Air Races (1964). Held annually each September in Nevada, these races are descended from the National Air Races of yesteryear. But a horrific reminder of the deadly risks of air racing occurred September 6, 2011, when veteran pilot Jimmy Leeward lost control of his WWII-era P-51 Mustang fighter plane and crashed into the crowd. Eleven people were killed, including the pilot, and more than 60 were seriously injured. The plane had been heavily modified to get more speed—five feet had been cut off each wing—and film footage revealed that a piece of the tail broke off shortly before the crash. The resulting controversy over the safety of air races prompted calls to keep spectators farther away from the planes. Race organizers intend to continue holding the annual event.

RED BULL AIR RACE WORLD CHAMPIONSHIP (2003–)

Taking place annually in locales all over the world, this aerial contest is a series of timed challenges with an emphasis on pilot skill over brute speed. Pilots are held to a strict list of safety rules: No crowd flyovers. No showboating. No accelerating to over 12 Gs. Penalties are incurred for flying too high through the gates or banking incorrectly during vertical knife-edge passes. Pilots maneuver through the circuit in small, custom aerobatic planes like the Zivko Edge-450. At 20 feet long and 25 feet wide, it has a top speed of 265 mph and is amazingly nimble in the air, ideal for navigating the slalom-style course, which is lined with pylon air gates that safely break apart if struck by a plane and can be quickly replaced.

Aviator jargon: When a pilot is hot for a dogfight, he's said to have his "fangs out."

DEATH BY CAR

The automobile accidents that took these celebrities' lives made them even more famous.

JAMES DEAN

The iconic movie star died September 30, 1955, in a nearly head-on collision in his new 1955 Porsche 550 Spyder on Old Highway 46 in the Central California farming town of Cholame. The 24-year-old actor, on his way to compete in a race in Salinas, had been pulled over for speeding two hours before.

ALBERT CAMUS

On January 4, 1960, the Nobel Prize–winning author of *The Stranger* was riding with his publisher, Michel Gallimard, when their 1959 Facel Vega FV3B went out of control and crashed near Paris. The 46-year-old Camus had an unused train ticket in his pocket, having decided to hitch a ride at the last minute.

BESSIE SMITH

On September 26, 1937, the "Empress of the Blues" was badly injured when her Packard slammed into a truck on Route 61 in Mississippi. A rumor that she died hours later because a white hospital refused to admit her inspired Pulitzer Prize–winner Edward Albee to write the play *The Death of Bessie Smith*. The truth was that she bled to death waiting eight hours for a "blacks-only" ambulance to take her to a "blacks-only" hospital in Clarksdale.

GENERAL GEORGE S. PATTON

On December 9, 1945, the four-star general was blindsided in his 1938 Cadillac Model 75 by a 2½-ton GMC military truck outside Mannheim, Germany. Patton, aged 60, had been out shooting pheasant with a friend. He died 12 days later.

JACKSON POLLOCK

On August 11, 1956, the painter, age 44, was driving his green 1950 Oldsmobile 88 convertible while drunk. He crashed, killing himself and a female passenger; his lover, Ruth Kligman, survived.

Only about 2% of the world's vehicles are fueled by natural gas...

JESSICA SAVITCH

The 36-year-old NBC news anchor drowned on October 23, 1983, when the rented blue station wagon she was in dove into the Delaware Canal. The driver, Martin Fischbein, perhaps confused by heavy rain, had taken the wrong exit out of the restaurant where they'd just had dinner. Although the water was shallow, the car flipped over, trapping Fischbein, Savitch, and her dog, Chewy, inside. All three perished.

HARRY CHAPIN

On July 16, 1981, the 38-year-old folksinger, whose hits included "Cat's in the Cradle" and "Taxi," was rear-ended in his VW Rabbit by a truck on the Long Island Expressway. The trauma triggered a fatal heart attack. Chapin was posthumously awarded the Congressional Medal of Honor for his work fighting world hunger.

DAVID HALBERSTAM

In April 2007, the Pulitzer Prize–winning author of *The Best and the Brightest* was on his way to an interview when the U.C. Berkeley graduate student driving him to the appointment made an illegal left turn into the path of an oncoming car. In the collision that followed, Halberstam was killed instantly.

* * *

COMIC CAR COLLECTOR

Jay Leno is almost as famous for his car and motorcycle collection as he is for his quips on late-night television. Leno's collection of 200 vintage rides is housed in a massive warehouse complex in Burbank, California, which also holds a workshop and a full-time staff of four mechanics and fabricators. He describes his taste as "eclectic," which means he buys anything that suits his fancy. His collection includes rare Bugattis and Duesenbergs, a Lamborghini Miura, a 1932 Packard Twin Six 12-cylinder coupe, and an antique three-wheeled, two-cylinder, chain-driven Morgan. His favorite? The fastest production car ever made, the McLaren F1.

SPEED WEEK

So you want to set a land speed record? This August, just head out to the Bonneville Salt Flats—nature's answer to your needs.

MILES TO NOWHERE

At the western end of Utah's Great Salt Lake Desert, the 46 square miles known as the Bonneville Salt Flats sit on a dried lake bed that began forming some 15,000 years ago. Every winter the flats fill with rainwater and then dry out under the harsh sun, leaving a level pan of stratified mineral layers, some as much as five feet thick. In 1907 Bill Rishel, president of the Utah Automobile Association, brought two fellow businessmen out to the Flats and drove a Pierce Arrow over them to test the surface. Subsequently, they invited American racer Teddy Tezlaff to run his Blitzen Benz on the salts. Before long, Tezlaff set a new speed record (which the established racing authorities refused to recognize).

At the time, European land speed record attempts were held at beaches like the seven-mile-long Pendine Sands in Wales, while Americans preferred Florida's Daytona Beach. But by the mid-1930s, the higher-speed vehicles had become too dangerous to run on narrow, slippery beaches. The vast white plains in Utah provided the solution, and speedsters began to flock to Bonneville. The Flats' reputation was firmly established in 1935 when Sir Malcolm Campbell broke the 300-mph mark for the first time there, followed by two more speed records in 1938 by other British drivers.

FAST AND FURIOUS

Meanwhile, Southern Californian hot-rodders began using the dry lake beds such as Muroc (now Edwards Air Force Base), El Mirage, and others to hold impromptu races. While they often formed racing clubs, their rules were not always well defined, and serious—even fatal—accidents weren't uncommon. To keep the local authorities from interfering with their sport, several clubs established the Southern California Timing Association (SCTA) in 1937, with the goal of bringing order and safety to the events.

When they ran out of room at the smaller lakes, the SCTA relocated to the Salt Flats in 1949 and established Bonneville Speed Week. Bonneville Nationals Inc. (BNI) was formed by SCTA to oversee specific Speed Week events. Considered the grand finale of all land speed racing events, Speed Week is held the third week of August—weather, wind, and surface conditions permitting.

HOW TO SET A RECORD

BNI Speed Week records pertain only to the United States. An older, internationally recognized organization, the Fédération Internationale de l'Automobile (FIA, and its sister organization, FIM, for motorcycles) has slightly different rules governing the actual runs—FIA's are more restrictive—which makes for good bar arguments when trying to decide who holds which record.

For SCTA/BNI record attempts, vehicles must be wheel-driven and powered by either piston, steam, or turboshaft engines, or electric motors. (Ground-scorchers that rely on thrust to push them, like a jet engine, also run at the Flats, but at separate events.) Beyond that one requirement, BNI sponsors have worked to make the events as inclusive and safe as possible. It's now possible to watch record-hopefuls from around the world compete in everything from cars to diesel big-rigs, along with futuristic "special construction" speedsters, motorcycles with sidecars, and even motorized bar stools (world record: 47.5 mph).

Competitors race against time, not each other, and only against vehicles in the same narrowly defined category and class designation. Attempts are made over a straight course between marker cones with timing indicators every mile (in years past, vehicles just followed a black line painted on the ground). The recorded speed attempt is calculated from the average speed out of two one-mile runs in opposite directions (known as "flying miles," designed to offset the effects of the wind). In 2010 a total of 381 cars and 181 bikes participated in Speed Week, with 3,108 runs over 3 courses.

WHO'S ON TOP?

• The overland speed record for a steam-powered car, 127.659 mph, was set in 1906—and stood for nearly 100 years. It finally fell on August 25, 2009, when a British Steam Car entrant, *Inspiration*, clocked a two-way average speed of 139.843 mph—a new record recognized by both BNI and FIA.

• The two-way record for an electric vehicle, 300.992 mph, was set in 2009 by Ohio State's *Buckeye Bullet*, fitted with an electric motor that was powered by hydrogen fuel cells. The next year, after switching out the fuel cells for batteries, the renamed *Buckeye Bullet 2* set the record for battery-powered vehicles at 291 mph.

• The record for a wheel-driven vehicle is held by the *Turbinator* (a turboshaft wheel-driven streamliner), driven by Don Vesco at 458.440 mph during the Bonneville World Finals in October 2001. It's also a record sanctioned by both BNI and FIA.

• Honorable mention: On August 12, 2002, Nolan White, driving the *Spirit of Autopower*, set a record speed of 413.156 mph in his blown-fuel, twin-piston-engine streamliner. But tragically, White was killed two months later when his three braking parachutes failed to deploy properly at the end of a 422-mph run at the BNI-sponsored World Finals. He was 71.

• The world land-speed record for a vehicle of any kind is 763.035 mph, set in 1997 at Black Rock Desert, Nevada, by Englishman Andy Green, a Royal Air Force pilot who broke the sound barrier in the twin turbofan (thrust-propelled) *Thrust SSC*.

*   *   *

FASTEST PLANE

According to *Guinness World Records*, it's the X-43A. Built by NASA as part of its Hyper-X program to test what happens to aircraft during hypersonic flight, this pilotless jet was designed to fly at speeds in excess of Mach 7. The third flight of the X-43A set a new world record of Mach 9.8. (Mach 1 is the speed of sound, approximately 760 mph at sea level, so a plane flying at Mach 9.8 is going 7,546 mph—almost 10 times the speed of sound.) Only 10 feet long, the craft weighs 3,000 pounds and is powered by a special type of engine called a "scramjet." The craft is almost wingless—its body is designed to provide most of its lift.

World's oldest subway: the London Underground, which opened in January 1863.

CRAZY CARL

From bicycles to cars to racetracks, Carl Fisher could promote anything. He even convinced people to buy swampland in Florida...

RAGS TO RICHES

Like the great showman and promoter P.T. Barnum, Carl Fisher was a man with big ideas and a genius for selling them to the public. Born in 1874 to a poor family in Greensburg, Indiana, Fisher dropped out of school at the age of 12 to take up bicycle racing. Five years later, he opened a bicycle shop with his brother in Indianapolis. With little cash for advertising, he resorted to promotional stunts to attract customers: He rode a bicycle on a tightrope stretched across Washington Street (wearing a padded suit for safety). He built a double-decker bicycle and cycled through the streets with children following, like the Pied Piper. He released 1,000 balloons, 100 of which carried coupons for a free bicycle. As a result of all the attention, Fisher's bicycle shop became the biggest in town.

UP IN THE AIR

When friend and champion bicycle racer Barney Oldfield came to town in his new automobile, Fisher teamed up with him to open the first automobile dealership in the United States. Fisher demonstrated the toughness of the new-fangled contraptions by pushing a seven-passenger car off the roof of a building. When the car landed safely on the street, Fisher drove off, waving farewell to a cheering crowd. (He had deflated the tires so the car wouldn't bounce.)

Another time, Fisher announced that he would be flying his new automobile over the city of Indianapolis. Thousands watched as Fisher rose into the sky behind the wheel of his Stoddard-Dayton, which dangled from an orange hot air balloon. Man and car floated away into the clouds, only to be greeted with enthusiastic cheers as he drove up in triumph an hour later, the balloon folded in the backseat. Newspapers across the nation carried the story. Fisher described the stunt: "I had taken the heavy motor out of the car before we went up. When the balloon landed a couple of miles away, my brother was there to meet us with an identical car. It was simple, yet no one ever seemed to figure it out."

A BRIGHT IDEA

In 1904 a friend brought Fisher a tank of compressed gas that he thought might make better headlights than the more-flammable kerosene currently in use. Fisher jumped on the idea, and the Prest-O-Lite Company was born, offering safe, bright acetylene gaslights for night driving. Soon Fisher had cornered the market, and when he sold the company to Union Carbide in 1913, he walked away with a cool $9 million in profit (about $195 million today).

With the money, Fisher moved onto his next project: building the world's greatest racetrack. The plan was to make the track the premier testing ground for new cars.

THE BRICKYARD

Fisher and partners Arthur Newby, Frank H. Wheeler, and James A. Allison built the Indianapolis Speedway, which became—and remains—the premier auto racing arena in the world. In June 1909, Fisher opened the Speedway with his usual flair: He held a balloon race.

The first day of auto racing two months later, however, was a catastrophe. The crushed rock-and-tar track caused numerous crashes, fires, injuries to racecar drivers and spectators, and six deaths. A disaster of that scale might have stopped the project in its tracks, but Fisher convinced his investors to resurface the Speedway with 3.2 million paving bricks, earning its famous nickname, "The Brickyard." The new and improved Speedway reopened on May 30, 1911, with 80,000 spectators who'd paid a dollar apiece. Thousands more watched from surrounding trees and the roofs of neighboring buildings. It was a huge success.

COAST TO COAST

Not one to rest on his laurels, Fisher had another vision: With the burgeoning success of the automobile, drivers were going to need roads—lots of them. At a dinner party for automobile manufacturers in September 1912, Fisher revealed his plan to build a gravel road that would stretch from San Francisco to New York City. "A road across the United States!" he told the auto executives. "Let's

In 1958 Ford designed the Nucleon concept car, which featured a built-in nuclear reactor.

build it before we're too old to enjoy it!" The Panama-Pacific International Exposition in San Francisco was planned for May 1915—the perfect target date for completion of the Coast-to-Coast Rock Highway, as Fisher called it.

The group began seeking contributions to come up with the estimated $10 million the project would cost. Frank Seiberling of Goodyear, Thomas A. Edison, former president Theodore Roosevelt, and current president Woodrow Wilson all sent checks. Industrialist Henry Bourne Joy helped Fisher raise the rest of the money using the slogan, "See America First." (He also changed the name to the more patriotic and less clunky-sounding Lincoln Highway.)

There was no stopping Fisher. Once he had his East-West road, he focused on building the Dixie Highway from the Upper Peninsula in Michigan to southern Florida. By 1916 the section from Indiana to Miami was open, and Fisher set his eye on a new project: Miami Beach.

FUN IN THE SUN

Snowbirds who escape the harsh winters of the northern United States and head for Miami Beach have Carl Fisher to thank for their place in the Florida sun. He saw the potential for 3,500 acres of bug-infested mango swamp to be turned into a resort destination. As humorist Will Rogers put it: "Carl was the midwife of Florida. Had there been no Fisher, Florida would be known today as just the Turpentine State. He rehearsed the mosquitoes till they wouldn't bite you until after you had bought."

Fisher dredged the swampland and covered it with sand, and built four hotels in this new place called Miami Beach. Ever the promoter, he bought a baby elephant named Rosie and photographed her posing as a golf caddy for visiting president-elect Warren G. Harding.

He put up billboards in the north splashed with photos of bathing beauties sunning themselves on sparkling white beaches. He placed a huge illuminated sign in New York City's Times Square declaring, "It's June in Miami."

When the Florida land boom took off, Fisher made money like he was printing it. By the mid-1920s his estimated worth was $100 million. Fisher immediately made plans to build a Miami Beach–

The Hells Angels motorcycle club took their name from the WWII B-17 airplanes.

type summer resort in Montauk, Long Island, for wealthy New Yorkers. When asked by associates why he didn't just rest and enjoy his fortune, he said, "You dudes can sit around here on your white pants if you want, but I can't. I've got to see the dirt fly!" In 1926 Fisher bought 10,000 acres in Montauk and began building homes, offices, and a luxury hotel resort in the manor style of English country homes. His slogan: "Miami in the winter, Montauk in the summer."

CRASH!

Carl Fisher's great ride came to an end on October 29, 1929. As with many speculators, his money was heavily invested in the stock market, and when it crashed, so did his fortune. He retired to a small cottage in Miami to wait out the Great Depression. But Fisher had one last project in him: building the famous Caribbean Club as a "poor man's retreat" on Key Largo. In 1948 it was immortalized on film as the setting for the Humphrey Bogart–Lauren Bacall film of the same name.

When Fisher died in 1939, he was a shell of his former ebullient self, broken by years of heavy drinking. He went to his grave thinking himself a failure, but that was not the opinion of his friends. Will Rogers said Fisher had done "more unique things, even before I heard of Florida, than any man I ever met." Howard Kleinburg, an author and Miami Beach historian, said, "If you look at Fisher's entire life, it's a marathon. It's a race. It was a race to achieve the top of whatever field he was in at the time. Everything he did he went into it with his heart, his soul, his money, and he would not stop until he reached the end. He wanted to be there the quickest and first."

Today, in a park on the north end of Miami Beach, stands a bronze bust dedicated to Mr. Miami Beach, as Fisher was often called, with these words: "He carved a great city out of a jungle."

* * *

VROOM IRONY

Gottleib Daimler (1834-1900), automotive pioneer and inventor of one of the earliest automobiles, did not like to drive.

THIS SUCKS

Doing a little traveling? Be careful if you hear a giant sucking sound.

HEADING OUT

Chris Fogg was a flight nurse transporting a patient from Twin Falls, Idaho to Seattle on a twin-engine Piper turboprop in June 2007. As they cruised at 20,000 feet, Fogg chatted with the pilot in the cockpit. With a loud popping noise, the window next to Fogg's right shoulder exploded, and he was partially sucked out of the window. His left arm and legs were still in the cockpit, but his head and right arm were outside battling 200 mph winds. The pilot put the plane in a steep dive down to 10,000 feet to equalize the pressure, and Fogg was able to pull himself back inside. They made an emergency landing in Boise 10 minutes later.

UP, UP, AND AWAY

In 2006 Meghan Mahoney of St. Louis was driving to visit friends when a fierce storm struck suddenly Interstate 74 in central Indiana. Before Mahoney could pull over, she was sucked out of her open sunroof (she wasn't wearing a seatbelt) and tossed 300 feet away. She survived the incident.

BUS-TED

Nicolas Stilwell of Ocala, Florida, was riding around Orlando in 2008 in a chartered limo called "The Ultimate Party Bus," celebrating a friend's 21st birthday. When another guest leaned over to say something to the driver, the bus door popped open. The bus was going 60 mph, and the turbulence outside created a vacuum that sucked Stilwell out the door. He was critically injured and lost a leg.

SPACE VAC

In 1960 Joe Kittinger was testing a pressurized suit in a high-altitude parachute jump from 20 miles up when he lost pressure in his right glove. Exposure to the near-vacuum present at the edge of space caused his hand to swell painfully to twice its size. Happily, three hours after his return to Earth, the hand returned to normal.

DWARF CAR RACING

It's half the size and half the price of a regular racing car—but with all the thrills!

DWARF CAR DADDIES

In 1979 Ernie Adams and Darren Schmaltz were coming home from watching sidehack (motorcycle-and-sidecar) races in Phoenix, when they started talking about how four-wheeled racers would corner better than the three-wheelers they'd just seen. They decided to build one with a retro racing car body for spectator appeal—the dwarf car was born. The first one, built by Adams, was a replica of a 1934 Ford coupe, but only five-eighths its size, with a 73-inch wheelbase and a height of 46 inches, powered by a Honda 350cc engine. Schmaltz built a replica 1933 Dodge coupe powered by a Kawasaki 350cc engine. Wherever the men drove the cars, crowds gathered, asking the same three questions: What are they? Where do they race? and How can I get one?

LITTLE CARS, BIG FUN

In March 1981, Adams and Schmaltz drove some laps in their cars around Arrowhead Speedway in Phoenix. The crowd went wild, and orders poured in. The two men decided to build only ⅝-scale replicas of American-made automobiles built from 1928 to 1949, with steel roll cages, full racing suspensions, and enough power to top 100 mph. When 12 of their cars raced at the Yavapai County Fair in Prescott, Arizona, in 1983, a new sport was born. In 1987 racer John Cain established Dwarf Car U.S.A., the first official sanctioning body for dwarf cars. Today the Western States Dwarf Car Association governs the West, and Team U.S.A. governs the East.

Dwarf car racing allows young drivers to break into the sport at a fraction of the cost. NASCAR champ Kurt Busch won the Nevada Dwarf Car championship when he was 17. He moved on to the slightly larger Legends cars, and his wins in both racing associations led to his eventual success on the NASCAR circuit.

Dwarf car racing continues to crank out champions. And with four national events per year and numerous regional meets, the little sport is still growing.

Austrian Dagobert Müller built the world's first air-cushion vehicle in 1915.

PRESSURE SUIT

Before 1933 any pilot who tried to fly to 40,000 feet would have had a death wish. Enter aviation pioneer Wiley Post.

AIMING HIGH

Wiley Post was a fearless, one-eyed aerial acrobat from Oklahoma (he lost the eye in an oil field accident as a young roughneck). Post first attracted attention on August 27, 1930, when he flew from Los Angeles to Chicago in a record 9 hours, 8 minutes, and 2 seconds. In 1933 he became the first person to fly solo around the world. But Post wanted not only to fly faster and longer, he wanted to go higher. To do that, he knew he would need oxygen and a pressurized cabin.

From sea level to 12,000 feet, the average person moves and breathes comfortably. Above that elevation, low oxygen and air pressure make it difficult to function. The lungs struggle, gases trapped in the body start to expand, the brain swells, and bubbles of nitrogen block blood flow. A person quickly becomes dizzy, nauseated, confused, and finally unconscious.

SUITING UP

Post's famous single-winged Lockheed Vega, the *Winnie Mae*, was made of wood and couldn't be pressurized, so Post teamed up with Russell S. Colley of the B.F. Goodrich Company to design the world's first practical pressure suit. With financial backing from Frank Phillips of Phillips Petroleum, Post and Colley built three prototypes out of rubberized parachute fabric. The first suit ruptured during a pressure test. The second suit's helmet got so tight during testing that Post had to be cut out of it. They pieced together the third suit from parts of the first two.

The final result consisted of three layers—long underwear, a rubber air-pressure bladder, and an outer layer of double-ply rubberized parachute fabric—topped off with pigskin gloves, rubber boots, and an aluminum helmet. The suit looked like a cross between a diving bell, a wet suit, and the Tin Man's costume. The outer "skin" was attached to a hinged frame with arm and leg joints that allowed Post to walk to and from the *Winnie Mae*.

JET STREAMER

On September 5, 1934, Post took his new suit and the *Winnie Mae* into the stratosphere. Somewhere above Chicago he set a new altitude record of 40,000 feet and discovered the jet stream. Meteorologists and pilots now know the jet stream is a fast-flowing air current on the edge of the stratosphere. Guiding the *Winnie Mae* into it made Post fly not only higher but faster. The plane had a top speed rating of 174 mph, so Post was stunned to see the speedometer show he was flying over 360 mph. He made 10 stratospheric flights before stress tests revealed the *Winnie Mae* couldn't handle such high speeds. Before Post could design a new plane, he and humorist Will Rogers were killed in a plane crash in Alaska. The *Winnie Mae* and the pressure suit were sold to the Smithsonian.

FULL PRESSURE

Over the next 20 years, a similar partial-pressure suit developed by the David Clark Company became standard gear for high-altitude test pilots. The mask provided pressurized oxygen, but the suit functioned only in the event of a loss of cabin pressure. It wasn't until the 1960s that the aviation industry realized it needed a flight suit offering more than partial pressure. In 1964 President Lyndon B. Johnson revealed the existence of a strategic reconnaissance plane that flew faster than the jet stream and higher than the stratosphere: the SR-71. It could fly almost four times the speed of sound—2,000 mph—at altitudes of more than 80,000 feet. However, flying at supersonic speed causes the air moving across a plane's fuselage to create a shock wave, pushing temperatures on the windshield and in the cockpit to 600°F. The Blackbird, as the SR-71 was nicknamed, carried cooling systems, but these weren't enough to protect the pilot.

Enter the Pilot Protective Assembly, a full-pressure flight suit that, updated over the decades, is still worn today. The PPA provides a pilot with a self-contained capsule of oxygen and a constant atmospheric pressure. Its built-in cooling system maintains body temperature until a pilot can lock into an onboard climate system. The suit also comes equipped with a parachute and a flotation device. With USAF planes often flying right up to the Kármán line—the very edge of space—the full-pressure flight suit continues to be standard-issue wear.

1st track to hold a NASCAR race outside the US: Stamford Park, in Ontario, Canada (1952).

CAR NAME QUIZ

Can you match these cars with their countries?
(Answers are on page 463.)

Round One. Match the car to the country it comes from:

1. Koenigsegg
2. Leblanc
3. ZIL
4. Tramonta
5. Hongqi HQD
6. Harper
7. Holland Car
8. Laraki
9. Shaka
10. Wallyscar
11. Timmis
12. Bolwell
13. Almac
14. Biscayne
15. Tata Nano

a. Spain
b. Tunisia
c. Argentina
d. Sweden
e. Ethiopia
f. Morocco
g. South Africa
h. India
i. China
j. Canada
k. Australia
l. Switzerland
m. Russia
n. New Zealand
o. Botswana

Round Two. Match the model to the make and where it's sold:

16. Montana
17. Corsa
18. Matiz
19. SLS
20. Transit
21. Beat

p. Pontiac
q. Ford
r. Chevy
s. Cadillac

(aa) India
(bb) Europe
(cc) Argentina
(dd) Mexico
(ee) Latin America
(ff) China

Bonus Question: What do these cars have in common?

Buick Excelle (China)
Daewoo Lacetti (Korea)
Chevy Optra (Canada)
Holden Viva (Australia)

QUEST FOR SPEED, PART III

For those seeking to break the next great speed barrier, the real question is: How do we keep all four wheels on the ground? (Part II is on page 303.)

BREAKING BARRIERS

Getting a car to go faster than the speed of sound took over a century to accomplish. Getting one to go faster than 1,000 mph involves more than just extra speed. The current low-level altitude speed record (under 300 feet) for an aircraft is 988.26 mph, set by a civilian-owned F-104 jet in the 1970s. That same jet is capable of Mach 2 up in the clouds, where it was designed to fly, but the physics of high speed at ground level are unforgiving. Chuck Yeager wasn't really sure what would happen when he took the Bell X-1 to Mach 1.06 (807.02 mph) in 1947 (would the pressure waves buffeting the craft rip it apart?) until he did it and survived. Land speed record teams today are never convinced that the pressure waves generated from going supersonic just four inches off the ground won't tear a car apart. Making the attempt is always a potentially deadly leap of faith.

DOING THE MATH

Getting the passing air to flow correctly around the wheels and over the body is the critical design challenge on a supersonic car. As on an airplane, uneven airflows can cause destructively unbalanced forces. Plus, the aerodynamic shape of the vehicle must behave well at both sub- and supersonic speeds. Super-computers are used to solve calculations involving computational fluid-dynamics that will predict how a vehicle will behave as it transitions from sub- to supersonic speeds. Additionally, chassis flex must be kept to a minimum over the 30-foot-plus length of the lightweight streamlined shell, and the wheels (aluminum-alloy, not rubber tires) must be capable of withstanding centrifugal forces generated by turning at 167 revolutions per second. Teams face diminishing returns the faster they go: As speed and acceleration increase, aerodynamic loads do too, which requires the car to be stronger and heavier, both of which then have to be overcome to get more speed.

Conditions are equally brutal for drivers. During acceleration, they experience forces up to 2.5 gs (2.5 times the pull of gravity at ground level), and negative gs if the speed is dropped too quickly at the end of a run. Either situation can cause blackouts, and negative gs can make the car uncontrollable. Powering down engines, popping parachutes, and applying brakes have to be sequenced very carefully over the two miles it takes for the vehicle to come to a stop.

THE CONTENDERS

- **Bloodhound SSC (U.K.).** Named after the Bristol Bloodhound, a Cold War–era British Mach 2.7 surface-to-air missile, the ground-hugging Bloodhound is 43 feet long, 9 feet tall, and close to 6.5 tons when fully fuelled. It has three engines that work in stages. A turbo fan jet (pulled from a Eurofighter Typhoon) takes the car up to 200 mph. At that point, a Cosworth Formula 1 racing engine, acting as a high-speed fuel pump capable of delivering 800 liters of fuel in 20 seconds, kicks in to start the custom, solid-liquid hybrid rocket intended to take the car to its ultimate speed. The combined power system produces about 133,000 hp, theoretically able to push the car to 1,000 mph in 40 seconds.
- **Aussie Invader 5R (Australia).** The Australian team has been working on this project for 10 years. Their Invader 5R is an elegant, 40-foot-long, 36-inch-diameter rocket on wheels. The plan is to power the car with a series of Atlas rocket engines previously used by NASA and intercontinental ballistic missiles. Under full load, the new engine design will produce 62,000 pounds of thrust (200,000 hp), accelerating the Invader 5R from 0 to 1,000 mph in 20 seconds.
- **North American Eagle (U.S.).** While the British and Australian teams designed their cars from the ground up, the North American team built theirs around a piece of military surplus, an obsolete Lockheed F-104 A-10 Starfighter. Not a bad choice, considering that in its day the F-104 was capable of better than Mach 2. It was affectionately known as a "man in a missile." The former

jet fighter is now the North American Eagle, a heavily modified and modernized ground speedster with 52,000 hp to push it along. The North American team figures that if they can get half that speed on the ground, the Eagle will be a serious contender for the land speed record.

FOR THE RECORD

Ideally, all the aerodynamic forces working to tear a car apart at supersonic speed are in perfect balance at peak performance when the machine comes screaming flat-out through the timing gates—a 3.4-second window of achievement for a decade's worth of labor and millions of dollars in investment. But there's one small detail that none of the teams can overlook: "The timekeepers will be looking for wheel tracks," as British team engineering director John Piper puts it. "No wheel tracks, no record; we can't do this in the air."

* * *

ROAD SCHOLAR

• The United States has 4 million miles of streets and roads.

• Each mile of a 4-lane highway takes up 17 acres.

• There are 1,214 rest areas along the U.S. Interstate System.

• The Interstate System goes through all but five state capitals: Juneau, Alaska; Dover, Delaware; Jefferson City, Missouri; Carson City, Nevada; and Pierre, South Dakota.

• The straightest road in the United States is a stretch of Highway 46 in North Dakota that runs 123 miles from Streeter (population 170) to Hickson (population 3,129).

• The stretch of U.S. Route 50 that crosses the center of Nevada was named "the loneliest road in America" by *Life* magazine in 1986.

• According to State Farm Insurance, the most dangerous intersection in America, determined by the number of crashes that occur there annually, is Flamingo Road and Pines Boulevard in Pembroke Pines, Florida.

1st traffic crossing pedestrian button: the corner of 105th St. & Euclid Ave, Cleveland (1948).

WATER WINGS

A brief history of seaplanes. Or are they flying boats?

EARLY DAYS

Many early airplanes were designed to take off and land in water, the idea being that water is a more forgiving medium than solid ground. French pilot and designer Gabriel Voisin flew the first manned seaplane over the Seine in Paris in 1905. Basically a glider with floats for wheels, it was towed by a boat until it caught enough wind to lift off. Voisin managed to fly 1,800 feet before dropping into the river, where he nearly drowned. A colleague captured the flight on film.

Further tinkering and testing led to the debut of the Canard Voisin in 1910, which caught the eye of the French military. Powered by a 60-hp radial engine, its main wings were set toward the rear of the fuselage, with a horizontal stabilizer near the front. The odd configuration, which gave the craft better stability, prompted its name—*canard* being French for "duck." Two years later, it became the first seaplane to be used in army exercises.

Greece was the first nation to use a seaplane as a war plane. During the Balkan War of 1912–13, a seaplane called the Astra Hydravion flew over the Turkish fleet and dropped four bombs, and then landed safely in a nearby bay.

CROSSING THE POND

The first American seaplane, designed by aeronautics pioneer Glenn Curtiss, took flight over San Diego Bay in 1911. Two years later, the *Daily Mail* of London offered a £10,000 prize to the first pilot to fly a plane across the Atlantic. American businessman Rodman Wanamaker was determined to see that the prize went to a U.S.-based team. He joined with Curtiss to open the Curtiss Aeroplane and Motor Company to develop and build two seaplanes capable of making the flight. Curtiss and Englishman John Cyril Porte designed two aircraft, dubbed the "Model H2s," and shipped them to England. They scheduled a transatlantic flight for August 1914, but the outbreak of World War I interrupted their plans.

As soon as the war ended, teams from England, France, and

the U.S. continued to vie for the prize. On May 27, 1919, Lt. Cdr. Albert Read landed his Curtiss-designed NC-3 Model #2 "flying boat" in Lisbon harbor and telegraphed back to the states, "We have successfully crossed the pond. The job is finished." Read flew his "Nancy," as the NC-series flying boats were called, in stages from Rockaway, New York, to Plymouth, England, in a series of flights lasting a total of 53 hours, 58 minutes, spread out over 23 days. His fame was short-lived—British aviators John Alcock and Arthur Whitten Brown pulled off the first nonstop transatlantic flight, from Canada to Ireland, only a month later. It took 16 hours, 12 minutes.

IMPERIAL AIRWAYS

Due to safety concerns and the lack of runways in many areas, early commercial airlines relied on seaplanes for flights over vast distances, particularly when crossing bodies of water. Seaplanes fall into two categories: *float planes*, which are conventional airplanes in most respects except that their wheels are replaced by pontoons that allow the craft to make a water landing, and *flying boats*, which use the airship's hull for buoyancy. Passenger and cargo cabins were set in the hull, and the resulting ships were some of the biggest, most powerful aircraft of their era.

Starting in 1928, the British carrier Imperial Airways began planning a route that would connect England with the most far-flung outposts of the British Empire: India and Australia. By 1936 a fleet of Short S-23 "C" class Empire flying boats were servicing a long route: Southampton to Marseilles, to Rome, to Athens, to Alexandria, to Baghdad, to Karachi, to Calcutta, to Rangoon, to Bangkok, to Singapore, and all the way to Sydney.

The Empire flying boats were considered among the handsomest planes ever built; they were certainly among the most luxurious. Nose to tail they were 88 feet long, with a wingspan of 114 feet. Four 920-hp Bristol engines could lift the craft's 18 tons out of the water in 17 seconds. With a top speed of 200 mph, the Empire flagship *Canopus* would cruise at 165 mph for 700 miles between refuelings. Up to 24 passengers could relax in the forward smoking lounge, sipping a Pimm's Cup offered by the steward and looking out the porthole windows at the ocean or land passing 11,500 feet below. The aft cabins converted into sleeping berths.

World's first automobile law: In 1901, the state of Connecticut set the speed limit at 12 mph.

Above them was a mail room carrying up to three tons of correspondence (the real bread-and-butter of the company), with the radio room set behind the pilot and navigator. By modern standards the pace was leisurely—it took six days of flying to reach Singapore—but compared to the only alternative, steamship travel, it was a breathtakingly quick way to go around the world.

PAN AMERICAN AIRLINES

Not to be outdone, Pan American Airlines in the United States turned to flying boats to provide service to Hawaii, Samoa, and China. The Pacific Ocean presented greater challenges to aviation because of the vast stretches of open water that had to be crossed between stops. Several seaplanes filled the bill, the Martin M-130 "China Clipper" being one of the most notable, but the greatest flying boat in the Pan Am fleet was the Boeing 314, considered the pinnacle of its class.

Weighing over 80 tons, the B-314 was 106 feet long, with a wingspan of 152 feet (about three quarters that of a 747 today). Its four Wright "Twin Cyclone" 14-cylinder radial engines generated 1,500 hp apiece, giving the B-314 a range of 3,500 miles at a cruising speed of 183 mph. Up to 74 passengers could be seated in the interior, but it usually carried 40 in seven elegant compartments, with a special honeymoon suite in the tail. A crew of ten served three-course meals in the 14-seat dining room, which doubled as a smoking lounge between meals. There was a special catwalk inside the massive fixed wing to allow access to the engines during flight. Over their lifetime, the B-314s made over 5,000 ocean crossings, traveling more than 12 million miles.

END OF AN ERA

By the mid-1940s, seaplanes had fallen out of favor with commercial airlines. The surge in construction of new runways and airports around the world during WWII, in addition to major innovations in land-based planes, made flying boats less and less practical. Eccentric industrialist and aviator Howard Hughes provided one last hurrah with the 1947 test flight of his gigantic flying boat named *Hercules*—better known today as the *Spruce Goose*.

Engineers also had high hopes for the Grumman G-73 Mallard, a large craft capable of landing on both land and sea, but only 59

Although they were available, until 1926, a pilot's license wasn't required to fly.

were made and they were used primarily by corporate bigwigs to commute between New York City and their mansions in the Hamptons of Long Island.

During the 1950s there were attempts by U.S. and U.K. designers to develop jet-powered seaplanes for military use, but none of the developed models, including the Saunders-Roe SR.A/1 and the F2Y Sea Dart, ever entered service. The U.S. Navy continued to use conventional seaplanes for sea reconnaissance well into the 1970s until another, more-efficient aircraft took their place: the helicopter.

SEAPLANES TODAY

Some of the old flying boats have been converted for use as tanker planes to fight forest fires, and float planes continue to have a valued niche in aviation. Coast guards around the world still keep them on hand for use in ocean search-and-rescue missions, because they have a greater range than helicopters. They're also used to travel to and from remote island and coastline communities.

* * *

DUMB CROOKS: VROOM EDITION

• When Amy Brasher, 45, of San Antonio, Texas, took her car in for an oil change, the mechanic discovered 18 packages of marijuana stuffed into the engine compartment. He called the police and she was promptly arrested. According to the Texas police, Brasher thought her drugs were safely hidden. It hadn't occurred to her that the mechanic would have to lift the hood of the car to change the oil.

• When a Seattle man tried to steal gasoline by inserting a siphon hose into what he thought was the gas tank of a motor home, he got the surprise of his life. Police arriving at the scene found the man rolling on the ground, clutching his stomach. He'd sucked on the end of the hose, only to find that what he was siphoning wasn't gas, but raw sewage—and he'd swallowed several mouthfuls of it before he figured it out. The owner of the motor home declined to press charges. Instead, he thanked the thief for giving him a laugh.

Before Studebaker made cars, it was America's largest producer of horse-drawn wagons.

CHASIN' IT, OLD SCHOOL

Today's big-screen car chases involve a lot of special effects, but these movies did it the old-fashioned way, with stunt drivers and actors risking their lives to give viewers a few seconds of adrenalin-laced excitement.

BULLITT (1968)

Steve McQueen, a green 1968 Ford Mustang GT 390 Fastback, and the vertiginous streets of San Francisco. Need we say more? SFPD Lieutenant Frank Bullitt (McQueen) pursues a pair of hit men in a 1968 Dodge Charger in a thrill ride that, after 40 years, remains the gold standard of screen car chases. McQueen did his own driving in the Mustang, while the Charger was manned by famed stunt driver Bill Hickman. McQueen scoffed at the idea of "undercranking" the camera to create the illusion of speed, telling stunt coordinator Carey Loftin that money was no object in creating "the best car chase ever done." In *Bullitt*, what you see is what really happened: two classic 400-hp muscle cars blasting down real city streets at speeds of up to 110 mph.

***THE FRENCH CONNECTION* (1971)**

Director William Friedkin must have nerves of steel. To shoot portions of the iconic chase scene in which police detective Popeye Doyle (Gene Hackman) commandeers a 1971 Pontiac LeMans to chase an elevated train through the streets of Brooklyn, Friedkin sat in the backseat of the car holding a camera over stunt driver Bill Hickman's shoulder. He explained, "The camera operator and the director of photography both had families with children, and I didn't." Friedkin chided Hickman to go faster—up to 90 mph—from Bay 50th to Bay 24th Street until he ran out of film. A gumdrop-style police beacon and blaring horn were used to warn bystanders. "The fact that we never hurt anybody in the chase run, the way it was poised for disaster, this was a gift from the Movie God," said Friedkin in a 2009 interview. "Everything happened on the fly. We would never do this again. Nor should it ever be attempted in that way again." The movie

America's first subway system was built in Boston in 1897.

went on to win five Oscars, including Best Picture, Best Actor, and Best Director.

GONE IN 60 SECONDS (1974)

Stunt driver and junkyard owner H.B. "Toby" Halicki wrote, produced, directed, and starred in this cult classic that earned him the nickname "Car Crash King." He bought most of the cars used in the movie for about $200 each—which was fortunate because 93 were totaled in the 34-minute car chase that ends the movie. It remains the longest chase in film history. Insurance adjuster and master car thief Maindrian Pace (Halicki) outruns most of the Long Beach police department in his yellow 1973 Ford Mustang Mach I, nicknamed "Eleanor." Production was halted while Halicki recovered from injuries resulting from hitting a telephone pole at 100 mph. He was hurt again in the chase's final jump, a 128-foot leap over another car, and he walked with a limp for the rest of his life. Halicki died in 1989 at 48, the result of a rigging accident that occurred while preparing a stunt for a sequel that was never filmed. A remake starring Nicolas Cage came out in 2000.

THE ROAD WARRIOR (1981)

Director George Miller spent most of his $4 million budget on the frantic chase that ends the film. The 10-minute scene features hopped-up muscle cars, XT and TT500 Yamaha dirt bikes, a nitrous-powered Ford F-100 Ute pickup armed with a crossbow cannon, VW-based "sandrail" dune buggies ridden and driven by hordes of leather-clad, mohawk-adorned, steroidal junkies intent on seizing a tanker truck full of gasoline driven by hero Mel Gibson. The semi pulling the tanker is a highly modified 1970s Mack R-600, with a huge cowcatcher-style ram welded across the grill and armored plates protecting the wheels. The cult classic cemented Gibson's reputation as a top movie star.

TO LIVE AND DIE IN L.A. (1985)

This often overlooked film features one of the most white-knuckle car chases ever made. Director William Friedkin told the stunt coordinator, Buddy Joe Hooker, that if they couldn't come up with a better chase scene than their previous work in *The French Connection*, he'd scrap the footage. The 10-minute chase features

Indiana has more miles of interstate highway per square mile than any other state.

a harrowing wrong-way sequence on an L.A. freeway that took six weeks to film and put the movie $1 million over budget. Actor William L. Petersen did most of his own driving in a 1985 Chevy Impala. This chase has it all—smashes, crashes, a close call with a train, a jackknifed truck, and a multicar pileup on the freeway as Chance (Petersen) dodges and outruns a menagerie of would-be assassins.

RONIN (1998)

Robert De Niro may get top billing, but Audi, BMW, and Peugeot are the real stars of John Frankenheimer's film, especially during the breathtaking sequence that has Sam (De Niro) and Vincent (Jean Reno) chase Deidre (Natascha McElhone) and her cohorts through the streets and tunnels of Paris in the face of oncoming traffic. Like *Bullitt*, the scene was done "at speed"—except that there are a lot more cars involved. Over 300 stunt drivers and 2,000 extras were employed to pull off what critics say is the most complicated chase sequence in movie history. The principal actors were often riding right alongside their stunt drivers for close-ups, and one of the stars—amateur race car enthusiast Skipp Sudduth—did most of his character's driving.

THE BOURNE SUPREMACY (2004)

During a dizzying chase sequence through Moscow's streets and subway tunnels, director Paul Greengrass put actor Matt Damon (Jason Bourne) inside the action by strapping him into the "Go Mobile," a device invented by stunt coordinator Dan Bradley. The Go Mobile is a mobile platform welded to the firewall of a car, with its own Formula 1–style cockpit complete with steering wheel, gearshift, clutch, and brakes. So while the stunt driver does all the driving up front and off camera, powering the vehicle around corners and executing death-defying maneuvers, the celebrity makes actions as if he's driving the car. The platform includes a camera mount that focuses on the back half of the vehicle—the chassis of a yellow taxi where Damon can be seen sweating through the front windshield. Damon's code name for the chase scenes was "N.A.R."—No Acting Required. When he finished his first ride in the Go Mobile, the actor purportedly told Bradley, "That's the most fun I ever had in a movie!"

The world's first electric trolley was introduced in Montgomery, Alabama, in 1886.

ITALIAN STALLION

Here's the skinny on one of the world's most famous sports cars and its notorious creator: Enzo Ferrari.

PRANCING HORSE

Born in Modena in 1898, Enzo Ferrari fell in love with racing when he saw Felice Nazzarro win on the streets of Bologna in 1908. The ten-year-old vowed to become a racer himself; but those dreams would be deferred when a flu epidemic killed his father and older brother in 1916. Then the family business collapsed while he served in the Italian army during World War I. When Ferrari came home in 1918, he faced a bleak future. He took a job at a small car company, working as a test driver on the side. A few years later, fortune smiled and he became a driver for Alfa Romeo.

In 1923 Ferrari had just won the first Circuito de Savio in Ravenna when he met Countess Paolina, the mother of deceased WWI flying ace Francesco Baracca. The countess gave him a "Prancing Horse" badge that had once decorated the fuselage of her son's fighter plane, and urged him to put it on his race cars for good luck. Ferrari tucked the *Cavallino Rampante* away for nearly a decade as he continued to race in competitions around Italy while helping to develop new models for Alfa.

SCUDERIA FERRARI

In 1929 Ferrari assembled a racing team of 40 drivers for Alfa Romeo, which he named *Scuderia Ferrari* (*scuderia* is Italian for "stable"), while working on developing race cars. In 1931 he quit racing himself to focus exclusively on car design. The result—Alfa Romeo 158 "Alfetta"—dominated the racing circuit for years.

But Ferrari chafed at being an employee and in 1939 left Alfa Romeo to form his own company. As part of the severance deal, he agreed not to use the Ferrari name on any car he made or raced for four years. Ferrari decided he would not rest until his own cars had toppled the Alfa Romeo dynasty.

The world's first nuclear powered submarine, the USS *Nautilus*...

FERRARI ROARS TO LIFE

World War II intervened to divert Ferrari from his goal, but as soon as the war ended he began planning his new race car. The Ferrari 125 S debuted at the Circuito di Piacenza road race in 1947, and the world of motor sports has never been the same. Powered by a 1.5-liter V-12 engine, it was the first in what would become a long line of high-powered sports cars bearing the soon-to-be legendary surname. Two years later, Ferrari unleashed the 166 Inter to the public at the Paris Auto Show, where the classy coupe was an immediate hit.

Meanwhile, Ferrari's racing team began piling up victory after victory: the Mille Miglia in 1948; Le Mans in 1949; and, led by driver Alberto Ascari, back-to-back Formula One World Championships in 1951 and 1952. In just a few short years, Ferrari race cars had become the class of the field and the cars to beat.

Scuderia Ferrari was almost destroyed by a disastrous crash in the 1957 Mille Miglia. Driver Alfonso de Portago lost control of his Ferrari 335S. It spun into the crowd lining the roadway, killing driver, co-driver, and nine spectators. The accident prompted new demands to eliminate open road races in Italy, and the public outcry prompted some carmakers to drop out of racing entirely. Ferrari himself was brought up on manslaughter charges, but he remained undaunted. The criminal charges against him were dropped in 1961 as *Scuderia Ferrari* began racking up even more victories. Their greatest achievements came at the 24 Hours of Le Mans race, where they took an unprecedented 14 wins, including six in a row between 1960 and 1965.

IL COMMENDATORE

Enzo Ferrari was never known as a mild man, and he hated to lose. He clashed with competitors, colleagues, and employees. Once he admitted that he thought of drivers as mere "accessories." Tony Brooks, a Ferrari team driver, said of his boss: "[He] would expect a driver to go beyond reasonable limits. You can drive the maximum of your ability but once you start psyching yourself up to do things that you don't feel within your ability, it gets stupid."

A former racer himself, Ferrari was cavalier about the mortal risks faced by his drivers, leading the newspaper *L'Osservatore Romano* to compare him sarcastically to Saturn, the god of harvest

...was built in Groton, Connecticut in 1954.

and reaping. Upon hearing about the death of driver Eugenio Castellotti, Ferrari supposedly responded, "And the car?" His tyrannical nature, both on and off the racetrack, earned him the nickname "*Il Commendatore*"—the Commandant.

THE GREAT WALK-OUT

Ferrari's disdain for customers was equally legendary. He claimed he only sold sports cars to the public to finance his racing stable, and thought the majority of his buyers only bought his cars for the prestige, not performance, which led him to sniff famously, "The client is not always right."

In 1961 his dictatorial nature almost destroyed him. When sales manager Girolamo Gardini complained that Ferrari's wife, Laura, was too involved in the company, Ferrari responded by firing him, along with his supporters, which included the manager of the racing team, the chief engineer, and the experimental development chief—essentially the core executives behind years of success. With one angry swoop, Ferrari had cleared the decks of his senior management. Was he out of his mind? How could he recover from such a loss of expertise, especially when they were being challenged in sales by the hot new Jaguar E-Type cars?

But Ferrari hardly missed a step. He replaced his former team with junior men eager for the challenge: engineer Mauro Foghieri and designer Sergio Scaglietti. They promptly brought out the new Ferrari 250, which American Phil Hill drove to victory at Sebring and Le Mans in 1961 and 1962, picking up a World Championship in the process. The Jaguar challenge had been dismissed with a flick of the wrist, and the Ferrari 250 went on to become one of the greatest cars of all time.

DECLINE AND FALL

Eager to continue funding his racing division without distractions, Ferrari sought to sell his factory. Ford Motor Company appeared on the verge of buying it when Ferrari abruptly called off negotiations. The dealbreaker? A stipulation in the contract that would have denied the Scuderia Ferrari team the right to compete against Ford cars at the Indy 500. Outraged at the botched buyout, Ford chairman Henry Ford II immediately challenged his engineers to develop a car capable of beating Ferrari in competition.

Ferrari will not manufacture more than 14 cars a day.

The result was the Ford GT40, which clobbered Ferrari at Le Mans four consecutive times from 1966 to 1969. Controlling interest in Ferrari's company was sold to Fiat in 1969, and a dispirited Ferrari stepped down as managing director in 1971. Fiat continued to invest in the racing team he had founded, and even managed to win a championship in 1975, but Enzo Ferrari would not score another win during his lifetime. He lived quietly in retirement until his death in 1988.

Since Ferrari's death, the company has rebounded, and today Ferrari remains synonymous with wealth, luxury, and speed. The 12-cylinder Ferrari Testarossa, which debuted in 1984, is one of the most iconic and easily recognizable sports cars in history.

In 2002 the company debuted "The Enzo," its fastest model to date and also the most expensive, at $1.8 million dollars. Enzo Ferrari's standards for performance continue to hold sway over the brand he founded—although the company's current management is by no means as stringent and ruthless as its founder. Carlo Benzi, a longtime Ferrari accountant, recalls, "For the 42 years I worked for Ferrari, I only saw him cry once, and that was at the tax office. If he had been in politics, Machiavelli would have been *his* servant."

* * *

RAILROAD RECORDS

• On April 3, 2007, the V150, a modified TGV (*Trés Grand Vitesse*, or "Very High Speed") French train set the world speed record of 357.2 mph for conventional railed trains.

• Fastest train of any kind is the JR-Maglev MLX01, a Japanese experimental train that went 361 mph on December 2, 2003.

• Every day, half a million passengers pass through New York's Grand Central Station, still the world's largest.

• The worst rail disaster in history occurred on December 26, 2004, when the *Queen of the Sea* train in Sri Lanka was engulfed and overturned by a tsunami, resulting in the deaths of as many as 1,700 passengers (only 900 bodies were recovered).

• Toilets were first installed on passenger trains in the 1850s.

World's first international underwater railway tunnel: Detroit, MI, to Windsor, Ont. (1891).

FINAL FATAL FLIGHT

Donald Campbell was a classic case of a racer who should have quit while he was ahead. Instead he pursued his speed dreams on land and water until the bitter end.

SIR MALCOLM

Donald Campbell (1921–67) had something to prove. His father, Sir Malcolm Campbell (1885–1948), dominated speed racing in the 1930s, setting records on land and water, always at the wheel of cars or boats called Bluebird. In 1935 Sir Malcolm set the world land speed record by going 301 mph in a car at the Bonneville Salt Flats in Utah. Two years later, he drove the Bluebird K3 speedboat to a world-record 126.33 mph on Italy's Lake Maggiore.

His son Donald had shown little interest in following in his footsteps, working instead as a small businessman making machine tools. That all changed in 1948 when his father died in his sleep before carrying out his plans for another water speed record attempt. When Donald heard that an American, Henry Kaiser, was out to break his father's record, he decided to take up the quest. "I just want to keep the old flag flying," he told Leo Villa, his dad's mechanic. "Get the record, and call it a day."

CHIP OFF THE OLD BLOCK

Donald Campbell initially met with frustration. On his first attempt, with no experience driving high-speed hydroplanes, he got in his dad's jet-powered Bluebird K4 on Lake Coniston in England and fell short of a world record by only 2 mph. On his second try, he hit a submerged railroad tie and ripped the stern out of the boat. Before he could build a new boat, another racer raised the bar by breaking his father's old record.

Campbell was undeterred. He bought a Metropolitan-Vickers Beryl jet engine, which delivered 4,000 pounds of thrust, built it into a new Bluebird, the K7, and took it to Ullswater in England's Lake District. On July 23, 1955, he set a new world water speed record of 202.32 mph. Friends were certain that now, with the ghost of his famous father thoroughly exorcised, Campbell would stay true to his word and give up racing.

JUST ONE MORE

He couldn't. Trying to beat the record had financially ruined him. The only way he could make money was by trading on his new fame. With each new attempt and each new record, endorsements and financing poured in, bankrolling the next effort. He became hooked on the quest for speed. For the next three years, Campbell methodically raised the water speed record, from 202 mph to 225, to 239, to 260.35 mph in 1959. He then became obsessed with the goal of breaking 300 mph.

Then in 1964 he accomplished the unthinkable. Switching gears, he took a jet car to Lake Eyre, Australia, a dry lake bed that, like the Bonneville Flats, makes a superb surface for speed racing, and stunned the world by setting a world land speed record of 403.1 mph. Then in December he went back on the water at Lake Dumbleung in Australia and broke his own world record in the K7 with a speed of 276 mph. Now he owned both world water and land speed records and, unlike his famous father, was the only person to have done so in the same year. It was his crowning achievement...and the beginning of his fall from grace.

FINAL BOW

Ignoring the advice of mechanics and friends, who felt that the Bluebird K7 was being raced far beyond its capabilities, Campbell bought a new, more powerful jet engine, the Bristol-Siddeley Orpheus, and installed it in his hydroplane. He went to Lake Coniston in November 1966 and on a test run took the K7 up to 280 mph with no difficulties. The elusive 300-mph barrier seemed within reach.

It was still dark on the morning of January 4, 1967, when Campbell made his first run at the record. When told he'd gone 297 mph, he radioed back, "Stand by. Am making my return run." Without waiting to refuel or let the wash from his first run settle down, he came roaring across the lake. The craft was clocked at 320 mph when it hit a swell, lifted out of the water, and tumbled bow over aft until it broke apart. Rescuers found Campbell's helmet and teddy bear mascot floating near the crumpled hull but not his body. That was not discovered until 2001. The obsessive compulsion for speed had killed him. He was 45.

Most expensive car to insure in the US: Cadillac Escalade. Least expensive: Ford Taurus.

"HIGH FLIGHT"

This poem is recited at the funerals of more military and civilian aviators and astronauts than any other piece of literature.

WHERE NEVER LARK, OR EVEN EAGLE FLEW

On August 18, 1941, 19-year-old John Gillespie Magee took his Spitfire Mk I to 33,000 feet above Lincolnshire, England. The young American had joined the Royal Canadian Air Force to fight in the Battle of Britain. Magee had been working on a poem describing his feelings about flying. Just as he broke through the clouds, he thought the words, "To touch the face of God," and knew his poem was complete. Magee wrote it out on the back of a letter to his parents and mailed it to them.

Three months later, Magee was killed in a midair collision, but his poem has endured. For many years when television stations signed off at night, the poem was narrated to footage of an F-104 Starfighter streaking through the sky, and after Space Shuttle *Challenger* exploded on takeoff in 1986, President Reagan quoted from it in his eulogy to the fallen astronauts.

HIGH FLIGHT

Oh! I have slipped the surly bonds of earth
And danced the skies on laughter-silvered wings;
Sunward I've climbed, and joined the tumbling mirth
Of sun-split clouds—and done a hundred things
You have not dreamed of—wheeled and soared and swung
High in the sunlit silence. Hov'ring there
I've chased the shouting wind along, and flung
My eager craft through footless halls of air.
Up, up the long delirious, burning blue,
I've topped the windswept heights with easy grace
Where never lark, or even eagle flew—
And, while with silent lifting mind I've trod
The high untrespassed sanctity of space,
Put out my hand and touched the face of God.

—John Gillespie Magee Jr. (1922–41)

THE FLYING MANTUAN

In the 1920s and 1930s Tazio Nuvolari was the indestructible iron man of both motorcycle and car racing.

BACKGROUND

Born in 1892 near Mantua, Italy, Tazio Giorgio Nuvolari always knew he wanted to be a racer. Both his father and uncle were champion bicyclists, his uncle Giuseppe having won several Italian cycling championships. It was Uncle Giuseppe who suggested his nephew give motor sports a try. But shortly after Nuvolari got his motorcycle-racing license in 1915, the 23-year-old found himself drafted into the Italian army. He finagled a job driving trucks and ambulances, and the occasional official limousine. One day an officer hopped into Nuvolari's car and barked some directions at him, adding, "*Subito!* Hurry!" Nuvolari proceeded to careen down the road at breakneck speed until at last he deposited his terrified passenger at his destination. On exiting the car, the officer told Nuvolari, "Listen to me. Forget driving. You are not cut out for this job."

Nuvolari didn't start racing seriously until 1920, when he was 28. From the start he switched back and forth between motorcycles and cars, doing well in both. But he was far more successful at first on a two-wheeler, winning the European Motorcycle Grand Prix and the European Championship in 1925, the Nations Grand Prix four years in a row (1925–1928), and the Lario Circuit race five times (1925–1929). His favorite mount was a Bianchi 350cc, which he nicknamed *Fresccia Celeste* ("Light Blue Arrow").

CAMPIONISSIMO

Ironically, it was a disastrous tryout for Alfa Romeo in a Grand Prix car that led to Nuvolari's reputation as the greatest motorcycle racer of his era. Called to Monza to try out for the Alfa team, Nuvolari ripped up the course for five laps, bettering the best laps of the other Alfa drivers. Then, on the sixth lap, he lost control and went flying into a barbed wire fence. The car was so badly damaged the Alfa team director, Vittorio Jano, banned Nuvolari from the team for five years.

...Fastest: Talladega Superspeedway, where the average speed is 188 mph.

Doctors told Nuvolari his injuries were so severe (cracked ribs, multiple lacerations) that he'd need bed rest for a least a month. However, the Nazioni Motorcycle Grand Prix was in 12 days. Among the entrants was the English champion Walter L. Handley, and Nuvolari always wanted to race against the top competition. Wearing a crude brace to support his ribcage, he was literally strapped to the seat of his Bianchi 350. Friends said that he looked like a mummy on a bike. The 300-kilometer (181-mile) race was a test of endurance for a healthy person; for someone in Nuvolari's condition it was an act of madness.

As predicted, the race turned into a fierce duel between the Englishman on his Rex-Acme and the Italian on his Bianchi. They traded the lead back and forth until the Rex-Acme's engine blew just before the finish and Nuvolari won the day. He said later, "During the last laps, there were some moments where I didn't see the track. I was hallucinating, and afraid I'd faint." His tough-willed bravado endeared him to Italian fans, who dubbed him "Campionissimo."

"WAIT THREE DAYS—THEN CRY"

In 1926 and 1927, Nuvolari won every major motorcycle race in Europe. He also suffered several serious accidents. One of the worst occurred at the Solitude Circuit near Stuttgart, Germany, where he was injured badly when fog caused him to miss a turn. However, he felt well enough the next morning to take a train back to Italy. At the border he ran into a Bianchi executive who was startled to see him alive. Evidently a German newspaper had printed the news of his death and the executive was coming to collect Nuvolari's body. The racer took it with great aplomb, saying, "If someone announces my death again, wait three days—then cry."

Nuvolari suffered two more bad accidents on his motorcycle that year, and he finally switched to racing cars exclusively. In 1927 in a Bugatti 35s, he won the Grand Prix of Rome and the Círcuito del Garda. Nuvolari, now known as the "Flying Mantuan," was ready to add to his legend.

SLY MANEUVER

He gave the new racing house of Ferrari its first victory at the

First arcade driving game: Taito's black-and-white *Speed Race*, released in 1974.

Trieste-Opicina in 1930. The following year saw him rack up three more wins: the Targa Floria, the Italian Grand Prix, and the Coppa Ciano. But 1932 was Nuvolari's banner season: Out of 16 races he won 7, with repeats of the races he'd won the year before as well as the Grand Prix of Monaco, Grand Prix of France, Circuito di Avellino and the Coppa Acerbo. His three Grand Prix wins earned him the Italian and World championships. Now, when newspapers wrote of his driving exploits, the word "great" was usually attached to his name.

Nuvolari often didn't have the fastest or best car in a race, but somehow he always seemed to find a way to win. In the 1930 Mille Miglia, a 1,000-mile open-road race across the Italian countryside, Nuvolari appeared to have fallen too far behind his archrival (and best friend) Achille Varzi to have a chance to win. Night fell, and when Varzi saw Nuvolari's headlights fade away behind him, he breathed a sigh of relief. Victory was surely his; he just had to baby his car the rest of the way. Only three kilometers from the finish, Varzi was startled to see Nuvolari's Alfa Romeo 1750 GS Spider Zagato appear suddenly beside him. The canny Mantuan had been driving through the night without headlights, carefully making up the distance between them without being noticed. With a jaunty wave, Nuvolari flicked on his lights and swept across the finish line.

FOUR-WHEEL DRIFTER

Cunning was only one weapon in the Flying Mantuan's bag of racing tricks. He was fearless and drove himself as hard as he drove his cars. He seemed to innately understand how to squeeze every inch of speed out of his machine. The great Enzo Ferrari recalled riding with Nuvolari as his mechanic when Ferrari was a young man, and being petrified by the way Nuvolari attacked the course. Nuvolari went into each turn at full speed, his foot pressing the accelerator to the floor, the back end of the car skittering out of control behind the front wheels. Why they didn't spin out and crash mystified Ferrari until it dawned on him: Nuvolari was using the centrifugal force of the car to power it through the turn at full speed without losing control.

Ferrari explained: "He put the car into a four-wheel drift. Throughout the bend the car shaved the inside edge, and when

The rubber in car tires is about 40% natural latex; the rest is synthetic rubber.

the bend turned into the straight the car was in the normal position for accelerating down it, with no need for any corrections." The four-wheel drift, sometimes described as a controlled skid through a turn, has been a staple of road racing for decades. Nuvolari may not have invented the technique, but he was clearly one of its first masters.

IMPOSSIBLE VICTORY

The German Grand Prix at Nurburgring in 1935 was meant to be a showcase for German automotive superiority. German drivers in their 8-cylinder, 375hp Mercedes-Benz W25s and 16-cylinder, 375hp Auto Union Tipo Bs had dominated racing in Europe the entire season; a sweep at Nurburgring was expected to be icing on the Kuchen. More than a quarter of a million Germans, including high-ranking Nazi officials, filled the stands, anticipating a great German victory.

Like the 43-year-old Nuvolari, his 265hp Alfa Romeo P3 was considered hopelessly out of date and underpowered. Oddsmakers thought him unlikely to place, much less win. Even so, Nuvolari had worked himself into the lead when one of his tires burst. By the time he got back on the track, the Italian was in last place. Somehow, he methodically worked his way back behind the leader, Manfred von Brauchitsch. The German tried to hold off the charging Italian, but fate intervened in the form of another flat tire, this time to von Brauchitsch's Mercedes-Benz. The stands were eerily quiet as Nuvolari took the checkered flag in front of the stunned crowd. An "Impossible Victory," as it was dubbed by newspapers, it was Nuvolari's finest hour.

THE RACE IS OVER

World War II effectively brought an end to Nuvolari's racing career. His last victory came in the 1950 Palermo-Montepelligrino Hill Climb, where the 57-year-old placed first in his class in his Cisitalia 204 Spyder Sport. Three years later he suffered a massive stroke and died. An estimated 50,000 mourners lined the streets of Mantua to pay their respects. Achille Varzi paid his old rival a final tribute: "He was not a master but the artist of driving. A master can teach; the art cannot be taught."

In the year after the release of *Smokey and the Bandit* (1977), Trans Am sales increased 36%.

HISTORY OF AIRSHIPS, PART IV

After the Hindenburg *disaster in 1937, the United States was left as the only major power still committed to using dirigibles. But the way forward was anything but smooth.* *(Part III is on page 323.)*

ROUGH START

After World War I, the U.S. Navy decided to piggyback onto the growing interest in airship development among Western powers by picking up the completion contract for an unfinished British R38. The British had modeled the airship after German "height climbers" for long-range patrol duties over the North Sea—up to six days of patrol time 300 miles from base at altitudes of 22,000 feet. At the time of her maiden flight, she was the world's largest airship: 700 feet long, 14 gas cells, six 350-hp engines, and a top speed of 71 mph.

Redesignated the ZR-2, she made four test flights in preparation for delivery to the States. Doubts about the craft's structural stability had begun to surface when on her final trial flight, August 23, 1921, the dirigible broke apart while attempting a tight-turn test and exploded over the English city of Hull, crashing into an estuary with the loss of 44 of her 49 crew members.

A week later, three dirigibles were destroyed in a hydrogen fire at the Rockaway Naval Air Station in New York. Then, on February 21, 1922, the U.S. Army's hydrogen-filled airship *Roma,* purchased from the Italian government and the largest semi-rigid airship in the world at the time, scraped some power lines on a test flight over Norfolk, Virginia. It burst into flames, killing 34 of the 45 crew members.

THE USS *SHENANDOAH*

The U.S. Navy had other airships in its fleet, like the semi-rigid airship C-7. Built after World War I for naval patrol work, it was small: 196 feet long, with a gas volume of 181,000 cubic feet and a crew of four. What makes this ship notable is that it was the first to be inflated with helium. The Navy promptly decided to fill all future airships with helium.

USS *Shenandoah* (ZR-1) was the first of four U.S. Navy rigid airships designed after the World War I Zeppelin bomber L-49, a "height climber" configured for altitude at the expense of other qualities. *Shenandoah* was planned for fleet reconnaissance work of the type carried out by European nations during World War I. The *Shenandoah* was long and skinny—680 feet long, 93 feet high—with a cruising range of 5,000 miles at 69 mph. She carried 20 gas cells within her rigid duralumin frame, a new alloy of aluminum and copper. Being helium-filled, *Shenandoah* had a significant edge in safety over previous airships, but it took much of the U.S. reserves to fill her 2.1 million-cubic-foot volume.

Shenandoah made the first coast-to-coast rigid airship flight in October 1924. On her return to Lakehurst Naval Air Station, the ship was deflated so that its helium could be transferred to the newly arrived ZR-3—the United States did not have enough of the gas to inflate two large airships at the same time.

Changes were made to *Shenandoah* that proved to be controversial: 10 of her 18 automatic-release gas valves were removed to reduce weight and helium leakage. On a flight over Ohio in 1926, the dirigible ran into a thunderstorm. A violent updraft carried her up beyond the pressure limits of the gas bags. The remaining automatic release valves could only handle altitude gains of 400 feet per minute, and the ship was rising at 1,000 feet per minute. At 6,000 feet, the airship broke apart. Although 14 died, 29 sailors survived by riding down to earth on the three remaining sections.

DOUBLE WHAMMY

The *USS Akron* and *USS Macon* were to be the largest helium-filled airships ever built: 785 feet long, 133 feet in diameter, with an envelope displacement of 6.8 million cubic feet. Each airship would be able to launch, retrieve, and service five biplane aircraft for scouting purposes. Through a T-shaped opening in the floor of the airship's hangar, a metal trapeze could be lowered, onto which the ship's five airplanes could be launched and retrieved using hooks attached to the top of the planes. Each of

States with the poorest road conditions: #1 Louisiana. #2 North Carolina. #3 Oklahoma.

the ship's eight 560-hp Maybach VL-2 engines drove a propeller at the end of a 16-foot outrigger that could swivel the propeller through a 90-degree arc. The reversible engines could deliver thrust in any direction.

On May 11, 1932, the *USS Akron* arrived in San Diego after a 77-hour flight from New Jersey. The docking to the stub mast did not go well for the inexperienced naval ground crew. The 400-foot-long docking ropes were dropped to the crew to stabilize the ship. After a mooring cable was dropped from the ship's nose to the mooring mast, the craft could then be winched down to the mast and secured. But the hot sun expanded the helium and made the ship too buoyant. A gust of wind jerked the tail into the air, threatening to stand the *Akron* on her nose at the mast. Tons of water spilled from ballast bags, causing the ship to suddenly rise. Most of the ground crew let go of their ropes as the *Akron* shot skyward but four clung to their ropes. One let go quickly and suffered broken bones from his 20-foot fall. Two others plunged 150 feet to their deaths. The ship rose to 2,000 feet with one sailor still dangling from his line, which he'd had the presence of mind to cinch around his body. The crew was able to haul him up to safety.

After her West Coast duty, *Akron* returned to Lakehurst. One year later, she departed for a routine training flight off the New Jersey coast. Within hours the ship was caught in a fierce storm. The low pressure caused the *Akron*'s barometric altimeter to read several hundred feet higher than the actual altitude, causing the crew, unable to see clearly due to the rain and wind, to fly the ship into the sea. The *Akron* carried no life jackets and only one rubber raft. Just three of the 76 crew members survived. The tragedy was compounded the next day when the blimp J-3 crashed while looking for survivors, killing two of its crew. The navy had lost the finest airship in the world and 75 men. Among them was Admiral William A. Moffet, known as the "Air Admiral," one of the leading proponents of naval aircraft.

Less than two years later, the *Akron*'s sister ship, the *Macon*, would go down off Monterey Bay, California, settling gently and sinking into the ocean after a controlled descent. This time there were adequate life rafts and preservers. Only two crewmen were lost.

The Bonnie and Clyde "death car" is on display in Nevada—a state the couple never visited.

The loss of its flagship dirigibles prompted the Navy to switch over to nonrigid airships. In June 1942, Congress authorized construction of 200 of them, and they performed successfully as convoy escorts in the Pacific, Atlantic, and Mediterranean theaters. But by the early 1960s, the Navy had retired all of them.

AIRSHIPS TODAY

British company Hybrid Air Vehicles is one of several aerospace firms developing 21st-century airships for the Pentagon. The traditional cigar shape has been replaced by a twin-envelope structure best described as a cataraft. The HAV "is a new vehicle," says company spokesman Gordon Taylor. "It's a hybrid because we're combining aerostatic lift (about 60 percent from helium), aerodynamic lift (air movement around the hull), a hovercraft landing system and vectored thrust (ducted fans in rotating cowlings). If you can get beyond the word 'airship'—because that has a lot of history—people think about them differently."

Unlike the dirigibles of old, the HAV doesn't require hundreds of ground crew to walk it in or out of its mooring. It can land and take off anywhere, in snow, sand, or water, and can be flown by a pilot or remotely like a drone. The HAV-3 is expected to be the first working model, a 300-foot-long unmanned surveillance ship capable of staying airborne over hot spots like Afghanistan at 20,000 feet for three weeks at a time.

* * *

ENZO FERRARI SPEAKS

The greatest race car designer of all time was rarely without a pithy thing to say.

- "Aerodynamics are for people who cannot build engines."
- "Race cars are neither beautiful nor ugly. They become beautiful when they win."
- "To finish first, you first must finish."
- "I build a young man's car that only rich old men can afford."
- "What's behind you doesn't matter." (When asked why one of his race cars was built without a rearview mirror.)

FAMOUS CARS: HOLLYWOOD EDITION

What happens to the cars from favorite TV shows and movies? Some are destroyed, some are stored on studio backlots, and some are displayed or sold to collectors.

EMMITT BROWN'S DELOREAN DMC-12

Details: Its license plate was OUTATIME. The speedometer went to 140 mph, but the car operated best at 88 mph. It was a time machine, the plutonium-fueled stainless steel invention of Dr. Emmitt Brown in the *Back to the Future* film trilogy (1985, 1989, and 1990). The studio used six cars in the series.

Where are they now? Universal Studios has two of the DeLoreans on display at their theme parks in Los Angeles and Orlando. Another hangs over the escalator in the Planet Hollywood restaurant in Honolulu. The fourth is being restored by a California collector. The whereabouts of the other two are unknown.

FERRIS BUELLER'S FRIEND'S DAD'S FERRARI

Details: The 1961 Ferrari 250GT California used by Ferris and his friends in the 1986 movie was *not* a real Ferrari. The Italian automaker made fewer than 100 250GTs, which cost $350,000 each. So the studio saved money by putting a lookalike fiberglass shell on an MG.

Where is it now? The fake Ferrari used in the movie was sold at auction in April 2010. Bonham's of London expected it to fetch around $50,000, but it ended up selling for $122,000 to an anonymous American bidder. Going price today for a real '61 Ferrari 250GT California? $10,976,000.

JED CLAMPETT'S JALOPY

Details: A whiskey barrel hangs from the hood, and a ladder made from tree branches is lashed to the side. But the most famous feature of this 1921 Oldsmobile flatbed is the rocking chair on top for Granny Clampett. Yessir, it's the truck that Jed drives out of the Ozarks in the opening credits of the TV sitcom *The Beverly Hillbil-*

lies (1962–71, CBS). (The truck actually belongs to Aunt Pearl, but she lets Jed keep it as long as he keeps Cousin Jethro, too.)

Where is it now? Ralph Foster Museum in Point Lookout, Missouri. The show's producer, Paul Henning, grew up nearby and donated the truck to the museum, which is known as "The Smithsonian of the Ozarks." You can also see wood-stump carvings, a barbed-wire collection, and a chair made from steer horns. For $10 you can sit in the *Hillbillies* truck. Another version hangs in Planet Hollywood at Disney World in Orlando.

THE MUNSTERS' KOACH

Details: Custom builder George Barris welded together three Model T Fords to make a suitably spooky ride for *The Munsters* (1964–66, CBS). It has seating for eight, and even a laboratory for Grandpa. The 18-footer rides on Anson Astro wheels and Mickey Thompson slicks, and is powered by a 300-hp 289 Ford Cobra V-8.

Where is it now? Barris has been customizing automobiles for shows since 1944. His shop/museum in North Hollywood is home to the Munsters' Koach and dozens of other one-of-a-kind vehicles, like the original Batmobile.

UNCLE MUNSTER'S DRAG-U-LA

Details: The Koach wasn't the only car in the driveway of 1313 Mockingbird Lane. When 378-year-old Grandpa Munster needed a break from the lab, he'd take his 350-hp "coffin-on-racing-slicks" dragster out for a spin. The gold leaf casket has a 360-cubic-inch Ford Mustang engine, can hit 180 mph, and has a parachute to slow it down. Grandpa's dragster got four miles per gallon (of embalming fluid). George Barris billed the studio $10,800 for it in 1964—about $75,000 today.

Where is it now? Planet Hollywood in Atlantic City.

URKEL'S BMW ISETTA

Details: On the TV show *Family Matters* (1989–97, ABC; 1997–98, CBS), hapless nerd Steve Urkel can never figure out how to be cool. His prayers are almost answered when his uncle gives him a red BMW as a gift—but the car turns out to be a three-wheeled, egg-shaped contraption called the Isetta. The car made several appearances but met its demise when it rolled off Paradise Bluff, the make-out spot where Urkel took his girlfriend Myra.

Where is it now? No one knows. However, an identical Isetta is on display at the Canton Classic Car Museum in Ohio.

FOZZIE BEAR'S 1951 STUDEBAKER

Details: Kermit the Frog cruised west in 1979's *The Muppet Movie* with Fozzie Bear at the wheel of this classic sedan, painted in psychedelic Day-Glo colors. The real driver crouched in the trunk and drove by remote control, using a video camera positioned in the hood.

Where is it now? There were two 1951 Studebaker Commanders used for the film. One was left unpainted and used for long shots; no one knows what happened to it. The psychedelic one is on display at the Studebaker Museum in South Bend, Indiana.

THE DUKES' GENERAL LEE

Details: Over the seven-year run of *The Dukes of Hazzard* (1979–85 CBS), the stunt crew used 321 original 1969 Dodge Chargers. The first, the Lee-1, was damaged beyond repair on its first jump, but appeared in the opening credits. The jump in question—where Bo and Luke jump the General Lee 82 feet over Sheriff Rosco P. Coltrane's Dodge Monaco—bent the body frame, so the crew painted the car green, gave it the number 71, and used it as a prop for three more episodes. Later the show's producer traded the Lee-1 and 50 other totaled Chargers to a junkyard for some transmission work. Most were crushed for scrap, but a few survived. They sat on the lot for 22 years.

Where is it now? In 2000 *Dukes* fans Travis Bell and Gary Schneider went searching for the original Lee and found the wreck in a junkyard in Georgia. It was badly rusted, all four wheels were gone, and an eight-foot tree had rooted itself inches from the passenger door. Bell eventually sold the car to Marvin Murphy of Florida, who agreed to spend $100,000 to restore it to its 1979 condition. Bell supervised the restoration right down to the hand-painted Confederate Flag. On November 11, 2006, Bell and Murphy brought the restored Lee-1 to the site of the first jump, 28 years to the day. It was driven off the trailer by John Schneider, who played Bo Duke (no relation to Gary Schneider). The car is now on display at the DuPont Registry Museum in St. Petersburg, Florida.

The safety glass in your car windows blocks up to 97% of UV rays.

ANGELS AND T-BIRDS

The year 2011 marks the centennial of U.S. Naval aviation. To celebrate, here is a brief look at the Navy's Blue Angels, together with the Air Force's Thunderbirds.

BACKGROUND

The Blue Angels and the Thunderbirds are fighter-jet demonstration squadrons that showcase the state-of-the-art air power and elite skill of the U.S. military. Both were created after World War II to bolster recruitment to replace the thousands of soldiers who had returned to civilian life, and recruitment remains their primary mission.

In 1946 Lt. Roy "Butch" Voris was ordered to lead a Navy flight exhibition team. Voris chose three more pilots and 11 mechanics to maintain four F6F Hellcats. The Blue Angels flew their first performance in June of that year. Their namesake was a Manhattan nightclub, which Lt. "Wick" Wickendoll, who flew the right wing slot, had seen in a *New Yorker* ad. (The club itself was named after a Marlene Dietrich movie.) The Navy had sponsored a contest to name the new team, but the pilots didn't like the suggested choices, which included "Blue Lancers," the favorite of Voris's superior, Captain Bill Gentner (his son had suggested it). Voris "accidentally" slipped the "Blue Angels" idea to a reporter, who published it, and a few days later Gentner reluctantly made it official. The Blue Angels' home base today is Pensacola, Florida.

Founded in 1953 at Luke Air Force Base in Arizona, the Thunderbirds took their name from a mythical Native American bird that shoots lightning bolts from its eyes and shakes the earth with the thunder of its wings—a good description of the F-16s they fly today. The squadron is based at Nellis Air Force Base near Las Vegas.

REQUIREMENTS FOR APPLICANTS

Thunderbirds: A minimum of 1,000 hours of jet-fighter experience and at least 10 years of active duty as a USAF officer. About 40 qualified applicants compete for two to four open spots each year. Most pilots fly with the team for about two seasons. So the transition process ensures that half of the team always has at least one year of experience.

Blue Angels: A minimum of 1,250 tactical jet flight-hours.

Both teams require their pilots to be comfortable in front of the public and the camera.

TRAINING

Thunderbirds: New pilots fly over 60 practice sessions, first in a T-38 Talon, then thirty sorties in an F-16. They start with solo maneuvers, and then move to "duets" and later to larger formations. It takes seven sorties before a new pilot can take off in the "Diamond" (more about that later) and 18 sorties before they can fly in a five-plane formation.

THE PLANES

Blue Angels: The plane is a modified FA-18 Hornet, a single-seat, twin engine attack-fighter capable of 17,000 pounds of thrust per engine with a top speed of 1,200 mph, or Mach 1.7. The nose cannon is replaced by a smoke canister, and an added fuel pump helps the plane fly upside down longer. A special low-friction paint helps gain maneuverability. Since 1947, the paint job has been the same: navy blue with gold accents, with the number on the tail and "U.S. NAVY" printed under each wing.

Thunderbirds: The "Fighting Falcon" can give 25,000 pounds of thrust, pushing the plane to 1,500 mph, with an airframe rated to nine times the force of gravity. A nimble dual-role (air-to-air, air-to-ground) single-seat combat fighter, the F-16C has a thrust-to-weight ratio of over 1:1, meaning it can fly straight up at great speed. Painted from nose-to-tail on the underside of the plane is a solid blue depiction of a Thunderbird. Slightly modified for air show use, these F-16Cs can be converted back to combat-readiness in 72 hours.

FLIGHT TRICKS

Both teams fly six planes in a demonstration. To close a show, all six fly together in this triangle shape.

• *Delta Formation.* Thunderbird (or Blue Angel) #1 leads the formation (#1 is also the commanding officer of the squadron; Blue Angels call this officer "Boss"). #2 and #3 fly behind and to the side of the Leader. #4 flies "Slot," directly behind the Leader. #5 is the Lead Solo, at the left corner, leaving the Opposing Solo, #6, to finish the triangle on the right. Thunderbird #5 wears his number upside down on his uniform, and upside down on the plane. Former #5 pilot Major Brian Farrar explains that since the Lead Solo spends so much time flying upside down—at least once on every maneuver over the crowd—this way they can ensure that pictures taken by the spectators come out right.

• *Diamond:* The #1 through #4 planes fly mostly in this signature formation (it's on both teams' official emblems). #1 leads, with #4 directly behind him; #2 and #3 fly wingtip-to-wingtip beside them. Every show ends with the two solos (#5 and #6) combining with #1 through #4 to create the Delta formation.

• *Double Farvel:* A Diamond, except #1 and #4 are upside down.

• *Echelon:* Four planes fly as one through rolls and loops, fanned out like a deck of cards, each plane's wingtip a few inches outside another's cockpit.

• *Low Break Cross:* The Diamond (#1 through #4) sneaks up from behind the crowd and roars overhead before pulling tight, high-G turns in four different directions. They circle back and cross again, in different directions, over "show center" at 500-mph.

• *The Solos:* While #1 through #4 are flying together, #5 and #6 (the Solos) display tricks like the "Knife-Edge Pass" (#5 and #6 fly directly at each other at a combined speed of 700+ mph, banking at the last second to converge over show center). After this aerial game of "chicken," they team up for the "High-Alpha Pass." Flying very low, the pilots pitch the noses of their planes up to 45 degrees, just below the point where the wings would stop generating lift. The effect makes the planes appear to crawl across the sky a few dozen feet above the runway. To stay airborne, they have to push the engines hard, so it's not only the slowest maneuver, it's one of the loudest.

PERFORMANCES

Each flight team performs around 70 shows per year to millions of spectators. To start a show, Blue Angel #7 narrates for the crowd while planes #1 through #4 taxi down the runway in the Diamond formation. They take off in unison, always just a few feet from each other while flying loops and rolls at 400 mph. The two Solos take off shortly after: #5 performs a "dirty" roll with his landing gear extended, while #6 screeches by a few feet off the ground before yanking the stick and showing how fast the Hornet can climb.

During a half-hour show, the Thunderbirds perform about 30 maneuvers; Blue Angels fly a bit longer and do close to 40 maneuvers. At times during the shows, these aircraft—56 feet long, 40 feet wide—travel 400 mph while only 18 inches apart.

Both teams use "heavy aircraft" to transport their support teams, gear, mobile repair stations, radio equipment, and public relations materials. The Thunderbirds use a C-5 or C-17, but the Blue Angels have a C-130 called "Fat Albert" that starts off each show with a few tricks of its own.

MAINTENANCE

Each pilot has their own plane, and each plane has its own maintenance team. Instead of inspecting their planes preflight like most pilots, as a show opens the pilots march to the planes in unison, sit down in unison, and salute in unison. They don't adjust the switches, they don't check the gauges, they don't adjust the seat height once they sit down. They have to trust that their maintenance team will have done all this for them. The maintenance and support teams—enlisted personnel who also serve two-year tours—are picked from the best in their branches of the military.

RISKY BUSINESS

The planes are high-tech, but the flying is strictly old school. Flying only a few feet apart at 350 knots (400 mph), #1 starts each maneuver, and the other pilots navigate by eyeballing his plane and following his lead. There's no "squawk-talk" on the radio; it's 100% concentration and human skill. The formation watches the leader more than they watch their instruments or the ground. When all goes right, this allows the teams to pull off the breathtaking aerial maneuvers for which they're justly famous.

...was given #53 in honor of baseball pitcher Don Drysdale.

Unfortunately, however, accidents are both a risk and a reality. On a training run in 1981, a Thunderbird leader had a plane malfunction during a loop, and the other three planes were so intent on watching him that they flew into the ground beside him. It became known as "The Diamond Crash." The #1 pilot's job carries so much responsibility that in May 2011, the leader of the Blue Angels resigned after taking his team on a maneuver too close to the ground.

BATHROOM HEROES

The Blue Angels and Thunderbirds never fly together. The Department of Defense limits them from performing within 150 miles of each other. But the officers play golf together, and the enlisted members play an annual softball game. Losers take home a red-and-blue toilet with "There's No Excuse For Lack Of Talent" written inside the bowl.

*　　*　　*

DRAGSTER TRIVIA

• The engine on a Top Fuel dragster is more powerful than the combined engines in the first 8 rows (24 cars) at the Daytona 500.

• The 17-inch rear tires on a dragster wear out after only 4 to 6 runs, or about 2 miles.

• A Top Fuel dragster accelerates from 0 to 100 mph in less than $^8/_{10}$ of a second, 11 seconds faster than a Porsche 911 Turbo.

• If a spark plug fails even momentarily early in a dragster's run, unburned nitro fuel will build up in the cylinders and blow the cylinders and block to pieces.

• A Top Fuel dragster leaves the starting line with a force nearly five times that of gravity, the same force of a space shuttle taking off from the launch pad at Cape Canaveral.

• A Top Fuel dragster can go from 0 to 300 mph before you finish reading this sentence.

• Under full throttle, a Top Fuel dragster engine consumes 1.5 gallons of nitro per second, the same rate of fuel consumption as a Boeing 747.

THE BIGGEST...

Some of the world's biggest vehicles, and the engines that move them.

PICK-UP TRUCK: International CXT

It's 9 feet, 3 inches tall, not counting the exhaust stack. Illinois-based International built the CXT on a chassis normally used by dump trucks, and the truck stands a foot taller than most garage doors. The 7.6-liter, inline-six diesel engine provides 220 hp and 540 pound-feet of torque, enough to haul six tons of cargo. The basic model costs $93,000.

HELICOPTER: Sikorsky CH-53E helicopter

For over 40 years, the U.S. Marines have used these three-engine helicopters to transport troops and equipment around the world, 16 tons at a time. It is 99 feet long and has a 79-foot main rotor. The tip of the 20-foot tail rotor (larger than most helicopter main rotors) sits 28 feet from the ground. It is capable of going 100 knots for 100 miles, hovering in place for five minutes, and then returning. And it's nimble. In 1968 a test-pilot put a CH-53E through barrel rolls and loops. It performed flawlessly, dropping only 250 feet of altitude during a loop.

SHIP: *Emma Maersk*

At 1,302 feet long—419 feet longer than the *Titanic* and 52 feet longer than the Empire State Building laid on its side—the *Emma Maersk* is the world's largest cargo ship. Launched in 2006, it can transport more than 15,000 standard 20-foot shipping containers. Its 180-foot-wide hulls are so large that officials in Panama have spent $5.2 billion widening the Panama Canal to accommodate the big boat. (The canal project will be completed in 2014.) Unfortunately, the Danish owner of the *Emma Maersk* has already ordered 10 megatankers that are 12 feet wider than the Emma, making the Canal modifications already obsolete.

LOCOMOTIVE: Union Pacific's "Big Boy"

A key part of the American supply chain in WWII, the Big Boy

The average car contains more than 44 pounds of glue.

line operated between Ogden, Utah, and Cheyenne, Wyoming. American Locomotive Company of Schenectady, New York, delivered the first of 25 Big Boy locomotives to Union Pacific in 1941. At 132 feet long and 1.2 million pounds, this steam engine had to be hinged to navigate turns. It used a wheel configuration called 4-8-8-4, in which the first and last sets of four wheels turn independently to allow better handling. The Big Boy had a 72-foot wheelbase, reached a top speed of 80 mph, held 30 tons of coal and 22,000 gallons of water, and generated nearly 6,000 hp. The Big Boys operated until 1959. Eight of the original Big Boys are on display around the United States, including the "4005" in Denver, which logged one million miles in its service life.

AIRPLANE: Antonov AN-225

The AN-225 made its debut at the 1989 Paris Air Show, carrying the Russian *Buran* spaceship on its roof. This airship can carry 551,000 pounds of cargo in its 140-by-21-foot cargo bay, twice the capacity of the U.S. military's C-5B Galaxy. After the breakup of the Soviet Union, the AN-225 became an air freighter (the first commercial voyage by this Cold War machine brought 216,000 meals to American soldiers in the Persian Gulf). Its wingspan is just shy of the length of a football field (290 feet), with a fuselage length of 275 feet, 7 inches. The cockpit sits 59 feet, 8½ inches above the runway. Its six ZMKB Progress Lotarev D-18T turbofans generate 309,540 pounds of thrust. Takeoff weight, fully fueled with no cargo: 1,322,750 pounds.

SHIP ENGINE: The RTA96-C Wartsila-Sulzer

Without question the largest engine ever built, this behemoth weighs in at 2,300 tons. It's a turbocharged two-stroke diesel with an 89-yard-long crankshaft generating 80 million watts of power. All this adds up to 100,000 hp and a top speed of 25.5 knots, or 28 mph. So what kind of ship needs an engine this big? The world's biggest, of course. This monster engine moves the *Emma Maersk* (see previous page).

JET ENGINE: General Electric's 90-115B

When GE tested this engine on a Boeing 747, only a single 90-115B was needed to keep the 700,000-pound airplane aloft (747s normally require four engines). The 90-115B's fan blades have an aerodynamic "swept-wing" configuration that forces more air into the compressor, resulting in over 100,000 hp and 127,900 pounds of thrust, enough to move 400-pound boulders near the runway. Hazard-testing has revealed the engine to be capable of maintaining 100% thrust without stalling while handling 4.5 tons of water per minute, three-quarters of a ton of hail in 30 seconds, or a 5.5-pound "bird ingestion" directly to the fan blades (a required test). Currently these engines fly Boeing's largest twin-engine jet, the 777-300ER.

OIL-DRILLING SHIP: *Discoverer Enterprise*

The 835-foot *Enterprise*, owned by Transocean, is the world's largest ultra-deepwater ship. It rises to 418 feet above the water line, weighs over 75 million pounds, and has living quarters for 200 crew members. The *Enterprise* is one of the few rigs in the world with two drilling stations rather than one, making it cheaper and faster than its competitors. Each station can start a well on the ocean floor 10,000 feet below sea level, and then keep on drilling for another 6.5 miles. Its six 7,000-hp engines are synchronized with a triple redundant positioning system that allows the *Enterprise* to keep drilling during a hurricane. The *Discoverer Enterprise* was the ship that finally sealed the disastrous 2010 BP oil leak in the Gulf of Mexico.

* * *

STUFFED!

Seeing how many college students could stuff themselves into a telephone booth was a fad in the 1950s. Volkswagen and Mini Cooper stuffing followed hot on its heels. Here are the latest record-breaking "stuffs."

Original Volkswagen Beetle: 17 people
Original Mini Cooper: 21 people
Smart Car two-seater: 19 people
Modern Mini Cooper: 25 people
New Volkswagen Beetle: 27 people

...It took 40 minutes to travel the 16 miles.

TOP DAREDEVIL: EVEL KNIEVEL

Dressed in his trademark red, white, and blue leathers, Evel Knievel jumped his motorcycle straight to superstardom in the 1960s and '70s. Here are some of the highlights... and lowlights...of his sensational career.

CALL ME EVEL

Robert Craig Knievel Jr. earned his nickname after a police chase in Butte, Montana, sent him to the county jail for reckless motorcycle driving in 1956, at the age of 18. The guy in the next cell was named William Knofel, and a witty jailer dubbed the two "Awful Knofel and Evil Knievel." Knievel's nickname stuck, though he later changed the spelling to "Evel" to make the name sound less, well, evil. In his teens and early 20s, Knievel was a ski jumper, pole-vaulter, rodeo rider, and minor-league hockey player who bounced from one failed business venture to another. In 1966, desperate to earn money for his growing family, he decided to create a motorcycle "thrill" show patterned after Joie Chitwood's Auto Daredevil Show, a traveling troupe that he'd seen years earlier. Knievel's act involved jumping his Honda 350cc motorcycle through flaming rings, over mountain lions, and across a 20-foot-long box filled with rattlesnakes.

SUCCESS HURTS

On February 10, 1966, Knievel attempted to leap his bike over another speeding motorcycle in Barstow, California, but was hit in the groin, tossed 15 feet into the air, and sent to the hospital with multiple fractures. This should have ended his daredevil career—but instead, it gave him his first brush with fame and set him on a course toward becoming the Guinness World Record holder for "most broken bones in a lifetime." Over his career, Knievel broke 433 bones, including his back twice and his femur five times. He endured 14 surgeries to replace or repair bones with steel screws, pins, or rods, spending a total of 36 months of his life in the hospi-

Evel Knievel was once fired from a mining job for making an earth-moving machine do a wheelie.

tal. In his later years, he treated his chronic back pain with a surgically implanted morphine drip. In 2007, at the age of 69, he died at home of pulmonary fibrosis. But for a generation of kids who grew up in the '60s and '70s, Knievel will always be known as the ultimate daredevil.

FLYING...AND FALLING

Here's a select list of Knievel's feats, flops, and bone-breaking errors.

HIT! May 30, 1967: Clears 16 cars on a Triumph T120 650cc at Ascot Park Speedway in Gardena, California.

MISS! July 28, 1967: Attempts the same jump with the same bike at Graham Speedway, Washington. He lands on the last vehicle and suffers a concussion.

MISS! August 18, 1967: Same jump, same bike, same spot, same result. Breaks left wrist, right knee, two ribs.

MISS! December 31, 1967: Tries to jump the fountains at Caesar's Palace, Las Vegas—a distance of 141 feet. Thrown over the Triumph's handlebars into the parking lot, suffers a crushed pelvis and broken femur, hip, wrist, skull, and both ankles. In a coma for 29 days.

MISS! May 10, 1970: Switches to an American Eagle 750cc. Tries to jump 13 Pepsi-Cola trucks in Yakima, Washington, but is thrown 50 feet. Breaks collarbone, both femurs, and right arm.

HIT! January 8, 1971: Leaps 13 cars to a sellout crowd of 100,000 at the Houston Astrodome on a Harley-Davidson XR750.

HIT! February 28, 1971: Sets a world record by jumping 19 cars on his Harley at the Ontario Motor Speedway.

MISS! March 3, 1972: After a successful jump at San Francisco's Cow Palace, is thrown over handlebars while making a quick stop and run over by his Harley. Result: broken back, concussion.

HIT! February 18, 1973: Jumps the Harley over a record-setting 50 stacked cars before a crowd of 35,000 at the Los Angeles Coliseum.

In 1961, 90% of kids who lived within a mile of their school walked or biked. In 2011: 31%.

HIT! August 20, 1974: Soars his Harley over 13 Mack trucks at the Canadian National Exposition in Toronto.

MISS! September 8, 1974: Attempts to fly over the quarter-mile-wide Snake River Canyon in Idaho on a steam-powered rocket, the Skycycle X-2. Is blown back into the canyon when his parachute deploys early; almost drowns.

MISS! May 26, 1975: Ninety thousand people at Wembley Stadium, London, watch him soar over 13 double-decker buses, only to crash in the landing, breaking his pelvis. He refuses a stretcher, saying, "I came in walking, I went out walking."

HIT! October 25, 1975: Leaps a personal-best 133 feet over 14 Greyhound buses at the Kings Island Theme Park in Ohio, drawing the largest TV audience ever for ABC's *Wide World of Sports*.

MISS! January 31, 1977: Inspired by the hit film *Jaws*, he plans to jump a tank of live sharks at the Chicago Amphitheatre. During rehearsal, he loses control of his motorcycle, breaks both arms, suffers a concussion, and seriously injures a cameraman, who loses an eye. Knievel never jumps again.

* * *

TOO MUCH IS NEVER ENOUGH

For billionaires who think they have everything, Yacht Island Design of Derby, England has come up with one more toy that is a must-have: a yacht that's a replica of the city of Monte Carlo, home to high-rolling casinos and luxury resorts. On first glance, the 500-foot *Streets of Monaco* looks like a floating city, complete with recognizable buildings like the famed Hotel de Paris. Winding around the four-story ocean liner is a go-kart racetrack reminiscent of the Grand Prix de Monte Carlo, plus there's a helipad, several tennis courts, pools with swim-in Jacuzzi bars, a library and a cinema. The *Streets of Monaco* also boasts a casino, an atrium with waterfalls connecting its upper and lower levels, and a restaurant with underwater views. There are seven guest suites, plus a three-story, 4,800 square-foot master suite Price: $1.1 billion.

First production car to have a wraparound windshield: the 1953 Cadillac Eldorado.

RACIN' IN THE SUN

Every other year in October, solar-powered vehicles push the limits of the possible in a grueling race across the Australian Outback.

BACKGROUND

The World Solar Challenge began in 1987 as a way for sustainable car designers to demonstrate the latest innovations. Using only solar power for fuel, teams from around the globe—including major auto manufacturers, research institutions, universities, and a few high schools—compete not only for the glory of winning but also to help create a sustainable future. The original intent of the race was to spur inventors to build efficient cars that could travel long distances at highway speeds. Since then, the racers have continued to expand on their inventions… and their expectations.

THE RULES

The field is limited to 30 participants. Each team is required to supply two to four drivers, as well as front and rear escort vehicles. The race begins in Darwin, the capital of Australia's Northern Territory, and heads south, primarily along the Stuart Highway, across the rugged outback to the finish line in the southern city of Adelaide some 1,900 miles away. Each day's racing starts at 8:00 a.m. and ends at 5:00 p.m. Because the race takes place on public highways, drivers are expected to abide by the rules of the road, although it's OK to cross lanes to better soak up the sun as long as no vehicles are coming from the opposite direction. Cars must also make a set number of 30-minute stops at various checkpoints. Batteries are fully charged at the beginning of the race but, except in the case of an emergency, cannot be replaced during the race.

Battery mass is limited for each type (lead-acid, NiCd, lithium ion, and so on) to an approximate maximum of five kilowatts per hour. In recent years, drivers have also been required to be seated upright as opposed to lying down. Otherwise, there is no limit for car design. Solar panel–covered cars resembling everything from slices of reflective toast to jet fighters to robotic insects have vied for the title of world's fastest solar vehicle. Some cars tilt to take advantage of the sun's position, while others rely on aerodynamics to reach the checkered flag first.

WINNERS

• In the inaugural race, Sunraycer, a collaborative effort from General Motors, AeroVironment, and Hughes Aircraft crushed the competition, traveling the sun-baked course in just over five days at an average speed of 41.8 mph. The $2 million concept car, which looked like a giant cockroach, beat its closest competitor, from Ford, by two days. Utilizing 8,800 solar panels, Sunraycer generated no more than 1,500 watts of electric power to the car's magnetic engine—about the same as a household toaster. The new Chevy Volt is a direct descendant of the Sunraycer.

• By the mid-1990s, Honda of Japan had pushed average speeds above 55 mph.

• UT Delft of the Netherlands dominated the new century, winning four Solar Challenges between 2001 and 2007. In 2005, UT Delft's Nuon 4 won the race with an average speed of nearly 64 mph. Operating at full power at high noon, some cars hit speeds topping 80 mph. The 2009 champion, Japan's Tokai Challenger, completed the race in 29 hours, 49 minutes, and cost under $300,000 to build.

NEW FOCUS

Also in 2009, the World Solar Challenge became synonymously known as the Global Green Challenge as it expanded to include classifications for alternative fuel as well as solar vehicles. With the speed and distance goals realized, focus has shifted to developing vehicles that are as practical as they are sustainable. When the globe's dependence on fossil fuels is finally broken through innovation or necessity, humanity will likely have a sun-drenched race through the heart of Australia to thank for it.

* * *

"The scientific theory I like best is that the rings of Saturn are composed entirely of lost airline luggage."

—Mark Russell

PRE-WRIGHT FLIGHT: ENGINE POWER

The invention of the steam engine in 1775 inspired aviation pioneers. These are some of the bright ideas they tried to get off the ground.

AIRCRAFT: Ariel (1842)
INVENTOR: William Henson (1812–88)
DETAILS: English lacemaker and aeronaut Henson started by building a small-scale model of the *Ariel*, a passenger-carrying airplane powered by a steam engine. The full-sized *Ariel* was to be 3,000 pounds, made of canvas, silk, metal, and wood. The 25-hp boiler would drive two rear-facing propellers, which Henson called "paddle-wheels." Henson's drawings are strikingly similar to those of modern aircraft: fixed wings, fuselage, landing gear, and tail section. He also predicted many of the modern uses for airplanes, which he thought could "convey letters, goods, and passengers from place to place through the air." His models flew successfully, albeit indoors and with the help of guide wires.

COULD IT FLY? Probably not. Engine-making was still a new science in the 1840s, and Henson's engine wasn't strong enough to power an eight-pound model, much less the actual ton-and-a-half *Ariel*. Henson scrapped his original plan and, partnering with another lacemaker named John Stringfellow, went back to the drawing board. The pair made several attempts to improve the *Ariel*, including a version with a 20-foot wingspan, but were ultimately defeated by their underpowered steam engine.

AIRCRAFT: Steam-planes (1848; 1868)
INVENTOR: John Stringfellow (1799–1883)
DETAILS: In 1849 Henson emigrated to New Jersey. Back in England, his former partner Stringfellow soldiered on. Within a year, he had built successful steam-driven fixed-wing monoplane models, and in 1868 he and his son exhibited a steam-powered

tri-plane at the Crystal Palace in London. His steam-planes lacked any vertical surface—essential for stability (in other words, a rudder)—but otherwise looked similar to airplanes that would finally take to the air 40 years later.

COULD IT FLY? Probably, if it had had more power. Stringfellow's steam-engines were strong enough to fly his small-scale models—one even sailed 40 feet after leaving its guide wire—but not a normal-sized plane. Stringfellow had created the first modern engine-powered airplane, but putting a person onboard would be left to another generation.

AIRCRAFT: Dirigible (1852)

INVENTOR: Jules Henri Giffard (1825–82)

DETAILS: The quest for controlled, sustained flight took a giant leap forward when French engine-maker Giffard turned his attention to aviation. He constructed a hydrogen-filled dirigible with a 10-foot propeller turned by a 3-hp, 250-pound steam engine. A large net covered the 144-foot-long, cigar-shaped balloon. A gondola hung from the net, large enough to hold the engine and at least two passengers. At the rear of the balloon was a vertical sail-like rudder.

COULD IT FLY? Absolutely. On September 24, 1852, Giffard took off from Paris and landed 17 miles away in Elancourt, averaging about 6 mph. Because Giffard's machine had engine power and maneuverability and could carry passengers, historians consider this the world's first powered aircraft. But his next experiment failed when the balloon tilted nose-up and slipped from the netting. The gondola fell to the ground with Giffard and a passenger inside, and the two received minor injuries. A planned 30-ton version never found funding.

AIRCRAFT: Planophore (1871)

INVENTOR: Alphonse Penaud (1850–80)

DETAILS: French engineer Penaud spent much of his life confined to a wheelchair because of a bad hip, which may explain why his thoughts were always on the skies. He successfully experimented with small, rubber-band-powered, propeller-driven aircraft. One large wing provided lift, and a modern-looking tail section with vertical and horizontal surfaces provided stability and steering. This type of tail section became known as a Penaud tail. The entire model weighed half an ounce.

COULD IT FLY? Possibly. On August 18, 1871, Penaud launched a 20-inch-wide model of his Planophore at the Jardin des Tuileries in Paris. The miniature aircraft climbed for two circles before descending to a safe landing. The flight lasted 11 seconds and covered 180 feet. Penaud applied to the Aerial Navigation Society of France for funds to build a full-size version but was rejected. Depressed that his dream would not be realized, he placed the drawings of his machine in a wooden coffin, sent them to fellow aeronaut Jules Giffard, and committed suicide. Penaud's design became popular as a children's toy.

AIRCRAFT: Aerodrome (1891)

INVENTOR: Samuel P. Langley (1834–1906)

DETAILS: During his tenure as secretary of the Smithsonian Institution, American astronomer Langley became the first person to systematically combine glider technology with adequately powered onboard engines. In 1891 he built the first of his steam-powered "Aerodromes." It had canvas wings stretched over a wood frame, an engine, and a Penaud tail, all supported on a central metal frame. For the next five years, Langley would improve and modify the aircraft, eventually switching to a gasoline-powered engine.

COULD IT FLY? Sort of. In 1896 Aerodrome #6 flew in three large circles, climbing 80 feet. Among the observers was Alexander Graham Bell, who calculated that the plane covered 3,000 feet in its 90-second flight, going over 20 mph. Seven years later, when the United States was preparing for the Spanish-American War, the War Department asked Langley for larger test models. His first two attempts fell "like a handful of mortar," as one observer put it, into the Potomac River. Test pilot Charles Manly wasn't hurt, but the project never recovered. The public saw the experiments as a waste of money, and Langley officially ended the Aerodrome contract—exactly nine days before the Wright brothers made their first successful flight.

AIRCRAFT: Katydid glider (1896)

INVENTOR: Octave Alexandre Chanute (1832–1910)

...Her car had a 30-horsepower engine—about the same power as a riding lawn mower.

DETAILS: Paris-born Chanute emigrated to New York at age six. He became a successful civil engineer and later designed the first bridge to span the Missouri River. Then his interests turned to aviation, a term he popularized. Chanute believed that science should be a collaborative effort, not a series of secretive competitions, so he took it upon himself to collect the entire history of aviation into one volume. Wilbur Wright called Chanute's 1894 book, *Progress in Flying Machines*, "the most significant work on aeronautical science of its time." But Chanute wasn't content just to write about other scientists—he wanted to build an airplane himself. In 1896 he organized a team of engineers and started making cutting-edge gliders like the *Katydid*. The frame was spruce, and the six wings—made of Japanese silk—were stacked vertically like a ladder. The "pilot" hung from the center of the rig, his legs dangling below. This was the *Katydid*'s only landing gear.

COULD IT FLY? Absolutely. The *Katydid* performed successfully in hundreds of manned glides, traveling up to 82 feet. This reliability allowed Chanute to perform detailed experiments on wing configuration and structural strength. And though Chanute's gliders had no engines, those studies led to his real breakthrough...

AIRCRAFT: Chanute-Herring biplane (1896)

INVENTOR: Octave Alexandre Chanute (1832–1910)

DETAILS: In 1896 Chanute's design team introduced the Chanute-Herring biplane, the culmination of his life's work. Its most important advancement was a wire-strut bracing system, which Chanute borrowed from his experience building bridges. The technique is still used in airplanes today. The biplane had no engine and no way to steer, and the pilot had to dangle from a harness beneath the craft, but it was the best glider yet.

COULD IT FLY? It glided once for 350 feet, and if Chanute had put an engine on it, it would have certainly become the world's first airplane. How can we be so confident? Because seven years later, two Ohio boys named Orville and Wilbur adapted this design, which they called the Double-Decker, strapped on a 12-hp gasoline-powered aluminum engine, and on December 17, 1903, made their historic first flight in Kitty Hawk, North Carolina.

THE WILD ONES

The bad-boy gang that inspired the story that inspired the movie that inspired a generation of bikers.

BOOZIN' AND BRUISIN'

When World War II ended, the tide of returning soldiers flooded the labor market, and many veterans found themselves jobless. The government tried to provide relief with a stopgap measure called the "52/20 program," which paid $20 a week for one year. Most veterans found their way back into regular jobs, but a minority couldn't make the transition back to civilian life. Some hopped on their motorcycles and set off to enjoy the freedom they'd fought so hard to preserve. They formed motorcycle clubs to race their bikes, drink beer, and have a good time. "We never tried to hurt anybody," one biker recalled, "because we'd all been hurt in the war. Believe me, baby, all of us had suffered in that war."

The Boozefighters MC (motorcycle club) traces its origins to an event that happened at a Class C motorcycle race in El Cajon, California, shortly after the war. A group of riders who'd come up from San Diego to watch the race, including John Cameron and Wino Willie Forkner, were drinking in the parking lot when Wino Willie "got a wild hair" to join the show on the track. Astride his Indian Chief motorcycle, he blasted through the crash wall at intermission and roared down the straightaway, finally spilling his bike after a lap of full-throttle drunk driving. The police tossed him in jail, and his gang, the 13 Rebels, tossed him out of their club. In retaliation, Wino Willie talked Cameron into forming their own club, calling it the Boozefighters because boozing and fighting were what had gotten Forkner into trouble. They settled on a uniform of white sweater with green sleeves, with an identifying patch of a "milk" bottle and gold stars. Ernie and John Roccio (later to become Class A speedway riders in Europe) signed on, along with Fatboy Nelson, Dink Burns, George Menker, and others. On July 4, 1947, the Boozefighters rumbled out of San Diego on their Harleys—and into infamy.

Lufthansa Airlines served preheated in-flight meals as early as 1928.

LOCK UP YOUR DAUGHTERS!

In 1947 Hollister, California, was a sleepy little farming town of about 4,500, tucked away inland near Salinas. The town was looking forward to the July 4th resumption of the motorcycle races that had been popular in the 1930s but interrupted by the war. What happened that Fourth of July weekend would shock the nation. As *Life* magazine reported:

> 4,000 members of a motorcycle club roared into Hollister, California, for a three-day convention. They quickly tired of ordinary motorcycle thrills and turned to more exciting stunts. Racing their vehicles down the main streets and through traffic lights, they rammed into restaurants and bars, breaking furniture and mirrors. Police arrested many but could not restore order.

The streets were littered with broken beer bottles as the bikers brawled, exposed themselves, and assaulted young women. The *San Francisco Chronicle* ran breathless reports on the reign of terror inflicted on the hapless town by the horde of drunken motorcyclists, led by the Boozefighters, along with other gangs like Satan's Sinners, the Galloping Gooses, and Satan's Daughters.

Accounts differ as to how bad the rampage actually was—the only arrests were for public drunkenness—but the photo published in *Life* of a paunchy, beer-toting Boozefighter astride his Harley, leering at the camera, became the indelible image in the public eye. Overnight, motorcycle clubs became "gangs" and anyone riding a motorcycle, an "outlaw."

REBEL ROUSER

A few years later, a short story about the incident by Frank Rooney, titled "The Cyclists' Raid," was published in *Harper's* magazine. Film producer Stanley Kramer and director Laslo Benedek knew they had an idea for a hit movie as soon as they read it, and hurried the film, which they titled *The Wild One*, into production. Marlon Brando, fresh off his star-making performance as the brutish Stanley in *A Streetcar Named Desire*, signed on to play the lead, Johnny Strabler.

In the film, Johnny is the leader of the Black Rebels, who gatecrash a legit motorcycle race. After a gang member steals the second-place trophy and gives it to Johnny, the gang heads for the quiet village of Wrightsville, where they race up and down main

The average car contains over 3,000 feet of electrical wires.

street and generally raise hell. Johnny falls for a pretty waitress at the local café, Kathie, who happens to be the sheriff's daughter. When her friend demands, "What are you rebelling against, Johnny?" he infamously replies, "Whaddaya got?" Kathie is intrigued by the brooding boy in the black leather jacket, cuffed jeans, and motorcycle cap, but he also frightens her. After riding on the back of Johnny's Triumph Thunderbird, her arms wrapped tightly around his waist, Kathie cries, "I've never ridden on a motorcycle before. It's fast. It scared me. But I forgot everything. It felt good!"

By the last frame, a sweet old man at the café bar has been killed, Johnny has been beaten up and jailed, and Kathie's budding bad-boy romance has no future. Before Johnny roars out of town, he gives her his trophy, the one he didn't win but still, a token to remember him by. The bad/good, cruel/sweet dichotomy in Johnny's character has led some film critics to say *The Wild One* introduced the concept of the antihero to Hollywood.

INFLUENCE

The reaction to *The Wild One* after its premiere in 1953 echoed the public outcry that had greeted the Hollister riot. Many moviegoers found it too violent. But the refusal of some theaters to screen it only elevated the film to cult status with youths. Sales of leather jackets, white caps, and Triumph motorcycles soared. Brando's sideburns became the new look, embraced by other sex symbols like Elvis Presley and James Dean. "I was as surprised as anyone," he recalled later, "when T-shirts, jeans, and leather jackets suddenly became symbols of rebellion." According to Beatles biographer Hunter Davies, the Fab Four were inspired by the film. Bass player Stu Sutcliffe saw the movie, and suggested the Beetles (the name of the rival gang) as the group's name. Reportedly John Lennon said, "Yeah, we'll spell it Beatles, as we're a beat group."

Triumph Motorcycle initially objected to the use of their motorcycles in the film, but now the company uses images of *The Wild One* to advertise their bikes, including a replica of the jacket Brando wore. In addition to influencing countless motorcycle clubs, the movie inspires other movie references to this day: In *Indiana Jones and the Kingdom of the Crystal Skull* (2008), Mutt Williams (Shia LeBoeuf) rides in on a 1950 Triumph Thunderbird 6T wearing the same outfit as Brando's Johnny.

The world's lowest street-legal car is the 19-inch-tall "Flatmobile."

VA-VA-VROOM!

For Hellé Nice, life in the fast lane came naturally. This daring French showgirl-turned-racing-champion turned heads and broke speed records during the 1930s.

BACKGROUND

The Automobile Age was just beginning when Mariette Hélène Delangle was born on December 15, 1900, in the rural village of Aunay-sous-Auneau, 47 miles southwest of Paris. In 1916 young Marie left home for the bright lights of the big city, changed her name to Helene Nice (later Hellé Nice, pronounced "El-ay Neece"), and by 1920 had made a name for herself on the cabaret scene as a dancer and model. By all accounts a superb dancer, she didn't rely on talent alone to make it to the top. Her act was loaded with sex appeal, and the nude postcards she sold on the side only made the lines to get into her shows longer. At 26 Hellé Nice was rich enough to have her own yacht, along with a quickly changing string of wealthy lovers. She had also picked up a passion for cars—fast cars.

SPEEDBOWL QUEEN

In 1929 a knee injury from a skiing accident put an end to Hellé Nice's showbiz career. So she turned her formidable passion and energy to car racing. On June 2, 1929, she entered her Omega Six car in the marquee race for women at the time, the Grand Prix Féminin—and won. In December she raced at Montlhéry (the French equivalent of the Indy 500) and set a new land speed record for women: 197.7 kph (122.85 mph). A reporter noted that she only took her foot off the accelerator when one of her tires blew, adding, "*Elle a du cran*" ("She's got guts"). In June 1930, she raced in her first open Grand Prix at LeMans, going up against the top male drivers of the day, and got on the podium with third place.

Glamorous, sexy, and controversial, Hellé Nice attracted publicity like a magnet and was dubbed by newspapers "the most famous woman in France." She became a Lucky Strike cigarette poster girl and spent the rest of 1930 racing at tracks in America.

The first Grand Prix race, in 1901, was won with an average speed of 46 mph.

(She was the first woman to race at Woodbridge, New Jersey, where the crowds adored her and called her the "Speedbowl Queen.") But 1931 found her back in France, where her new lover, Baron Philippe de Rothschild—a racing fan himself—introduced her to Ettore Bugatti. Bugatti, whose sleek racing cars were considered the top of the line, signed her to his team, provided her with a gleaming powder-blue Bugatti Type 35C (which became her trademark), and set her loose.

FASTEST WOMAN IN THE WORLD

Over the next five years, Hellé Nice competed in over 70 sanctioned Grand Prix, Rally, and Hill Climb races. She won so many women-only events that she is the undisputed women's champion of the '30s. Other notable women drivers, such as Kay Petre of England and Elizabeth Junek of Czechoslovakia, also competed in open races against men and did well, but none as successfully as Hellé Nice. Some of her accomplishments:

- First place, 1933 Women's Grand Prix at Montlhéry
- First place, Ladies' Cup, 1935 Rally at Monte Carlo
- Third place, 1933 Coupe des Alpes, where she was the only woman driver out of 121 entrants
- Third place, Italian Grand Prix at Monza
- Second place, Ventoux Mountain Climb, Provence, where again she was the only woman in the race
- Third place, 1936 Sao Paulo Grand Prix
- Women's land speed records in 1929 and 1937
- 10 speed records during the 1937 Yacco Endurance Trials at Montlhéry that still stand today

TOO HOT TO HANDLE

For Hellé Nice, the 1930s were a party that had no end. Her life was a swirl of lavish soirées, luxury hotels, high-society lovers, and auto races in Europe and North and South America. As one of the few women on the Grand Prix circuit and by far the most glamorous, she was swarmed by paparazzi wherever she went. Hellé Nice loved to play to her audience. She often raced without a hel-

The windshields on NASCAR race cars are made of the same material as fighter-plane canopies.

met so her blond hair was more visible to the spectators. Sometimes she wore only a swimsuit behind the wheel. Once, after a toughly contested win, she paused to powder her nose before driving her Bugatti into the winner's circle. The photo appeared in newspapers around the world.

THE ROAD TO RUIN

Hellé Nice had no way of knowing, but the Sao Paulo Grand Prix of 1936 was the beginning of the end of the good times. She was in second place behind Brazilian champion Manuel de Teffé when a bale of hay tumbled onto the track and she hit it going over 100 mph. Her car flew into the air and crashed into the grandstand, killing 6 people and injuring 34 others. Hellé Nice was thrown from the car and injured so badly that she was in a coma for three days. It took her months to recover, and when she did, the racing world had changed. With war in Europe looming, there was little interest in racing and she couldn't get a sponsor. Racing virtually came to a halt until the war's end, and it wasn't until 1949 that the Rally and Grand Prix circuit began to revive. Hellé Nice assumed that she could go back to her life as before. She was wrong.

FAST LIFE, FASTER EXIT

The 1949 Monte Carlo Rally heralded the grand return of professional auto racing, and scores of drivers and sponsors descended on the tiny Mediterranean principality. Hellé Nice was attending a gala the night before the race along with other drivers when Louis Chiron, a highly respected Grand Prix champion, publicly accused her of being an agent for the Gestapo during the war. There is no record of what Hellé Nice said in her defense, but it didn't matter: Her reputation was destroyed. Her lover, former mechanic Arnaldo Binelli, left her. Her sponsors dropped her, and her own family shunned her. She fled to Nice, where she changed her name and lived out her life on charity from a foundation that helped former cabaret performers. By the time she died in 1984, Hellé Nice was living in a rat-infested attic, toothless and alone. Among her few possessions were some racing trophies, a shabby leopard-skin coat, and a box of clippings. One of them was a poem from a newspaper: "When he died, nobody cared, nobody cried. Where he went, how he fares, nobody knows, nobody cares."

A PLACE IN RACING HISTORY

So was Hellé Nice a Nazi collaborator? The jury's still out. Chiron never substantiated his accusation, but there's no record of Hellé Nice trying to disprove the charge. She was probably the lover of Fritz Huschke von Hamstein, a top German Grand Prix driver before the war and an SS officer during it. Perhaps it was a case of guilt by association, though she never saw him again after the war began. But she was no hero of the French Resistance, either—she spent the war living quietly with Binelli in the south of France, waiting it out. When biographer Miranda Seymour tracked the story all the way to the German national archives in Berlin, she found no record of Hellé Nice ever being listed as a Nazi agent. Whatever the truth may be about her wartime activities, some things remain unchallenged: Hellé Nice was one of the best race car drivers, male or female, of her day, and one of the most colorful personalities the sport has ever seen.

* * *

EZ-FAST-SPEED-PASS-PAY-TAG

Nobel Prize-winning economist William Vickrey first proposed the idea of electronic tolling in 1959. The idea was to place an electronic transponder under a car to make it easier to assess and collect different toll amounts based on the amount of traffic at any given time. Vickrey theorized that traffic congestion could be alleviated by charging more when traffic was heavy. That idea didn't catch on, but the technology did. Today toll booths have cameras and scanners that detect a small transponder in the car and instantly deduct the toll from a prepaid account set up by the driver—the systems are variously called E-Z Pass, FasTrak, Fast Lane, Lee Way, E-Pass, O-Pass, I-Pass, and Tolltag. But taking it to another level, a Canadian company called Skymeter recently rolled out a "financial-grade GPS" device that can automatically pay tolls, parking-meter fees, and parking-garage charges.

MORE CAR STARS

Can you match the movie synopsis to the title? *(Answers are on page 463.)*

1. In the summer of 1962, college-bound teen obsesses over a beautiful blonde driving a white Thunderbird on the streets of Modesto, California.

2. Women compete with Ferraris and Lotus Fords for the affection of Formula One drivers in Monaco.

3. When shop-class bullies vandalize a '58 Plymouth Fury with a deadly past, it seeks vengeance.

4. Shop-class buddies build a tricked-out 1973 Corvette Stingray, only to have it stolen. One of them goes looking for the car in Vegas, accompanied by a hooker-in-training.

5. Zany characters (played by an all-star cast) compete in a road race from Connecticut to California in their Ferraris, Lamborghinis, and Rolls-Royces.

6. Reckless boys and their scantily clad female cousin wreak havoc in their '69 Dodge Charger while trying to save the family farm.

7. Sheriff's teenage son takes girl crush on a joyride in a stolen orange '67 Camaro. Smokies give chase.

8. Housewife wants to be a drag racer, despite the fact that women just don't do that.

9. Two wild women take a fateful road trip in a '66 Thunderbird convertible.

10. Bounty hunter pursues a woman driving a car full of counterfeit money belonging to white supremacists.

A. *Thelma and Louise*

B. *Heart Like a Wheel*

C. *Pink Cadillac*

D. *The Dukes of Hazzard*

E. *Christine*

F. *American Graffiti*

G. *Corvette Summer*

H. *Eat My Dust!*

I. *Cannonball Run*

J. *Grand Prix*

New York's first female taxi driver: Wilma Russey (1915).

MUSCLE CAR HALL OF FAME

In the 1960s and '70s, muscle cars were the American Dream: very fast vehicles with powerful V8 engines that the average Joe could drive off the showroom floor.

DETROIT MUSCLE

Muscle cars were a uniquely American phenomenon. In a sense they were the car industry's adoption of the classic hot rodder's philosophy—take a small car and put a huge engine in it. There have always been fast, powerful cars: the English had their Bentleys, Germans their Daimlers, Italians their Bugattis, Americans their Packards and Duesenbergs. The problem was, only the wealthy could afford them.

The muscle car changed all that. Truly classic ones were built on the frame of a midsize sedan a grandmother would have been happy to drive. Suspensions, braking and steering were upgraded to handle faster speeds, but in these cars the engine was the real story. Monster V8s with huge displacements and horsepower to spare did the impossible: they turned humble family transportation into high-performance sports cars that anyone could buy. It was American auto ingenuity at its very best.

ROCKET SCIENCE

The first muscle car was the 1949 Oldsmobile Rocket 88 (some may argue that it's a tie with the Hudson Hornet). The Rocket 88 featured the first high-compression overhead valve V8. It was revolutionary at the time but fairly anemic by later standards: 135 hp, 303 cubic inches. What made the car go like, well, a rocket was that Oldsmobile had dropped that big engine into a lightweight body used by smaller 6-cylinder cars. The results were dramatic: the car became a sensation when it won 8 of 10 races on the NASCAR circuit in 1950. By mid-decade every one of the Big Four car makers—GM, Ford, Chysler, and American Motors—were one-upping each other with new models offering better performance, crisper handling and bigger engines.

Indy 500's winning purse in 1911: $14,250. In 2011: $13.4 million.

END OF THE ROAD

What caused the end of the muscle car era? Several factors combined to turn these cars into dinosaurs. The necessity to equip them with catalytic converters and other emissions controls due to rising concern about air pollution led to a steady decline in horsepower. Insurance rates soared as auto insurers realized that drivers with powerful cars were more likely to have accidents. And during the oil crisis of 1973, the public began moving toward more economical cars that weren't such ga-guzzlers. But for 30 years muscle cars were a much-loved part of the automobile landscape in the United States. Here are 10 standouts of the genre, listed by year of release:

1963 CHEVROLET IMPALA SS

In the early 1960s, Chevrolet's "409" engine was so famous that it found its way into the classic Beach Boys' hit of the same name. Street racers liked to set their 409s in a lightweight "bubble top" Chevy Bel Air 2-door hardtop. In 1963 Chevy ramped things up by bringing out the Z11 option package for its Impala model. The 409 had grown to a 427-cubic-inch behemoth rated at 430 hp, although drag racing enthusiasts insisted it was closer to 500 hp. Because of its angled valves the engine became known as the "porcupine head motor." To keep curb weight down and speed up, the hood, fenders and bumpers were made out of aluminum. As a result, it clocked in the 14s in the quarter-mile and could go 0 to 60 mph in 6.6 seconds. Only 50 Impala SS cars with the Z11 package were made, and the 7 that remain today are collector's items.

1964 FORD THUNDERBOLT

Ford tried to keep pace with lighter, faster competitors by shoving its biggest engine, a big-block 427, into one of its smallest models, the two-door Fairlane. The front end of the frame was highly modified to handle the hood bulge needed to house the motor, but this was still a car a buyer could technically walk into a showroom and buy off the floor. The T-bolt was no family sedan, however. Anything that got in the way of racing was stripped out of it. No armrests, no sun visors, not even a radio or heater. The big-block was rated at 425 hp but with modifications put out closer to 500

Dr. Ernst Pfenning of Chicago, IL, became the very first owner of a Model A on July 23, 1903.

hp. When driver Gas Ronda won the NHRA 1964 World Championship with a time of 11.4 seconds in the quarter mile, the Thunderbolt's reputation was made.

1966 OLDSMOBILE CUTLASS 4-4-2

What set this car apart from other muscle cars was its smooth handling and acceleration. Yet it still delivered the requisite power and thrills, earning it the deserved reputation as the most balanced muscle car of its day. The standard 400-cubic-inch 350-hp engine was often upgraded with a "tri-power" carburetor arrangement that put another 10 hp under the hood. It could knock off the quarter-mile in 14.8 seconds, and go from 0 to 60 in 7 seconds.

1968 DODGE CHARGER R/T

The Charger was a different animal compared to its chunkier muscle car brethren, with a pinched waist "coke-bottle" body and aggressive blackout front grill with hidden headlights. It handled more nimbly than most muscle cars yet still competed strongly in speed and power. The top option package came with the fabled Chrylser 425-hp Hemi engine, which ran the car through the quarter-mile in 13.8 seconds. The car got a huge boost in 1968 when it was featured in the car chase in the movie *Bullitt*. Sales of the Charger that year were six times that of the previous year.

1968 PLYMOUTH ROADRUNNER

By 1966 muscle cars had become so laden with upgrades and options that they'd become luxury machines. Plymouth decided to bring the muscle car back to its cheap and fast roots. To appeal to younger buyers, the carmaker licensed the car's famous cartoon namesake, which appeared not only in decal form on the body but in the horn's "beep-beep." Sales gimmicks aside, the rest of the car was all business. The top power option featured a 425-hp, 426-cubic-inch Street Hemi V8 that could run the quarter-mile in 13.5 seconds. Most impressively, the Road Runner had a sizzling top speed of 140 mph. Plymouth thought they might sell 2,000 units the first year—instead they sold 45,000. The Road Runner is today considered the most important muscle car after the Pontiac

French inventor Gustave d'Amécourt coined the word "helicopter" in 1861.

GTO because it brought muscle cars back to populist (read "inexpensive") roots.

1969 PONTIAC GTO

Known as the "Goat," the GTO is probably the most famous of all muscle cars. Its split grill front-end design certainly made it one of the easiest to recognize. Again, an automaker took a midsized car, the Pontiac Tempest, and wedded it to a jaw-poppingly large engine. The engine was a Ram IV 400-cubic-inch V8 listed at 370 hp but probably closer to 400. This one burned up the quarter-mile in 13.7 seconds; 0 to 60 in 6.1 seconds. The 1969 version was nicknamed "The Judge," after a popular tagline "Here come da Judge!" from the TV show *Laugh-In*. More GTOs were sold than any other kind of muscle car, and to this day it is the car most associated with the style.

1970 AMERICAN MOTORS "REBEL"

The Rebel name first appeared on the 1957 AMC Rambler Rebel, considered the first lightweight muscle car. Then it disappeared until 1966, when it was resurrected with a vengeance in a series of two-door hardtops that culminated in 1970 with a version called "The Machine." Developed in partnership with Hurst Performance, the Rebel Machine came with a 390-cubic-inch V8 pounding out 340 hp, yielding a street-legit time of 0 to 60 mph in 6.8 seconds, as well as an impressive quarter mile in 14.4 seconds. Top speed was 127 mph. Designed to go head to head with the GTO, the car came in patriotic red, white, and blue. Only 2,000 were built, but aficionados, like Jack Nerad of *Driving Today* magazine, think it "somehow, someway deserves to be considered among the greatest cars of all time."

1970 PLYMOUTH HEMI-CUDA

Although Plymouth launched the Barracuda line in 1964, the car really grabbed the attention of muscle car buyers in 1970 with the arrival of the Hemi-Cuda. Powered with a 425-hp, 426-cubic-inch hemi-block V8 engine, the Hemi-Cuda seemed tailor-made for muscle car lovers, although it was reputedly tricky to handle. One of the more unusual features was its shaker scoop, so named because it stuck up through a hole in the hood and "shaked" whenever the engine did. The Hemi-Cuda tore up the quarter mile in a sizzling 13.4 seconds, and went from 0 to 60 in 5.6 seconds.

1970 BUICK GSX

This car's massive 455-cubic-inch engine rated at 360 hp (that most testers thought ran closer to 400 hp) nestled under the hood of a midsize Buick Skylark. That it was offered only in two colors—Apollo White or Saturn Yellow—with a dramatic black stripe down the middle made the car instantly recognizable. It had a full racing package: fat tires, front and rear spoilers, a hood tachometer, and a heavy-duty suspension. Considered the ultimate Buick muscle car, this supercar ran the quarter mile in 13.38 seconds, and went 0 to 60 in 6.5 seconds.

1970 CHEVROLET CHEVELLE SS

This muscle car had the distinction of being one of the most powerful stock cars anyone could buy. The 454-hp LS6 engine had the highest factory horsepower rating of any engine in history. The results showed in its performance on the track: 0 to 60 in six flat, 13.7 through the quarter-mile. Sleekly styled, the Chevelle SS was hugely popular, although it may have represented the high-water mark of the muscle car era. In 1971 GM converted all its engines to unleaded fuel, and new emissions controls resulted in a dramatic drop in horsepower and speed across the board. The Age of the Muscle Car was nearing its end. By 1973 the Chevelle SS was out of production.

*　　*　　*

THIS IS YOUR CAPTAIN SPEAKING

The plane thumped, and the pilot came on the intercom. "Ladies and gentlemen, I apologize, but that thump you just felt was the Number 1 engine malfunctioning. No cause for concern, we can continue safely with just our remaining engine. However, instead of a two-hour flight, our trip will now take four hours."

Everyone groaned at the delay. Then a passenger grumbled, "I hope the second engine doesn't malfunction. Then we'll be up here all day!"

ANSWER PAGES

CELEBRITY YACHT QUIZ

(Answers for page 89)

1-g—Paul Allen's *Octopus*

Good things come in pairs—at least that's what the billionaire software pioneer and Microsoft co-founder Paul Allen thinks. The 414-foot *Octopus*—the 12th-largest yacht in the world—is one of two megayachts that Allen owns. (The other is the *Tatoosh.*) Octopus sports two helicopters and a pair of submarines, and costs $200 million a year to maintain.

2-m—Humphrey Bogart's *Santana*

Bogart sailed the 55-foot yacht almost every weekend around Catalina Island, from 1945 until his death in 1957. Bogie once explained his passion for sailing by saying, "An actor needs something to stabilize his personality, something to nail down what he really is, not what he is currently pretending to be." He also said, "The trouble with having dames on board is you can't pee over the side."

3-d—Jimmy Buffet's *Cosmic Muffin*

Billionaire aviation pioneer Howard Hughes bought a Boeing 307 Stratoliner aircraft in 1939. So what's that have to do with a yacht? The *Cosmic Muffin is* the Stratoliner. Rendered unflyable by Hurricane Cleo in 1964, it was bought by private pilot Ken London for $62 and converted into a boat. First christened the *Londonaire*, it was renamed *Cosmic Muffin* by its subsequent owner, the laid-back "Margaritaville" singer-songwriter, Jimmy Buffet. It's currently on display in Ft. Lauderdale, Florida.

4-i—Al Capone's *Flying Cloud*

Part yacht, part speedboat, the wooden *Flying Cloud* was built in 1928 for Ransom Olds of Oldsmobile motorcar fame. It was bought by the infamous gangster in 1930, just a year after he ordered the brutal St. Valentine's Day Massacre. Capone was

The Japanese research submarine *Shinkai* 6500 can dive 21,414 ft., the deepest of any vessel.

indicted the following year on federal tax evasion charges and lost the *Flying Cloud* to the IRS.

5-b—Johnny Carson's *Serengeti*

Upon retiring in 1992 after 30 years as host of *The Tonight Show*, Johnny Carson became a globe-trotter. He even learned Swahili before visiting Tanzania in 1993, and became so enamored with the place that he named his 130-foot yacht after the famed African plains of the region.

6-j—Johnny Depp's *Vajoliroja*

The actor bought this 156-foot yacht for $33 million dollars in 2006. Named after his long-time partner Vanessa Paradis and their two children, Lily Rose and Jack, the *Vajoliroja* (pronounced vah-jolly-rojah) features finely crafted Honduras mahogany woodwork. Its Edwardian design has been described as "Art Deco meets the Orient Express."

7-c—David Geffen's *Rising Sun*

In 2010 the media mogul bought out co-owner Larry Ellison's share of this 453-foot superyacht, currently the eighth-largest in the world. Built in 2004 for $200 million, the boat has 82 rooms on five stories. The basketball court on the upper deck doubles as a helipad.

8-n—Ernest Hemingway's *Pilar*

Hemingway loosely based *The Old Man and the Sea* on Gregorio Fuentes, first mate on his 1934 custom 38-foot fishing yacht. The famous boat is currently on display on the tennis court of Hemingway's former estate, Finca Vigia, in Cuba. Fuentes died in 2002 at the age of 104, never having read the book he influenced.

9-a—Saddam Hussein's *Ocean Breeze*

The former Iraqi dictator's 270-foot luxury yacht features several swimming pools, a movie theater, a helipad, and even a mini-submarine—and it can be yours for a cool $30 million. The Iraqi government put it up for sale in 2011.

From 1900 to 1920, more than 200 different makes of cars were produced in Indiana alone.

10-f—Howard Johnson's *Riptide*

The renowned hotelier and restaurateur purchased the teak-and-brass Elco MY 54 cabin cruiser new in 1939. Ironically, he had to sell it two years later to cover gambling losses incurred from betting on a boat race. Despite supposedly being cursed, *Riptide* had better luck—it went on to star in its own television series, *Riptide* (co-starring Perry King) from 1984 to '86.

11-e—Dmitry Medvedev's *Sirius*

The president of Russia spent $42 million for the 177-foot *Sirius*, which features whirlpool baths, a gym, and six guest rooms. Kremlin spokesman Viktor Khrenikov justified the presidential extravagance by saying, "The president could use her during the 2014 Olympics on the Black Sea."

12-o—Aristotle Onassis's *Christina* O

The Greek shipping magnate named his 325-foot yacht after his daughter Christina. Built in 1943, *Christina* O was originally a Canadian convoy escort during World War II. Onassis turned it into a floating corporate HQ, from which he ran his business empire until his death in 1975. The *Christina* O features 18 guest cabins, sports and music lounges, and a saltwater swimming pool that converts to a dance floor. It's currently available for rent, at $65,000 to $85,000 per day.

13-k—Marge Schott's *DSV*

Before becoming the controversial owner of the Cincinnati Reds, the wealthy heiress commissioned the *Double Schott 5*, aka the *DSV*, in 1956. Later owned by TV personality Arthur Godfrey, the boat was host to celebrities like Jackie Gleason, JFK, and Marilyn Monroe. All of the ship's logs belong to a single memorabilia collector, except for "#3," which has mysteriously disappeared, allegedly because Kennedy and Monroe appear in it together.

14-p—Elizabeth Taylor's *Kalizma*

Purchased in 1967 by Taylor and then-husband Richard Burton, the 165-foot *Kalizma* was named after Burton's daughters Kate,

Liza, and Maria. The 100-plus-year-old Edwardian yacht served admirably in both world wars for the Royal Navy, and is currently owned by Indian liquor tycoon Vijay Mallya.

15-l—Donald Trump's *La Diva*

Curiosity seekers hoping to catch a glimpse of Donald Trump's 105-foot luxury yacht, *La Diva* (formerly *Ivana*), are out of luck. A mysterious exhaust leak caused the craft to burst into flames while docked in West Palm Beach, Florida, in 2010. Three firefighters trying to extinguish the blaze were hospitalized.

16-h—Tiger Woods's *Privacy*

The disgraced golfer tried to offer the unfortunately named $25 million 155-foot yacht to ex-wife Elin Nordegren as part of the couple's $100 million divorce settlement, but she rejected it. As of this writing, the *Privacy* is for sale.

PUZZLERS

(Answers for page 152)

LEAVING ON A JET PLANE

Solution: *In 5 hours, they will be 600 miles apart.*

Remember algebra? Time (x) = distance (d)/speed (s)

Speed of the Air Force One = 650 mph

Speed of the Air Force Two = 530 mph

For every hour in the air, Air Force One gains 120 miles on Air Force Two (650 – 530 = 120)

Time (x) = 600 miles (d) / 120 mph (s)

Time (x) = 5 hours

MECHANICS MANIA

Decoder:

A B C D E F G H I J K L M N O P Q R S T U V W X Y Z
p m h b d z g u i o x s w a f q n y c j l e r v k t

Solution:

MCVVU = wheel
JIU OIUZVW = oil filter
SRUIQEVW = cylinder
WJZJW = rotor
DWNYV ANE = brake pad
DNZZVWR = battery
IGQIZIJQ = ignition
LANWY AUHG = spark plug
EWIXV DVUZ = drive belt
WNEINZJW = radiator
BHOOUVW = muffler
ZWNQLBILLIJQ = transmission

ALL ABOARD!

Answer: Davis

Logic: Johnson lives in Los Angeles. The brakeman's neighbor, who lives halfway between Los Angeles and Seattle, earns three times as much as the brakeman. Therefore, neither Johnson nor Smith are the brakeman's neighbor. So Davis must be his neighbor. Davis beats the fireman in billiards. The passenger whose name is the same as the brakeman's lives in Seattle. Davis lives halfway between Seattle and Los Angeles. So it must be Smith who lives in Seattle and Smith who is the brakeman. Since Davis is not the brakeman and he is not the fireman, whom he beats in billiards, he must be the engineer.

CRASH COURSE

(Answers for page 168)

1. Trick question: It's **(b)** *and* **(c)**. Booze is a contributing factor in 32 percent of all fatal accidents, but between midnight and 3 a.m., that figure shoots up to 66 percent.

2. (b) Sorry, guys. When it comes to avoiding car accidents, women are the superior sex. Men are twice as likely as women to cause a crash. According to a 2007 AAA study, men are also 77% more likely to die in a car accident than women. That year, 14,512 male drivers were killed on U.S. highways compared to 5,865 females. However, women are catching up—slowly. Between 1975 and 2007, the chance of a woman being killed in a car crash climbed 1% while dropping 11% for men over the same period.

3. (d) Forty percent of vehicles on U.S. highways are prone to rollovers, including SUVs, pickups, and vans. While front and side airbags have saved numerous lives in front and side impact crashes, drivers in a rollover may not be so lucky. Ejections due to the driver not wearing a seatbelt account for more than 80% of the fatalities in rollover crashes, while only 25% of those who buckle up die.

4. (a) According to the insurance industry, attorneys (and judges) are the worst drivers. Dog groomers and bartenders made the top five, along with financial-industry workers and government employees.

5. (d) Unless there are ****ing snakes on your ****ing plane, you are far safer in a commercial jet than in a car.

6. (c) Known as El Camino de la Muerte ("The Road of Death") to locals, the North Yungas Road connecting La Paz to Coroico, Bolivia, is far and away the world's deadliest roadway. Each year, 200 to 300 people perish on the single-lane road that snakes to over 15,000 feet in the Andes before steeply descending to just under 4,000 feet in the Amazon rainforest. By contrast, the most dangerous stretch of road in the U.S.—Missouri's Highway 21—had just over 30 fatalities from 1991 to 2001.

7. (d) According to the Insurance Institute for Highway Safety, the Mitsubishi Lancer has resulted in more insurance losses for everything from vehicular and property damage to medical payments than any other vehicle on the market at the time. If you want to be safe, buy a convertible Corvette—it had the fewest reported losses of any car tested.

8. (b) Psychology professor Paul Atchley of the University of Kansas found in a 2010 study that college-age drivers believed texting while driving to be less likely to cause an accident than "talking on the phone," "being inattentive," and "drunk driving." But in reality, says Atchley, texting while driving is "probably the most dangerous thing you can do other than driving with your eyes closed." It increases your chances of having an accident by 2,400%, far higher than talking on a hands-free phone, talking with passengers, or even driving while drunk.

What's a "coffin car?" That's railway jargon for a passenger car with an engineer's cab.

9. (d) All 50 states have some form of seatbelt law. But 59% of drivers who die in car crashes were not wearing one.

10. (b) On average, one auto accident happens every 4.8 seconds in the U.S. That comes out to 6.5 million crashes per year, with 46% them of them resulting in injuries.

MOVIE QUOTE QUIZ

(Answers for page 216)

1) Rex Kramer (Robert Stack) in *Airplane* (1980)

2) Bob Falfa (Harrison Ford) in *American Graffiti* (1973)

3) Jean-Pierre Sarti (Yves Montand) in *Grand Prix* (1966)

4) Boolie Werthan (Dan Aykroyd) in *Driving Miss Daisy* (1989)

5) Frank Towns (James Stewart) in *The Flight of the Phoenix* (1965)

6) Elwood (Dan Aykroyd) in *The Blues Brothers* (1980)

7) Alan Shepard (Scott Glenn) in *The Right Stuff* (1983)

8) Mrs. Rosen (Shelley Winters) in *The Poseidon Adventure* (1972)

9) HAL (Douglas Rain) in *2001: A Space Odyssey* (1968)

10) George Hanson (Jack Nicholson) in *Easy Rider* (1969)

11) Lightning McQueen (Owen Wilson) in *Cars* (2006)

12) Max (Mel Gibson) in *Mad Max* (1979)

13) Thelma and Louise (Geena Davis, Susan Sarandon) in *Thelma & Louise* (1991)

CAR STARS

(Answers for page 268)

1–C; **2**–D; **3**–E; **4**–G; **5**–H; **6**–B; **7**–F; **8**–A.

World's smallest car: The Peel P50, built in England in 1963....

TV SPY RIDES QUIZ

(Answers for page 302)

1-f. Hot off the James Bond craze started by *Dr. No* in 1962, *The Man from U.N.C.L.E.* needed its own sizzling car for top spy Napoleon Solo (Robert Vaughn). Creators turned to automotive designer Gene Winfield of Aluminum Model Toys to create the futuristic AMT Piranha. It featured plenty of gadgets along with gullwing doors and a Chevrolet Corvair chassis. The car cost about $35,000 to build. AMT got the exclusive rights to sell 1:25 scale models of the car.

2-e. At the end of each episode of *Mission: Impossible*, just before the final credits, muscleman Willy Armitage (Peter Lupus) would drive up in a nondescript, dark-colored Ford F1 panel van to pick up the spy team at a preassigned extraction point—mission accomplished.

3-h. Star Patrick McGoohan wanted a Lotus Elan for his hip spy series *The Prisoner*, but when a Lotus marketing director showed him both the Elan and the Seven, McGoohan picked the Seven instead. It's just as well—*The Avengers*' Emma Peel (Diana Rigg) was already driving an Elan convertible.

4-b. We pity the fool who tried to take on *The A-Team* or its ride: a 1983 GMC Vandura G-1500. The V8 Vandura came complete with a flash suppressor that fired 5.56 x 45mm NATO rounds as well as a Ruger AC556 automatic rifle with a folding stock.

5-d. "Black Beauty," the 1966 Imperial Crown driven by the Green Hornet (Van Williams) and sidekick Kato (Bruce Lee) was a rolling arsenal with front and rear laser guns, rocket pods, and a grille-mounted gas gun.

6-a. When he wasn't talking to Agent 99 (Barbara Feldon) on his shoe phone, Agent 86, a.k.a. Maxwell Smart (Don Adams) of *Get Smart* could often be found trying to foil KAOS in his red 1965 Sunbeam Tiger. Adams liked the car so much that he chose one as his own personal vehicle, although his came without a machine gun or an ejector seat.

...It seated one, did about 35 mph, and weighed 130 lbs.

7-c. Before he was tapped to play the debonair 1970s Bond, Roger Moore played a similarly suave Simon Templar in the popular British series *The Saint*. Templar did his spy driving in his "Swedish ride," a sleek 1962 Volvo P1800. Apparently, the use of the term "Swedish ride" on the show was a jab at British sportscar make Jaguar, who declined to provide a car for the series because the executives didn't see it "ever really taking off."

8-g. While partner Emma Peel was oh, so hip in her Lotus Elan, dapper secret agent John Steed (Patrick Macnee) preferred driving vintage Bentleys in the early years of *The Avengers*, specifically racing or town cars from 1926 through 1928 like the Bentley Blower and, most famously, the Speed Six. Later in the series, he moved on to a pair of yellow Rolls-Royces.

DO YOU KNOW NASCAR?

(Answers for page 353)

1–b. As a driver, Darrell Waltrip got tired of hearing his crew chief yell, "Green! Green! Green!" over the two-way radio at the start of every race. He wanted something more original and came up with his own "boogity-boogity" catchphrase.

2–a. Darlington is a tough racetrack, and in order to stay in the groove, drivers have to go high and, as they put it, "get into the wall." That takes off paint, and sometimes even numbers, and leaves a telltale black stripe on passenger-side doors.

3–c. When a driver breaks the rules, NASCAR officials will call him into the Big Red Trailer to discuss the consequences.

4–a. Stop 'n' Go is the penalty handed out by race officials to a driver who goes too fast coming into the pit lane. He's required to wait a full second before getting back on the track, which can be a costly delay.

5–b. The contact patch is the section of a tire's surface that actually makes contact with the track.

6–b. Darrell Waltrip coined the term "using the chrome horn" for

The US Navy has two hospital ships, named *Mercy* and *Comfort*. Each hold 1,000 patients.

the not-so-subtle technique of using the bumper to tell the car in front of you to get out of the way.

7–a. The Big One is a crash involving 10 to 15 cars during a major race like the Daytona or Talladega 500.

8–c. When your car is running like Jack the Bear, it's operating at peak efficiency, and you're probably winning the race.

9–a. A sand bagger is any driver who qualifies at a slower speed than his car is capable of on purpose so he can fool the competition with faster speed in the actual race.

10–c. All kinds of patching materials are used to smooth or fill a racetrack surface, but they're all called "bear grease."

11–c. A fabricator is a sheet metal worker whose specialty is shaping and molding car bodies. Most racing teams have two of them.

CAR NAME QUIZ

(Answers for page 395)

Round One

1-d; 2-l; 3-m; 4-a; 5-i; 6-o; 7-e; 8-f; 9-g; 10-b; 11-j; 12-k; 13-n; 14-c; 15-h

Round Two

16-r (ee); 17-r (cc); 18-p (dd); 19-s (ff); 20-q (bb); 21-r (aa)

Bonus Question

They are the same car sold under different names.

MORE CAR STARS

(Answers for page 448)

1–F; **2**–J; **3**–E; **4**–G; **5**–I; **6**–D; **7**–H; **8**–B; **9**–A; **10**–C.

THE LAST PAGE

FELLOW BATHROOM READERS:

The fight for good bathroom reading should never be taken loosely—we must do our duty and sit firmly for what we believe in, even while the rest of the world is taking potshots at us.

We'll be brief. Now that we've proven we're not simply a flush-in-the-pan, we invite you to take the plunge: Sit Down and Be Counted! Log on to *www.bathroomreader.com* and earn a permanent spot on the BRI honor roll!

If you like reading our books...

VISIT THE BRI'S WEBSITE!

www.bathroomreader.com

- Visit "The Throne Room"—a great place to read!
- Receive our irregular newsletters via e-mail
- Order additional *Bathroom Readers*
- Face us on Facebook
- Tweet us on Twitter
- Blog us on our blog

Go with the Flow…

Well, we're out of space, and when you've gotta go, you've gotta go. Tanks for all your support. Hope to hear from you soon. Meanwhile, remember…

Keep on flushin'!